LUCREZIA BORGIA

A Biography

LUCREZIA BORGIA

A Biography

RACHEL ERLANGER

LONDON
Michael Joseph

*For my husband,
the only biochemist ever to become an expert
on Lucrezia Borgia,
and for our three children.*

First published in Great Britain by
Michael Joseph Limited
52 Bedford Square, London WC1B 3EF
1979

ISBN 0 7181 1820 0

Printed and bound in Great Britain by
Redwood Burn Limited, Trowbridge & Esher

Contents

Grateful acknowledgment is due the following for permission to use material appearing in this book:

To SCALA/Editorial Photocolor Archives Inc., for the fresco by Pinturicchio, *The Disputation of Saint Catherine*; the portrait of Cesare Borgia by an unknown artist; and the detail of Julius II from the fresco *The Mass of Bolsena*, by Raphael.

To Editorial Photocolor Archives, Inc., for the detail of Francesco Gonzaga from the painting by Andrea Mantegna, *The Virgin of Victory*; the photographic view of the Castello Estense in Ferrara; the terra-cotta bust of Charles VIII by an unknown artist; and the portrait by Titian of a woman presumed to be Vannozza dei Cattanei.

To Alinari/SCALA for the portrait of a cardinal presumed to be Pietro Bembo; the portraits of Alfonso d'Este and Ercole I d'Este by Dosso Dossi; the portrait of Isabella d'Este by Leonardo da Vinci; and the detail of Pope Alexander from a fresco by Pinturicchio in the Borgia apartments, the Vatican.

Acknowledgments

I would like to express my appreciation to Professor Frank Mac-Shane, chairman of the writing department of the School of the Arts at Columbia, for giving me insight into the craft and discipline required of a writer; to my sister and brother-in-law, Frances and Peter Harris, for always being available with help and encouragement when I needed them; and to my dear friends Harriet Bressack and Maureen de Biccari for reading practically everything I have ever written and criticizing it "without fear or favor." I would also like to thank Professor Samuel Lieberman, the chairman of the Queens College Department of Classical and Oriental Languages, and Stephanie Russell, of the Graduate Center of the City University, for translating many of the letters and quotations that appear in the text; Dr. Alex Charlton for giving me advice about the medical problems of Lucrezia and Alexander; my agent Carl Brandt and my editors Elizabeth Backman and Janet Hansen for being generally helpful; Carolyn Barax for typing the manuscript; Signorina Nazarena della Torre of the staff of the Castello Estense in Ferrara for obtaining permission for me to visit Lucrezia's apartment, which is normally closed to the public; and Mollie Mervis and the other members of the staff of the Paul Klapper Library for letting me renew and re-renew the books I needed. I am also grateful to the following libraries and special collections in Italy and the United States: the Archivio Segreto Vaticano and the Biblioteca Nazionale in Rome, the Biblioteca Ambrosiana in

Milan, the Biblioteca Oliveriana in Pesaro, the Biblioteca Municipale in Spoleto, the Archivio di Stato in Mantua, the Archivio Segreto Estense in Modena, the libraries of Columbia University and the New York Public Library. Finally I would like to thank Simon & Schuster for permission to use the translation of a sonnet by Barbara Torelli which appears on page 281 and of a statement by Bembo on page 214; Sidney Alexander and Collier books for permission to quote from Mr. Alexander's translation of Guicciardini's *History of Italy*; the Modern Library and Random House for permission to quote from Burckhardt's *Civilization of the Renaissance*; Arturo B. Fallico, Herman Shapiro, and the Modern Library for permission to quote from the translation of Petrarch's *De remediis utriusque fortunae*; Charles S. Singleton and Anchor Books for permission to quote from Mr. Singleton's translation of *The Book of the Courtier*; Neil Mann and Abelard-Schuman for permission to quote from the English translation of Anny Latour's *The Borgias*; Harper & Row for permission to use the excerpt from Guicciardini's *Ricordi*, which appears on page 28 of this text; Geoffrey Parker and the Folio Society of London for permission to quote from Mr. Parker's translation of Burchard's *Diary*; Florence Gragg and G. P. Putnam's Sons for permission to quote from Ms. Gragg's translation of the Commentaries of Pius II; Lawrence Binyon and the Viking Press for permission to quote from Mr. Binyon's translation of *The Divine Comedy*; Barbara Reynolds and Penguin Books for permission to quote from Ms. Reynolds's translation of the *Orlando Furioso*; Rudolph B. Gottfried and Indiana University Press for permission to quote from Mr. Gottfried's translation of Pietro Bembo's *Gli Asolani*; Bernard and Barbara Wall and Harcourt Brace Jovanovich for permission to reproduce the Walls's translation of the Spanish sonnets, which appear on page 215 of this text and the poem by Bernardo Accolti on page 112; Indiana University Press for permission to quote from Morris Bishop's translation of Petrarch's *Italia Mia*; E. P. Dutton & Company for permission to use Edmund Gardner's translation of an excerpt from the *Orlando Innamorato*, which appears on page 142 of this text, the translation of Ercole Strozzi's funeral poem to Cesare, which appears on page 272, and the translation of Strozzi's sonnet to Barbara Torelli which appears on page 281; and Haskell House for permission to quote from Mr. Gardner's translation of Ariosto's *Epithalamium*.

Author's Note

A bibliography of the sources used in the text appears at the end of this work. The following authors are referred to more frequently than any of the others.

Johann Burchard — He was the papal master of ceremonies during the reigns of Sixtus IV, Innocent VIII, and Alexander VI. In his *Liber Notarum* he recorded the day-to-day life of the papal court. He is not to be confused with

Jacob Burckhardt — the nineteenth-century Swiss historian whose *Civilization of the Renaissance in Italy* is probably the most acclaimed work on the period ever written.

Niccolò Machiavelli — He was secretary to the second chancery of the Republic of Florence during much of Alexander's reign, and he knew and admired Cesare Borgia. In *The Prince* he described, not what a ruler ought to be, but what he had to be if he wished to succeed. In the less well-known *Discorsi*, he sought to apply classical principles of government to the Italian politics of his day.

Francesco Guicciardini   He, too, was a civil servant of the Florentine Republic. Later he became papal governor of the Romagna. Although he had very little to say that was good about anybody, it was the priests—*questa caterva di scellerati* ("this swarm of scoundrels") as he called them—whom he hated most. His *History of Italy* has done more to blacken the reputation of the Borgias than any other single work.

Ferdinand Gregorovius   Gregorovius was a German historian who lived in Rome during the nineteenth century. Although neither the first nor the best, his *Lucrezia Borgia* is certainly the most famous of the biographies which have sought to reassess Lucrezia's character.

MONEY

In 1500 the gold ducat weighed approximately 3.45 grams, which would give it a worth of almost twenty dollars in the 1978 gold market. The slightly heavier chamber ducat was equivalent in value to the florin. Since the average annual wage of an unskilled laborer was fifteen florins and that of a skilled laborer thirty-three florins, whatever the intrinsic worth of a florin or ducat, to the ordinary man of the sixteenth century it seemed a very large sum indeed.

Prologue

The wedding was celebrated in the Vatican on December 30, 1501. Although not quite twenty-two, the bride had already had two husbands. Long before she was out of her teens, epigrams describing her scandalous conduct had been circulating throughout Rome. The Venetian diarist, Girolamo Priuli, was only repeating the general view when he described her as a courtesan who had bestowed her favors on her father and two of her brothers. Her new husband had to be coerced into marrying her by the threat that if he didn't, his father would, in order to save his state. In Victor Hugo's *Lucrèce Borgia*, upon which Donizetti's opera is based, she continues her debauchery in Ferrara and makes liberal use of the Borgia poison to destroy her enemies. But poets like Bembo and Ariosto, who knew her there, praised her for her virtue, her patronage of the arts, and her good government. And when she died, the husband who had married her so unwillingly told his nephew that he could not write of her death without tears, "knowing myself to be deprived of such a dear and sweet companion."

One of the problems in writing about Lucrezia is to reconcile the two halves of her life: the young woman whom Edward Gibbon would call the Messalina of modern Rome and the universally respected duchess of Ferrara. If she was really as depraved as she was said to have been in Rome, what made her change? And if she wasn't, how did she acquire her reputation?

Descendants of Rodrigo Borgia

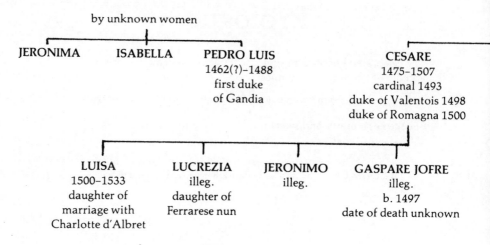

by unknown women

JERONIMA	ISABELLA	PEDRO LUIS		CESARE
		1462(?)–1488		1475–1507
		first duke		cardinal 1493
		of Gandia		duke of Valentois 1498
				duke of Romagna 1500

LUISA	LUCREZIA	JERONIMO	GASPARE JOFRE
1500–1533	illeg.	illeg.	illeg.
daughter of	daughter of		b. 1497
marriage with	Ferrarese nun		date of death unknown
Charlotte d'Albret			

Descendants of Lucrezia Borgia

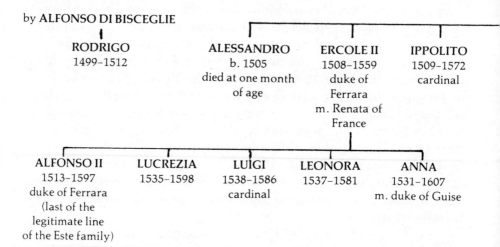

by ALFONSO DI BISCEGLIE

RODRIGO	ALESSANDRO	ERCOLE II	IPPOLITO
1499–1512	b. 1505	1508–1559	1509–1572
	died at one month	duke of	cardinal
	of age	Ferrara	
		m. Renata of	
		France	

ALFONSO II	LUCREZIA	LUIGI	LEONORA	ANNA
1513–1597	1535–1598	1538–1586	1537–1581	1531–1607
duke of Ferrara		cardinal		m. duke of Guise
(last of the				
legitimate line				
of the Este family)				

by **VANNOZZA DEI CATTANEI**
1442–1518

possible offspring by
unknown woman

GIOVANNI (JUAN I)
1486–1497
second duke of
Gandia
m. Maria Enriquez

LUCREZIA
1480–1519

GEOFFREDO (Jofre)
1482–1517
m. 1) Sancha of Aragon
2) Maria de Mila

GIOVANNI BORGIA
infans Romanus
duke of Camerino
and Nepi
b. 1498, still
living in 1548
date of death unknown

JUAN II
1494–1543
third duke of
Gandia

ISABELLA
1497–1557
nun

Saint **FRANCESCO BORGIA**
1520–1578
fourth duke of Gandia
third general of the Order
of Jesuits

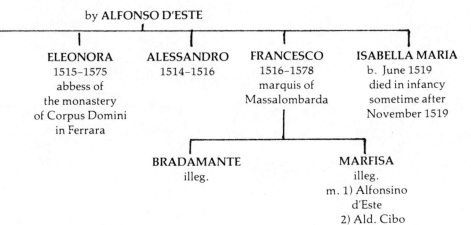

by **ALFONSO D'ESTE**

ELEONORA
1515–1575
abbess of
the monastery
of Corpus Domini
in Ferrara

ALESSANDRO
1514–1516

FRANCESCO
1516–1578
marquis of
Massalombarda

ISABELLA MARIA
b. June 1519
died in infancy
sometime after
November 1519

BRADAMANTE
illeg.

MARFISA
illeg.
m. 1) Alfonsino
d'Este
2) Ald. Cibo

Rome

I well know that as you are now to reside at Rome, that sink of all iniquity, the difficulty of conducting yourself by these admonitions will be increased.

Lorenzo the Magnificent in a letter to his son Giovanni, the future
Pope Leo X, March 12, 1492.

In 1492 Lucrezia Borgia was a child of twelve, living in the palace of the Orsini on Monte Giordano overlooking the Tiber. That her father had already been a cardinal of the church of Rome and her mother his longtime concubine when Lucrezia was bórn shocked virtually no one. In the more than 1,100 years since the western church had imposed a mandatory vow of celibacy upon the clergy, in every time and in every place, the majority of priests had ignored that vow. For a long time after marriage was first forbidden, they'd continued to take wives. When the laws against marrying grew stricter, they'd sought respite by taking concubines.

So widespread had the practice of taking a concubine become by the Renaissance, that in 1490 a high Roman prelate reported scarcely ever finding a priest or a member of the Curia without one. And King Ferrante of Naples complained that the Holy City was filled with the sons and daughters of cardinals. In addition to Lucrezia, Cardinal Rodrigo Borgia had fathered six other children; three by Lucrezia's mother and three by other mistresses. Cardinal Giuliano della Rovere, Rodrigo's bitterest foe in the Sacred College, had several illegitimate daughters and at least one son. Giuliano owed his cardinal's hat to his uncle, the late and generally unlamented Pope Sixtus IV. Although Sixtus was openhanded with his nephew, he was even more openhanded with two other young men who, although he also referred to them as his nephews, were commonly believed to be his sons. One epigrammist attributed sixteen illegitimate children to the then reigning pope, Innocent VIII, and considered it only fitting that Rome should call him father. A more conservative writer said that the pope had sired seven children. Actually, Innocent seems to have had only two. Rather than call them his niece and nephew, he was the first pontiff to openly acknowledge his children as such. The pope's son received numerous honors and emoluments. An anonymous Veronese chronicler reported seeing Innocent's daughter ride through Rome in great pomp, "not incognito, but as the daughter of the Pope."

Two of Innocent's granddaughters were married in the Vatican. After the marriage of one of them, the pope's master of ceremonies, Johann Burchard, wrote in his diary that the rule forbidding the presence of women at a papal banquet had been violated. Although Burchard described the affair as "widely noted and not kept secret," few appeared to share his dismay. Perhaps it was because like Stefan Infessura, another indefatigable diarist, the rest believed that "nothing good was done in Rome in those days." Countless, Infessura wrote, were the acts of sacrilege, the robberies, and the murders committed in the city.

Nor was this lawless behavior limited to any one class or group. After the servants of one of the cardinals had a fistfight with some Roman youths, members of the cardinal's household went through the neighborhood armed with crossbows and stones assaulting everyone on whom they could lay their hands. The retainers of another cardinal joined in the fracas over a Greek courtesan that ended with forty persons being wounded and an old man being burnt to death. For a price, a group in the Curia headed by two apostolic secretaries would forge papal bulls granting dispensations to all who needed them. When the forgers were discovered and sentenced, the relatives of one of them offered to pay the Curia the 12,000 ducats that their kinsman had earned from his forgeries in exchange for a pardon. But the case had attracted so much attention abroad that the pope, fearful of the scandal a pardon would cause, ordered the young man hanged. Usually, however, Innocent was only too eager to accept money settlements for the most heinous crimes. "God desires not the death of the sinner, but that he pay and live," Cardinal Borgia, the pope's vice-chancellor, was supposed to have said.

The precarious state of papal finances had compelled the Holy Father to pawn his miter and to omit the distribution of palms on Palm Sunday. In an effort to replenish his exhausted treasury, Innocent not only sold pardons, he also resorted to the creation and sale of offices. Emulating Sixtus IV, who had declared that a pope needed only paper and ink to get the sum he wanted, the Holy Father created a college of fifty-two *plumbatores* (or sealers of papal bulls) and charged each of them 2,500 ducats for his office. Since the plumbatores intended to make this up by charging exorbitant fees for their services, they had no objection to paying. The pope gained another 62,400 ducats by increasing the number of papal secretaries to twenty-six. As one of them wrote, "Henceforth, this office which had hitherto been bestowed as a reward for industry, faithfulness and eloquence became simply a marketable commodity."

In truth, there was very little in Rome that wasn't marketable. "Our churches, priests, altars, sacred rites, our prayers, our heavens, our very God are purchasable," moaned one disillusioned young scholar.

With the exception of a small minority, the members of the clergy were men who had entered the church not because of any special calling to the priesthood, but because they were second sons earmarked for a religious life since birth. And every great Italian family was prepared to offer gifts and bribes to get its second son named to the College of Cardinals. During Innocent's reign, as during the reigns of most of his predecessors, there was a Cardinal Orsini, a Cardinal Colonna, a Cardinal Savelli, and a Cardinal Sforza. When the news that the fourteen-year-old Giovanni de Medici was to be made a prince of the church became public, an epigram accused the pope of giving the purple to *"un ragazzetto,"* ("a little boy") "in order to unite the Medici to his son Franceschetto," which was, of course, true. The appointment followed the marriage of the pope's son to Giovanni's sister Maddalena. What the epigrammist neglected to mention, however, was that Innocent had at first objected to the extreme youth of the future cardinal. Whereupon Lorenzo dei Medici, one of the most outspoken critics of the depravity of Rome, added two years to his son's age!

Other cardinals entered the Sacred College under equally dubious circumstances. Following an unsuccessful attempt to wrest the Turkish crown from Sultan Bajazet II, the sultan's brother Prince Dschem fled to the Isle of Rhodes. Soon afterward the sultan offered the grand master of the Knights of Rhodes an annual stipend of 45,000 ducats if he would retain Dschem indefinitely. By bestowing a cardinal's hat upon the grand master, Innocent managed to have the valuable prisoner transferred to the Vatican. Although the sultan was at first nonplussed—he financed an unsuccessful attempt to poison the pope's drinking water—he later sent the Holy Father 135,000 gold ducats to defray the cost of keeping Dschem for three years. As a further token of his appreciation, he offered to send the pope a fragment of the holy lance which had pierced the side of Jesus.

The majority of the cardinals doubted the relic's authenticity and advised the pontiff to receive it with a minimum of fanfare. Innocent, however, chose to ignore their advice. On May 31, 1492, the Feast of the Ascension, he bore the crystal casket containing the relic in a solemn procession from the Porta del Populo to the Vatican. Standing upon the loggia of the portico, the Holy Father blessed the thousands massed in the square below, while Cardinal Borgia held the lance high above his head for the crowd to behold.

The reception of the holy lance was Innocent's last public act. He had suffered from gout and urinary infections during much of his reign. By mid-July 1492, it was obvious that he was dying. Invariably, the death of a pope meant the total breakdown of public order in Rome. After the death of Sixtus IV, barricades had sprung up all over the city, and, as was the norm on such occasions, the great Roman barons tried to seize control of the city. The powerful Colonna family raised a force of more than 2,000 men who marched across the city to their palace on the Piazza of the Sainted Apostles shouting "Colonna, Colonna!" Not to be outdone, their traditional rivals, the Orsini, armed two squadrons of horsemen who rode through the neighborhood surrounding their headquarters on Monte Giordano shouting *"Orso e chiesa!"* (literally "bear and church," a play on words intended to remind the people that the Orsini were the defenders of the church, whereas the Colonna had always supported the emperor). While a Roman mob demolished the palace of the late pope's "nephew" Count Girolamo Riario, the count's wife, Caterina Sforza, rode across the Tiber to take possession of the Castel Sant' Angelo, the ancient fortress which many considered the key to the city. Crowds plundered the corn exchanges on the Tiber and broke into the banks owned by Sixtus's fellow countrymen, the Genoese. So great was the pillage that only eleven cardinals risked leaving their palaces to attend the pope's funeral. Because Burchard, who as the papal master of ceremonies was in charge of the corpse, could find no one to give him a change of linen, the Holy Father had to be buried in the same underpants in which he'd died.

When it became obvious that Innocent was dying, Cardinal Borgia, as vice-chancellor, asked the pope for permission to take over the Castel Sant' Angelo in the name of the College of Cardinals. Innocent was about to give his consent when Cardinal Giuliano della Rovere strode into the sickroom to remind him that the vice-chancellor was a Catalan and wished to see a renegade Neapolitan cardinal made pope. "If we weren't in the presence of His Holiness, I would show you who is vice-chancellor," Borgia growled. "If we weren't here, I'd show you I'm not afraid of him," Giuliano replied.

Since a display of physical violence was out of the question, the two cardinals had to content themselves with an exchange of insults. According to one correspondent, they ended by calling one another Marranos (Jews who had converted to Catholicism in order to escape persecution) and white Moors.

The intensity of their discord reflected the intense conflict within the College of Cardinals when, on August 6, 1492, the princes of the church met to elect a new pope. The man that they were going to elect would be the spiritual leader of western Christendom, the successor of Saint Peter as Keeper of the Keys. "The head of the world . . . the spouse rector and pastor of the Universal church," one of the bishops called him in an address to the twenty-three cardinals gathered in the Sistine Chapel. The cardinals listened politely while the bishop implored them to "set aside ambition, rivalry and all ill-will . . . and trust in Christ our Lord." But it was not thus that popes were chosen. Describing the conclave of 1458, Aeneas Sylvius Piccolomini, the future Pope Pius II, wrote: "The richer and more influential members of the college summoned the rest and sought to gain the papacy for themselves and their friends. They begged, promised, threatened. . . . Many cardinals met in the privies as being a secluded and private place. . . ."

After the conclave of 1484 agreed upon Innocent VIII, Burchard reported that all the cardinals rushed into the cell of the pontiff-elect to get him to sign their requests for favors. Christ's vicar, after all, had much to bestow: offices and benefices worth thousands of ducats a year as well as castles and land and all the trappings of the cardinalate he was renouncing to ascend the papal throne. As a result of the famous donation of Pepin given to the popes in the eighth century, the pope was, moreover, not only the spiritual leader of all Christendom, but the temporal head of the papal states. His dominion over that disorderly hodgepodge of semi-independent cities and provinces stretching across central Italy from Rome to Ancona brought him an annual income of 100,000 florins. It also made him one of the five most important princes on the Italian peninsula.

At a time when most of the rest of Europe was consolidating into nations ruled by kings, Italy remained as fragmented as it had been in the Middle Ages. After the fall of Constantinople in 1453, the then reigning pope had joined the rulers of Venice, Milan, Florence, and Naples in a league designed to keep peace among the numerous warring states. By 1492, however, that league was crumbling. In 1485 and again in 1490, Innocent had clashed with King Ferrante of Naples over the papal tribute. Now Naples and Milan were at loggerheads because Ludovico Sforza of Milan, longtime regent for his nephew Gian Galeazzo, had refused to turn the rule of the duchy over to the young duke. Since Gian Galeazzo was married to Isabella of Aragon, the granddaughter of King Ferrante, Ferrante had protested to Ludovico. Although nothing overt had as yet occurred, Ferrante's troops could cross the border into the Romagna and reach the outskirts of the duchy of Milan in a matter of hours. To discourage such an undertaking, Ludovico had signed an agreement with Charles VIII of France. Because the king's Angevin ancestors had once ruled Naples, Charles considered the kingdom lawfully his. Should he wish to take it by force, Ludovico promised to finance his expedition and to give it free passage through northern Italy. Florence supported Naples, Venice could not make up its mind whom to support, and each of the opposing factions saw the conclave of 1492 as an oportunity to elect a pope favorable to its own interests. Ludovico instructed his brother Cardinal Ascanio Sforza to spare no expense to guarantee the election of a pro-Milanese pope. Ferrante put aside 200,000 ducats to insure the election of Giuliano della Rovere.

By the time the conclave opened that August, however, Giuliano seems to have concluded that he had little chance of gaining the two-thirds majority needed for election; hence, he threw his support to the elderly and respected Cardinal Costa. Ascanio and the Milanese faction supported the younger but equally respected renegade Neapolitan, Cardinal Oliviero Carafa. As for Rodrigo Borgia, though he was certainly among that select group of cardinals considered *papabile*, or "papal material," few thought he had much chance of being elected. Not only was he a Spaniard in a college controlled by Italians, he had no direct support from any of the Italian or European powers.

And so the voting began. Until it was over the cardinals would remain isolated in their cells in the Sistine Chapel, protected from all intruders by a select corps of Roman noblemen and foreign ambassadors. Each cardinal was allowed three votes; the winning candidate needed to receive sixteen of the votes cast to carry the election. After the conclave of 1484, Burchard had drawn up a list of what was needed to keep the princes of the church comfortable while they deliberated. Among other amenities it included a seat for the discharge of the stomach, two urinals, four boxes of sweets for provisions, one vessel of sugared pine seeds, marzipan, cane sugar, biscuits, a lump of sugar, a water jug, and a salt cellar. Because there were no facilities for cooking in the chapel, the cardinals had to have their food prepared at their palaces and then brought to them in wooden vessels. So that they would not take too long voting, custom decreed that their rations be cut each day they continued in session. Were the conclave to last more than a week, the princes of the church would be restricted to a diet of bread, wine, and water.

At the first scrutiny, Cardinal Carafa, the Milanese candidate, received nine votes. Cardinal Costa, the candidate of Naples, received seven votes, as did Cardinal Michiel, who was also acceptable to Naples. Although officially supported by neither side, Rodrigo Borgia also received seven votes. Giuliano della Rovere received five. The second scrutiny saw very little change in the voting pattern. Cardinal Carafa once again received nine votes, Cardinals Costa and Borgia received eight each, Cardinal Michiel seven, and Giuliano della Rovere five. By the third scrutiny, however, the Neapolitan faction had switched to Cardinal Michiel. He and Cardinal Carafa, the Milanese candidate, received ten votes each. Since neither side had any idea where it was going to get the additional six votes needed for election, and since neither showed any desire to compromise, the conclave appeared hopelessly deadlocked.

By then it was Friday morning, August 10, 1492. What with the nine days of mourning following Innocent's death and other ceremonies, the interregnum had already lasted a fortnight. During that fortnight over two hundred people had been murdered in the city, not to mention the usual looting and pillaging inevitable at such a time. From the moment the Romans learned that the voting had begun, thousands gathered in the Piazza San Pietro each day, waiting to hear of the election of a new pope who, they hoped, would put an end to the disorder. Since the ballots of the cardinals were burnt after being counted, every time the people saw smoke issuing from the chimney of the Sistine Chapel, they expected to hear the announcement of the new pope's name. When on Friday morning they were once again disappointed, many must have decided to go home. Although there was always the possibility of another vote toward evening, few in the crowd would want to return at that hour.

Unsafe by day, Rome was doubly unsafe after dark, for then the only light in the narrow *vias* and *vicolos* came from the lamps that glowed before the holy images at every street corner. Hence, there could have been only a handful of men and women in the Piazza San Pietro when at six o'clock the following morning the stones blocking a walled-up window on the first floor of the Vatican palace started falling. A cross was extended over the heads of those in the piazza, and a barely discernible figure began the ancient chant: *"Annuncio vobis gaudium magnum papa habemus."* ("I announce to you with great joy that we have a pope.")

While those who knew of the deadlock within the Sacred College strained to hear which of the two front-running cardinals had carried the election, another figure appeared at the window and let fall a stack of crumpled white slips of paper. Each bore the identical, hastily scribbled message: "We have for pope Alexander VI, Rodrigo Borgia of Valencia."

Rodrigo Borgia

The French and those who dwell in the remoter parts of Christendom think that the Pope is not made like other men, but is like one sent down from heaven who cannot be moved by human feelings and has not, as Saint Paul says, a law in his members contrary to the law in his mind.

Sigismundo dei Conti,
The Story of His Times

"I am pope and vicar of Christ!" The rich, melodious voice of the pontiff-elect quivered with joy as he was helped into his papal vestments for the first time.

On that hot August morning in 1492, when church bells all over the city joined the great bell of the Capitol in proclaiming the news of his election to the Romans, men and women everywhere—in the shops and in the palaces, in the outdoor markets and in the grimy hovels that clung to the sides of the ancient ruins—left what they were doing and hurried to Saint Peter's to give thanks that the long interregnum was finally over. That evening the magistrates of the city organized a torchlight procession in honor of the new pope and bonfires glowed in every piazza. "Even Mark Antony did not receive Cleopatra with such splendor," said one dazzled observer.

But if the people rejoiced, the ambassadors and correspondents dispatched by the various Italian states to report on the conclave appeared bewildered. Obviously, the election was "the work of the Holy Spirit," the correspondent of the Estense of Ferrara told the Duchess Eleanora. But, of course, he didn't expect to be taken seriously. In subsequent letters he eschewed all mention of supernatural influence and concentrated instead upon what the newly elected Alexander VI had paid for his office. The chair of Peter had cost the

pope 150,000 ducats, the correspondent told Duke Ercole. This included a 6,000 ducat "gift" to the moribund ninety-five-year-old
Cardinal Gherardi, whose vote had apparently swung the election,
and a 2,000 ducat "gift" to the adviser of the seventeen-year-old
Cardinal de Medici.

Immediately after Alexander's election, said Stefan Infessura, "he
distributed his wealth to the poor. He gave Cardinal Orsini his palace, the castle of Monticilli and that of Soriano. He named Cardinal
Ascanio vice-chancellor of the Holy Roman church. He gave Cardinal Colonna the abbey of Saint Benedict of Subiaco with all its castles." In fact, Infessura declared, there were only five cardinals who
declined to receive anything, and he spoke of four mules laden with
silver seen going from the palace of the pontiff-elect to the palace of
Cardinal Ascanio.

The Florentine ambassador in Rome also compiled a detailed list
of what each of the cardinals had received in exchange for his vote.
Moreover, he seemed convinced that Alexander would never have
been elected without the help of Ascanio Sforza. Although at first
the ambassador was at a loss to explain what had motivated Ascanio, he later concluded that it must have been greed. The cardinal
from Milan had offered to help elect Borgia because he coveted the
office of vice-chancellor, which had a commercial value of 100,000
ducats or better.

And it was this opinion—that Rodrigo Borgia had bought the
votes of his fellow cardinals "partly with money and partly with
promises of offices and benefices" and that Ascanio Sforza, "cor-
rupted by his boundless appetite for riches," had induced them to sell
their votes—that was later taken up by Francesco Guicciardini and
incorporated into the Borgia legend. The truth, however, is more
complex. For if Rodrigo Borgia was guilty of simony, it was not as
Guicciardini would have us believe, "simony in a manner unheard of
in those times," but the same willingness to reward his supporters
that had characterized every pope elected within the last forty years.
And although it is true that he could not have been elected without
the help of Ascanio Sforza, what had motivated Ascanio was not so
much his "boundless appetite for riches" as the need to find a new
candidate who would break the deadlock which had developed at
the end of the third scrutiny.

Next to Cardinals Carafa and Michiel, the cardinal who received
the most votes in that scrutiny was Rodrigo Borgia. Ascanio had

voted for Borgia as his second choice in all three scrutinies, as had a number of other cardinals associated with the Milanese faction. There were, however, four cardinals who had voted for Carafa who had given neither of their remaining votes to Borgia. Were Milan to shift its support from Carafa to Borgia, Ascanio felt certain he could persuade those four cardinals to follow suit. One of them had, in fact, made Borgia his second choice in the first two scrutinies. There was in addition another cardinal who had never voted for Carafa who had given Borgia his vote in the earlier scrutinies. Assuming that he, too, could be induced to once again cast his vote for the vice-chancellor, Borgia would have thirteen votes pledged to him. And once he had that many votes, Ascanio felt confident it would be a simple matter to win over three of the remaining uncommitted cardinals, thus giving Borgia the necessary two-thirds majority.

To understand why Ascanio felt so confident that he could persuade these men to vote for his candidate, it is necessary to forget the legends that have transformed the Borgia pope into a libidinous monster and to see him as he appeared to his contemporaries at the time of his election. To the majority he seemed the most capable member of the Sacred College—conscientious, hardworking, and dignified. During the thirty-six years he had been a cardinal, he had seldom missed a consistory, and when he had, it was because he was ill or away from Rome. He had held important posts under five popes and had served as papal legate in Spain and Italy. According to the papal secretary and chronicler Sigismundo dei Conti, who knew him well, "few people understood etiquette as well as he did; he knew how to make the most of himself and took pains to shine in conversation and to be dignified in his manners. In the latter point his majestic stature gave him an advantage. Also, he was just at the age, about sixty, when Aristotle says men are wisest; robust in body and vigorous in mind, he was admirably equipped for his new position."

That he was also the father of a numerous brood was not held against him. How could it be after the example of Innocent and when so many princes of the church were fathers in both senses of the word? Far more important in the eyes of both the cardinals who voted for him and the world at large was his proven ability as an administrator and diplomat, what one writer called "his brilliant skill in conducting affairs."

Although innumerable critics of the Holy See, including Dante, had considered the temporal power of the popes the source of all that was wrong with the papacy, in 1492 it was obvious that only by continuing to be a strong temporal power could the papacy hope to survive. This does not mean that the contradiction inherent in the pope's twofold role did not remain. As vicar of Christ he was called upon to be all values, convictions, inflexible resolution, and integrity. As temporal head of the papal states he was expected to be all compromise and accommodation, a man who adjusted his principles to reality and frequently had to use means that ill befitted a Christian pastor. But not only were the cardinals untroubled by the dichotomy; the majority seemed convinced that sufficient practical experience enabling one to use those means when the occasion demanded was a prerequisite for anyone who aspired to the papacy.

That Cardinal Borgia was prepared to reward those who voted for him was taken for granted. Borgia was no idealistic reformer bent on changing the existing order of things, but a practical politician eager to be elected. Nevertheless, had the cardinals thought only of what they would receive in exchange for their votes, they could have just as easily voted for a candidate supported by Naples. Ferrante of Naples, after all, had put aside 200,000 ducats to insure the election of Giuliano della Rovere or a candidate he favored. And Giuliano was not one to balk at using money to swing a papal election. At the conclave of 1484 he had promised 25,000 ducats to one of the cardinals if he would vote for the future Innocent VIII. On Friday afternoon, August 10, 1492, when Ascanio Sforza was campaigning for Borgia, Giuliano, who had more than once said that he would prefer anyone to a Borgia pope, must have campaigned just as hard for his candidate and made just as many promises. But in the final analysis, the majority of the cardinals felt more comfortable voting for Borgia, not because he was offering them more, but because they knew him well enough to realize that despite the support he was getting from Ascanio and the Milanese, he was too independent ever to allow Ascanio to rule him. Rather than thinking of Borgia as pro-Milanese, they tended to think of him as anti-Neapolitan; hence, he was a good compromise candidate, ready to oppose further encroachments by the meddlesome King Ferrante of Naples, yet not so closely bound to Milan as to be unable to act on his own.

Guicciardini tells us that although Ferrante dissembled his grief in public at Alexander's election, he informed the queen, his wife (shedding tears which he usually could control even at the death of his children), that a pope had now been created who would prove most pernicious for Italy and all Christendom. The majority of Italians, however, was more optimistic. Burchard noted that on the day of Alexander's coronation "the greatest honor was done him throughout the city by the Roman people with triumphant arches and with more than ever was done any other pope."

All the splendor of the Renaissance was apparent that day as well as all the contradictions between this Christian ceremony and the pagan means used to celebrate it. In front of one of the houses along the route taken by the pope, a protonotary had erected an arch with an inscription in gold letters upon a blue background: *Cesare magna fuit nunc Roma est maxima: Sextus Regnat Alexander: ille vir: iste Deus.* ("Rome was great under Caesar, greater far under Alexander. The first was a mortal; the latter is a God.") Other arches hailed *Divi Alexandri Magni Coronatio* ("the coronation of the great God Alexander"), *Alexandro Pientissimo* ("Alexander the most pious"), *Alexandro Invictissimo* ("Alexander the invincible"), *Alexandro Magnificentissimo* ("Alexander the most magnificent"). And everywhere, on the arches and the doorposts, on the flags and banners, as much in evidence as the cross, was the new pope's coat of arms: the red bull of the Borgias grazing upon a field of gold. Near the Piazza San Marco, one of the cardinals had placed a gigantic papier-mâché bull with water flowing from his horns, eyes, ears, and nostrils, and wine streaming from his forehead.

Rodrigo Borgia was not the first of his line to ascend the papal throne. In 1455, his maternal uncle Alonso de Borja ("Borgia" in the Italianized version of the name) had been elected pope and had taken the name of Calixtus III. Like Rodrigo in 1492, Alonso was a last-minute choice. The supporters of the Orsini and the supporters of the Colonna, the two opposing factions in that conclave, were so evenly matched that neither could hope to elect its candidate. As a compromise they decided to elect a non-Italian.

Alonso de Borja came from Jativa, a dusty little Catalan town encircled by low Moorish walls, at the foot of one of the carob-dotted mountains south of Valencia. Although the Borgias would later claim links to royalty, they belonged, in fact, to the lesser Spanish nobility. Alonso's sister Isabella married Jofre de Borgia, a member of another branch of the same family. Rodrigo, their second son, was born in a three-story house on the Plaza Borja in Jativa on New Year's Day 1431. When he was ten, his father died, and his uncle Alonso, who was then bishop of Valencia, invited Isabella Borgia and her six children to join him in the episcopal palace. Even after Alonso was made a cardinal and left for Rome, Isabella and her family continued to live in Valencia. Rodrigo, who as a second son was automatically destined for the church, attended the university where he majored in jurisprudence. Then, when he was about twenty, his uncle sent him to the University of Bologna to study liberal arts and sacred law.

Alonso would later complain that no sooner was he elected pope than Rodrigo's mother demanded that her sons be aggrandized "at the cost of the purse of Saint Peter." Despite his complaints, the new pope gave in readily enough, not only to her demands, but to the demands of all his other sisters, cousins, and aunts. Not long after his election, he made the then twenty-five-year-old Rodrigo and his cousin Luis de Mila cardinals. A year later, he gave Rodrigo the vice-chancellorship, next to the papacy the most important and lucrative post in the hierarchy. At around the same time, Calixtus named Rodrigo's older brother, Pedro Luis, captain-general of the church, commandant of the Castel Sant' Angelo, and governor with the title of duke of Spoleto, Foligno, Orvieto, and Nepi. When the prefect of Rome died, the pope also gave this office to his nephew.

In general, the Italians took a certain amount of papal nepotism for granted. No man was immortal and a pope was no exception to this rule. As Lorenzo de Medici would remind Innocent VIII a few years later: "the nobility of his character did not constitute a legacy. Only the honors and benefits with which he had endowed his kinsman could be regarded as his estate." Besides, as everyone knew, the members of the Curia and the Roman barons were so treacherous that, save for the pope's kinsmen, there was no one upon whom he could depend to carry out his policies. But it was one thing to see an Italian pope give honors and benefits to his relatives and another thing to see those same honors and benefits going to Catalans. Though the Italians distrusted all foreigners, they had always been most suspicious of the Catalans. A Roman friend of Piero de Medici was only reflecting the general view of the pope's appointments when he wrote: "The Catalans are masters here and God knows how different their nature is from ours."

Despite the widespread grumbling over the *"peste Catalana,"* or "Catalan plague," as the Romans called the pope's relatives, those Italians who had dealings with Rodrigo respected him for his ability and his conscientious attitude toward his work. In the opinion of the cardinal of Siena, the renowned humanist Aeneas Sylvius Piccolomini, the new vice-chancellor, although young in years, was old in judgment. Rodrigo's brother, Pedro Luis, on the other hand, came to symbolize the greediness and the arrogance that the Romans had always attributed to his countrymen. When Calixtus was dying, Pedro Luis's enemies decided that this would be a good time to get rid of him. Before they could find him, however, Rodrigo and a fellow cardinal managed to get him out of Rome. When he left, the Romans were storming through the Spanish quarter, burning and looting the houses. Rodrigo's own palace had been looted a few days before. Nevertheless, after helping his brother to escape, he returned to Saint Peter's to pray for his uncle. Calixtus died in his arms. A little over a week later, Pedro Luis died of malaria. Although most of Rodrigo's remaining kin had long since left Rome and although the feeling against the Catalans was still at its peak, the twenty-seven-year-old cardinal appeared determined to hold on to the office of vice-chancellor. And he was much too practical to allow considerations of principle to get in the way of his determination.

At the conclave that followed the death of Calixtus, the two most important contenders for the papal tiara appeared to be the cardinal of Bologna and Rodrigo's old friend the cardinal of Siena, Aeneas Sylvius Piccolomini. When neither candidate succeeded in mustering enough votes at the first scrutiny, Guillaume d'Estouteville, the wealthy cardinal of Rouen, went around making extravagant promises to the members of the Sacred College in order to get them to vote for him. Hearing this, Aeneas Sylvius asked Rodrigo if he was one of those who had sold his vote.

"What would you have me do?" Rodrigo answered. "The thing is settled. Many of the cardinals have met in the privies and decided to elect him. It is not to my advantage to remain with a small minority out of favor with a new pope. I am joining the majority and I have looked out for my own interests. I shall not lose the chancellorship; I have a note from Rouen assuring me of that. If I do not vote for him, the others will elect him anyway, and I shall be stripped of my office."

Although Aeneas pointed out that Rouen had also promised the chancellorship to a Frenchman and that he was much more apt to honor a promise to a fellow countryman than a promise to a Catalan, Rodrigo voted for Rouen at the next scrutiny. When, however, neither Aeneas nor Rouen received enough notes for election and the cardinals decided to try a method called "by accession," Rodrigo was the first to accede to the cardinal of Siena. His accession prompted several other cardinals to switch to Aeneas, thus giving him the necessary two-thirds majority. Naturally the new pope, who chose to reign as Pius II, was sufficiently grateful to allow Rodrigo to keep the chancellorship.

Portraits of Rodrigo Borgia, of which the best and most famous is the fresco by Pinturicchio in the Borgia apartments, reveal a stout, impressive-looking man, neither light nor dark, with exceptionally large, fleshy hands, an aquiline nose, and full lips. Although he certainly does not appear handsome by modern standards, there must have been something in his appearance that the portraits do not capture, for even when he was in his sixties, people spoke enthusiastically of Rodrigo Borgia's physical beauty. When he was in his twenties, he was considered so handsome, so lively and amiable and well spoken, that according to his tutor Gaspar of Verona, he had only to look at beautiful women to attract them to him "with greater force than a magnet attracts iron."

Since the handsome young cardinal was as susceptible to the charms of the ladies as they were to his, it was inevitable that his behavior should eventually cause talk. A few days after attending a baptismal party in Siena, he received the following indignant letter from Pius II.

Beloved Son:

We have learned that Your Worthiness, forgetful of the high office with which you are invested, was present from the seventeenth to the twenty-second hour, four days ago, in the gardens of Giovanni de Bichis, where there were several women of Siena, women wholly given over to worldly vanities. Your companion was one of your colleagues whom his years, if not the dignity of his office, ought to have reminded of his duty. We have heard that the dance was indulged in in all wantonness; none of the allurements of love were lacking, and you conducted yourself in a wholly worldly manner. Shame forbids the

mention of all that took place, for not only the things themselves but their very names are unworthy of your rank. In order
that your lust might be all the more unrestrained, the husbands,
fathers, brothers, and kinsmen of the young women and girls
were not invited to be present. You and a few servants were the
leaders and inspirers of this orgy. It is said that nothing is now
talked of in Siena but your vanity, which is the subject of general ridicule.

After once again reminding the young cardinal of the high office he
held, the pope left it to him to judge whether it was becoming to his
dignity to court young women and during the whole day to give no
thought to anything but sensual pleasures.

Pius himself came from Siena, and his family still lived there.
After he had time to reflect upon the story he had heard, he must
have realized that there wasn't a nobleman in Siena who would
meekly surrender his wife and daughters to a handsome young cardinal and an elderly lecher for five hours. Nor would Giovanni di
Bichis, in whose garden the party was held, have allowed the two
cardinals to exclude the young women's escorts. In a letter which the
pope sent to Rodrigo a few days later, Pius admitted that he had
probably been too quick to believe everything he'd been told. But he
must have believed some of it, for he implored Rodrigo to abstain
from such occasions in the future, and "to take care of his honor
with greater prudence."

At the Council of Basel, Pius, who before the age of forty had
been something of a rake himself, had spoken out against sacerdotal
celibacy. Although his advice to Rodrigo was well meant, one wonders if the pope could have followed it himself in his younger days.
Certainly Rodrigo found the demands of the flesh too strong and the
opportunities for satisfying them too tempting. In 1462, his first
child, Pedro Luis, was born. In 1464, while in Ancona with Pius, the
thirty-three-year-old father became ill. The prognosis was not good,
said the correspondent of Mantua, because the vice-chancellor "had
not slept alone." Whether the lady who shared his bed was the
mother of his son, we do not know. Nor do we know who was the
mother of his first two daughters, Isabella, born in 1467, and Girolama, born in 1469; or whether, in fact, the girls had the same
mother.

Illegitimacy was widespread during the Renaissance, and the Italians made little distinction between legitimate and illegitimate children. Like most fathers of illegitimate children, Rodrigo provided for his offspring. Isabella and Girolama were brought up in Rome; Pedro Luis spent much of his childhood in Spain. In 1472, Rodrigo also went to Spain where, as papal legate, he granted the dispensation which allowed Ferdinand of Aragon to marry Isabella of Castille. When he returned to Italy toward the end of 1473, he was forty-two years old, an age when many a man who has spent his life flitting from woman to woman decides it is time to settle down and raise a family. Had he been a secular, he probably would have taken a wife. Because he was a priest, he took a concubine.

A cracked and discolored tombstone in the right wall of the atrium of Saint Mark's in Rome tells us that Vannozza dei Cattanei, "mother of Cesare of Valentois, Juan of Gandia, Geoffredo of Squillace and Lucrezia of Ferrara," was born in 1442. Hence, she must have been just past thirty when she became the mistress of Rodrigo Borgia. Since in those days most young women married before they were out of their teens, one of the numerous unsolved mysteries concerning Lucrezia's mother is how she happened to still be unmarried at such a relatively advanced age. One possible answer is that she didn't possess a dowry large enough to attract a suitable husband.

During the Renaissance many families of Lombard painters and sculptors traveled to Rome to work on the churches and palaces then being built. Vannozza belonged to one such family. Her father, Jacopo, was an obscure Brescian painter who came to the Holy City during the reign of Paul II. A close relative, Antonio da Brescia, did some of the sculpture for the windows and doors of Palazzo Venezia. Since Rodrigo Borgia was constantly embellishing the palace he had built for himself on what is now the Corso Vittorio Emanuele, he may have first met his future mistress when visiting the workshop of either her father or one of her relatives.

Although there are no well-authenticated portraits of Vannozza, most writers assume that she was beautiful, for how else could she have held the interest of Rodrigo Borgia for almost ten years? The women of Lombardy are slimmer and fairer than the women of Rome. Hence, it may have been from Vannozza that her daughter Lucrezia inherited her slender frame and her blonde hair and gray-blue eyes. And it may have also been from Vannozza that Cesare inherited the regular features that led many to consider him the handsomest man of his time.

In a document written in 1483, Rodrigo refers to Vannozza's mother, Menica, as the "widow" of Jacopo (pinctor). Had Menica been widowed when Vannozza was still a child, she could very well have been too poor to provide an adequate dowry for her daughter. Without one, even the most beautiful girl would find it impossible to get a husband. Even if Vannozza did have a dowry, the prospect of a liaison with one of the wealthiest and handsomest of the princes of the church would dazzle this family of modest means. Nor would they consider it dishonorable. The ancient Romans had made no great distinction between a wife and a concubine and something of this attitude carried over into the Renaissance.

But although the liaison would not discredit Vannozza, it could discredit her lover. Perhaps because he remembered the admonition of Pius II—that he guard his honor prudently—the now middle-aged cardinal decided that for appearance' sake his mistress needed to have a husband. In 1474, he married her to Domenico di Rignano, an elderly and apparently complaisant lawyer. Rodrigo then gave the couple a house on the Piazza Pizzo di Merlo, which was close to his palace. In summer, when plague threatened Rome, Vannozza would join her lover in the fortress of Subiaco, one of the numerous benefices he had acquired during his years as vice-chancellor. There, sometime between August and October of 1475, Cesare was born. Because his mother was married at the time, he was legally the son of Domenico di Rignano, and it was not until 1493 that Rodrigo, in a secret bull, acknowledged him as his own child. By 1476, when Cesare's brother Giovanni, or Juan, was born, Domenico di Rignano was dead. Hence, Rodrigo immediately acknowledged this new son as his. The little boy's mother was still a widow when, on April 18, 1480, Lucrezia was born at Subiaco. Then, in 1481 or in the early part of 1482, Geoffredo was born. Not long after his birth, Vannozza married Giorgio San Croce, and Rodrigo apparently terminated his relationship with her. Because in later years he frequently expressed doubts as to whether Geoffredo was really his son, some have assumed that he terminated his relationship with Vannozza because she was unfaithful to him, but there is really no way of knowing. He could have discontinued their relationship because he was seriously thinking of making a bid for the papacy and having a mistress would compromise his chances.

Whatever his reasons for breaking with Vannozza, Rodrigo continued to show an interest in her. In the Secret Archives of the Vatican there is one folder with the provocative title *Lettere scritte di diverse dame a Papa Alessandro VI* ("Letters written by various women to Pope Alexander VI"). Three of them are from Vannozza. If we strip away the formal salutations, which were obligatory when writing to the pope and which even Lucrezia used, there is an air of cozy intimacy to these letters. This Holy Father, at whose feet Vannozza humbly throws herself, is someone she knows very well indeed.

"I beg Your Holiness to grant me the privilege of coming to see him for I have many things to say in which I know Your Holiness will take pleasure, especially the good news about the signor duca [Giovanni duke of Gandia, their second child], and the beautiful little son that has been born to him," she tells the pope in one letter. In another, written when she is recovering from an illness, she informs His Beatitude that as she is feeling better, she will be happy to visit him the following Sunday or whenever is most convenient. "And if you will deign to grant me this [audience], I inform you that, truly Sainted Father, I believe it will free me from my illness which in truth, most Holy Father, was not slight and I also have some things to tell you which mean a great deal to me."

Ferdinand Gregorovius, in his analysis of Vannozza's subsequent letters to Lucrezia, thought they disclosed "a powerful will and a mind both rude and egotistical." Certainly there is evidence of these qualities in the letters to her former lover. "Furthermore, Holy Father, I am unhappy that Your Holiness does good for me but someone else benefits. Therefore, I beg Your Holiness to take precautions with Msgr. Carpaccio because it seems to me he doesn't care," she tells the pope in the same letter in which she speaks of the birth of their grandchild. And yet when she signs her first and most formal letter "that one who day and night prays for the life of Your Holiness," it seems no mere conventional ending but an effort to break through the necessary formalities and express her real feelings.

Although Vannozza was extremely proud of her children and although they always treated her with great respect, after her marriage to Giorgio San Croce she played only a minor part in their upbringing. Because it was felt that a new husband might be tempted to appropriate the inheritance of his stepchildren, Roman law had stipulated that when a widow remarried, she must relinquish the guardianship of her children. During the Renaissance, a mother generally transferred custody to her late husband's kin. If, however, she had had her children out of wedlock, her own kin were expected to look after them. Vannozza's relatives were simple people. Even had her mother been young enough to care for four children, Rodrigo would probably have wanted to be in charge of their upbringing. He could not, of course, keep them with him, so he asked his cousin Adriana de Mila to act as their governess.

Adriana was the daughter of his mother's cousin Pedro de Mila. Some say Don Pedro was one of the counselors of King Alfonso of Aragon; others believe he was one of the many Catalans who settled in Rome after the election of Calixtus. In any case, he was sufficiently important to marry his daughter to an Orsini: Ludovico, lord of Bassanello, by whom she had one child, Orsino. In 1483, when Adriana undertook the care of the Borgia children, Ludovico was already dead, and she and the seven-year-old Orsino were living in the Orsini palace on Monte Giordano. Adriana was a strong-minded, imperious woman, so strong-minded indeed, that she was sometimes described as doing only what she wanted to do. She was also intelligent and kind and completely devoted to Rodrigo. Equally important, she was a Catalan.

Although by then Rodrigo had lived in Italy for twenty-seven years and although he spoke Italian fluently, he still used Spanish a good deal of the time. Many of his letters were written in the Catalan dialect; even those written in Italian contained numerous Catalan expressions. With the exception of a German master of his household and a Greek scholar, virtually all the members of his court were Spanish. Hence, it was only natural for him to want his children raised as Spaniards. Under Adriana's tutelage all four learned to speak Spanish as well as they spoke Italian. Although Rodrigo later sent Cesare and Juan to Italian universities, they went there in the company of their Spanish preceptors. Lucrezia, whose step was so light that she seemed not to touch the ground when she walked, learned Spanish dances. And when, shortly before her eleventh birthday, her father decided to look for a husband for her, it was a Spanish husband that he sought. On February 26, 1491, he betrothed her to Cherubino Juan de Centelles, lord of Val d'Ayora in the kingdom of Valencia. Under the terms of the nuptial contract, she was to be sent to Valencia within a year's time and to be married within six months after her arrival. There was nothing unusual in such an early marriage. Bianca Maria Sforza, the illegitimate daughter of Ludovico Sforza of Milan, had married when she was eight. Lucrezia's half sister Girolama had married at thirteen; her half sister Isabella at sixteen.

Even while Lucrezia's father was negotiating her marriage contract with Don Cherubino, however, he was also considering another bridegroom, Don Gasparo de Procida, son of the count of Aversa and heir to his title. Perhaps because Rodrigo found Don Gasparo's credentials more impressive, the contract with Don Cherubino was annulled and in April 1492 a new contract betrothing Lucrezia to Don Gasparo was drawn up. Since the twelve-year-old bride-to-be had seen neither Don Cherubino nor Don Gasparo, the change in bridegrooms meant nothing to her. Had her father not been elected pope, she might very well have gone to Valencia to marry her count and lived, if not happily, at least inconspicuously ever after.

Those who knew Rodrigo Borgia described him as *uomo carnalesco*, by which they meant that he was a man of warm and affectionate nature devotedly attached to his own flesh and blood. During his years as vice-chancellor, they had seen him diligently exploit his contacts to obtain titles and benefices for his children. Thus, he had used the close ties with Ferdinand of Aragon, established during his trips to Spain in 1472, to bestow the dukedcm of Gandia, a leading city of Valencia, upon his eldest son Pedro Luis. When Pedro Luis died unexpectedly, both his dukedom and his fiancée, Maria Enriquez, a first cousin of the king, passed to his younger brother Juan. Cesare, who though the eldest of Rodrigo's children by Vannozza was nevertheless his second son and as such destined for the church, was made apostolic protonotary, canon of the cathedral of Valencia, archdeacon of Jativa, and rector of Gandia when he was only seven. Geoffredo, who Rodrigo was also thinking of making a priest, became archdeacon of the cathedral of Valencia before he was eleven. Hence, it was only natural for many to fear that as pope Rodrigo would be even more nepotistic than his uncle had been.

To allay those fears, the newly elected Alexander VI assured the envoy of Ferrara that he intended to keep his children at a distance. He would do his utmost to preserve peace and to be a father to all without distinction, he informed the Florentine envoy. And at the time that he said it, he probably meant it. The first indication that his resolution was weakening occurred at the consistory of August

31. After rewarding all those who had voted for him, he gave his vacated bishopric of Valencia to the eighteen-year-old Cesare and made a nephew, Giovanni Borgia of Monreale, a cardinal. Then on September 3, an event occurred that in due time thrust his daughter into the limelight and prepared the way for her sinister reputation.

On the surface it appeared an ordinary business transaction. Franceschetto Cibo, the son of the late pope, had been given the castles of Cerveteri and Anguillara by his father. Since Franceschetto was married to Maddalena de Medici and wished to reside in Florence, Maddalena's brother arranged for him to sell the castles as well as some other lands he had been given near Rome to Virginio Orsini for 40,000 ducats. What all three parties to the deal chose to ignore, however, was that the castles were papal fiefs that could not be sold without the consent of the pope. And of all the possible buyers, the one the pope would least like to have own them was Virginio Orsini.

Ever since the Middle Ages, the Roman barons had been divided into two opposing factions, one headed by the Colonna family and the other by the Orsini. Because the two factions were "constantly under arms before the eyes of the Pope," and "there was constant quarreling between them," it was clear to Machiavelli that the other Italian powers used them to keep the papacy weak and infirm.

From the Orsini headquarters at Bracciano, north of Rome, Virginio Orsini commanded between ten and twenty thousand vassals. One of the new castles he had acquired from Franceschetto Cibo overlooked the Via Aurelia; the other commanded the Via Cassia and the Via Clodia. It was along these roads that food was brought to Rome from the sea. To put the castles into the hands of so powerful an enemy of the papacy as Virginio Orsini—a man who six years before had threatened to hurl Innocent VIII into the Tiber—was not only to give him and his vassals easy access to the city, but also to give him the opportunity to divert Rome's food supply whenever he chose.

Nor did the damage end there. The Orsini, like the Colonna and innumerable other barons in the papal states, were condottieri who sold their military services to the highest bidder. At the same time that Virginio Orsini bought the castles, he was chief condottiere for Ferrante of Naples. Since, moreover, Alexander was convinced that Ferrante had provided much of the purchase money, the sale in effect gave the king easy access to Rome and control of her food supply.

Equally galling from Alexander's point of view, the entire transaction had taken place in the palace of Giuliano della Rovere.

At the time of his election, the pope had found both Rome and the papal states in chaos. Like the good administrator that he was, he immediately set about restoring order. Burchard tells us that he appointed four commissioners to hear complaints and that on Tuesdays he heard complaints himself. "You would be astonished to see how he grants his public audiences to private individuals, even to poor widows, and with what patience and forbearance," the bishop of Perugia wrote to a friend. Alexander also appointed inspectors for the prisons and, in the opinion of Burchard, who rarely had a good word to say for the new pope, he administered justice "in an admirable way." One normally hostile observer praised him for never letting workmen wait for their wages, teachers for their salaries, nor soldiers for their pay; another noted that through Alexander's vigilant care "there arrived in Rome a quantity of grain so great that the oldest man did not remember ever having seen a more copious affluence." But of what use were these measures when two of the principal roads to Rome were in the hands of her enemies, and her food supply was menaced?

In an audience with the Florentine orator Francesco Valori on September 22, Alexander let it be known that he would be compelled to take action against those involved if the sale were not immediately rescinded. Somewhat later he sent briefs to all the powers of Europe denouncing the Orsini and asking for help in opposing them.

Nor was the pope the only one upset by the sale. To Ludovico Sforza and his brother Ascanio, the involvement of Piero dei Medici in the transaction meant that Naples and Florence had reached an understanding at the expense of Milan. To counteract this dangerous agreement, Ascanio urged the pope to join Milan and Venice in a treaty of mutual protection. And what better way to to seal their pact than with a marriage between the pope's daughter and a member of the Sforza family? The bridegroom Ascanio proposed was his second cousin, the recently widowed twenty-eight-year-old Giovanni Sforza, lord of Pesaro and count of Contignola.

Alexander wasn't sure that he wanted Giovanni as a son-in-law; on the other hand, he wasn't sure that he didn't. Although he had been elected with the help of Giovanni's relatives in Milan, he did not really approve of the treaty Ludovico Sforza had signed promising to support a French invasion of Naples. In fact, the pope disapproved of all foreign invaders and he believed that the best guarantee of peace was to maintain the status quo. On the other hand, he could not tolerate the Neapolitan king's interference in the matter of the castles. Because Alexander was essentially a negotiator rather than a warrior, he hoped to put enough pressure on Ferrante to force him to cancel the sale. If, however, the king decided instead to use his strengthened position to invade the papal states, Alexander would have need of both the Milanese army and of Giovanni Sforza, who was an accomplished condottiere in his own right.

After thinking the matter over, the pope asked Giovanni to come to Rome incognito at the end of October. Secrecy was essential, not only because the pope did not wish to have the Neapolitans know what he was up to, but also because Lucrezia was already betrothed to Don Gasparo. In Italy such agreements were considered almost as binding as the actual marriage ceremony. But Alexander had already annulled one betrothal. Given his vast wealth, his extensive knowledge of the law, and the power of his great office, he would find a way to annul another.

Meanwhile, although he would tell his daughter about this second change in bridegrooms, she would have no say in the matter. Not because her father was indifferent to her welfare—"The Pope loved his daughter *in superlativo grado*," said the Ferrarese ambassador—but marriages were alliances between families, and the most loving of fathers had no qualms about using his sons and daughters to cement diplomatic treaties or to increase the family wealth. "I took Clarice as my wife, or rather she was given to me," said Lorenzo the Magnificent of his marriage to Clarice Orsini. By the same token, the twelve-year-old girl in the palace on Monte Giordano would be expected to follow her customary routine, not knowing whether at the end of her father's complicated negotiations she would find herself countess of Pesaro or countess of Aversa.

Lucrezia

Day, night, hour, tide, time, work, play,
Alone, in company, still my care hath been
To have her match'd.

Shakespeare, *Romeo and Juliet*,
act 3, scene 5

Nothing in our civic life is more difficult than marrying off our daughters well.

Guicciardini, *Ricordi*

Her earliest memories were of the house in the Piazza Pizzo di Merlo, one of those dimly lit three-story Roman houses with beamed ceilings, rush-covered floors, bare, whitewashed walls, and the inevitable picture of the Madonna before which a lamp glowed constantly. Because her mother was already a widow when she was born, there was no conflict involved in calling the frequent and altogether splendid visitor with the wonderfully rich voice papa. Nor would she find it unusual that he did not live there, for she had, after all, no basis of comparison. And if for a time after she was removed from those familiar surroundings the three-year old girl was understandably bewildered, and if she clutched her doll and refused to answer when spoken to, the pain of separation would soon be eased by the genuine concern of the woman who now replaced her mother, by the presence of her brothers, and the eagerly awaited visits of her father.

There were books on child care that advised fathers to behave coldly toward their daughters lest the little girls acquire a premature taste for masculine society. Rodrigo Borgia, however, was no great reader. And even if he had read those books, he was much too elemental a man to pay attention to such rubbish. He adored his small blond daughter, and he made no effort to conceal his feelings.

And it was perhaps Lucrezia's gratitude for this reassuring love and her desire to prove worthy of it that were at the root of the almost fatal compulsion to please that characterized her all her life.

Save for the emphasis on Spanish language and culture, the education she received in Adriana's house differed scarcely at all from the education received by most upper-class Italian girls in those days. According to Jacques de Mailles, the *loyal serviteur* of the Chevalier Bayard, who met Lucrezia in 1512, "she spoke Spanish, Greek, Italian, French, and a little Latin very correctly and she wrote and composed poems in all these languages." She also learned to play the lute, to dance, to draw, and to embroider so well in silver and gold that she would later amaze the Ferrarese with her skill. Her father's master of the household was a noted Latin scholar; his secretary was an equally noted Greek scholar. Although both these men undoubtedly had a hand in educating the Borgia children, in Lucrezia's case at least the instruction in the humanities seems to have been fairly superficial. Besides an annotated copy of Dante and a handwritten edition of Petrarch, both standard books in the library of every well-educated young woman, the seventeen books she brought with her to Ferrara when she was twenty-two dealt mainly with religious subjects. They included among others a life of Christ in Spanish, a book called the *Dodexe del Christiano* in the Valencian dialect, a breviary, a book of psalms, and a book of the epistles of Saint Catherine of Siena.

Even if she had been a prodigy of humanist scholarship, she wouldn't have been expected to do very much with her education except to become a wife and mother. "Men and women ought to receive the same education with this difference," said the renowned humanist Ludovico Dolce, "that whereas the education of the man has as its goal the welfare of the state and the prince, that of the woman has as its goal the management of her household." To prepare little girls for their housewifely role, Dolce recommended giving them miniature household utensils. Even the most exalted princesses learned to cook, to look after the linens, to do needlework, and to keep the household accounts. Since any exposure to the outside world involved a possible threat to their chastity, they generally completed their education at home or at some reputable convent. Their brothers, on the other hand, in preparation for the worldlier role in store for them, generally completed their education at one or more of the numerous Italian universities. Cesare, the most brilliant of the Borgia children, left for the Sapienza of Perugia in 1489, when he was fourteen. Juan followed almost immediately.

That same year their thirteen-year-old former playmate Orsino Orsini, the son of their governess Adriana de Mila, was affianced to fifteen-year-old Giulia Farnese, the youngest daughter of a family of provincial nobles whose headquarters were at the castle of Capodimonte on Lake Bolsena. As was so often the case then, the decision to affiance Giulia to Orsino had been made by their respective fathers many years before. Since neither father was alive in 1489, Rodrigo offered his palace for the signing of the nuptial contract on May 20 and the civil marriage the following day. The two principals were seeing one another for the first time. The fifteen-year-old Giulia was already famous for her beauty. *Giulia Bella*, the Romans would call her a few years later, was not only beautiful, but brilliant, "endowed with gentleness and humanity." Blond was the preferred hair color then, and legend has it that Giulia was blond. But a letter written to Cesare describes her as *fusco* ("dark complected") with black eyes, a round face, and *quidem ardor* ("a certain vivacity").

Her barely pubescent bridegroom was a typically gawky thirteen-year-old boy with nothing to distinguish him from other boys his age save his listlessness. No one asked this ill-matched couple what they thought of one another. Although the civil ceremony did not permit them to consummate their marriage, it involved an exchange of rings and was considered binding. A year later the religious ceremony took place and Orsino's bride joined his mother and Lucrezia in the palace on Monte Giordano. Lucrezia was ten at the time and had never lived in such close proximity to a married couple before. What she saw of the relationship between Giulia and Orsino was certainly not calculated to arouse any great enthusiasm for married life.

To help launch the couple, Rodrigo had secured a *condotta* in the papal army for the young husband. It was fairly modest as *condottas* went, but then Orsino was only fourteen. He was given command of two men and received 300 ducats a year for his service. A month before his *condotta* came up for renewal the following year, one of Giulia's cousins sought to replace it with a more lucrative *condotta* under the command of Orsino's kinsman, Virginio Orsini. At around this time Orsino lost an eye, just how is not clear. The ex-

perience was sufficiently unnerving for the fifteen-year-old condottiere to resolve to make a pilgrimage to the Holy Land. Not only his
mother and Rodrigo, but all his friends urged him to reconsider.
Orsino, however, was adamant. Since he was still a minor and could
not touch his money without his mother's consent, he besieged her
with requests for funds with which to make the trip. Adriana ignored these requests, apparently hoping that if she did so long
enough, Orsino would forget *"questa fantasia"* as she called his decision to go to the Holy Land.

Then one day while negotiations for his new *condotta* were still in
progress, Orsino suddenly left his wife and mother and retired to the
family estate at Bassanello. If Adriana did not send him the 300
ducats he needed to visit the Holy Sepulcher, he would take out a
loan against the estate, he informed her. Rodrigo wrote to him.
Giulia's brother Angelo went to see him. But neither the one nor the
other could dissuade him. Finally, after eight days of fruitless talk,
Adriana agreed to give him the 300 ducats he needed for the trip,
provided he would allow "two men of good will" to accompany him.
Orsino then went to Bologna to meet one of them. From Bologna it
was assumed he would go to Venice to board a ship bound for the
East. Instead he went to Florence. Once the money was procured to
make the trip, he seemed to have lost all desire to go. Nor is the
reason for this sudden change of heart difficult to comprehend. He
was, after all, little more than a child. What with the trauma of losing an eye, the responsibilities, sexual and otherwise, associated
with a new wife, and the prospect of a new *condotta,* he felt overwhelmed. Surrounded as he was by forceful adults all intent upon
shaping his future, the only way out he could think of was to make a
pilgrimage to the Holy Land. His was a typical adolescent rebellion
against having his life laid out for him before he'd had any chance to
decide what he really wanted to do. Certainly the news that his wife
was pregnant, which may have reached him while he was at
Bassanello, could only have aggravated his feeling of being
hemmed in. When, however, all objections to his proposed trip were
removed, the preposterousness of the means he had chosen to evade
his responsibilities must have struck him.

Eventually Rodrigo persuaded him to resume his *condotta* with
the pope. It was renewed in April 1492 and again in May 1493 when
the number of men under Orsino's command was increased to

twenty-five. Orsino did not, however, return to the palace on Monte Giordano. Instead, he decided to spend his free time at Bassanello. Giulia remained with Lucrezia and Adriana. There was nothing unusual in her situation. Italy was filled with young wives whose husbands expressed their resentment at being forced into marriage by spending as little time with them as possible. Giulia was a sweet-tempered gentle young woman, and Lucrezia came to think of her as a beloved older sister.

Like most young noblewomen, the two were ardently devoted to what the Swiss historian Jacob Burckhardt called "the national passion for external display." Lorenzo Pucci, a relative of Giulia's who visited her one day just after she had washed her hair, wrote a letter to his brother describing how she let it down and had it dressed: "It reached down to her feet; never have I seen such beautiful hair. She wore a headdress of fine linen and over it a sort of net light as air with gold threads woven in it."

For Lucrezia who was blond there were elaborate rituals to enhance her blondness. The celebrated virago Caterina Sforza had in fact compiled a book, *Esperimenti,* in which among other arcane matters she described the most reliable methods for making the hair "blonde and beautiful," and there were other works as well. A recipe used by the Countess Nani called for two pounds of alum, six ounces of black sulphur, and four ounces of honey, the whole to be diluted to achieve a shade called *filo d'oro.*

"What shall I say of the color of their hair?" asked an unknown poet. "That each one wants long and blonde and beautiful. / But for this one must sit in the sun. / What does it matter? / Everything for this. / They pay scant attention to their household / and pass three hours looking at themselves / Drying themselves and curling themselves."

Clothes, of course, were equally important. One of Matteo Bandello's *Novelle* describes the women of Milan, "their dresses covered with wrought gold, so many trimmings, embroideries and precious jewels, so that when a dame goes forth from her door it reminds one of the ascension at Venice." After describing Giulia's hair, Lorenzo Pucci went on to speak of her clothes: "She wore a lined robe in the Neapolitan fashion as did Madonna Lucrezia who, after a little while, went out to remove it. She returned shortly in a gown almost entirely of violet velvet."

Besides washing and drying their hair and making up their faces, Lucrezia and Giulia must have also spent much time fussing over Giulia's new baby and talking about Lucrezia's approaching marriage to the count of Aversa. Rodrigo's palace was nearby, and he enjoyed visiting them and listening to their talk. After he was elected pope, he tried to think of a way to continue these impromptu visits. Since he could no longer come to the palace on Monte Giordano without attracting attention, he decided to look for a palace nearer the Vatican for his daughter. The palace of Santa Maria in Portico owned by Cardinal Zeno stood on the left side of the steps of Saint Peter's, almost directly opposite the Palace of the Inquisition. Soon after Alexander's election he obtained the use of this palace and had it furnished for Lucrezia. Some time before the spring of 1493, she and Adriana and Giulia moved in.

The gossips and the pope watchers knew why Lucrezia was there. She was the pope's daughter. They also knew why Adriana was there. She was Lucrezia's guardian. But they refused to believe that Giulia was there because her husband had deserted her. Observing their still-virile sexagenarian pontiff and the numerous children he had fathered, they decided that he had probably sent Orsino away so that he could have the beautiful Giulia for himself.

"Madonna Giulia, *'Sposa di Cristo'* " ("the Bride of Christ"), one Roman writer called her. "Giulia Farnese, 'the Pope's concubine,' " Burchard called her in his diary, and Infessura referred to her in the same way. To the Ferrarese ambassador, Gianandrea Boccaccio, she was "Madonna Giulia Farnese about whom so much is whispered." The correspondent of the marchese of Mantua called her *"una bella cosa a vedere* ['a beautiful thing to see'] and the Pope's favorite." After visiting her and Lucrezia in the winter of 1493, Lorenzo Pucci informed his brother that Giulia's baby resembled the pope. Nor was the gossip confined to Italy. In Germany, it was rumored that Alexander had a cypress grove in which he entertained "Giulia Farnese and other loose women."

There isn't any real proof that Giulia ever was Alexander's mistress. On the other hand, there isn't any real proof that she wasn't, save the pope's treatment of Giulia's daughter Laura. Though gossips like Lorenzo Pucci spread the word that Alexander intended to give Laura a huge dowry, the *uomo carnalesco* who, no matter how compromising the circumstances, always found a way to provide for his own flesh and blood, never did anything for this supposed "love child." What is indisputable, however, is that the pope's well-known susceptibility to feminine beauty led him to behave in a very unpopelike fashion in Giulia's presence. The man who at twenty-seven had made himself the laughingstock of Siena by reason of his extravagant attentions to pretty women, at sixty-one could not resist constantly flirting with Adriana's exquisite daughter-in-law.

The orphaned seventeen-year-old Giulia who, like her new husband, had at first no doubt seen Rodrigo Borgia as a father substitute, could not have taken long to realize the ambivalent nature of his feelings toward her. Though past sixty, Rodrigo was still an unusually attractive man and his elevation to the papacy could only have enhanced his attractiveness. Giulia's husband, on the other hand, was a surly adolescent who, despite his wife's much-praised beauty, persisted in regarding her as more of an encumbrance than anything else. Although modesty forbade Giulia from voicing her suspicions concerning the pope's feelings toward anyone, the atmosphere must have been charged with fantasies on both sides.

Giulia's family, either because they sensed Alexander's delight in her beauty or simply because her position in Lucrezia's household gave her easy access to the pope, were constantly urging her to obtain favors for them. Giulia, in turn, seems to have taken a naïve pride in using her influence. According to Lorenzo Pucci, "she was alive to all her opportunities," and she wanted her sister Geronima, who was married to Pucci's brother Giannozzo, "to see her magnificence just as much as Geronima herself wanted to see it." But even when Giulia was being most coquettish, she must have sensed that Alexander's interest in her was relatively shallow compared to his overwhelming love for Lucrezia.

Pinturicchio began work on the frescoes in the Borgia apartments while Giulia and Lucrezia were living in the palace of Santa Maria in Portico, and legend has it that Lucrezia served as the model for the figure of Saint Catherine in that fresco in the Hall of the Saints known as *The Disputation of Saint Catherine*. Legend also has it that the artist painted Alexander on his knees before Giulia Farnese dressed as the Virgin. However, the fresco of Alexander on his knees shows him praying not before the Madonna but alongside an empty tomb, the triple tiara on the ground before him. Moreover, the sweet-faced Madonna with the chestnut hair who appears, not with Alexander but in the circle over the door of the Hall of the Saints, resembles scores of other Madonnas painted by Pinturicchio. Though all this would seem to cast doubt on the legend that Lucrezia served as the model for Saint Catherine, there is, nevertheless, a marked resemblance between the childlike figure of the saint with her long blond hair and earnest blue eyes and some of the descriptions of the pope's daughter.

Niccolò Cagnolo of Parma, for instance, would later describe her as "of medium height and graceful in form. Her face is rather long, the nose well cut, hair gold, eyes of no special color, her mouth rather large, the teeth brilliantly white. Her neck is slender and fair; her bust admirably proportioned." However, two medals struck in 1502, which are considered authentic portraits of Lucrezia, show her with a wider face, a more aquiline nose, and a smaller chin than the girl in Pinturicchio's fresco. A silver shield in the church of San Giorgio in Ferrara shows the same aquiline nose, the same receding chin.

Although Lucrezia was more than ordinarily attractive, she was not a great beauty like Giulia Farnese. Rather she had what one lady who saw her in 1502 described as *"dolce ciera,"* "a sweet face." The Ferrarese ambassador Gianandrea Boccaccio, who knew her when she was living in the palace of Santa Maria in Portico, was struck not so much by her appearance as by her gaiety. "She had," he said, "a smile that lit up her features in a thousand different ways. Never did gentle creature seem happier to be alive." And yet, although her face and indeed her whole appearance reflected her happiness, in the depths of her small being the ambassador thought he detected a shade of sadness, an inexplicable taste for solitude.

Was it the memory of that early and unexplained separation from her mother or a growing awareness of her ambiguous position as the bastard daughter of the pope? There is really no way of knowing what caused this fleeting sadness. But whatever the cause, in those days it was only the most ethereal of clouds in an otherwise bright blue sky, for Lucrezia was, after all, surrounded by people who loved her, and she was still too young to realize that even those who loved her best would ignore her interests if it served their purpose to do so.

It was not customary for a suitor to see the lady he was courting until the pair were officially betrothed. If, however, as some historians think, Giovanni Sforza did catch a glimpse of Lucrezia when he came to Rome on October 31, 1492, he must have thought that, given the arbitrary way in which his bride had been chosen for him, he could have fared considerably worse. The signor of Pesaro was so close-mouthed about the reason for his trip to the city that even such an acute observer as the Ferrarese ambassador at first assumed that he was there to arrange a match with someone else. Lucrezia's Spanish fiancé, Don Gasparo, however, was under no such illusion. He and his father arrived in Rome the same day as Giovanni and immediately announced that they would resist any attempt to dissolve Lucrezia's betrothal to Don Gasparo. "Moreover," said the correspondent of the marchesa of Mantua, "they claimed to have the support of the King of Spain and they were confident that the Holy Father would not do anything without his majesty's approval." By November 8, however, Alexander had persuaded them to agree to the dissolution of the betrothal. Supposedly, the dissolution cost the pope 3,000 ducats. Soon after it was effected, Giovanni Sforza returned to Pesaro and sent his procurator to Rome to negotiate with the pope. The nuptial agreement was signed on February 2, 1493. By its terms Lucrezia was to go to Pesaro within the year, and she would bring her husband a dowry of 31,000 ducats. Alexander also obtained a *condotta* in the papal army and a high salaried post in the army of Milan for his future son-in-law.

When news of Giovanni's good fortune reached Pesaro, the jubilant bridegroom-to-be invited all the nobles of his small realm to a celebration at his palace. "They danced in the great hall, and the couples hand in hand issued from the castle led by Monsignor Scaltes, the Pope's plenipotentiary, and the people in their joy joined in and danced away the hours in the streets of the city."

The only existing likeness of Giovanni Sforza is that on a medal struck ten years after his marriage to Lucrezia. It shows a slender sensitive-looking man with an aquiline nose, long, flowing hair, a short, well-tended beard, and a grim expression about the eyes and mouth. The signor of Pesaro appears a tense, humorless man, but perhaps it was his unfortunate alliance with the Borgias that made him so. Perhaps when he first came to Rome, he was more relaxed and easygoing.

Lucrezia's prospective bridegroom was the eldest of two illegitimate sons born to Costanzo Sforza, lord of Pesaro and nephew of the celebrated condottiere Francesco Sforza of Milan. Since Costanzo's marriage was childless, when he died in 1483, his vicar-general arranged for the eighteen-year-old Giovanni to inherit his father's titles and to govern jointly with the latter's widow. She, however, found her young co-ruler so proud and harsh and generally difficult that in 1489 she retired to a castle she owned in Parma. By then Giovanni had also fallen out with his father's vicar. And this vicar, too, left Pesaro.

The domain that Giovanni was left to govern on his own was one of numerous small fiefs of the papacy in that section of Italy between the Appennines and the Adriatic known as the Romagna—"those atrocious governments that succeeded the democratic city-states of the Middle Ages," Stendhal would call them. Like his fellow tyrants throughout the region, Giovanni was an absolute ruler whose principal concern was not his subjects but himself. Within his small state he and his wishes were what counted. In the great world of Italian politics, however, he and his wishes counted for very little, indeed, until his betrothal to Lucrezia. "He will be a great man as long as this pope lives," Boccaccio wrote to the duke of Ferrara. And it was the thought of his future greatness as much as the size of Lucrezia's dowry that caused the twenty-eight-year-old signor of Pesaro to celebrate as he did when he heard that the nuptial contract had finally been signed.

In Rome, meanwhile, his not yet thirteen-year-old bride-to-be was receiving the congratulations of the ambassadors of the various princely houses. She was, of course, still too much the child to deal with these notables on her own. She merely smiled and thanked them while Adriana heard their requests for favors and promised to relay them to the pope. "We will make him a cardinal," Adriana promised, when asked to use her influence to obtain a cardinal's hat for Ippolito d'Este, the fifteen-year-old son of the duke of Ferrara.

Alexander, however, had more important things on his mind that winter, for the question of the castles was still unsettled and Rome appeared on the brink of war. In January, Cardinal Giuliano della Rovere, at whose palace the original deed of sale had been signed, left Rome for his fortress at Ostia. This fortress, which stood at the mouth of the Tiber, was considered impregnable. From there the cardinal was in a position to stop Rome's maritime commerce, and from there he could serve as a liaison between the armies of the king of Naples and the pope's enemies in the north. To meet the threat, Alexander summoned his chief condottieri to Rome and ordered that the gates of the city be watched. All that winter he seemed to fear an attack upon his person. One day while en route to the papal hunting lodge midway between Rome and Ostia, he heard a cannon go off. Without waiting to find out the reason for the bombardment, which was actually meant as a salute, the pope ordered his entire party to return to Rome. On February 27, when he and his cardinals went to the basilica of Santa Maria Maggiore, several squadrons of men-at-arms, armed with long lances as if for combat, rode behind him on the return trip.

Whatever Alexander's fears, however, they were not allowed to interfere with preparations for the wedding. While he conferred with his condottieri and arranged for new fortifications, his daughter was busy with her trousseau. Besides linen, and silver and gold plate and other household items, every bride was expected to bring a complete wedding outfit to her new home. A merchant of Pescia noted that the wedding outfit he had given his daughter included several rose-colored skirts embroidered with silver, a number of petticoats of Alexandrine silk, some crimson waistbands fringed after the Venetian style, silver damask girdles trimmed in white or green leather, cloth caps with silver scales, an embroidered bodice with azure-blue sleeves, red shoes and colored hose, as well as a Book of Hours, a coral necklace, a string of pearls with a gilt pendant, a sapphire and diamond clasp, a picture of the Virgin, and a garland for the hair fashioned of peacock feathers interspersed with silver and pearls. A pope's daughter would, of course, be expected to have a far more splendid trousseau. Much of what it eventually included would be in the form of gifts: from the bridegroom, from the cardinals, from the various princes, and from anyone else who wished to curry favor with the pope. There would be pearls and rubies and diamond rings; furs, hats, scarves, belts, bonnets, handkerchiefs, and ivory combs; gold-embroidered pillowcases and carved mirrors; a jasper vase worth 66 ducats; a set of enamelled dishes; five pieces of gold brocade; and a silver lavabo worth 800 ducats. All of the gifts would be displayed on her wedding day. Although Lucrezia was supposed to be married on April 24, the Feast of Saint George, the date was later changed, then changed again. Finally, it was announced that she would be married in the Vatican on June 12, 1493.

The chroniclers of Pesaro tell us that the bridegroom set out for the Holy City "with a following of 120 men-at-arms, fifty horsemen and many bishops. " On Sunday, June 9, 1493, he and his entourage arrived at the Porta del Populo. The entire Roman senate, the ambassadors of all the great powers, and his three prospective brothers-in-law were there to greet him.

Alexander's promise to keep his children at a distance had long since been forgotten. Geoffredo, the youngest, who was only twelve and had originally been destined for the church, was being mentioned as a prospective bridegroom for the granddaughter of the king of Naples, should the dispute between Ferrante and the pope ever be settled. Despite Alexander's frequently voiced doubts as to whether this son was really his, he would sometimes go out of his way to show off the boy. On February 16, 1494, for example, he introduced him to the ambassadors of Florence and Naples, and according to Virginio Orsini's correspondent in Rome who was present at the time, both men were enchanted by Geoffredo's astute replies and generally winning manners. The eighteen-year-old Cesare also enchanted his elders. The Ferrarese ambassador Gianandrea Boccaccio found him "lively and merry and fond of society," and since he was very modest, he presented "a better and more distinguished appearance than his brother, the Duke of Gandia." Cesare had been named bishop of Valencia a short time before, but he made no secret of his distaste for the priestly life. When Boccaccio visited him at his palace, "he was on his way to the chase dressed in a costume altogether worldly, that is silk and armed. He had only a little tonsure like a simple priest."

After the death of his half brother, Pedro Luis, Cesare had thought that as the next eldest he would be the one to inherit all of Pedro Luis's titles. When he was bypassed in favor of his younger brother Juan, his anger and disappointment were such that he frankly stated that he felt like killing Juan "for having the dukedom of Gandia." But although most of those who met Cesare recognized his superiority, the sixteen-year-old Juan was his father's favorite—*il dretto occhio* ("his right eye"). There seemed, in fact, to be nothing the pope would not give him.

Since Maria Enriquez, Juan's betrothed, was a first cousin of the kind of Spain, Alexander wished to send his son to Valencia with jewelry befitting the husband of a royal bride. For months a famous Roman goldsmith did nothing but set jewels and buy every kind of precious gem for the pope's son. According to Boccaccio, there were "great pearls in infinite numbers, rubies, diamonds, emeralds and sapphires all in perfect condition." But the sixteen-year-old Juan was having a good time in Rome and seemed in no hurry to leave. The Turkish price Dschem was living in the Vatican then and for some reason Juan delighted in the company of this cruel-tempered, middle-aged man with the hooked nose and glittering blue eyes. On May 5, for example, Juan and Dschem, both sporting turbans and long flowing Turkish robes, rode in front of the cross when the pope visited the basilica of Saint John Lateran.

For Lucrezia's wedding Juan planned to wear a Turkish robe made of cloth of gold and a collar of rubies and pearls. Not wishing to be overshadowed by this dazzling brother-in-law, Giovanni Sforza also planned to appear in Turkish garb. Because the signor of Pesaro was not a wealthy man, he had been forced to borrow money to cover the cost of his wedding expenses, and he had used Lucrezia's 31,000-ducat dowry as security. But even his bride's dowry was not sufficient to cover the cost of a collar of pearls and rubies. To appear without jewelry on his wedding day, however, was unthinkable, and so Giovanni had asked his former brother-in-law, the marquis of Mantua, to lend him a gold collar for the occasion. But if the need to scrounge thus in order to keep up with his new in-laws humiliated him, the humiliation must have soon been forgotten on that warm Sunday morning in June when Giovanni rode through the streets of Rome with his distinguished escort and felt himself the cynosure of all eyes.

Preceded by Mambrino, "the priest"—a jester in velvet suit and golden cap—and announced by the joyous sound of fifes and trumpets, the wedding procession moved slowly down the Via del Corso, past the basilica of Saint Mark, through the crowds in the Campo dei Fiori, across the Ponte Sant' Angelo, to the palace of Santa Maria in Portico, where the bride was waiting for them. As soon as the trumpets announced the approach of the wedding procession, Giulia and Adriana sent Lucrezia out to stand on one of the loggias overlooking the Piazza San Pietro. It was her first public appearance, and the piazza was filled with people eager for a glimpse of the pope's golden-haired daughter. Although all those upturned faces must have at first bewildered her, she had been too carefully coached to show it. Instead, she stood there smiling down at them, a slender, graceful, still childish figure awaiting the bridegroom she had never seen. As soon as Giovanni caught sight of her, he reined in his horse, and, in the age-old gesture of the knight saluting his lady, acknowledged her presence. As she had been taught to do, Lucrezia curtsied in return, and the procession continued on its way to the Vatican, where the signor of Pesaro would throw himself at his father-in-law's feet. In a short Latin speech, which he had doubtless rehearsed innumerable times, he would dedicate himself and his small state to the service of the papacy.

While Giovanni was giving this speech, Lucrezia must have been discussing her bridegroom's appearance with Giulia and Adriana. Certainly during the long, lazy afternoons while Giulia and Lucrezia waited for their hair to dry or worked on their embroidery, Giulia had explained the sexual responsibilities of a wife to her friend. And if, after glimpsing her bridegroom, Lucrezia expressed a certain uneasiness about fulfilling those responsibilities, Giulia and Adriana were there to reassure her and to turn her mind from thoughts of what followed the wedding to thoughts of the wedding itself.

Weddings have always provided a convenient excuse for conspicuous consumption. "What man, no matter how miserable his condition, does not marry in style?" asked Giovanni Pontano, the humanist secretary of Ferrante of Naples.

At the banquet given in 1473 by the cardinal of San Sixtus to celebrate the marriage of Ferrante's daughter Eleanora to Ercole I of Ferrara, oxen roasted whole in casings of sweetmeats were followed by gilded sheep and innumerable chickens, ducks, and pheasants. After these came gigantic pies from which children in allegorical costumes emerged. "Who would have expected the Church of God to have so much silver," said Infessura, referring to what the eight-hour feast must have cost the cardinal.

When Caterina Sforza married Girolamo Riario, the "nephew" of Pope Sixtus IV, the end of each course was announced by the appearance of a triumphal chariot from which a child emerged to recite verses or tell funny stories. Leonardo da Vinci designed the costumes for the wild men in the tournament celebrating the marriage of Ludovico Sforza to Beatrice d'Este. In addition to the presentation of an allegory, *The Struggle of Chastity with Love*, at the wedding of Beatrice's half sister to Annibale Bentivoglio, lord of Bologna, there were 800 barrels of wine, 30,000 pounds of meat, and a castle made of sweetmeats housing a live pig whose loud grunting and frantic efforts to break free provided even more entertainment than the elaborately staged allegory.

Compared to these extravaganzas, Lucrezia's wedding was a fairly subdued and inexpensive affair. Rather than use the Sala dei Pontefici in which Innocent had celebrated the weddings of his granddaughters, Alexander chose to use the rooms adjoining the newly decorated but still unfurnished Borgia apartments. The walls of these rooms were hung with velvet coverings and tapestries for the occasion, and the great papal throne used in public consistories was decorated with brocade and set in the middle of a platform in the Sala Reale, or "Great Hall," where the celebration would take place. To either side of the throne stood five consistorial chairs with shoulder pieces of crimson, blue, and green velvet. On a lower platform, two similar chairs, their backs decorated with narrow strips of gold brocade, had been set against a wall between a pair of windows. A hundred cushions in various colors were scattered in front of these seats. The Sala Reale was reached by way of a smaller room where the couple would exchange their vows. Here, too, a throne had been placed, not upon a platform, but with four steps as an approach to it across the width of the room.

On the morning of June 12, Juan Borgia, resplendent in his new gold Turkish robe, arrived at the palace of Santa Maria in Portico to fetch the bride. Lucrezia's wedding dress was rumored to have cost 15,000 ducats, an expensive outfit to be sure, but not nearly as expensive as her brother's, which the correspondent of the marchesa of Mantua estimated had cost three times that amount. In fact, those who described the wedding seem to have been so dazzled by Juan's outfit that they scarcely mentioned Lucrezia's. Like most Roman brides, she probably wore white satin, although red velvet trimmed with fur and embroidered with gold thread was also popular. Her dress had a small train which was carried by a Negro girl. Slaves, both black and white, were common in all the Mediterranean countries. Elegant ladies usually preferred having black slaves to offset their own whiteness. Burchard tells us that one of Innocent's granddaughters, who followed immediately after Lucrezia, also wore a dress with a train "borne by a Negress." Behind these two came Giulia Farnese, Adriana de Mila, and about 150 other Roman ladies. Led by Juan Borgia, they made their way to the room where the ceremony was to take place. When the pope heard that they had arrived, he proceeded through the apartments to the same room and seated himself upon his throne. One by one the ladies passed before him, but, says Burchard, "despite my admonishments none of them genuflected except for the pope's daughter and a few others close to her."

The Borgias were noted for their perfect manners. Lucrezia had been carefully taught how to behave toward a pope—when to curtsy, how many steps to move forward and backward—and she invariably accorded her father the deference due his great office. But the other ladies must have been too excited by the presence of the splendid figure in the narrow-sleeved white overgarment and crimson satin hood to remember what was expected of them. And although Burchard might be scandalized by their neglect of protocol, Alexander appeared too delighted by the proximity of all these bejewelled ladies with their fashionably exposed bosoms to notice. After he had greeted the last one, Juan and Lucrezia stepped forward to kiss the pope's foot. They were followed by the ladies who once again passed in single file before the papal throne. A few of the more prominent ladies remained kneeling by the pope while the others moved back to stand by his right. Among the prelates and other male guests at the pope's left stood Cesare, an insignificant figure in ecclesiastical black who must have resented the stellar role accorded to his younger brother.

When all the ladies had kissed the papal foot, the bridegroom stepped forward in his Turkish robe and borrowed gold collar. He and Lucrezia knelt on cushions before the pope, and Alexander's notary asked them if they were prepared to take one another as man and wife. Although they had never so much as exchanged a word, they both assured the notary that they did so "most willingly." Their replies were the signal for the bishop of Concordia to kneel beside them and slip the ring given the bride by her bridegroom on the ring finger of her left hand and a second ring on her index finger. During this ceremony, the commander of the papal army held an unsheathed sword over the heads of the newly wedded pair. The sword, a tradition at Renaissance weddings, was supposed to remind the bride of what awaited her should she forget her marriage vows. It was lowered as soon as the rings were in place on her fingers. The bishop then delivered a short sermon on the sacrament of marriage and the ceremony was over. Juan once again took his sister's arm and led her and the other wedding guests into the Sala Reale where the pope seated himself on his throne and most of the rest of the company found places on the cushions scattered on the floor.

After verses and a comedy were presented, it was time for refreshments. Says Burchard:

> An assortment of all kinds of sweets, marzipan and drinks of wine in about a hundred basins and cups was brought and carried around with napkins by chamberlains and grooms. They first served the pope and the cardinals, then the bridegroom and the ladies, whilst others went to the clergy and the rest, and finally they flung what sweets remained amongst the people outside, in such abundance that more than a hundred pounds of sweets were crushed and trampled underfoot.

Sweets were a great luxury then, and the papal master of ceremonies obviously disapproved of such wastefulness. But even as a cardinal, Alexander had been prodigal with the masses. There was, for example, the bullfight he had organized in the Piazza Navona to celebrate the fall of Granada.

According to Stefan Infessura, who also described Lucrezia's wedding in his diary, not all of the leftover candies were thrown to the masses. Some of them were tossed *"in sinu multarum mulierum,"* which some have translated as "into the laps of many of the ladies" and others have translated as "into their bosoms." Wherever the candies landed, Infessura obviously disapproved, for he ends his description of the proceedings *"et hoc ad honorem et laudem omnipotentes Dei et Ecclesie Romane"* ("and this in honor of almighty God and the Roman church").

The medieval church saw woman as *Eva rediviva,* "the temptress responsible for Adam's fall." To antipapalists, such as Infessura, as well as to old-fashioned priests, such as Burchard, and reformers, such as Savonarola, the presence of so many women at a wedding ceremony in the traditionally all-male halls of the Vatican was an indication of the depths to which God's church had fallen. Although as a young man Alexander's mentor Pius II, the former Aeneas Sylvius Piccolomini, also had mistresses and fathered illegitimate children, when he was elected pope, he had turned his back upon his former life. "Forget Aeneas, look at Pius," he told his critics. Alexander was, however, too devoted a father to follow Pius's example. He was, moreover, much too balanced a person ever to become an ascetic or a fanatic. But this devotion to his children and this balance, which would have seemed admirable in a layman, were exasperating in a clergyman, for they led him into actions which, while not always outrageous in themselves, were so inconsonant with the office he held as to outrage large numbers of Christians and provide ready ammunition for his critics.

Following the afternoon celebration, a select handful of those who had crowded into the Sala Reale were invited back for the wedding supper. Each of the cardinals invited had a woman sitting next to him, Burchard reported. When the guests had finished dining, the wedding gifts were presented to the bride. The ladies then danced, and a comedy was given which Infessura, who wasn't present, described as "lascivious," and Boccaccio, who was present, called "worthy." When it was over, says Infessura, "the Pope himself personally escorted his daughter and her spouse to the palace of Santa Maria in Portico which is to the left of the steps of Saint Peter's where the said spouse was united with his wife."

It makes Alexander sound unbelievably prurient, but in truth he was doing no more than was expected of him, for it was customary then for princely marriages to be consummated before witnesses. In a letter to the duke of Milan, two of those present described the first union of Alfonso d'Este of Ferrara and his bride Anna Sforza:

> Then the bride and groom were put to bed and all of us surrounded their bed and began teasing them. In Don Alfonso's corner was the Marchese of Mantua with many others who harrassed the bridegroom. Don Alfonso had a stick in his hand with which he defended himself. Madonna Anna took it all good humoredly, though both bride and groom must have found it strange to see so many people gathered round their bed. . . . Finally we left, and in the morning we wanted to know how things had gone, and we found that they had slept well.

If the bride was very young, however, consummation could be postponed. In the *Heptameron*, Marguerite of Navarre tells the story of Alexander de Medici, who married a bastard daughter of the emperor Charles V. "Since she was still so young that it would not have been seemly to sleep with her, the Duke treated her very gently while waiting for her to mature." The eleven-year-old Caterina Sforza, on the other hand, was twice sent to bed with her much older bridegroom before being returned to her stepmother because she was too delicate to continue living as a wife. Although Infessura says that Lucrezia's marriage was consummated on her wedding night, other sources make it clear that it wasn't. Lucrezia was, after all, only thirteen and may not yet have reached her menarche. Certainly, Alexander loved his daughter enough to want to ease the abrupt transition from childhood to womanhood this early marriage had forced upon her.

Nor would the delay in consummating the marriage impose any special hardship on the bridegroom. Like all patriarchal societies, Italy was a bulwark of the double standard. The wife was expected to remain faithful to her husband so that he could be sure the children she bore him were really his. The husband was free to roam. The higher up the social scale he was, the greater the number of available women. Marguerite of Navarre tells us that "to spare" his youthful bride, Alexander de Medici "was amorously involved with several other women of the city whom he went to see while his wife slept."

The pope had asked that Giovanni and Lucrezia live in the palace of Santa Maria in Portico for at least a year, and he seems to have expected that the marriage would be consummated before the year was over. Lucrezia, meanwhile, continued to keep Adriana and Giulia with her so that in many respects her life after marriage must have seemed no different from what it had been before. But although she continued to retire to her virginal bed, the presence of this husband with whom she would one day have relations could only intensify the growing awareness of her own body and the vague desire to love and be loved that normally herald the onset of puberty. If Giovanni Sforza was at all considerate of his young bride, if he noticed what she wore and how she did her hair, or took time to sit and talk with her, the thirteen-year-old girl would not find it difficult to focus all her undefined yearnings upon him.

As the Ferrarese ambassador had predicted, the signor of Pesaro was now a great man in Rome. Four days after his marriage, he and his brother-in-law the duke of Gandia rode out "as if they were two kings" to welcome Don Diego Lopez de Hare, the ambassador of the king of Spain. According to Infessura, the ambassador had come to reproach the pope for his simony and the venality of the Curia. Moreover, "his king had expelled the Marranos from his kingdom as enemies of the Christian faith and he marvelled that the Pope as head of the Church had received them in Rome; therefore the king exhorted the Holy Father to expel them from the lands subject to the Church."

Although it is true that Alexander, like many of the popes before the Counter Reformation, was hospitable to the Jews, he was, in fact, frequently accused of being a Jew or a Marrano by his enemies. Burchard, who was present at the meeting with the Spanish ambassador, makes no mention of any complaints about the Marranos. What seems more likely is that besides making formal obeisance to the pope on behalf on his king, the Spanish ambassador emphasized Spain's interest in the affairs of Naples and the house of Aragon.

Ever since the coronation of Charles VIII, the young French king had stated repeatedly that he had as much right to Naples as he had to France and that his army would one day invade the kingdom. As Charles saw it, the treaty signed with Ludovico Sforza in 1492 had no other end in view. In the troubled days after the flight of Giuliano della Rovere to Ostia when Alexander feared a Neapolitan attack upon Rome momentarily, the pope had encouraged one of his cardinals to write to the king of France urging him to begin the invasion. But, says Sigismundo dei Conti, "if Alexander had the cardinal write this way, it was not because he wished Charles to come, but because like so many popes before him, he hoped to profit from the terror inspired by the mere mention of the French."

Charles, however, took the cardinal at his word. Because Naples was a papal fief, only the pope could invest its rulers. Although Innocent VIII had promised the investiture to Ferrante's son Alfonso, the king of France decided to seek it for himself. So that he would be free to send his soliders to Naples, he decided to placate all his enemies. In January 1493, he signed a treaty with Ferdinand of Spain; on May 21 of the same year, he signed a treaty with Maximilian, the heir to the Holy Roman Empire. Two weeks later, he informed Ludovico Sforza that he had selected him to head the forthcoming invasion of Naples, the famous *impresa di Napoli* as it came to be called. Then, on July 11, the king's ambassador arrived in Lyons en route to Italy where he planned to seek first the cooperation of the other Italian states and then ask the pope to approve the investiture of Charles as king of Naples.

Ferdinand of Spain had no great love for his cousin Ferrante of Naples. In fact, he believed that because Ferrante was illegitimate, his father had had no right to bestow the kingdom of Naples upon him in the first place. Nevertheless, even Ferrante was preferable to the French. Although the king of Spain had signed a treaty of friendship with Charles VIII, he made up his mind to help resolve Ferrante's differences with the pope before the French ambassador arrived in Rome to demand investiture for his king. With Spanish assistance the matter of the castles was finally settled. By the terms of the settlement, Virginio Orsini was to keep the castles he had illegally bought, but as a sign of the pope's rights over them, he was to pay Alexander 35,000 ducats. To consolidate the Holy Father's ties with Spain and Naples, Geoffredo Borgia was to marry Ferrante's granddaughter Sancha, and Juan Borgia was to go to Spain as soon as possible to marry Maria Enriquez.

On August 2, Juan set sail for Barcelona. Before he left, the pope sent him a letter of advice written in the Valencian dialect urging his son to treat his new bride well, and warning the seventeen-year-old bridegroom against going out at night, playing dice, and most important of all, touching the revenues of his duchy without the approval of his advisers. Juan's ship had not yet reached Civitavecchia when a messenger arrived bearing a second letter. In it Alexander told his son how to care for his skin and hair and ordered him to put on gloves at once and not to take them off until he reached Barcelona. "Salt ruins the skin," wrote the pope, "and in our country people prize beautiful hands."

Rome is hot and muggy during the summer, and hot, muggy weather meant plague in those days. At around the same time that Juan left for Barcelona, Giovanni Sforza used the weather as an excuse to ask his father-in-law's permission to return to Pesaro. Lucrezia was still very much the child under Adriana's tutelage, and Giovanni may have looked forward to getting away from this household where he did not feel himself the master. Unfortunately, his homecoming did not turn out to be the joyous occasion he had pictured. No sooner did he arrive in his little state on the Adriatic than he was greeted by the many bills he had run up in preparation for his wedding. Since he lacked the wherewithal to pay them, he wrote to his father-in-law asking for a 5,000-ducat advance on the 31,000-ducat dowry he had been promised. On September 15, the pope sent his reply. He had discussed the matter with Giovanni's cousin Cardinal Ascanio Sforza, he told his son-in-law. The two of them had agreed that when the weather was cooler and healthier, Giovanni should return to Rome to consummate his marriage with his wife. Afterward, he would receive not the 5,000-ducat advance, but the entire dowry.

Lucrezia was young and attractive, and her husband was in desperate need of her dowry. Nevertheless, he appeared in no great hurry to return to Rome. Nor was he the only laggard lover with whom Alexander would have to contend that fall. According to reports the pope had received from Spain, Juan Borgia, too, had not yet consummated his marriage. Instead of spending his time with his wife and "being a good companion to her" as his father had advised, he spent his time chasing after prostitutes and gambling.

In a world of arranged marriages, the reluctance shown by Juan and Giovanni was neither unusual nor, from a modern standpoint, incomprehensible. Husbands did not, after all, court their wives. Rather than being the eagerly anticipated gratification of a mutual desire, the first union was an act performed with a stranger. And like Lucrezia, that stranger was usually extremely young and embarrassingly innocent compared to her bridegroom who, even if he was in his teens, had already had considerable experience with courtesans and may have had a mistress or two. Since, moreover, the purpose of marriage was procreation not pleasure, he had been warned against seeking the same satisfaction with his bride that he sought with other women. She, in turn, had been cautioned against showing too much enthusiasm, not only because it would make her appear a whore, but because coitus that was too passionate was believed to be unfruitful.

Though some husbands managed to find enjoyment in the marriage bed despite these restrictions, others regarded "this discrete and conscientious voluptuousness," as Montaigne called it, something of a chore.

Ludovico Sforza was betrothed to Beatrice d'Este, the daughter of the duke of Ferrara, when he was twenty-nine and she was five. While waiting for her to grow up, he took a beautiful Milanese noblewoman as his mistress. Since by the time Beatrice came of age, he really loved his mistress, he found all sorts of excuses for postponing the wedding. When he finally married the then fifteen-year-old Beatrice, her anxious father informed his wife that "the result which we had desired did not follow." Eventually, however, Ludovico did get around to sleeping with Beatrice, and for a time, the forty-year-old bridegroom even fancied himself in love with his rambunctious teen-aged bride. Juan Borgia also consummated his marriage, and in February 1494, he was able to tell the pope that Maria Enriquez was pregnant. What happened when Giovanni Sforza returned to the palace of Santa Maria in Portico in mid-November of 1493, however, we do not know. Certainly, whatever happened was not so enjoyable that he could not bear to be parted from his wife, for on November 23 he accompanied the pope and Cesare when they made their triumphal entry into Orvieto.

The papal party remained in Orvieto for almost two weeks, passing their days "in ceremonies and spectacles and their nights in parties and banquets and balls and discussing affairs of state after dinner." December 19, they were back in Rome. Giovanni remained there only long enough to celebrate Christmas with Lucrezia and her family, then once again set out for Pesaro. Whatever the reason he gave for taking leave of his wife so soon after being reunited with her, it must have seemed legitimate to the pope, for Alexander raised no objection to his departure. If Lucrezia was surprised or upset, she kept her feelings to herself. Not only was she still too young to have any idea of what to expect from her husband, but the example of Giulia and Orsino had convinced her that she could expect precious little.

Burchard tells us nothing about the Christmas festivities that preceded Giovanni's departure. No matter how joyous they may have been, Christmas of 1493 was not a joyous season for the pope. Like a nightmare from which he could not awaken, the deadly situation taking shape in France grew ever more ominous. Less than a week after the signing of the agreement with Virginio Orsini on August 2, the French ambassador had arrived in Rome to demand investiture for his king. Although by then Alexander had made up his mind not to support Charles, he was much too adroit a diplomat to say so. He would be willing to examine all claims to Naples, he told the ambassador. However, the French must realize that since two other popes had granted the investiture of Naples to Ferrante it would be unjust to take it away from him without first making a thorough investigation. When the French envoy asked if the Holy Father would be willing to grant the French free passage through the papal states, Alexander told him that that also would depend upon the results of the investigation.

His reply did not deter the French. To prod Alexander into making a firmer commitment, Charles announced that he would deprive the papacy of its share of the revenues the church collected in France by withholding his country's obedience to the Holy See. The king also threatened to call a council to depose the pope. There had been three ecclesiastical councils between 1402 and 1449, all of them intended in one way or another to limit papal power. To discourage further councils, Pius II had promulgated his bull *Execrabilis*, which declared any appeal to a general council as a superior authority to the pope to be anathema. But the denunciation did not prevent disgruntled kings and cardinals from continuing to threaten a council whenever they had a disagreement with the pope. Because Charles was busy with preparations for the *impresa di Napoli*, he could do nothing to implement his threat that winter. The young king had put aside between 500,000 and 600,000 ducats to cover the first costs of the invasion, and he counted on moving some of his troops by Christmas. In November, Ludovico Sforza, whom Guicciardini calls "the guide and director of all the French dealings with the Italians," granted the king and his army free passage through the duchy of Milan. On December 28, Charles informed the pope that since Alexander had not yet said anything about the investiture of Naples or papal aid to the French army, France would continue to withhold her obedience.

Meanwhile, Ferrante of Naples berated the pope for his lack of commitment to the Neapolitan cause. In a characteristically vituperative letter to his envoy in Rome, the king accused Alexander of breaking all his promises and doing nothing to hinder the French. "And in such confusion of affairs likely to lead to new disturbances," says Guicciardini, "began the year 1494—a most unhappy year for Italy, and in truth the beginning of those years of misfortune, because it opened the door to innumerable horrible calamities, in which, one could say, for various reasons, a great part of the world was subsequently involved."

The Invasion of Charles VIII

While I sing O God the Redeemer
I see all Italy being set afire
By these Frenchmen who with great force
Are coming to lay waste to each and every place

Matteo Maria Boiardo

May God forgive him who invited the French into Italy, for all
our troubles have arisen from this.

Alexander VI

I confess that I did great wrong to Italy, but I did it to keep myself in the place in which I find myself, and I did it unwillingly.

Ludovico Sforza

The year 1494 began in a mood of sinister foreboding. Everywhere rumors spread that "in various parts of Italy there had appeared things alien to the natural course of nature and the heavens.
"One day a lone pilgrim was observed shouldering a heavy
wooden cross through the silent countryside on the outskirts of
Siena. Suddenly he paused and shook his fist at the city. Another
day a flock of birds belonging to a species hitherto unknown in Siena
circled over the bell tower of the Palazzo Pubblico. In a number of
places men found images of the saints covered with sweat. Near
Arezzo, armed phantoms were reported riding through the sky
astride giant steeds. At Puglia, one night during a thunderstorm, a
flash of lightning revealed three suns surrounded by clouds. And
from the pulpit of Santa Maria del Fiore in Florence, Girolamo
Savonarola announced the coming of a new Cyrus, "a man who will
invade Italy in a few weeks without drawing his sword. He will pass
over the rocks and the mountains and the fortresses will fall before
him."

To Savonarola, the king of France was an instrument of divine
judgment, the incarnation of the "fiery sword" that the Florentine reformer had once beheld in a dream. But to those who knew Charles
VIII, the twenty-four-year-old monarch seemed an unlikely choice

for so heroic a task. "The French king," wrote the Venetian ambassador, "is insignificant in appearance; he has an ugly face, large lustreless eyes which see badly, an enormous hooked nose and thick lips which are always open. He stutters and has a disagreeable twitching in his hands which are never still."

When, in 1492, Ludovico Sforza entered into an alliance with this grotesque young man, who surrounded himself with mistresses and slept on rose-scented sheets, it was because he wished to compel King Ferrante of Naples to give up the idea of deposing him. To the French chronicler Philippe de Comines, Ludovico seemed a very shrewd man but a very apprehensive one. "And," said Comines, "he is very dejected when he is afraid (and I speak as one who has known him and negotiated many matters with him); he is a man without faith if he sees profit in breaking it."

Had Ludovico's nephew Gian Galeazzo not married Ferrante's granddaughter Isabella, Ludovico would have had little to fear, for the lawful duke of Milan was a dull and ineffectual sort. "*Incapacissimo*," Guicciardini calls him. But Isabella had enough capacity for them both, and she had no intention of seeing her husband's claims to the duchy of Milan pushed aside by his uncle. In the opinion of her contemporary, historian Paolo Giovio, she set "the first spark to the conflagration of war that was to consume Italy." Certainly her appeals to her father and grandfather and their frequent letters in her behalf terrified Ludovico. As he later confided to his brother Ascanio, he allied himself with Charles VIII, not because he wished Charles to have Naples, but because the threat of a French invasion would compel the king of Naples to attend to his own affairs instead of meddling in the affairs of others. And, if later, it should become necessary to restrain the French, there was always the threat of the emperor to fall back on.

A prince, says Machiavelli, "ought never to make common cause with one more powerful than himself." Unfortunately for Italy, Ludovico failed to take into account either the power or the tenacity of Charles VIII. In a world where self-interest, or what Guicciardini calls "*il mio particolare*," was the universal rule, Charles clung to the moribund ideals of the Middle Ages. Like his distant ancestor Saint Louis, he dreamed of leading a crusade against Islam, a crusade that would end with Constantinople once more in Christian hands and France the arbiter of Europe. As the king saw it, the conquest of

Naples was a necessary preliminary to his great undertaking. "To better and more easily accomplish this . . . and at the least cost for the future," he wrote, "we must recover the kingdom of Naples which borders the lands held by the infidels and which was usurped from our predecessors of the house of Anjou." To Comines, the king was "a weak body wedded to his own will." But his will was strong and he had the French army behind him. Since, moreover, he was convinced that what he was doing was in the interest of Christendom, neither the pope nor Ludovico nor the emperor nor anyone else was going to restrain him.

His claims to the investiture of Naples assumed new urgency when on January 27, 1494, the pope received word of the death of King Ferrante. *"Sine luce, sine cruce, sine Deo"* ("without light, without the cross, without God"), Burchard wrote in his diary. With Ferrante dead, Alexander could no longer fend off the king of France with vague promises to investigate his claim. He had to agree to crown either Ferrante's son Alfonso or the French monarch. Although the pope had never really considered giving the crown to Charles, it was not until March 21, four days after the king had formally announced his intention to set out for Italy, that Alexander issued a papal bull supporting Alfonso.

Despite the pope's sincere commitment to the Neapolitan cause— he would rather lose his miter, his state, and his life than abandon Alfonso, he later told Ascanio Sforza—Alexander was not so altruistic as to overlook the advantages that might accrue to his children from his decision. In fact, his demands for money and titles for his sons appeared so excessive to Alfonso that for a time negotiations between the two were at a standstill. Finally, however, an agreement that found favor with both king and pope was reached. On April 18, the College of Cardinals met in a secret consistory that lasted from five in the morning until almost two the following afternoon. When it was over, the pope proclaimed Alfonso the lawful king of Naples. Ignoring the protests of the French ambassadors and their threats to summon a council to depose him, the Holy Father drew up a bull appointing his nephew Cardinal Giovanni Borgia of Monreale papal legate to the new king's coronation.

Alexander was never a man who found it easy to keep secrets, and he was in the habit of confiding his most carefully guarded diplomatic maneuvers to his children. Hence, Lucrezia and her husband must have known of the decision of the consistory even before it was made public.

When the signor of Pesaro had returned to Rome at the end of January, he had found his palace the center of an active and lively court. "The majority of those who wish to curry favor with the Pope pass through these doors," reported one observer. Under Adriana's tutelage, his thirteen-and-one-half-year-old wife was learning how to deal graciously with this stream of supplicants—whom to heed and whom to ignore. It was customary then for those seeking favors from the pope to bring him gifts, and Alexander usually shared his gifts with his children. During the Lenten season, for example, he divided several wheels of cheese and some carp between Cesare and the residents of Santa Maria in Portico. Occasionally, Lucrezia received more expensive gifts, such as jewelry or perfume. In addition to benefiting from these gifts, Giovanni also had other less tangible indications of Alexander's favor. On March 14, he headed the escort sent to the Lateran gate to greet the Neapolitan ambassador. On Palm Sunday, he occupied the place of honor at the celebration of mass in the Sistine Chapel. On Easter Sunday, he was one of three dignitaries who gave the pope the water with which to wash his hands. But the signor of Pesaro no longer derived any pleasure from these honors. How could he when each day the breach between the pope and the Sforzas seemed to grow wider?

"You speak to me of Italy, but I have never seen its face," Giovanni's cousin Ludovico supposedly told a Florentine citizen who accused him of endangering his country by his dealings with the French.

Like Ludovico, Giovanni felt no loyalty to that amorphous entity known as Italy. But he did feel an intense loyalty to the house of Sforza. And he could not see how he could continue to serve as a condottiere of Milan and a condottiere of the pope when one was supporting France and the other was supporting Naples. He was also concerned about what would happen to Pesaro in the war which everyone now thought inevitable. Because he lacked the courage to take an independent stand, Giovanni continually besieged both his father-in-law and his cousin Ascanio with questions. The questions so exasperated the pope that Alexander accused his son-in-law of wishing to know the outcome of events before they happened. Ascanio also grew impatient, especially after he learned that

Giovanni had been trying to help his former in-laws, the Gonzagas, obtain a cardinal's hat for one of their family. To see a Gonzaga made cardinal would be "a knife in his heart," Ascanio informed his cousin. How could Giovanni be so stupid as to assist an enemy of his own house at a time when it was so necessary that the Sforzas present a united front?

Although temporarily chastened, Giovanni continued to press for a solution to his personal dilemma. "Holy Father," he told the pope one day in the presence of Ascanio, "everyone in Rome believes that Your Holiness has entered into an agreement with the king of Naples, who is an enemy of the state of Milan. If this is so, I am in an awkward position, as I am in the pay of Your Holiness and also of the state I have named. If things continue as they are, I do not know how I can serve one party without falling out with the other, and at the same time I do not wish to offend. I ask that Your Holiness may be pleased to define my position so that I may not become an enemy of my own blood, and not act contrary to the obligations into which I have entered by virtue of my agreement with Your Holiness and the illustrious state of Milan."

Giovanni took too much interest in the affairs of the papacy, his father-in-law replied. He should choose in whose pay he wanted to remain according to his contract. The pope then ordered Ascanio to write to his brother Ludovico about the matter. In desperation, Giovanni also decided to write to his cousin in Milan. "My lord, if I had foreseen in what a position I was to be placed, I would sooner have eaten the straw under my body than have entered into such an agreement," he told Ludovico.

Still unwilling to take the responsibility for making a decision, he beseeched his powerful relatives to make it for him. "I cast myself in your arms," he wrote. "I beg Your Excellency not to desert me, but to give me help, favor and advice on how to resolve the difficulty in which I am placed so that I may remain a good servant of Your Excellency. Preserve for me the position and the little nest, which, thanks to the mercy of Milan, my ancestors left me, and I and my men-of-war will ever remain at the service of Your Excellency."

Since Neapolitan troops would pass through Pesaro on their way to Milan and since the French might also go through Pesarese territory on their way to Naples, before Giovanni resigned his post as a condottiere in the papal army, he wanted a guarantee from Ludovico that the resignation would not cost him his "little nest." Ludovico, however, was too self-centered to give much thought to the plight of such a relatively unimportant person as his provincial cousin. He had used him when he needed him. But the marriage with Lucrezia that was supposed to bind her father to the Sforzas had done no such thing, and now the signor of Pesaro must fend for himself. Without a guarantee from Ludovico, Giovanni dared not resign his post in the papal army. And so for the present he remained in Rome.

A feeling of crisis once again pervaded the city. As in the troubled days after Giuliano della Rovere had fled to Ostia, armed guards surrounded the pope whenever he appeared in public. At the Castel Sant' Angelo, masons worked on a new outer wall for the fortress, while others helped build a corridor that would run from the Vatican to the castle, thus providing the Curia with a means of escape should one be needed. Not only did the French report these preparations to their king, they constantly sought to win over the members of the great Roman families and the more important cardinals. Five days after Alexander announced that he would grant the investiture of Naples to Alfonso, they succeeded in persuading Giuliano della Rovere to flee his fortress at Ostia and head for France. Although Giuliano had long been a friend of Naples, both Ludovico Sforza and the French were shrewd enough to realize that once Alexander threw his support to Naples, Giuliano's hatred of the pope would make him eager to support France. With Ludovico's assistance, the cardinal reached his bishopric at Avignon in May. On June 1, he entered Lyons, where Charles greeted him affectionately. In the months that followed, he, who had never hesitated to use money to influence a papal election, became one of the most vociferous supporters of a council "to depose this simoniacal pope."

Although Giuliano's defection was certainly a blow to Alexander, it in no way changed his plans. On the Sunday before the cardinal left Ostia, the pope had sent his master of ceremonies, Johann Burchard, to Naples to attend to the details of Alfonso's coronation. On April 30, Burchard was summoned to the royal palace to demonstrate to the king how he must salute, kneel, and bare his arms and shoulders to take the oath of office. No hint of approaching war marred the coronation in the cathedral of San Gennaro on May 8 when, with his right hand on the Bible and his left on the crucifix, Alfonso swore to be faithful to the Holy Roman church and received his investiture from the hands of the papal legate. "Long live King Alfonso," the crowd shouted at the sight of the newly anointed monarch ascending his throne.

A few days later, the pope's son Geoffredo married the king's illegitimate daughter Sancha. When the wedding feast was over, the twelve-year-old bridegroom and his seventeen-year-old bride retired to Sancha's palace accompanied by the bride's father and the papal legate. While Alfonso and the legate waited in an antechamber, the youthful pair were undressed and placed side by side in the marriage bed. After a sheet had been thrown over them to cover their nakedness, the king and the legate were summoned. In their presence Sancha's maids of honor uncovered the pair to their navels. According to Burchard, Geoffredo "embraced his wife without shame." The king and the legate remained with them an hour chatting and then left.

While Geoffredo was being introduced precipitously to the responsibilities of married life, his fourteen-year-old sister was preparing to leave Rome for Pesaro. Lucrezia's marriage contract had stipulated that she leave "within the year" after her wedding. Even before the change in the pope's foreign policy, Giovanni had found living in Rome a burden and had constantly sought excuses to get away. Hence, it was only natural for him to wish to take his wife to Pesaro as soon as the marriage contract would permit. Although Alexander no longer had any legal right to keep Lucrezia with him, under normal circumstances the delight he took in his daughter's company might have tempted him to insist that she remain notwithstanding. As it was, the threat of plague made him eager to have her leave. On May 31, Lucrezia and her husband set out for Pesaro. With them were Adriana de Mila, Giulia Farnese, Giulia's lady-in-waiting Juana Moncada, and another Lucrezia, Lucrezia Lopez, a young Spanish noblewoman who would remain in Pesaro with the pope's daughter. Giulia and Adriana would return to Rome in July. A few days out of the city, they were joined by Francesco Gacet, a canon of Toledo, who frequently served as Alexander's confidential agent.

Their journey, which can be accomplished in a matter of hours today, took over a week. Since the only vehicles then in use were the four-wheeled peasant cart and a contraption with a movable front carriage, descended from the artillery cart, those who could afford to do so invariably traveled on horseback. Because of the scarcity of accommodations and the danger from bandits, each lap of their journey along the narrow, unpaved roads had to be timed so that nightfall would find them within reach of food and lodging. But despite the long hours on horseback and the primitive inns at which it was sometimes necessary to seek shelter, both Giulia and Lucrezia found the trip an exciting adventure. For Giulia, it represented a change from the enclosed life at Santa Maria in Portico. For Lucrezia, it was her first real separation from her father. And, as is so often the case with children of oversolicitous parents, the pang she felt at leaving him was soon tempered by a certain relief at being free of the prison of his concern.

Although Lucrezia was not then or ever in love with her husband nor he with her, the two seemed to get along reasonably well. Now that they were headed for his beloved Pesaro, Giovanni felt himself more in control, and he regaled the party with stories of how eager his subjects were to see their new countess. With that naïve narcissism so typical of pretty young women, both Lucrezia and Giulia could scarcely wait to show off their clothes at the balls and celebrations which Giovanni assured them would follow their arrival in his capital.

The route they took went through the olive tree–covered hills and the walled *castelli* of Umbria, then descended into the Marches and the duchy of Urbino. In early June the freshness of an Italian spring has not yet given way to the hot dustiness of summer. As they cantered along past meadows edged with poppies where now and again a solitary shepherd could be heard summoning his sheep, or stopped to rest in a grove of shade trees, all the world must have seemed bright and young and filled with promise. And in that bright, green world, it was easy to forget that the French were even then preparing to cross the Alps. It was easy to think only of parties and jewels and coiffures.

At Fossombrone where the foothills of the eastern Appennines merge into the coastal plain and the Adriatic can be seen sparkling in the distance, representatives of the duke and duchess of Urbino gave them a "sumptuous welcome," Giovanni wrote the pope. Although it was raining when they left the town, the rain did not deter the Pesarese from showing up in droves to greet their new countess. There were as many men as there were women and they manifested the greatest possible joy and happiness at seeing her, her husband reported. Unfortunately, many of the flowers they tossed in her direction landed in the mud, and Lucrezia and the others were so thoroughly drenched by the time they reached the ducal palace that they could think of nothing save getting dry.

But the next morning the sun shone and the round of balls and parties that Giovanni had promised them began. Although Alexander was then busy preparing for a meeting with King Alfonso, his concern for his daughter made him eager to be informed of everything she and her companions did. Since mail sent by ordinary couriers usually took weeks to reach its destination, the Holy Father provided special messengers who covered the route from Rome to Pesaro in three or four days. Yet no matter how often Lucrezia and the others wrote, it never seemed often enough. "Giulia, dearest daughter, I received your letter which if it had been longer and more prolix would have made me even happier," he told his supposed mistress at the end of June.

Realizing how lonely he was without his feminine entourage, the women corresponded faithfully, assuring him that they missed him, begging him to leave plague-ridden Rome, and providing him with stories of their new surroundings, the people they met, and the parties they attended. Pesaro lies on a plain between two mountains on the right bank of the River Foglia, facing the Adriatic. In the fifteenth century, the sea lapped at the town's eastern wall and spilled over into the moat surrounding the Rocca Costanza, the dome-shaped fortress begun by Giovanni's father and named for him. Many of the town's 6,000 inhabitants lived in houses dating back to the tenth or eleventh century, gloomy, crumbling structures whose dingy Gothic façades constrasted sharply with the solid rose-tinted brick fronts of the occasional newer buildings. Few of the houses, new or old, were more than one story high. Fewer still had glass windows. The majority depended upon squares of linen to keep out the cold and the rain. The streets were as irregular as the buildings, a maze of narrow, tortuous alleyways where the sun seldom penetrated. The only really large open space was the vast rectangular Piazza del Populo before Giovanni's palace. Although this rambling two-story palace lacked the marble-encased doorways and the sumptuous wall decorations to which Lucrezia had grown accustomed in Rome, in her first letter to her father she described it as a "beautiful and commodious house."

Adriana, too, found the palace "beautiful and capacious," and the women of the town "good-looking enough." To her daughter-in-law, the city was a "jewel." In a run-on sentence that took up most of her two-page letter to the pope, Giulia declared Pesaro the equal of Foligno in beauty but superior to that town in civility, praised the loyalty of Giovanni's vassals as well as Lucrezia's dignified bearing when she received them, and then went on to describe the parties, the singing and the dancing, and the Latin eulogies that had marked the arrival of their party in Pesaro. So magnificently had she, Lucrezia, and Giovanni been attired on one of these occasions, she told the pope, that many declared they had never seen the like of it in those parts. "For we looked as if we had despoiled Florence of brocade." Like Adriana and Lucrezia, Giulia assured Alexander that she missed him, but in her case the protestation sounds like a passing thought inserted into a breathless account of her good times because she knew it was expected of her, whereas in Lucrezia's case it is obvious that she was genuinely concerned for her father. "We understand that at present things are going badly in Rome," she wrote him, " . . . and I implore Your Beatitude to leave and if that is not practical to take the greatest possible care, and Your Beatitude must not impute this to presumption but to the very great love I bear and be certain Your Holiness that I will never be at peace unless I have frequent news of Your Holiness."

The effort to sound grown-up and to maintain the necessary formality in writing to a papa who was also Il Papa, "the father of all," broke down somewhat in the next letter, which provided a brief sketch of one of the visitors to her palace. This visitor, Caterina Gonzaga de Montevecchio, had a reputation as a beauty.

> I will describe her beauty to Your Beatitude because I am certain you will have accepted it because of her great fame. First she is six inches taller than Madama Giulia with a beautiful white complexion, beautiful hands and a beautiful figure. However she has an ugly mouth and the ugliest teeth, a long face, ugly-colored hair and many facial expressions that are very masculine; she speaks well. I had wanted to see her dance, but I wasn't very satisfied. In short in every way she does not measure up to her reputation.

Though Giulia's estimate of Caterina's charms was considerably more generous, her generosity did not deceive the pope.

> In devoting so much time to describing the beauty of this person who is not worthy to unlace your shoes [he wrote], you are, we know, comporting yourself with great modesty. The reason is obvious to us, for you have been informed that everyone else who has written us has told us that she seemed a lantern compared to your sun. When you make her appear so beautiful, we comprehend your perfection, of which truly we have never been in doubt.

As long as things went well and Alexander heard from the women regularly, he could be an amused and amusing correspondent. When, however, at the beginning of July a rumor that Lucrezia was dying spread through Rome, he became frantic and immediately dispatched a special messenger to Pesaro. The letter he addressed to his daughter soon afterward reveals his anxious state of mind.

> Dona Lucrezia dearest daughter,
> Truly you have given us four or five days of great distress because of the bitter news prevailing in Rome that you were dead or truly so sick that there was no hope of your surviving. You can imagine how much grief this caused us because of the immense and cordial love we bear you, greater, indeed, than for any other person in the world. Until we saw a letter in your own hand which was badly written and shows us that you are not well, we had no rest. We thank God and our glorious Lady for having removed you from danger, and rest assured we shall never be happy until we have seen you in person.

Alexander would probably have found the separation from his daughter intolerable even under the best of circumstances, but he found it even more intolerable when, as he put it in letter to Adriana, "the French are coming by land and sea" and the country around Pesaro "is filled with men-at-arms." One of the matters the pope intended to discuss at his meeting with Alfonso was the king's plan to send the greater part of the Neapolitan army, under the command of Alfonso's son Ferrantino, into the Romagna. Besides opposing the first moves of the French, Ferrantino and his army intended to threaten Milan. Although Giovanni Sforza had been a condottiere of Milan since his marriage, the Milanese had not been paying his salary very regularly. Moreover, said Alexander in a letter to Lucrezia, "we are of the opinion . . . that . . . the state of Milan seeing that we are allied with King Alfonso and knowing that the said Signor Giovanni has no alternative save to do as we wish will not want to give him his money." Hence, Alexander urged that Giovanni accept the command of a Neapolitan brigade. Since the pope would soon be meeting with Alfonso, he asked Lucrezia to send him her husband's reply immediately. The pope also wished to know whether Giovanni would be averse to allowing Lucrezia to return to Rome with Adriana and Giulia while he remained in Pesaro "getting his men-of-arms ready for war and guarding his city and state." The situation was a delicate one, for the power of a Renaissance husband over his wife was absolute. Although her father could ask him to allow her to leave, he could not command her departure. Apparently Alexander did not even wish to ask if he could help it. Instead he relied upon Adriana de Mila to ascertain his son-in-law's intentions by whatever means she considered most suitable. "And if you think it necessary for us to write him, let us know immediately, because we will write him anything that is necessary," Alexander told his cousin.

The pope's letters to Adriana were at once affectionate and peremptory. She was *"madama nepote carissima"* ("madam my dearest relative") whom he trusted completely, but she was also subject to his orders and he expected her unquestioning obedience. He was planning to meet with Alfonso in five or six days, he told her in a letter dated July 8. If she and Lucrezia and the others returned to Rome immediately, he would make it his business to be back in the city by the 25th, otherwise he would remain with Alfonso a few more days. The pope then went on to discuss where the women would be housed when they returned to Rome.

If Adriana received his letter, it must have been long after there was any possibility of her carrying out the orders it contained. At six o'clock on the morning of July 12, she and Giulia and Giulia's lady-in-waiting Juana Moncada left Pesaro for Capodimonte, the fortress near Lake Bolsena owned by Giulia's family. Since it was not safe for women to travel alone, the pope's confidential agent Francesco

Gacet traveled with them. Realizing how much their departure would upset the pontiff, Giovanni Sforza hastened to write him a letter of explanation. A few days before their departure, Giulia's brother Cardinal Alessandro Farnese had sent word to his sister that their older brother Angelo was dying. If Giulia wished to see him alive, she and Adriana must head for Capodimonte immediately. "God knows how I tried to dissuade them, especially when I realized that they would be departing without the knowledge of Your Holiness," Giovanni told his father-in-law. But when another and even more urgent message arrived from the cardinal, Giulia had insisted upon leaving forthwith.

Since Alexander set out for his meeting with Alfonso on July 12, Giovanni's explanation could not have reached him until much later. By then the pope had already heard from Giulia and Adriana. They had found Giulia's brother dead, Alexander told Lucrezia in a letter dated July 24. "His death caused the cardinal and Giulia such distress that both fell sick of fever." Alexander had provided physicians and everything necessary and he prayed to God and the glorious Madonna that they would soon be restored. "But of a truth," he wrote his daughter, "Don Giovanni and yourself have displayed very little thought for me in this departure of Madonna Adriana and Giulia, since you allowed them to leave without our permission; for you should have remembered—it was your duty—that such a sudden departure without our knowledge would cause us the greatest displeasure. And if you say that they did so because Cardinal Farnese commanded it, you ought to ask yourself whether it would have pleased the Pope. However, it is done; but another time we will be more careful and will look about to see where our interest lies."

In a letter to the pope written toward the end of June, Lucrezia had told him that she thought of Adriana as a mother and Giulia as a sister. After they left, she spoke of the loss of their "sweet and loving counsel." Their departure forced Alexander to abandon his plans for bringing his daughter to Rome and made him even more apprehensive about her welfare. Any slackening off of her letters to him brought an immediate protest. "For several days we have had no letter from you," he told her on the 24th. "Your neglect to write us often and tell us how you and Don Giovanni, our beloved son, are causes us great surprise. In the future be more heedful and diligent."

Nor did Lucrezia's reply satisfy the pope. She was indifferent and deceitful, he told her, and what was even worse, she showed no desire to return to him. Furthermore, her explanation of Giulia's departure differed markedly from the explanation she had given Cesare. So incensed was the pope by what he interpreted as a lack of filial devotion on her part that he ordered the bearer of his letter to deliver a stern oral reprimand to his daughter. The reprimand put Lucrezia "in a great melancholy," she told her father. But years of dealing with this excitable and overly anxious parent had taught her how to handle him. Because she had injured her right arm, her last letter had been written by one of her chancellors, she reminded him. Surely her father must realize that the style of a chancellor was different from the style of a woman and that he must not allow himself to become embittered, "because he will see that in the future I will continue to do my duty toward him." As for the discrepancies between what she had written him and what she had written Cesare, they were really very slight. If His Holiness would deign to reread her letter, he would understand "that I have no other desire save to be at the feet of Your Beatitude of which I hope I am worthy, because until I am there, I will never be content, and of this Your Beatitude can rest assured."

Lucrezia saw very little of her husband that summer, for at the pope's insistence, he had agreed to command a brigade in the Neapolitan army. To reconcile what he was doing with his loyalty to the house of Sforza, Giovanni had also agreed to keep his cousins in Milan informed of everything the Neapolitan commanders were planning. In a letter written to Ludovico Sforza on August 2, 1494, Giovanni assured him that he had given all available information about troop movements in the Romagna to the Milanese envoy and had spoken to him at great length about the arrival of the duke of Calabria. "Should any word of what I am doing leak out, I will find myself in greatest peril, for I am committed to serving the pope," the signor of Pesaro warned his cousin.

Lucrezia, of course, knew nothing of her husband's double-dealing. Alexander continued to keep her informed of his plans, and she seems to have taken it for granted that Giovanni was as devoted to the Neapolitan cause as she was. If her father had any inkling of what was going on, he said nothing.

His meeting with Alfonso had left the pope confident of eventual victory. "We have had an interview with the Illustrious King Alfonso who showed us no less love and obedience than he would have shown had be been our own son," the pope wrote Lucrezia. "I cannot tell you with what satisfaction we took leave of each other. You may be certain that His Majesty stands ready to place his own person and everything he has in the world at our service." Not until Charles crossed the Alps on September 2 did Alexander realize how woefully inadequate were Alfonso and "everything he had in the world."

The army that accompanied Charles across the Alps was the most formidable that Italy had ever seen. "Before 1494," says Guicciardini, "wars were protracted, battles bloodless . . . and although artillery was already in use, it was managed with such want of skill that it caused little hurt." Because most Italian commanders were mercenaries, they and their troops were more interested in holding prisoners for ransom than in mowing one another down, and they rarely took the offensive. What cannons they had were equipped with stone cannonballs, which generally shattered on impact. But the French used iron cannonballs and, says Guicciardini, "their cannon were hauled on carriages drawn not by oxen as was the custom in Italy, but by horses." And these horses "marched along with the armies right up to the walls." The weapons they carried "were set into position with incredible speed; and so little time elapsed between one shot and another and the shots were so frequent, and so violent was their battering that in a few hours they could accomplish what previously in Italy used to take many days."

Nor was the use of "this diabolical rather than human instrument," as Guicciardini described the cannon, the sole reason for the success of the French. The typical Italian mercenary was a leisurely fighter who would not think of going into combat after nightfall. Rather than fight in well-ordered squadrons, he and his fellows "scattered throughout the countryside retreating most of the time to the security of river banks and ditches." The French and their Swiss infantrymen, on the other hand, faced the enemy without ever breaking ranks. To Giacomo Trotti, the Ferrarese ambassador in Milan, they appeared "arrogant and insolent" and "more bestial" than any soldiers he had ever seen.

That Duke Ercole of Ferrara should give the French free passage through his territory seemed incomprehensible to Alexander. "Italy ought to be left to the Italians and every man ought to feel safe in his own state," he told the duke's Roman representative Pandolfo Collenuccio. And, said Collenuccio, "He spoke with such vehemence of word and gesture that it was obvious he spoke from the heart, and many times his eyes filled with tears."

But Ercole d'Este of Ferrara, like his son-in-law Ludovico Sforza and like Ludovico's cousin Giovanni and most of the other petty tyrants of the Romagna and their neighbor the doge of Venice, was too concerned with his own private interests to give any thought to the welfare of Italy. Nor were the Roman barons any more patriotic.

After the flight of Giuliano della Rovere, papal troops had seized Ostia. On September 18, soldiers in the pay of the Colonna and Savelli families suddenly attacked the fortress. After driving out the papal governor, they raised the French flag. The capture of Ostia opened the Tiber to enemy vessels and once again endangered Rome's food supply. "The Pope," said Sigismundo dei Conti, "had an enemy in his own house; his army was insignificant and he could not expect any effectual help . . . from any other European power." Of the great Roman families only the Orsini were still loyal to him.

Among the condottieri of the Orsini serving in the papal army was Giulia's husband, Orsino. Like Giovanni Sforza and numerous other papal condottieri, Orsino received orders to join the duke of Calabria in the Romagna. The eighteen-year-old commander left his family estate at Bassanello in early September. He had gotten as far as Civita Castellana in the Roman *campagna* when he suddenly complained of feeling ill. After ordering his troops to go on without him, he returned home. One of his kinsmen warned him that the duke of Calabria considered his illness feigned and suggested that Orsino "purge himself of this contumacy" by proceeding to the duke's camp immediately. Orsino, however, had no intention of doing any such thing. Not only did he remain at Bassanello, he wrote a letter to his wife ordering her to join him. At the time Giulia was still at her family's estate at Capodimonte. Before leaving for Bassanello, she wrote to the pope, whereupon Alexander forbade her to join her husband and ordered her and Adriana to come to Rome instead.

For those who take it for granted that Giulia was Alexander's mistress, the reason for his order is obvious: He wanted her in his bed. But Giulia had been at Capodimonte since July. And although Alexander had written to her, until he heard of Orsino's command, he had seemed perfectly content to have her remain there. And while his sudden insistence that she come to Rome could have been prompted by a reawakening of sexual desire, it could also have been prompted by the conviction that if Giulia went to Bassanello, Orsino would never rejoin his troops in the Romagna.

Whatever the pope's reasons for ordering her and Adriana to Rome, his order created a furor at Capodimonte. Although Giulia's brother Alessandro had received his cardinal's hat from the pope and although he felt beholden to him, he could not see how, as head of the family, he could legitimately allow his sister to ignore her husband's request that she join him at Bassanello. The cardinal would do anything for the pope but this, Alessandro informed Alexander in a letter.

Soon afterward Adriana left for Rome. She had hoped to persuade Alexander to rescind his order. Instead he made her promise to bring Giulia to the city. But when Adriana returned to Capodimonte and told Giulia's brother of her promise, the cardinal would not hear of it. He was convinced that not only would it be dishonorable, it would also be a great error to break with Orsino over such a thing and so publicly, Adriana wrote the pope. Rather than do so, both Alessandro and the pope's emissary Francesco Gacet urged Alexander to summon Orsino to Rome where, with the assistance of Virginio Orsini, the matter could undoubtedly be settled.

From the tone of Gacet's letter, it is obvious that whether the gossip about Giulia and the pope was true or not, everyone at Capodimonte was embarrassed by it. In fact, Alessandro, the future Pope Paul III, must have felt himself as much its victim as Giulia. Although Sigismundo dei Conti wrote that Giulia's brother had been named to the College of Cardinals at the request of the Romans, the gossips took it for granted that he had received his cardinal's hat as a reward for the sexual services of his sister. To them he was Il Cardinale della Gonnella ("the petticoat cardinal"). Were he to allow Giulia to go to Rome against the wishes of her husband, they would have a field day. Nor would there be any hope of keeping the matter secret, for as Adriana had pointed out in her letter to the pope, should Orsino's wishes be ignored, he was determined to let the world hear of it.

Were Giulia to go to Rome instead of Bassanello, Orsino would throw away a thousand lives had he so many and all such goods as he had, his adviser, Fra Teseo Seripando, warned her in a letter written a few days later, and he spoke of Orsino's rage and discontent and how it was leading him to do abnormal things. Although the friar was seeking to placate Orsino, he could not seem to do so, "for he has decided [that] you shall not go to Rome, but shall come here as I have said. Should anything else befall, he will be like the devil."

To be wanted desperately is always agreeable. Certainly Giulia was sufficiently impressed by her husband's sudden desire to have her with him to give the pope's special messenger, Navarrico, a letter in which she declared that she would not leave without Orsino's permission. Her letter infuriated the pope. And although she may never have been Alexander's mistress, from his reply it is clear that what infuriated him was not that she was disobeying him, but that she preferred her eighteen-year-old husband to him. He wrote her on October 22:

> Thankless and treacherous Giulia,
> Navarrico has brought us a letter from you in which you signify and declare your intention of not coming here without Orsino's consent. Though we judged the evil of your soul and that of the man who guides you, we could not believe that you would act with such perfidy and ingratitude in view of your repeated assurances and oaths that you would be faithful to our command and not go near Orsino. But now you are doing the very opposite, risking your life by going to Bassanello with the purpose no doubt of surrendering yourself once more to that stallion. We hope that you and the ungrateful Adriana will recognize your error and make suitable penance. Finally, we herewith ordain under penalty of excommunication and eternal damnation that you shall not leave Capodimonte or Marta and still less go to Bassanello—this for reasons affecting our state.

Adriana, who the pope said, had "finally laid bare the malignity and evil of her soul," was also forbidden to leave Capodimonte under penalty of eternal damnation. As for Cardinal Farnese, Alexander let him know that he would never have believed that after all he had done for him Giulia's brother would so quickly "prefer Orsino to us." So that Alessandro would have an excuse for ignoring Orsino's commands, the pope was sending him a papal brief expressly forbidding Giulia to go to Bassanello. Finally, Alexander wrote to his emissary Francesco Gacet informing him of his decision to excommunicate Giulia and Adriana if they continued to prefer "that monkey," as the Pope called Orsino, to him. Furthermore, said Alexander, he was sending an archdeacon to Orsino to warn him that if he did not either return to camp or come to Rome within three days, he, too, would be excommunicated.

Not only did the threat of excommunication keep Giulia and Adriana from going to Bassanello, it must have also persuaded Orsino to rejoin his troops, for at the end of November he wrote to ask Alexander for money to pay them. And once Orsino was back in the field, the pope seemed to lose all interest in having Giulia and Adriana come to Rome. The two women were still at Capodimonte when, in the middle of November, he sent Cardinal Alessandro to Viterbo as his legate. Viterbo is an ancient town in the Alban hills about fifty kilometers north of Rome. On November 27, Adriana, Giulia, and Giulia's sister Geronima decided to visit the cardinal there.

All that month the French had been moving rapidly down the Italian boot toward Rome. So rapidly, indeed, that unbeknown to the women they had already entered Viterbo. Giulia and Adriana and their party were a mile from the city when they were accosted by one of the French captains, a certain M. Allegre. Upon learning their identity, he took them prisoner and led them to the neighboring town of Montefiascone where their ransom was set at 3,000 ducats. When Alexander heard of what had happened, he immediately set about negotiating their release. On December 1, an escort of four hundred French soldiers brought them to the gates of Rome where they were received by the pope's chamberlain.

"It is said that Giulia spent Sunday night in the apostolic palace," Pandolfo Collenuccio told the duke of Ferrara.

And Giacomo Trotti, the duke's ambassador in Milan, wrote that when Giulia and Adriana entered Rome, the pope had gone to meet them "arrayed in a black doublet bordered with gold brocade, with a beautiful belt in the Spanish fashion and with sword and dagger. He wore Spanish boots and a velvet biretta, all very gallant."

Trotti had received his information from Ludovico Sforza, who claimed to have gotten it from his correspondents in Rome and Florence. A week later, the ambassador reported that Ludovico had publicly stated to his senate that the pope had allowed three women to come to him, "one of them being a nun of Valencia, the other a Castilian, the third a very beautiful girl from Venice, fifteen or sixteen years of age." However, Trotti must have been skeptical for he told the duke that in Milan the same scandalous tales were spread about the pope as were spread about the Torta (a family of condemned traitors) in Ferrara.

Even as the sixty-three-year-old pontiff was supposedly arranging his numerous assignations, he was also trying to keep Charles from entering Rome. Although the French had already taken Viterbo and Fundi and numerous other towns in the papal states, the pope seemed determined not to grant them free passage through the Holy City. When, however, on December 19, his ally Virginio Orsini opened his great fortress at Bracciano to Charles, Alexander realized that further resistance was pointless. On New Year's Eve 1494, the king and his troops crossed the Ponte Molle and entered Rome through the Porta del Populo. To one eyewitness, Charles seemed more deformed than anyone he had ever seen: "Quite small, hunchbacked and with the ugliest face a man ever possessed. . . ." At the king's side rode Cardinal Giuliano della Rovere, who was known to the Romans as the cardinal of San Pietro in Vincoli, and Cardinal Ascanio Sforza. All along the Via Lata (now the Via del Corso), Burchard reported seeing "fires, torches and lights seemingly in every house, with people repeatedly shouting *'Francia! Francia! Colonna! Colonna! Vincola! Vincola!'* " While Charles and his army took over the left bank of the Tiber, Alexander and Cesare and a few of the cardinals still loyal to the pope remained locked in the Vatican, protected by a thousand horsemen and a small number of foot soldiers. Everyone in Rome was "very anxious," said one writer, because it was learned that the French "had plundered the Jews and done great harm."

By the following week the disturbances in the city so alarmed the pope that he and his son and five of the cardinals fled through the underground passageway to the Castel Sant' Angelo. In answer to the king's repeated demands that the fortress be turned over to him, Alexander announced that if it were attacked, he would take his stand on the walls with the most sacred relics of the church. A group of rebel cardinals led by Giuliano della Rovere urged Charles to summon a council to depose the pope. But even Ludovico Sforza realized that Charles was not the man for such a task. "The king would do well to begin by reforming himself," he was heard to remark.

When Alexander and Charles finally met, the highly intelligent and experienced man of sixty-three easily got the better of the naive and not overly bright boy of twenty-four. The pope had to agree to give Charles free passage through the papal states. He also let the king have the Turkish prince Dschem and turned Cesare over to him as a hostage. But he skillfully avoided any commitment to invest Charles with the kingdom of Naples. And although Comines tells us that a proclamation calling for the deposition of the pope had already been drafted, Charles readily tendered his obedience to the Holy See in exchange for cardinal's hats for three of his advisers.

On January 30, two days after the king and his troops left Rome, Cesare escaped from his French guards. When Charles protested to the pope, Alexander expressed his regrets, but did not offer to send anyone as hostage in his son's place. In truth, the loss of Cesare made very little difference to the French. Their march south encountered so little resistance that, according to Alexander, they conquered the country "with chalk," by which he meant that their soldiers had nothing to do but the quartermaster's work of marking the doors of the houses in which the troops were to be billeted. Their easy victories so terrified King Alfonso that he had nightmares in which he heard "all the trees and rocks calling France." By the time Charles arrived at the gates of Naples, Alfonso had abdicated and his son Ferrantino, to whom he'd left his kingdom, had set sail for Ischia.

To the tired French soldiers, Naples with its fabled harbor, its mild climate, and its beautiful and accommodating women, seemed an earthly paradise. Beguiled by the pleasures of this newly found Eden, Charles and his men forgot that the ostensible purpose of their expedition was a crusade against the Turks. Not until it was too late did they realize that those dark-haired southern beauties, for whom they had relinquished the crusade, bore death on their lips. *Le mal de Naples* ("the sickness of Naples"), the French called it. To the Neapolitans it was *il morbo gallico* ("the French disease"). "Syphilis, the Sinister Shepherd," the Italian doctor, Girolamo Fracastoro, would call it in his famous poem.

"Not only did the evil befoul the human race with pimples and ulcers," said Sigismundo dei Conti "but also attacked the joints of the body, eating into the marrow. The pains . . . were so intense that the sick screamed endlessly. . . . Many remained marked, some on the arms, others on the legs, and many died a horrible death." The disease is thought to have existed in Europe before the return of Columbus from the New World, but not in the same virulent form. Camp followers and deserters would soon spread it to every part of Europe. Six years later the first cases appeared in China—the final bitter fruit of the *impresa di Napoli*.

The Italians were so disillusioned with their own rulers that at the first arrival of the French, the people had treated them like saints, supposing "all faith and virtue" to be in them, Comines reported. But the favorable impression did not last "partly because of the slanderous reports . . . charging us that we forced women and robbed and carried away money and whatsoever we could lay hands on."

Although Comines denied the charges "touching women," most Italians, including Giulia's brother Alessandro, believed them. During the French occupation of Rome, "the cardinal was eating his heart out because Giulia was still in the city," one bishop told a relative of the Farnese serving in the French army. Although the bishop did not mention Giulia's supposed affair with the pope, it must have been of that he was thinking when he wrote that it seemed unfitting that she remain in Rome "and things might occur that would bring small honor to all."

Just when Giulia got the horse and escort she had demanded in order to leave the city, we do not know. Soon after Charles and his troops reached Naples, she and her mother-in-law joined Orsino at Bassanello. Although Adriana later served as the manager of the papal household at a salary of fifty gold ducats a month and although she accompanied Lucrezia to Ferrara in 1502, she was never again as closely involved with the fate of the Borgias as she had been before 1495. And whatever Alexander's relationship with Giulia up to that time, there is no evidence of any relationship thereafter. Once it was no longer a question of keeping Orsino from his troops, Giulia at Bassanello with her husband was apparently not that difficult for the pope to accept. Lucrezia at Pesaro was another matter.

The winter that had been so hectic for Alexander had been relatively tranquil for his daughter. After the French forced the Neapolitan troops out of the Romagna at the end of October, Giovanni returned home with his men. Although no spark of passion, however transitory, seems ever to have been ignited between husband

and wife, he was kind to his young bride and tried to make Pesaro as agreeable as possible to her. As a Sforza, he could not, of course, honestly share her concern for her father and brother in Rome. Whether he went as far as his cousin Ludovico, who told the Ferrarese ambassador that he was hourly expecting a courier bringing news that Alexander had been taken and beheaded, there is no way of knowing. Certainly, the knowledge of how traitorously he had served his father-in-law gave him reason to wish Alexander out of the way. But Giovanni must have been careful to keep his thoughts to himself, for there is no evidence that Lucrezia ever suspected how he felt. In any case the problem of his divided allegiance was unexpectedly solved when his cousin Ludovico suddenly decided to switch sides.

Ludovico's nephew Gian Galeazzo had died in October. Some said his uncle had poisoned him, but there was really no proof one way or the other. With Gian Galeazzo out of the way, Ludovico quickly took the dukedom for himself. Had French troops not been in Milan, he would have never gotten away with it. But Ludovico was not one to feel obligated to his benefactors. By the end of the year the spectacular successes of the French king and his army had begun to alarm him. Nor was he the only one alarmed. The Venetians, say Comines, had "thought it to their profit that war should arise between the King and the House of Aragon, but they supposed it could not have ended so soon as it did, and that it should but weaken their enemies, not utterly destroy them."

To check the French before they swallowed the entire peninsula, Venice and Milan offered to join the pope in a so-called Holy League. Not long after they approached him, Alexander sent his son-in-law a letter addressed to the doge urging him to hire the signor of Pesaro as a condottiere of the new league. To the pope's disgust, Giovanni announced that before accepting such a post, he intended to go to Milan to discuss the matter with Ludovico. Although Ludovico was now Alexander's ally, the pope did not trust him, nor did he like to be reminded of Giovanni's devotion to him. Should Giovanni go to Milan, he would be excommunicated, Alexander informed his son-in-law. Although the threat of excommunication kept Giovanni from visiting his cousin, it did not keep him from writing a fervent and adulatory letter to him. "As I am a Sforza, I wish to live and die with Your Excellency," he told Ludovico.

Apparently this single-minded devotion to the house of Sforza was no more pleasing to the Venetians than it was to the pope. Even after the Holy League between the Emperor Maximilian, Spain, Venice, Milan, and the papacy was formally announced two months later, the republic made no move to give Giovanni his *condotta*. When the signor of Pesaro wrote to his father-in-law demanding to know what had happened, he received a stern letter rebuking him for his self-interest. Although Alexander did not mention espionage in this letter, he did tell his son-in-law that the examples of the past, and especially of the last year in the service of the duke of Calabria, had made others wonder whether he would not do the same thing in the future. Moreover, said the pope, if his own son the duke of Gandia "served us in the same way you have until now, we would not want him in our service. I exhort you therefore to abstain from bargaining for a salary and to prepare yourself to serve well and loyally, putting aside ostentation and vanity."

Obviously, Alexander was exasperated with this pusillanimous son-in-law. But for Lucrezia's sake, if for no other reason, Giovanni's interests had to be attended to. On May 9, the signor of Pesaro received a letter from his father-in-law congratulating him on his appointment as a condottiere of Venice and ordering him and his troops to come to Rome. The same day a letter ordering him to send Lucrezia to Rome also arrived. Meanwhile, however, Charles and his army had worn out their welcome in Naples. After leaving a few battalions behind to hold the kingdom, the French headed north. Since the pope wished to avoid another encounter with Charles, he moved his court to Orvieto. When the king sought to meet him there, Alexander moved on to Perugia. And it was there rather than in Rome that the eagerly awaited reunion with his daughter finally took place.

Escorted by eighty horsemen, Lucrezia and her husband passed through the Porta Mazia on June 16, 1495. The streets of Perugia wind their way up a lofty hill overlooking a wide valley, which spreads out on all sides from the city's ramparts. When Lucrezia's party reached the vast piazza at the summit of this hill, they beheld the pope standing at one of the windows of the Palazzo dei Priori, his hand raised in a blessing.

Lucrezia had passed her fifteenth birthday two months before. Although she had been married a year, she was still a child with a child's instinctive and uninhibited reactions. At the sight of that majestic and dearly beloved figure, the admiration she felt for her father and her pride in their relationship must have all but overwhelmed her. To refuse his request that she accompany him to Rome would have been unthinkable. Since Giovanni would be away in the service of the league, there wasn't even a reason for her to do so. The end of June found her back in the palace of Santa Maria in Portico under her father's affectionate and oversolicitous care.

On the sixth of July occurred the celebrated battle of Fornova between the retreating French army, commanded by Charles VIII, and the forces of the Holy League, commanded by Gianfrancesco Gonzaga, marchese of Mantua. It was a famous victory, but just whose victory has never been established. Because the Italians were not driven from the battlefield, the marchese assumed that the victory was his and commissioned Andrea Mantegna to paint the superb *Madonna della Vittoria* now in the Louvre. Because Charles and his troops were able to cross the River Taro and continue on to Asti, the French assumed the victory was theirs. Whoever the real victor, Lucrezia's husband had nothing to do with the outcome. Although he was in the service of the league, he and his troops did not participate in the battle.

The same day that the French and Italian armies clashed at Fornova, Ferrantino appeared before Naples and once again took possession of the city. Soon afterward Giovanni joined his wife in the palace of Santa Maria in Portico. That February he and Lucrezia held a number of receptions in their palace. Among those who attended was Giovanni's former brother-in-law, Gianfrancesco Gonzaga, the thirty-year-old hero of the battle of Fornova. A time would come when this swarthy soldier with the African countenance and his slim golden-haired hostess would turn to one another for emotional support. But that time was more than nine years off. At this, their first meeting, they exchanged the usual pleasantries and then presumably forgot each other's existence.

In March, Giovanni was sent to Naples to help rid the kingdom of the remaining French outposts. He remained there until the end of April when he once again returned to Rome. The signor of Pesaro was cold and pinched by nature, and the open affection he saw between his wife and her father made him uncomfortable. He longed to take Lucrezia back to Pesaro where he, not Alexander, was master.

But he knew in advance what his father-in-law's reply to such a request would be. By then it was almost a year since Lucrezia had come to Rome, and her husband was beginning to suspect that the pope planned to keep her there indefinitely. Legally, of course, Giovanni had every right to insist that she return to Pesaro, but he was too dependent upon Alexander to risk an open conflict with him.

Giovanni's first wife had been Maddalena Gonzaga of Mantua. Because he was still on such good terms with her family, he must have confided some of what he felt to their envoy in Rome, Gian Carlo Scalona, for on April 27, Scalona wrote Maddalena's brother the marchese that "the Signor of Pesaro perhaps has something in his household that others do not realize." A few days later, this same envoy informed the marchese that Giovanni had abandoned Rome in desperation, "leaving his wife under the apostolic mantle" and giving the impression that he would never return.

However desperate he may have sounded, the signor of Pesaro had a perfectly valid reason for leaving the city at that time. Since there had been a flare-up of hostilities in Naples, he had been recalled to duty by the league. He and his men remained in the Naples area until the beginning of August when the last French battalion finally capitulated. There being nothing more to do, they returned to Pesaro. And it was then that Giovanni's intention to stay away from Rome indefinitely became clear. Although he gave no reason for his prolonged absence, he must have hoped that it would force Alexander to send Lucrezia to him. Instead it set the stage for the ugly finale of their tepid marriage.

Divorce and
Other Strange Matters

The reign of Pope Alexander is full of startling and portentous
events; his antechamber was struck by lightning, the Tiber over-
flowed and flooded the city; his son has been horribly murdered,
and now the Castle of Sant' Angelo has been blown up.

Malipiero, *Annali Veneti*

During the three years that Lucrezia had been married to Giovanni Sforza, he had seldom remained with her for more than a few
months at a stretch. Hence, when he took leave of her at the end of
April 1496, she had no reason to view this renewed absence with
alarm or to suspect that it would be different from the others. And if
she felt a certain anxiety at seeing him go off to war, the anxiety
must have been short-lived. This tentative self-centered husband of
hers had, after all, never really engaged her affections. She had,
moreover, much to occupy her that spring. Less than three weeks
after Giovanni and his troops headed down the Appian Way toward
Fondi, she prepared to welcome her brother Geoffredo and his wife
to Rome.

Either because he was the youngest child in a large family or because he sensed that he was the child by whom his father set the least
store, Geoffredo had a frantic desire to impress his elders. They in
turn were alternately amused and touched by his efforts. His cousin
Cardinal Giovanni Borgia of Monreale, who had been present on
Geoffredo's wedding night, called him gracious and full of spirit and
declared that he would have paid heavily to have others see the
twelve-year-old bridegroom as he had seen him.

Whatever Geoffredo's sexual prowess, he was still a child. After his marriage he had continued to be ruled by his preceptor Don Ferrando Dixer. Besides Don Ferrando, the young husband also had a large number of men-in-waiting who, although ostensibly charged with serving him, were really there to keep an eye on him. His seventeen-year-old wife had a number of older women to look after her. But whereas Geoffredo took his supervision for granted, Sancha was not so easily controlled. A normal marriage would have transferred her from the authority of her father to the authority of her husband. Marriage with a twelve-year-old made her feel that she was free to do as she pleased, and it was not long before rumors of mismanagement and scandal in her household began to reach Rome.

Never a model of rectitude himself, Alexander found such behavior in a daughter-in-law intolerable. As usual when he was displeased, he did not hesitate to invoke the authority of his high office. A series of angry pastoral letters accused Sancha of receiving men in her rooms and her ladies-in-waiting of being no better than she was. The entire court was undisciplined and licentious, the pope declared. Rather than grovel, Sancha's majordomo met the attack head on. The only man besides her husband who entered her rooms, he assured the pope, was "a man of good-will well past his sixtieth birthday." The majordomo also sent the pope a number of affidavits attesting to the good behavior of Sancha and every member of her household.

Although these affidavits labelled anyone who criticized the princess "a vile and wicked man worthy of great punishment," they failed to convince the pope. In October, Alexander replaced Geoffredo's preceptor and dispatched a certain Alberto Magalotti to supervise his son's household. The following winter when the arrival of the French forced King Ferrantino to leave Naples for Ischia, Geoffredo and Sancha went with him. It may have been Alexander's continuing dissatisfaction with the manner in which their household was run that led him to summon the young couple to Rome soon after Ferrantino regained his throne. Because the pope's new daughter-in-law had a reputation as a beauty, the gossips immediately assumed that Alexander had summoned her to Rome so that he might judge her beauty for himself. According to these same gossips, Sancha's imminent arrival was making Lucrezia jealous. "The countess of Pesaro is anything but pleased," they declared, implying that she was afraid of competition.

Certainly Lucrezia and her twelve ladies-in-waiting made an effort to look their best on that sunny afternoon in May when they rode across the city from the palace of Santa Maria in Portico to the Lateran gate to greet Geoffredo and his wife. Before them rode two pages, one mounted on a horse covered with crimson velvet, the other on one covered with precious gold brocade. Since Cesare had dispatched runners to all the cardinals requesting them to send chaplains and men-at-arms, the reception at the gate turned into one of those flamboyant pageants so dear to the Renaissance heart. After Lucrezia had affectionately greeted her brother and his wife, all three went to the basilica of Saint John's Lateran to pray before the high altar. Accompanied by the entire cortege of men-at-arms, cardinals' stewards, ambassadors, and ladies-in-waiting, they then made their way across the city from Saint John's to the Coliseum, past the ruins of the Forum to the Church of Saint Mark, then on to the Campo dei Fiori from whence they followed the Via Recta to the Ponte Sant' Angelo, the traditional approach to the Vatican.

Their itinerary gave all Rome a chance to compare the two princesses: the dark-haired, green-eyed Sancha, mounted on a horse caparisoned in alternate bands of velvet and black satin; the golden-haired Lucrezia on a mule caparisoned entirely in black satin. Apparently the pope was as eager as everyone else to see how they looked together, for Burchard tells us that Alexander stood at one of the windows of the Vatican Palace awaiting their arrival. As soon as he saw the first of their party enter the great courtyard where distinguished guests customarily dismounted, he hastened to join his cardinals in the Hall of the Pontiffs. There a raised seat had been prepared for him at the center of the left wall. Thrown over this seat was a green carpet depicting the Savior laying his fingers on the side of Saint Thomas. When Geoffredo, Lucrezia, and Sancha entered accompanied by the members of their cortege, including Alexander's master of ceremonies, Burchard, Geoffredo made the customary obeisance to the pope, kissing his foot and hand. Alexander then took his son's head in both his hands, bowing his own head over him but not kissing him. He followed the same procedure with Lucrezia and Sancha, after which Geoffredo kissed the hands of each of the eleven cardinals in the room. Sancha followed her husband's example in kissing the hands of the cardinals, and, says Burchard, "they took her head in their hands as if they wanted to kiss it."

After the last cardinal had lingered over Sancha's dark, perfumed head, Geoffredo took his place beside his brother Cesare. Lucrezia, who had been standing next to her father, seated herself on a crimson cushion lying on the floor to his right, Sancha on a similar cushion to his left. As might have been expected, the sight of these two pretty young women crouched at his feet aroused an irresistible urge to play the gallant in the still youthful heart of the pope. Burchard tells us that as their ladies-in-waiting advanced one by one to kiss the papal foot, Alexander exchanged "humorous and teasing remarks" with his daughter and his daughter-in-law.

The tight prim soul of the master of ceremonies was further outraged two days later, the Sunday of Pentecost, when Alexander and his family went to Saint Peter's to hear mass. The sermon that day was preached by a Spaniard who even Burchard found "wordy and wearisome." But to the master of ceremonies not even the most intense boredom justified violating protocol. To his horror he observed Lucrezia and Sancha and many of their ladies-in-waiting standing on the marble staircase on which the canonics usually sang the epistle and the Evangile, "and they occupied the whole stairway and the floor around it which aroused great disgust and scandal among us [i.e. the priests] and the populace."

Was it Sancha who had suggested that the women, the majority of them teen-agers like herself, alleviate their boredom by occupying the places reserved for the canons? Although all of the historians of the Borgias emphasize her bold and independent ways, not much is known about this Aragonese princess. It used to be thought that she had served as the model for the young woman in pale blue in the left front quadrant of Pinturicchio's *Disputation of Saint Catherine* and that the young man standing next to her was Geoffredo. But Pinturicchio completed his fresco in 1495, a year before Sancha came to Rome. Since there are no other likenesses, we must accept the word of her contemporaries that she was beautiful. Her subsequent behavior gives the impression that she could be loyal, kind, and considerate, which is probably why she and Lucrezia became such good friends. On occasion she could also be hot tempered and arrogant, and it must have been her arrogance that made the gossips so relish tearing her reputation to shreds. Even had she been docile, however, the very fact that this attractive young woman was married to a boy of fourteen would have probably been enough to set tongues wagging, especially since a man so much better suited to her in both age and appearance was to be found in the pope's own household: Sancha's tall, blond, strikingly handsome twenty-one-year-old brother-in-law, Cesare.

Although Cesare had not yet taken his priestly vows, Alexander had made him a cardinal-deacon in the fall of 1493. The cardinal of Valencia, as he was called, spent more time at the chase than he did in church, and his escape from the French had given the Romans a presentiment of the bravado that would later become his hallmark. Not only had he managed to get away so swiftly "that he was sleeping that night in Rome," but by an ingenious ruse he had also managed to save his luggage.

> In his departure from Rome with King Charles [says Burchard], they had arranged for nineteen mules to follow him, laden with his goods and apparently wearing rich trappings; amongst them were two beasts carrying his valuables. On the first day out, however, when His Majesty and the cardinal [of Valencia] were still on their way to Marino, these beasts had remained behind and returned to the city in the evening whilst the cardinal's servants made the excuse at the king's court that the mules had been seized and despoiled by some thieves.

As a consequence, people who had never taken much notice of Cesare before began attributing other daring and often ruthless exploits to him. When, at the beginning of April, sixty Swiss soldiers in the French army were attacked by two thousand Spaniards while they were standing in St. Peter's Square, the rumor spread "that the Cardinal of Valencia had ordered the massacre of the Swiss to avenge himself on them for brutally and unlawfully pillaging his mother's house during the period when the King of France was in Rome."

Surely such a man would have no qualms about stealing his brother's wife. Nor in the view of the gossips did anyone else hesitate to cuckold the unfortunate Geoffredo. In time, every presentable young man seen speaking to Sancha was presumed to be her lover. And when, in August, Juan Borgia, duke of Gandia, returned to Rome, it was immediately taken for granted that he, too, must be sharing his sister-in-law's bed.

Alexander's favorite son was then twenty. Leaving his pregnant wife and the year-old Juan II in Gandia, he had set sail for Italy in late July. Shortly before sunset on the evening of August 10, he arrived at the Porta Portense mounted on a bay covered with golden ornaments and little tinkling silver bells. His red velvet cap was adorned with pearls; both the sleeves and the front of his brown velvet waistcoat were embroidered with pearls and other precious gems. Those who saw him ride through the Trastevere to the Apostolic Palace would later find it easy to believe the rumor that this extravagantly dressed youth with the jaunty air had brought a "magnificent" young Spanish woman as a gift for his father. But whether this rumor or the subsequent rumors concerning Juan's relations with Sancha had any basis in fact there is no way of knowing.

Now that the pope had all his children with him, the presence of these attractive young people in the Vatican was bound to give rise to all sorts of stories and to dismay those who believed that Christ's vicar ought to at least pay lip service to the principle of sacerdotal celibacy. "Once anointed priests called their sons nephews, but now they speak no more of their nephews but always and everywhere of their sons," said Savonarola in an obvious jab at the pope.

But the jabs of Savonarola had no more effect upon the pope than the stories spread by the gossips. He had brought his sons to Rome, not only because he wanted them close to him, but because he needed them to carry out his policies. The perils of using them (and Lucrezia) in this manner would not become apparent until later.

In the summer of 1496, Alexander's principal concern was to strengthen the temporal power of the papacy. The invasion of the French had taught him that his spiritual authority counted for nothing unless it was backed by temporal might. It had also taught him that in an emergency he could count on no one. The College of Cardinals, the great Roman barons, and his feudatories in the Romagna had proved equally unreliable. By appointing four Spanish cardinals to the Sacred College the previous winter he had already begun the process by which he hoped to bring that body under his control. When in the summer of 1496 the last French outpost in Naples surrendered to the Holy League, Alexander decided to take full advantage of the lull in hostilities to break the power of the Roman barons.

> More irksome than plague, pope or emperor
> More irksome than famine, Frenchman or Spaniard
> More irksome, rough and ruinous to Rome
> Are Savelli, Orsini, Cenci and Colonna.

Thus a popular contemporary epigram characterized these obstreperous noblemen. Although the Colonna had raised the French flag at Ostia in 1494, they had later supported the Holy League, whereas the Orsini were still in the pay of the French. Because the family also controlled the strategic castles of Cerveteri and Anguillara and because Virginio Orsini's decision to turn Bracciano over to Charles had forced Alexander to grant the king's troops free passage through Rome, the pope decided to make the Orsini his first target. The previous February he had proclaimed Virginio Orsini a rebel. When on August 2, Virginio and his son Gian Giordano were taken prisoner by the Neapolitans, Alexander insisted that King Ferrantino renege on his promise to release them. With the leaders of the clan under lock and key in the Castel del Uovo in Naples, it must have seemed to the pope that his campaign against these troublesome nobles must surely be successful.

Although Alexander would have to rely on mercenaries to do the fighting, he was loathe to entrust the leadership of such an undertaking to a condottiere who, like Virginio Orsini at the time of the French invasion, might be tempted to switch sides at the last minute. Instead, he proposed to make his son the duke of Gandia captain-general of the church and to put him in charge of the campaign against the Orsini. Nothing in the duke's background qualified him for such a task. His principal interests had always been women, clothes, and gambling. Alexander had, moreover, another son who was passionately interested in military matters, a son whose brilliance impressed all who met him. But although the pope's letters to Juan reveal an awareness of his son's shortcomings, Alexander was determined that Juan, not Cesare, should lead the campaign against the Orsini. Like many a doting father, he must have hoped that by giving his son responsibility, he would make a man of him.

Because Juan was as yet untried in battle, Alexander engaged the celebrated condottiere Guidobaldo da Montefeltro, duke of Urbino, to serve as his lieutenant. Giovanni Sforza had just returned to Pesaro a short time before, and the pope was also eager to have him take part in the campaign. "We are surprised that when the Duke of Urbino and others who are not as closely tied to us as your lordship come to serve us of their own free will, you refuse to do so," he wrote to his son-in-law on September 17. "Wherever you may find yourself on receipt of this letter, we exhort you to come to us bringing as many soldiers as you have." If only the signor of Pesaro came quickly, he would receive his entire salary, including that part owed to him by the duke of Milan, Alexander assured him.

Giovanni was perpetually in need of funds; nevertheless, he did not budge. And although his refusal to return to Rome must have troubled his wife—it may have even reminded Lucrezia of the time that Orsino Orsini had deserted Giulia and sought refuge at Bassanello—there seemed to be nothing either she or her father could do about it.

On Sunday, October 23, Guidobaldo of Urbino arrived at the Porta Asinaria. After the obligatory triumphal entry, he made his residence in the Vatican. The following Wednesday a booted and spurred Juan Borgia knelt before his father and took the corporal oath sworn by the captains-general of the church. Accompanied by Cardinal Lunate, the legate appointed "to assist in reducing the lands of the Orsini to papal obedience," and by the duke of Urbino, the new captain-general set out along the Via Cassia the following morning "in charge of a great number of troops, arms and artillery."

Within a month his army had besieged and captured ten of the Orsini castles, including the strategic castle of Anguillara which commanded the northern route to Rome. The pope, meanwhile, continued to urge Giovanni to "put his troops in contact with those of the duke of Gandia." In answer to his father-in-law's plea, the signor of Pesaro mobilized a few of his own men, but neither he nor they left for the front. Instead, Giovanni sent his chancellor to Rome to speak to the pope. In a letter dated December 30, Alexander professed to understand and accept the reasons this chancellor had given him for Giovanni's strange behavior. Less than a week later, however, the pope's sympathy appears to have been exhausted. In a papal brief dated January 5, 1497, he ordered his son-in-law to present himself in Rome within a fortnight. The tone of this brief must have convinced Giovanni that he could procrastinate no longer. On January 15, he informed the duke of Urbino that he was setting out for Rome forthwith "so as not to cause His Beatitude further indignation."

When he arrived there, both Lucrezia and her father made a great fuss over him. According to one correspondent, Lucrezia appeared "very happy and quite mad about her husband." Although subsequent events would belie the word *mad*, she was unquestionably happy to have him back. During the Renaissance, as during the Middle Ages, it was generally assumed that a man belonged to himself, but a woman belonged to a man. Whereas a Renaissance husband was free to do more or less as he wished, innumerable treatises on marriage told his wife that her most important task was to please her husband. In the opinion of Fra Cherubino da Siena, the author of a widely read treatise on marriage: "A wife ought to fear, serve and counsel her husband. That is to say it behooves her to be constantly in fear of displeasing him in act, word or gesture."

If despite her efforts her husband appeared indifferent to her, it would be only natural for her to consider herself a failure and to suspect that he had found another woman. Giovanni's return to the palace of Santa Maria in Portico relieved his sixteen-year-old wife of such worries. It also spared her the humiliation of an open and public rejection, as had been the lot of her friend Giulia for so many years. To be rejected thus openly was indeed the nightmare of every young noblewoman married for reasons of state or family advancement to a man who did not love her. Only three weeks before Giovanni's return, Beatrice d'Este, the twenty-two-year-old wife of his cousin Ludovico, had died in childbirth. Ludovico's loud and ostentatious grief sprang not so much from love of Beatrice as from guilt over his liaison with one of her ladies-in-waiting. So public had been his affair with Lucrezia Crivelli that Burchard referred to her as Ludovico's "concubine."

By the time Giovanni arrived in Rome, the papal army, which had set out from the Holy City so confidently and taken so many castles, was on the verge of being driven from the field. On January 9, the troops of the church had begun to assault the Orsini headquarters on Lake Bracciano with scaling ladders. The fortress was under the command of Virginio Orsini's sister Bartolomea, one of those courageous and domineering women whom the men of the Renaissance honored with the title of virago, or "manlike." The cold weather and the rain worked in her favor, eventually compelling the papal forces to retreat. While they were preparing for a new assault, Bartolomea amused herself by sending her enemies a donkey to which she'd attached an enormous placard requesting that he be allowed to pass for he came "as ambassador to the duke of Gandia." Tied to the animal's tail was a letter mocking the young duke.

The arrival of reinforcements led by one of Virginio's Orsini's illegitimate sons compelled the papal troops to withdraw entirely. They were trying to regain the Via Cassia when they found themselves trapped in a narrow valley. On January 24, they met the army of the Orsini at the foot of Monte Termini between Soriano and Bassano de Sutri. Although Burchard tells us that the troops of the church were heavily defeated "in great dishonor," both the Orsini historian, Francesco Sansovino, and Sigismundo dei Conti say that the battle was closely fought. During the course of the fighting, the duke of Urbino was captured and Gandia received a wound in the face. Later, he and the papal legate Cardinal Lunate had great difficulty making their way back to Rome.

Although the pope wished to continue his campaign against the Orsini even after the defeat of his troops at Soriano, the Venetians persuaded him to make peace. On February 5, a treaty was signed in the Vatican Palace. The pope agreed to restore all the castles taken from the Orsini save Anguillara and Cerveteri. They in turn agreed to pay the Holy See 50,000 ducats and to abstain from waging further war on the papacy. Later, much would be made of Alexander's failure to ransom the duke of Urbino. Since a captured condottiere almost invariably paid his own ransom, there was, however, nothing unusual in the pope's behavior.

His plans for subduing the Orsini thwarted for the moment, the pope turned his attention to the fortress of Ostia. The French had held this fortress at the mouth of the Tiber since the fall of 1494. During that time they had done all they could to interfere with the provisioning of Rome. Hence, an attempt to retake Ostia was long overdue. To help retake it, Alexander engaged Gonsalvo di Cordova, the celebrated general, to whom, according to Guicciardini, Spanish vanity had given the title El Gran Capitan. On February 19, Gonsalvo arrived at the Lateran gate. Both Giovanni Sforza and the duke of Gandia were on hand to greet him. Two days later, the general set out for Ostia with six hundred Spanish horsemen and a thousand poorly armed foot soldiers. When the Italians laughed at the appearance of his troops, he replied that they were so naked the enemy had nothing to gain from them. Soon afterward they were joined by a contingent of Italian soldiers led by the governor of Rome.

Although Burchard tells us that Giovanni Sforza and the duke of Gandia were present at mass in the Sistine Chapel on February 26, they and their troops also participated in the siege of Ostia. The signor of Pesaro and his brother-in-law were, in fact, becoming a familiar twosome used by the pope on both military and ceremonial occasions. Rather than make them friends, this forced intimacy accentuated their differences. In Spain, Juan had left a reputation as "a very mean young man full of false ideas of grandeur and bad thoughts, cruel and unreasonable." Like Gonsalvo di Cordova and the duke of Urbino, Giovanni must have resented having to defer to this unpleasant young upstart merely because his father happened to be pope. During the time that he and Juan were encamped before Ostia, their constant quarreling resulted in an open rift between them.

Despite their differences, however, the two served as honorary escort for Gonsalvo when on March 15 El Gran Capitan returned to Rome in triumph after having retaken Ostia. They were again seen together four days later on Palm Sunday when Burchard tells us one stood to the right of the pope and the other to his left during the services in the Sistine Chapel. Because there was a shortage of palms, they were the only ones besides cardinals and ambassadors to receive them. But this signal honor failed to soothe the troubled heart of the signor of Pesaro. All during Holy Week while pilgrims from every part of Europe converged upon the city and ceremony followed ceremony at the Vatican, Giovanni continued to brood over his wrongs until finally he reached a decision. The sun had not yet risen over the Alban hills on Good Friday when he awakened his wife to tell her that he was going to confession at Sant' Onofrio on the Janiculum.

Sant' Onofrio is but a short distance from the Vatican. According to the Venetian chronicler Marino Sanuto, when Giovanni arrived there, two horses were waiting for him. Rather than go to confession as he had said he would, he mounted one of them "and set out for Pesaro leaving his wife in Rome." According to other sources, Giovanni never even went to Sant' Onofrio. Once out of sight of Santa Maria in Portico, he and a small escort headed for the *campagna*. They reached Pesaro that same night "worn out," as Giovanni put it, "by an early start." The following day, which was Holy Saturday, his secretaries informed the Milanese ambassador Stefano Taverna that the signor of Pesaro had fled because of "dissatisfaction with his father-in-law." The ambassador, however, considered this explanation misleading. In a letter written to Ludovico Sforza soon afterward, he told him that in his opinion the real reason for Giovanni's flight was something more serious, something concerning "his wife's lack of modesty which had already put the Signor of Pesaro into a state of great discontent." How this "lack of modesty" manifested itself the ambassador did not say. Since, moreover, Giovanni had left a message for Lucrezia urging her to join him after Easter week, the signor of Pesaro could not have been all that displeased with his wife.

Even Ludovico suspected that there were other reasons for Giovanni's abrupt departure, and it was not long before he demanded to know what they were. Giovanni would explain everything, he assured his cousin, but not until he had received an answer from Rome. The answer he was awaiting was, of course, the answer from Lucrezia. Meanwhile, every correspondent in the city seemed to have his own theory about the reasons for Giovanni's flight.

The signor of Pesaro had fled because he feared that otherwise he would be poisoned, said the Mantuan ambassador Gian Carlo Scalona in a letter to Francesco Gonzaga. But Gian Lucido Cattanei, the correspondent of Gonzaga's wife, Isabella, assured her that he could find no evidence of a plot nor did he believe that one existed. Nevertheless, the rumors of foul play continued.

In an account of Giovanni's flight written somewhat later by Battista Almerici and Pietro Garzetti, two chroniclers of Pesaro, it was Cesare who was the villain. The scene these chroniclers paint is in the best cloak-and-dagger tradition. Lucrezia is in her room speaking to Giovanni's chamberlain when Cesare knocks, whereupon Lucrezia directs the chamberlain to hide behind a screen. Cesare enters and tells Lucrezia of a plot to kill Giovanni. As soon as her brother leaves, Lucrezia asks the chamberlain to warn her husband he must flee. "This the chamberlain immediately did," say the chroniclers, "and Giovanni Sforza threw himself on a Turkish horse and rode in twenty-four hours to Pesaro, where the beast dropped dead." Why Lucrezia did not warn her husband herself is never explained.

In the account written by Bernardo Monaldi, another chronicler of Pesaro, it is the pope who has decided "either to take Giovanni's wife away from him or to kill him, but he, having been warned by his wife, returned here on horseback." Gregorovius, who first discovered these chroniclers, found them "confusing and full of mistakes," so that there is no reason to assume that they knew any more than, for instance, the Milanese ambassador or the correspondents of the Gonzaga. Hence we are left with the question of why Giovanni decided to flee Rome that Easter.

When Giovanni had left the Holy City in the spring of 1496, it had been with the intention never to return. Back in Rome once more, he found himself subject to the same pressures that had made life there so intolerable for him during his previous stays. If anything, those pressures had worsened, for now he had to contend not only with his father-in-law, but with his brother-in-law, the duke of Gandia, a young man he could not abide. Since by the terms of Giovanni's marriage contract he ought to have been free to take Lucrezia to Pesaro whenever he pleased, he must have felt himself more put upon each day that he remained in the Holy City. When on Good Friday he mounted his horse and headed for the Appennines, it was because he could not bear to be in Rome another day. Had he feared for his life, he would not have gone to Pesaro, for paid assassins could have tracked him down there almost as easily as they could have pursued him in Rome. Nor would he have urged Lucrezia to follow him. Although neither Ludovico nor the Milanese ambassador believed Giovanni's secretaries when they said that his dissatisfaction with his father-in-law had prompted him to take off so precipitously, this is the obvious explanation. By urging Lucrezia to follow him, he made it clear that he was not fleeing Alexander's wrath but defying him. And filled as Giovanni was with a sense of his own wrongs, he could not understand the impossible position in which he had placed his wife.

A young woman could not simply get on a horse and cross the Appennines as he had done. Even had Lucrezia been motivated by passionate love of her husband, without Alexander's permission she would have found it impossible to obtain the escort she needed to get to Pesaro safely. Since, instead, the only reasons she had for wishing to join her husband were reasons of propriety and duty, it was only natural for her to abandon the effort and allow herself to be guided by her father.

On April 1, the pope's special messenger Lelio Capodiferro arrived in Pesaro with a letter for Giovanni. "Your own good judgment can tell you how deeply grieved we are by your unexpected departure from the city; and since in our opinion there is no other remedy for an act of this nature, if you wish to safeguard your honor, we exhort you most strongly to return here as soon as possible," Alexander told his son-in-law.

He wanted his wife sent to him, Giovanni replied, whereupon Alexander let him know that unless he came to Rome, he would never see his wife again. Nor should Giovanni think that he could count on help from his cousins in Milan. The pope had spoken to both Ascanio and Ludovico and they had assured him of their support. But Giovanni had no one else to turn to, and so he wrote letter after letter to Milan imploring his cousins to help him. Once he realized that they regarded his dissatisfaction with his father-in-law as insufficient cause for flight, he began to hint at other weightier reasons for what he had done. Although he was at first evasive about just what those weightier reasons were, he later promised to tell all to Cardinal Ascanio when Ascanio went on pilgrimage to Loreto. "And I do this in spite of my unwillingness to make this matter public," he declared. What Giovanni failed to realize, however, was that no matter how shocking he made his revelations, the exigencies of politics required that his cousins support the pope. And not only was Alexander unwilling to allow his daughter to go to Pesaro, he would not countenance what he regarded as a case of lese majesté on the part of one of his vassals, even though that vassal happened to be his son-in-law.

The political and diplomatic advantages the pope had expected from Lucrezia's marriage to the signor of Pesaro had never materialized. Nor had Giovanni been of much use militarily. Besides finding him a lackadaisical and unwilling soldier, the pope had found him whining, treacherous, and not overly bright. To a father as adoring as Alexander, the thought that he had wasted his beloved daughter on so poor a creature must have been intolerable. As long as Giovanni had been willing to allow Lucrezia to remain in Rome, Alexander had been willing to put up with his limitations. When, however, the signor of Pesaro chose to defy him and to insist that Lucrezia come to Pesaro, the pope decided to find a way to end the marriage. On May 26, he signed two writs of divorce directed at his son-in-law. To serve them he chose one of the ablest lawyers in Italy, Fra Mariano da Genazzano, the director of the Augustinian order.

When Fra Mariano had preached in Florence, the renowned humanist Angelo Poliziano had praised his sonorous voice, his refined expressions, and his well-turned sentences. "Never have I met a more discreet and agreeable man," he had declared. "Mariano is moderation itself." Like the pope, Fra Mariano preferred doing unpleasant things in a pleasant manner. Upon his arrival in Pesaro he presented Giovanni with two alternatives. He could say that he had never consummated his marriage, or he could say that the marriage had been invalid from the start because Lucrezia had never legally freed herself from her obligation to marry Gaspar de Procida. In any case, said the friar, it was the pope's will "that by no means was Giovanni to be allowed to rejoin the aforesaid Madonna Lucrezia whom he wished to send to Spain."

The divorce proceedings show the pope at his most artful and his most dishonest. Certainly, a lawyer as well versed in canon law as da Genazzano must have warned the pope that the second of the alternatives he was offering his son-in-law—Lucrezia's prior commitment to Don Gasparo—had little chance of being accepted by the ecclesiastical court, which passed on requests for divorce. But to offer Giovanni no other excuse for dissolving his marriage save nonconsummation by reason of impotence was too harsh—at least at the beginning. Once Alexander had induced his son-in-law to agree to the less compromising of the two alternatives, it would be easier to persuade him to accept the other should accepting it prove necessary. Meanwhile, the pope assiduously spread the story of Giovanni's inadequacy.

That a man of Giovanni's nervous temperament could have been inhibited by the imagined presence of his father-in-law hovering over the marriage bed judging his performance is, of course, possible. That he was so inhibited that he never succeeded in having relations with his wife seems unlikely. Giovanni's first wife had died in childbirth, and we know that he had at least one illegitimate daughter. A few months after his marriage to Lucrezia, he had been told that receipt of her dowry depended upon his consummating his marriage; and at the time the divorce proceedings began, he had received a substantial part of that dowry. In fact, his reluctance to part with it was the principal reason he did not wish to see the marriage dissolved.

After being presented with the writs of divorce, Giovanni was understandably shaken, and he asked Fra Mariano for a week in which to think things over. In Rome, meanwhile, his seventeen-year-old wife appeared equally shaken by this new development. Less than two weeks after her father sent Fra Mariano to Pesaro, she and her ladies-in-waiting suddenly left the apostolic palace. "Madonna Lucrezia has left the palace *insalutate hospite* [without informing her host] and gone to a convent known as that of San Sisto where she now is," Donato Aretino reported in a letter to Cardinal Ippolito d'Este. "Some say she will turn nun, while others make different statements which I cannot entrust to a letter."

When Ascanio Sforza asked Alexander for an explanation of his daughter's sudden departure, the pope assured him that he had sent her to San Sisto because he wanted her in a religious and honest place until her husband made up his mind about the divorce. If this was indeed the case, Alexander soon changed his mind. On June 12, Gian Lucido Cattanei reported that the pope had sent the sheriff to get her. The sheriff, or *bargello*, as the Romans called him, never got past the prioress; Lucrezia remained in San Sisto, and Alexander realized that for the first time in her seventeen years his adorable golden-haired daughter was showing a mind of her own.

That Lucrezia should have thought of becoming a nun was only logical, for the convent was the one place where a Renaissance woman could escape the authority of both husband and father. Being a nun was, moreover, the only alternative a woman had to being a wife and mother. Frequently, it was not an alternative she selected of her own free will. Because a bride of Christ could bring her spouse a comparatively small dowry, the convents had become dumping grounds for young women with dowries too meager to attract any other husband, and these unwilling nuns were responsible for the frequent comparisons between religious houses and houses of ill repute. But for every convent with a reputation for bawdiness, there was another with a reputation for sanctity, a place where women who had found the male-dominated world too much for them could seek refuge. San Sisto was one of these.

When Lucrezia sought refuge there, she was a young person in the midst of a life crisis. Like most well-brought-up young women, she had been taught to believe in the sanctity of marriage. The sword that had been held over her head on her wedding day, the ring her husband had placed upon her finger, the oath she had sworn, the documents she had signed had all attested to the indissolubility of her union with Giovanni. And now here was her father urging her to divorce him.

Were the ecclesiastical court to grant the divorce on the basis of Lucrezia's prior commitment to Don Gasparo, she would play a relatively passive role in the proceedings. But should it become necessary to resort to a plea of nonconsummation—and from the beginning Lucrezia must have realized that this was a distinct possibility—she would be required to testify that she was a *virga intacta* ("an intact virgin") and submit to an examination by a qualified midwife. If her marriage had indeed been consummated, her horror at being asked to do this would be unbounded—all the more so because the father who asked it of her was no ordinary father but the Holy Father of all Christendom, the anointed representative of Christ on earth. Nor would the procedure be very much more palatable if the marriage had never been consummated, for it would still involve public disclosure of her most intimate secrets and cause incredible humiliation for her husband.

To realize that none of this mattered to her father as long as it resulted in a divorce was to see that indulgent parent in a new light. If Lucrezia seriously thought of becoming a nun at this time, I believe it was in part because she regretted her own weakness in allowing her father to talk her into signing an appeal for a divorce. "You persuaded me to agree to give testimony that will make me a laughingstock," she seemed to be telling him, "but it's not going to do you any good. When the time comes I simply won't testify. And instead of remarrying as you no doubt wish me to, I'll become a nun."

In the first heat of anger Alexander sent the *bargello* to bring her home, but when that didn't work, he decided to bide his time. Lucrezia was young and fun-loving and did not really care for her husband. Eventually her enthusiasm for religious life would pall, and she would realize that it was wiser to let her father dissolve the marriage and find her a new spouse than to bury herself in a nunnery. Meanwhile, the pope continued to press for a divorce. On June 14, Cardinal Ascanio Sforza informed his brother Ludovico that Alexander had told him that both the pope and his sons Cesare and Juan had agreed that they could not permit Lucrezia to remain in the hands of a man like Giovanni. The marriage had never been consummated and could and should be annulled.

Before it could be annulled, however, Alexander would be faced with the greatest tragedy of his life: the loss of his beloved son Juan, "the hope and glory of his line." According to a letter received by Marino Sanuto, the pope was exercising "all his ingenuity to give this son a state in Italy." After King Ferrantino of Naples had died of dysentery the previous December, the pope had erected the territories of Benevento, Terracina, and Pontecorvo into a duchy for his son. To get Ferrantino's successor, Frederic of Aragon, to agree to what he was doing, the pope discharged the new king of all his back church dues. He also appointed Cesare as legate to the king's coronation. Although a number of cardinals opposed Cesare's appointment, his mother was understandably pleased. To celebrate her son's appointment, she decided to give a dinner party in his honor on June 14.

Vannozza was then fifty-five. Her second husband and the son she had borne him had both died in 1486. Not long afterward she had married for a third time. Carlo Canale, her new husband, soon found that marriage to the discarded mistress of a prince of the church had its advantages, for the then Cardinal Borgia got him an appointment at the papal court. Vannozza, meanwhile, began investing the money left her by her second husband in real estate. By 1497, she was the lessee of several taverns in Rome and had made enough money to buy herself a country home with a large, shady garden and abundant vineyards. It was in one of these vineyards on the then virtually deserted slopes of the Esquiline Hill opposite the fifth-century church of San Pietro in Vincoli that she gave her dinner. Besides Juan, Cesare, and Geoffredo, the all-male guest list included their cousin, Cardinal Giovanni Borgia of Monreale, Cardinal Ascanio Sforza, and a few other clergymen. While the company was at the table, a masked man arrived and seated himself next to Juan. Since this same masked man had been visiting the young duke at the Vatican almost daily for about a month, no one thought anything of his sudden appearance that night. Vannozza's guests watched the sun go down over the ruins of the Forum, which in those days were clearly visible from the Esquiline, then lingered awhile to enjoy the soft Roman twilight before Cesare suggested that as it would soon be dark he and Juan had best be starting for home.

The two brothers had gotten as far as the palace of Cardinal Ascanio close by the Tiber when Juan suddenly announced that he wished to go "in pursuit of further pleasure." With the masked man astride his mule's crupper and one groom in attendance, he galloped off in the direction of the Piazza degli Ebrei. Upon his arrival there, he ordered the groom to wait for him in the piazza for an hour. If he was not back by then, the man was free to go home. According to one report, the duke spent the next hours with Madonna Dalmatia, a well-known Roman courtesan. When the next morning neither he nor the groom had returned to the Vatican, Juan's servants decided to speak to the pope. Although Alexander was obviously uneasy over his son's absence, he told himself that Juan had gone off with some girl and did not wish to be seen leaving her house in daylight. However, when evening brought no sign of the duke, he began to suspect the worst. The news that his son's missing groom had been so brutally attacked that he had lost the power of speech only served to confirm the pope's fears. By now thoroughly distraught, he ordered his servants to search the city.

Among the scores of persons they questioned was Giorgio Schiavi, a wood dealer who recalled having seen four men dump a corpse into the Tiber around midnight on the evening of the fourteenth. As a result of his testimony, three hundred fishermen began plumbing the river. Around the hour of vespers one of them brought up the body of the duke, still fully dressed with his gloves under a belt containing thirty ducats. Juan's throat had been cut and he had been stabbed eight times in various parts of the legs, head, and trunk. His soggy mud-encrusted corpse was taken by boat to the Castel Sant' Angelo to be washed, cleaned, and dressed. When it arrived there, Marino Sanuto, who had stationed himself on the bridge so as to get a better view, reported hearing a "thunderous cry" which he assumed had come from the pope. Says Burchard:

> Upon learning that his son had been thrown like dung into the river, the pope shut himself away in a room . . . weeping most bitterly. . . . From the Wednesday evening until the following Saturday morning the pope ate and drank nothing; whilst from Thursday morning to Sunday he was quiet for no moment of any hour. At last however . . . after being exhorted by . . . friends, His Holiness agreed to begin ending his mourning insofar as he was able, since he understood that otherwise he would bring greater harm and danger to himself through it.

His eyes were still red and swollen from weeping and lack of sleep when on the nineteenth he appeared before a plenary session of the consistory. "The blow which has fallen upon us is the heaviest that we possibly could have sustained," he told the assembled cardinals and ambassadors. "We loved the Duke of Gandia more than anyone else in the world. We would give seven tiaras to be able to recall him to life. God has done this in punishment for our sins, for the Duke had done nothing to deserve this mysterious and terrible death."

Although the letter officially announcing his son's death emphasized that the pope did not know "by whom the murder had been committed or what had been its cause," in the opinion of the public any number of persons had reasons for wanting the duke out of the way, including Giovanni Sforza and his brother Gian Galeazzo, as well as their cousin Ascanio Sforza and Juan's former lieutenant, the duke of Urbino. Because of Juan's supposed affair with Sancha, Geoffredo, too, was suspected of having killed his brother. But the pope labelled such a suspicion "incredible." He was also persuaded that Giovanni Sforza was not the criminal "and equally so that neither Giovanni's brother nor the Duke of Urbino was guilty," he told the consistory. Upon learning that Ascanio Sforza had stayed away because he feared the rumors associating him with the crime, Alexander assured the Spanish ambassador that he looked upon Ascanio as a brother. In fact, the only one with a motive for killing his son whom Alexander did not absolve by name were the Orsini.

The Orsini had bitterly resented Alexander's campaign against them, and they had regarded the appointment of so inexperienced a soldier as the duke of Gandia to lead the campaign as an affront. Since Alexander had been responsible for Virginio Orsini's imprisonment in the Castel del Uovo in Naples, they must have also blamed his subsequent death in prison upon the pope. By murdering the duke of Gandia, not only would they be avenging Virginio's death in the manner best calculated to hurt the pope, but they would also be ridding themselves of the man appointed to destroy them. "Evidence linking the Orsini to the crime had been uncovered but the more they [sic] got verified, the more careful the Pope became not to let the matter be known before the right time," the Milanese ambassador in Rome told Ludovico Sforza in a ciphered dispatch dated June 21. The following December Marino Sanuto reported that the pope had "acquired the certainty that they (the Orsini) had murdered the duke."

"It seems that His Holiness declares himself more openly than before in accusing the Orsini of having killed the Duke of Gandia," the Ferrarese orator in Florence wrote on December 22. But Alexander ordered the investigation into his son's murder closed twenty days after it began, and he never reopened it. "Although he could name the authors of the cruel death of his son, yet he tolerated the misdeed for the good of Italy, to avoid the renewal of an intestine war," he told the Venetians in March 1498. Because in the end Cesare was the one to benefit most from his brother's death, popular opinion would later hold him responsible for the murder. But at the time he was not even mentioned as a suspect. Nor is there any real evidence linking him to the crime.

Juan had wished to remain in Gandia, but his father had ordered him to return to Rome to lead the campaign against the Orsini. Hence, the pope's conviction that they had killed his son must have left Alexander with the feeling that in a certain measure he was responsible for Juan's death. In his agony he saw the loss of his son as God's way of punishing him for the worldliness of his reign, and he vowed to reform both himself and the church he headed. "We renounce all nepotism," he told the consistory. "We will begin the reform with ourselves and so proceed through all the ranks of the Church till the whole work is accomplished."

But the habits of a lifetime were not thus easily broken. Even as the pope swore to renounce nepotism, he continued to press for the dissolution of Lucrezia's marriage. It grieved him to speak of it, he told the consistory, but since the marriage had not been consummated owing to impotence, a decree of nullity to end a union of this kind would be an act of righteousness.

If he was using questionable means to get rid of his son-in-law, his son-in-law was using equally questionable means to get back at him. Soon after being served with the writs of divorce, Giovanni had gone to Milan. As usual he hadn't been able to decide what to do and had looked to Ludovico for advice. There was really only one thing to do, Ludovico informed him: Giovanni must prove beyond the shadow of a doubt that he wasn't impotent. He could do this by asking that Lucrezia be brought to some neutral place, such as Cardinal Ascanio's castle at Nepi, in the company of a group of witnesses agreeable to both parties. In the presence of these witnesses the signor of Pesaro could then demonstrate his virility upon his wife. Or, if he did not wish to subject Lucrezia to so public a demonstration, he could prove his virility upon certain women of

Milan in the presence of the papal legate, Giovanni Borgia of Monreale.

The suggestion was not as preposterous as it sounds. In fact, the court records of the Renaissance include numerous instances in which husbands refuted charges of impotence by proving their virility before witnesses in a brothel or upon their wives behind a bed curtain. The most famous of these cases occurred in Mantua where Vincenzo Gonzaga, a prince of the reigning house, gave an audience of ambassadors and cardinals proof of his virility upon a *virga intacta*. Before a man agreed to such a public demonstration, however, he had to be absolutely certain he wasn't going to muff it. Either because Giovanni had reason to believe that he might fail or because the very idea of such a demonstration was repugnant to him, he refused to consider it. Meanwhile, as if to compensate for not demonstrating his virility, he grew increasingly shrill about proclaiming it.

"I do not want to agree to this dissolution for no man under God could do so," he wrote his cousin Ascanio, "and even were I to give my consent it would be invalid owing to the things that have passed between me and the said Madonna Lucrezia as I explained at greater length to His Excellency the most illustrious Lord Duke [Ludovico] things that I do not care to repeat here, and that I shall not repeat unless I am obliged to."

Giovanni had told Ludovico that he had known Lucrezia "an infinite number of times" but that the pope was taking her back "because he wanted her for himself," Antonio Costabili, the Ferrarese ambassador in Milan, wrote in a dispatch dated June 23.

By then the signor of Pesaro was a man at the end of his tether. He had been made to look ridiculous and he no longer cared what means he used to get back at the man who had placed him in such an uncomfortable position. Nevertheless, there is no reason to think that when he told Ludovico that Alexander wanted his daughter for himself, he didn't believe what he was saying. For why else, he would ask himself, was the pope so adamant about keeping Lucrezia in Rome? From the very beginning of his marriage it must have seemed to Giovanni that he had been forced to compete with his father-in-law for Lucrezia's love. All the resentment and inadequacy he had felt in the face of so awesome a competitor found an outlet in this final bitter accusation.

"*Se non è vero è ben trovato*" ("Even if it's not true, it's a good invention") is an old Italian saying. Giovanni was speaking only of intent not of act. But as his words passed from one mouth to another, intent became act and in no time at all, not only Alexander, but Juan and Cesare, too, were said to have partaken of Lucrezia's favors.

Giovanni Sforza had murdered the duke of Gandia "because the duke had commerce with his wife, the sister of the duke and daughter of the pope," a Roman friend of the Venetian chronicler Malipiero told him soon after Juan's murder.

The royal house of Salerno would never admit a woman "commonly reputed to have slept with her brothers," its prince told the representatives of the king of Naples when Alexander sought to marry Lucrezia to the prince's son.

Cesare had murdered the duke of Gandia or had had someone else murder his brother for him "through envy or jealousy over Madonna Lucrezia," Machiavelli would say years later in his *Florentine Histories*, and Guicciardini would give a similar explanation for the murder in his *History of Italy*.

At the time that these rumors of incest began, Lucrezia was still in the convent of San Sisto. Although she was sufficiently realistic to know that the divorce proceedings would make her the subject of gossip, she could not have had any idea of the bizarre turn the gossip had taken. Certainly the news of her brother's murder, which must have reached her while she was at San Sisto, would make the world outside the convent walls appear more threatening than ever. Just as certainly it would dispel any anger she may have still felt toward Alexander.

The commission that the pope had appointed to reform the church met every morning that June, and the grief-stricken pontiff seemed eager to change his ways. In July, Cesare left to attend the coronation of King Frederic of Naples. In August, the pope sent Geoffredo and Sancha to their principality of Squillace. "The pope does not wish to have his children around any longer and he intends to send Madonna Lucrezia . . . to live in Valencia," said a correspondent of the duke of Ferrara on August 7.

But the Orsini were acting up again, and war between them and the Colonna seemed imminent. With Juan dead, Alexander had need of a new captain-general of the church to subdue these troublesome vassals. Save for the members of his family, there was no one he could trust. On August 20, Ascanio Sforza reported that Cesare wished to surrender his cardinal's hat. Obviously he intended to take Juan's place as captain-general of the church.

For the vicar of Christ to permit his son to be released from his ecclesiastical vows so soon after that same vicar had announced plans to release his daughter from her marriage vows would be, to say the least, bizarre. Perhaps because Alexander was still mindful of his promise to renounce nepotism, he at first refused even to consider Cesare's request. But Cesare would not take no for an answer. On September 24, Ascanio reported that the pope's son "showed himself daily more active in his endeavors to procure release from the cardinalate." And by then Alexander seems to have found the idea more appealing. Nor given the dual nature of his office could it have been otherwise. "Truly we . . . cannot stand with one foot in Heaven and the other on Earth," a chronicler of Piacenza had written. Despite Alexander's good resolutions, he, like all the Renaissance popes, was first and foremost a great secular prince with both feet planted firmly on earth. As a member of the Curia, he had spent his entire adult life immersed in the struggle for power, and not even the most profound sorrow could long extinguish his determination to use every means at his disposal to hold on to what he had. Although the opposition of the king of Spain made the pope decide to wait before releasing Cesare from his cardinal's vows, that October he was already looking around for a wife for his son. The need to subdue the Orsini also made the need to reform the church appear less urgent. When the commission Alexander had appointed after Gandia's death suggested increasing the powers of the College of Cardinals, especially with regard to the alienation of church lands, the pope tactfully but firmly ignored its suggestions. Meanwhile, another papal commission was trying to decide whether sufficient grounds existed for dissolving Lucrezia's marriage.

From the beginning Giovanni had made it clear that he would never agree to a divorce. Rather than put pressure upon him to change his mind, Alexander decided to put pressure upon Giovanni's cousins in Milan. To Ludovico, Giovanni's predicament had always seemed little short of hilarious, and it was obvious that he had no intention of allowing it to jeopardize his relations with the pope.

Hence, he must have made no effort to defend his cousin when Alexander suggested that a "specific malpractice" might be responsible for Giovanni's inadequacy. Nor would the duke of Milan seek to refute the Pope's legal arguments in favor of divorce. Instead, Ludovico must have relayed them to his cousin. Eventually, he persuaded the signor of Pesaro to write to the papal commission on divorce requesting that his marriage to Lucrezia be annulled on the grounds that his wife had never freed herself from her obligation to marry Gasparo de Procida.

After reading Giovanni's letter, Cardinal Antonio San Giorgio, one of the most distinguished jurists on the commission, informed the pope that such grounds for divorce were "neither just nor honest nor in accord with law." Since the cardinals already had Lucrezia's appeal for a divorce in which she stated that she had been transferred to Giovanni's family for over three years and was still "without nuptial intercourse and carnal knowledge and that she was prepared to swear to this and submit herself to the examination of an obstetrician," they could pass sentence upon this; or if both parties agreed, the pope could dissolve the marriage by means of a papal bull.

Aided and abetted by the pope, the Sforzas once again went to work on their cousin. To extend his supreme clemency and to demonstrate the high esteem and good will he felt for the house of Sforza, Alexander was prepared to remit Lucrezia's entire dowry and to make it a gift, Ascanio told his cousin, if only Giovanni would forget about Gasparo de Procida and agree to one of the alternatives suggested by Cardinal San Giorgio. If, however, the signor of Pesaro refused to do this, the pope's clemency would turn to severity.

Giovanni had always been more interested in holding on to his wife's dowry than he had been in holding on to his wife. Once he knew that the 31,000 ducats were his to dispose of as he saw fit, he told Ludovico that he was willing to agree to a divorce by sentence. Since such a divorce would not require a humiliating confession of impotence from him, it seemed a small price to pay for the dowry.

But the wily old fox in the Vatican would have none of it. What he wanted, and what he had undoubtedly wanted from the beginning, was a signed statement from Giovanni that he had never "known" Lucrezia: *quod non cognoverim Lucrezia.* Only with such a statement could the pope reestablish his daughter's reputation as a *virga intacta* and get her a new husband, he told the Milanese ambassador.

The letters between the Vatican and Milan and between Milan and Pesaro commenced once more. This time, however, Giovanni stood firm. Nothing, he announced, would get him to sign such a statement. "I would prefer to lose my estate and life itself rather than my honor," he had once told Ascanio. For a while that autumn it looked as if he had meant it. But honor is a nebulous thing, whereas Giovanni's estate brought him a substantial income. When Ludovico warned him that failure to sign a confession of impotence would compel Milan to withdraw its protection from Pesaro, Giovanni capitulated. "If His Holiness wishes to establish his own kind of justice, I cannot gainsay him. Let him do what he wishes, but God is higher," he told his cousin.

The great hall of his palace was filled with doctors and theologians when Giovanni signed the confession on November 18, 1497. "The signor of Pesaro has written in his own hand: I never knew her. . . . While it seems he must be impotent for otherwise a sentence of divorce could not be granted, he says that he wrote this in obedience to the duke of Milan," Pandolfo Collenuccio told the duke of Ferrara. Although Giovanni had the consolation of knowing that his former in-laws, the Gonzaga, had offered him another match, it was, nevertheless, a supremely humiliating moment.

The marriage was formally dissolved on December 22. That morning Lucrezia appeared before the divorce commission to hear herself readmitted to the company of *virgae intactae.* Because she had never learned very much Latin, she must have memorized the short Latin speech in which she thanked the commission "with such elegance and sweetness," said the Milanese ambassador, "that had she been Tullius [Cicero] himself, she could not have spoken more to the point or with greater grace."

Lucrezia had never loved her husband. Even if she had slept with him, she scarcely knew him save in the biblical sense. As her father had always assumed she would, she had soon realized how foolish it was to shut herself off from the world for the sake of this comparative stranger. She was never one to pout and sulk or throw tantrums. Once she had agreed to divorce Giovanni, the inherent graciousness of her nature required that she put the best possible face on what she was doing.

But the experience would leave her with a realization of how little voice she had in her own destiny. And it would destroy the unlimited confidence she had once placed in her father. For the first time in her seventeen years she had glimpsed the darker side of his character: the deviousness and the iron will behind the genial exterior. Even in his love for her it must have seemed to Lucrezia that she could detect something selfish and self-serving. She was still too young to realize that no love is entirely unselfish, and her ingenuousness must have made her disillusionment with her idol all the more poignant. Although she might hope that the husband he chose to replace Giovanni would be someone she could love more than she had loved the signor of Pesaro, she knew now, as she had not known at the time of her first marriage, that her interests and her desires would in no way influence the choice.

Alfonso of Bisceglie

No grief surpasses this
(And that thy Teacher understands full well)
In the midst of misery to remember bliss.

Dante, *Inferno*, canto 5, lines 121–123

The court had declared her a *virga intacta,* but the divorce proceedings and the rumors of incest caused many to see her as a second Messalina or a Thaïs. Seizing upon random scraps of information, the tales of her misconduct—the ubiquitous *si dice*—grew ever more unsavory as they passed from mouth to mouth and from city to city. The mysterious disappearance of Pedro Calderon, known familiarly as Perotto, is a case in point. Perotto was a chamberlain of the pope. He was young and handsome and one of Alexander's favorites. On February 8, 1498—a little over a month after Lucrezia's divorce—he suddenly vanished. Six days later, Burchard reported that Perotto had been found in the Tiber "where he fell against his will" (*"non libenter"*). According to the master of ceremonies, various comments were made about this incident in Rome. What they were he doesn't say.

An entry in the diary of Marino Sanuto for February 20 repeats the story of Perotto's disappearance but gives the chamberlain a companion—"a young woman belonging to the retinue of Madonna Lucrezia, the daughter of the Pope. Penthisilea by name, she was formerly a creature of the Pope, and she too was found drowned in the river. The reasons for this are not known."

Was the body of Penthisilea discovered after the body of Perotto, and is this why Burchard doesn't mention her? What exactly does Sanuto mean by "a creature of the Pope"? Does he mean that Penthisilea was Alexander's mistress, or does he mean that she was a young woman with whom the pope liked to flirt just as he liked to flirt with Sancha and every other attractive female that crossed his path? And if Penthisilea was his mistress, did she eventually make it clear that she preferred the young and handsome Perotto to her corpulent sixty-six-year-old lover? And did her preference for his chamberlain so enrage the pope that he decided to get rid of them both? These are but a few of the questions raised by the entry in Sanuto's diary. But neither Sanuto nor anyone else provides any answers.

The next time Perotto is mentioned is in a dispatch to the marchese of Mantua written by Cristoforo Poggio, a secretary of the Bentivoglio family of Bologna. Perotto was in prison for having impregnated the daughter of the pope, Poggio told the marchese on March 2. Penthisilea is now forgotten, and on March 15, a Ferrarese correspondent in Venice brings the story of the illicit pregnancy to its logical conclusion. "It has been vouchsafed from Rome that the daughter of the pope gave birth to a child," the correspondent informed Duke Ercole.

If Lucrezia gave birth in March, she must have become pregnant during her stay in San Sisto. Had Alexander used Perotto to deliver messages to his daughter while she was there? Later, the prioress would complain that Lucrezia and her ladies in-waiting had introduced a note of unaccustomed worldliness into the life of that tranquil convent. Was Sister Girolama alluding to an affair between Lucrezia and her father's messenger? And was Penthisilea the lady-in-waiting who helped Lucrezia to dress in such a way as to conceal her pregnancy when, during her sixth month, she appeared before the cardinals on the divorce commission to hear herself described as a *virga intacta*? And how did Cesare feel about the man who had dishonored his sister?

An answer to the last question is provided in a report written over a year later by Paolo Capello, the Venetian envoy in Rome. "With his own hand and under the mantle of the Pope, Cesare murdered Master Perotto so that his blood spattered in the face of the Pope of whom Master Perotto was a favorite."

But Capello did not arrive in Rome until June 1499, some sixteen months after the event of which he writes, so it is only natural to wonder where he got his information. With so many uncorroborated stories to choose from and so many discrepancies between one story and another, it is, in fact, impossible to decide what really happened, let alone how or why it happened. Renaissance Rome was such a lawless place—there were so many private vendettas— Perotto could just as well have been murdered for some reason unconnected with Alexander and his family. When Giorgio Schiavi told the pope's servants that he had seen a corpse dropped into the Tiber on the night the duke of Gandia disappeared, they had asked him why he hadn't reported the crime earlier. Because he'd seen a hundred bodies dropped into the Tiber at that point without anyone getting in the least excited about it, he had replied.

If, as some think, the story of Perotto's involvement with Lucrezia was concocted to discourage potential suitors, it failed to achieve its purpose. Lucrezia's first suitor, Roberto di San Severino, the heir of the prince of Salerno, had dropped out of the running even before the Perotto story began circulating, not because Roberto's father objected to the reputation of the future bride, but because Naples and Milan objected to the prince's ties with France. Soon after Alexander agreed to look elsewhere for a husband for his daughter, King Frederic of Naples confiscated the principality of Salerno and bestowed it upon his nephew Alfonso of Aragon, the illegitimate son of the late King Alfonso II. Frederic then proposed that the new prince of Salerno replace the heir of the former prince as Lucrezia's suitor.

By then Alexander's difficulties with the Orsini and the Colonna were increasing daily. Strengthening his ties with Naples would give him greater freedom to deal with his troublesome barons. It could also pave the way for a marriage between Cesare and Frederic's daughter Carlotta, a marriage which the prospective ex-cardinal and his father both desired. Nevertheless, it was not the pope's nature to commit himself to anything until he had examined the alternatives. All that winter he continued to encourage suitors for his daughter's hand. There was Francesco Orsini, duke of Gravina, whom the pope appeared to favor because an Orsini in the house of Borgia would be one way to put an end to the feud between the two families. There was Caterina Sforza's son Ottaviano, a young man apparently undaunted by the fate of that other Sforza who had married

Lucrezia. And there was a signor of Piombino whom nobody seems to have taken very seriously.

Winter turned into spring, and spring was on the verge of becoming summer. Gian Lucido Cattanei had just written the marchesa of Mantua that it looked as if Alfonso was out of the running because the pope had nothing good to say about either the young prince's intellect or his worth, when on June 20 the contract affiancing Lucrezia to him was signed. Alexander agreed to give his daughter a dowry of 40,000 ducats; King Frederic gave his nephew the territories of Quadrata and Bisceglie and the title of duke of Bisceglie, which he would use henceforth along with his previous title of prince of Salerno.

Because by then Alexander knew that he could not bear to be separated from his daughter, the contract also stipulated that she remain in Rome during his lifetime and that Alfonso reside there during the first year of the marriage. Although this seems a rather unusual request, there is no record of any opposition from either the bridegroom or his family.

In an unsigned epigram that recalled both Giovanni Sforza and Gasparo de Procida, the Roman humanist Fausto Evangelista Capodiferro sought to warn the seventeen-year-old bridegroom of what lay in store for him:

> *Non pereire alii vivunt, Alphonse mariti*
> *Spe duo fraudantur te tua poena manet*
> *Nec te Parthenopes duxisse ab origine nomen*
> *Juvert, aut quod stirp regia: jura cadunt.*

> ("The other husbands are not dead, Alfonso, they live. / Two are cheated of their hopes and your punishment awaits you. / It will help you neither to have drawn your name from Parthenope / Nor to be of royal stock: Your rights, too, will be trampled on.")

Alfonso of Bisceglie was the brother of Geoffredo's wife, Sancha. Comines called their father, Alfonso of Calabria, "the cruellest, most vicious and commonest man" that he had ever seen. The son, on the other hand, was of an open and unassuming nature, gentle, carefully educated, and so good-looking that to the Roman chronicler Talini he appeared "the handsomest young man ever seen in the Imperial city."

Soon after the marriage contract was signed, he set out for Rome accompanied by fifty cavalrymen. Because Alexander wished his entrance into Rome to be as secret as possible, the prince left all but seven of his horsemen behind at Marino. He arrived at the gates of Rome on July 15, and, said Ascanio Sforza, the "secret" of his presence immediately became known all over the city. After being received by the pope's emissaries, he rode up to the palace of Santa Maria in Portico to be presented to his bride.

The Italians call it *un colpo di fulmine*—literally, "a thunderbolt"—that miraculous and overpowering phenomenon known as love at first sight. Was it Alfonso's youth and good looks or his easy forthright manner, so different from the bumbling awkwardness of Giovanni Sforza, that drew Lucrezia to her new bridegroom? Whatever it was, she made no effort to conceal her feelings. "The daughter of the Pope appears most pleased with Don Alfonso," Gian Lucido Cattanei wrote soon afterward. And Alfonso appeared equally pleased with the slim golden-haired young woman with the bright smile who was to be his wife. After six glorious days spent getting to know one another, these two gentle, young creatures were married in the Vatican on July 21, 1498.

Although Lucrezia's long, blond hair and slender figure must have made her seem more child than woman despite the elaborate wedding gown she wore—the jewel-studded silk stomacher embroidered in black velvet, the girdle of pearls, and diadem of chased gold—she was no longer the bewildered little girl thrust into a world of adults that she had been at the time of her marriage to Giovanni Sforza. For four years she had been mistress in her own house; she had attended banquets and receptions where cardinals and ambassadors had been her dinner partners. She was at ease in society and those who met her came away charmed by her graciousness. Nevertheless, it would be only natural for memories of that other marriage and its ugly aftermath to intrude upon her wedding day. When once more the unsheathed sword was held over her head while Alfonso's ring was slipped on her finger, she must have prayed that no further scandal would defile her name, that her marriage to the beautiful boy who knelt beside her would last a lifetime.

According to Burchard, the wedding celebrations the following day "were conducted quietly without any great pomp though everyone knew of the event." While the guests were being seated, the retainers of Sancha and the retainers of Cesare suddenly began quarreling over who should have precedence. Swords were drawn, and two bishops who tried to mediate "received many punches." The fisticuffs so alarmed Alexander's servants that they fled, leaving the pope, who was apparently also trying to pacify the combatants, "in the thick of the fray." Since none of the chroniclers offers any reason for the outbreak, there is no way of knowing whether it resulted from a falling out between Sancha and Cesare or from some private feud between their retainers. In any case, peace was finally restored; Alexander's servants returned, and the wedding supper began. Although Alexander delighted in the company of women—he particularly enjoyed watching young women dance—he was mindful of the rule that forbade a pope to sit at table with them. And so he dined in solitary splendor, waited on by two of his cardinals and by his daughter-in-law, Sancha, who poured his wine. After the meal ended, she and Lucrezia danced for him, probably the Spanish dances that he loved best. Later, a play was presented in which Cesare appeared as a unicorn.

The year 1497 had seen seventeen cases of the French disease at the papal court, and the pope's son had been one of them. In fact, Cesare's private physician, Gaspar Torella, had just dedicated a treatise on the disease to his illustrious patient. In this treatise, Torella hailed Cesare as a benefactor of the human race, because by contracting syphilis he had given his doctor an opportunity to understand the nature of the disease and to devise a treatment. Although the treatment was the best then available, it did not cure Cesare. However, the pains in the groin and the pustules that would plague him later had not yet made their appearance. As he cavorted about the stage in his unicorn's costume that evening, Cesare must have been feeling particularly gay and carefree. His father's objections to his surrendering his hated cardinal's hat had long since been overcome. Now it was only a matter of time before he was released from his vows and took Carlotta of Aragon as his wife. His wish to marry Carlotta had nothing to do with love—the princess was being educated at the French court, and Cesare had never seen her. But Carlotta was the legitimate daughter of a king. Marriage to her would make Cesare prince of Altamura and Taranto, and these territories would provide him with an income sufficient to compensate for the 35,000 ducats a year he was surrendering along with his cardinal's hat.

"Cum Numine Caesaris Omen; Jacta est Alea" ("Under the auspices of Caesar the God; the die is cast")—these were the devices engraved on Cesare's sword. Like his namesake, the twenty-three-year-old cardinal of Valencia was wildly ambitious and shamelessly vain. To renounce the cardinalate to become just plain Cesare Borgia when one brother had been duke of Gandia and another was prince of Squillace would have been unthinkable.

Lucrezia knew that her marriage to Alfonso had been arranged to facilitate Cesare's marriage to Carlotta, but she was so delighted with her new husband that she must have felt almost grateful to her father for having used her thus. That the failure of his plans would have the most terrible consequences for her and Alfonso, she could not, of course, foresee.

Burchard notes that Lucrezia's marriage was consummated that night. And most blissfully consummated, it would appear from the young couple's continued absorption in one another. It was a delectable time for Lucrezia, that first year with her beloved, a year when she began to branch out and build a life of her own, independent of her father and his circle. Poetry has always had a unique appeal for lovers. With Alfonso's encouragement Lucrezia began to invite poets and writers to the palace of Santa Maria in Portico and soon had formed a small literary court of her own.

Frequently in attendance was her husband's former tutor, the famous blind scholar Raphael Brandolinus Lippus, as well as the neo-Petrarchan poet Serafino Aquilano and his friend, Vincenzo Calameta. Later, the flamboyant and popular Bernardo Accolti, who called himself "L'Unico Aretino" or sometimes simply "L'Unico," joined the group. The courtly tradition was still strong then, and L'Unico chose Lucrezia as the inaccessible lady to whom he "made love" in his poems.

Another poet who also frequented the palace of Santa Maria in Portico was Fausto Evangelista Capodiferro, the same poet who had penned the unsigned epigram warning Alfonso of what awaited him if he married Lucrezia. Despite Capodiferro's ambivalent attitude toward the Borgias, like L'Unico he sometimes "made love" to Lucrezia in his poetry:

There was once born a Lucrezia more
   chaste than the Lucrezia of old
This one is not the daughter of mortal man
   But is born of that same Jove.

Side by side with such poems in his notebook, however, were
other poems that Lucrezia never saw, poems in which Capodiferro
dwelt upon long nights haunted by incestuous phantoms and the
hapless shades of those unfortunate women who had loved the bull.
The bull to whom he was alluding in Lucrezia's case was not,
however, the bull for whom Mirra and Biblis and Pasiphaë had
pined, but the bull in the Borgia coat of arms, that blood red beast
whose aggressive virility made him such an appropriate emblem for
Alexander VI. How with such a father, a father whom Capodiferro
compared not only to the Minotaur but to Jove himself, could
Lucrezia love any other man, especially an untried lad of seventeen?
Must she not be forever dissatisfied, forever longing for what she
could   not   have?   Although   certainly   not   meant   as   such,
Capodiferro's poems were a tribute to the overwhelming force that
Alexander communicated, a force that seemed to make him more
akin to those wild sensual gods of pagan antiquity than to the gentle
Prince of Peace whose anointed vicar he was.
   But the splendidly virile bull, the Jove-like figure who ruled over
the Vatican, was also a devoted and domesticated paterfamilias who
fussed over his daughter in very un-Jove-like fashion. And whatever
her unconscious longings, on a conscious level it was obvious that
she frequently felt stifled by his excessive concern.
   This devoted father rejoiced and must have also been a trifle
anxious when, in early January, Lucrezia told him that she was
expecting a child. Renaissance women did not coddle themselves
during pregnancy. Vannozza had joined her lover on the steep and
windy heights of Subiaco when she was more than six months
pregnant with Lucrezia. Lucrezia, in her turn, saw no need to curtail
her own activities. On February 17, she and her ladies-in-waiting
decided to spend the day in the vineyards of one of the cardinals.
They were all healthy, exuberant teen-agers, delighted to escape the
confining atmosphere of Santa Maria in Portico. Spotting a stretch
of level ground, Lucrezia suggested that they have a race. The

ground proved not quite as level as it had appeared. As she tripped and fell, she brought one of her ladies-in-waiting down on top of her. The pain was so intense that Lucrezia fainted and had to be carried into the house. At nine that evening she aborted. Whether the fetus was male or female there was no way of knowing, Gian Lucido Cattanei wrote the marchesa of Mantua.

Venus was jealous of Lucrezia's happiness, said Capodiferro, in an attempt to console her for her loss. Alexander, too, appeared in need of consolation, for he had been eagerly awaiting the arrival of this new grandchild. The pall that descended over the Vatican was, however, of short duration. Two months later, Lucrezia announced that she was again pregnant. But even as she and Alfonso congratulated one another on their good fortune, events beyond their control, deals and counter deals in France and Spain and in the Vatican, what is best described by that frazzled old cliché "a tangled web of intrigue," were setting the stage for a shift in papal policy that would destroy their youthful idyll.

The delight they took in one another was, after all, merely a happy coincidence. They had been married to make it easier for Cesare to marry Carlotta of Aragon. When in February 1498, Cesare had first been proposed as a possible husband for Carlotta, her father had immediately made it clear that he opposed the match. Although Frederic based his opposition to Cesare on his still being a cardinal, there were any number of other reasons why the king could have found the pope's son a less than ideal spouse for his daughter.

For one thing, Frederic had had the opportunity to witness Cesare's extravagant and promiscuous life-style at close range when the young cardinal had served as legate to his coronation. In fact, one observer had predicted that Cesare's frequent demands for money would end by driving "the poor king" into the arms of the Turks. Were he to give his daughter to Cesare, Frederic must have shuddered to think of the dowry he would be expected to provide. That the prospective groom had contracted the French disease while he was in Naples did not help matters, nor did Carlotta's announcement that she had fallen in love with a Breton nobleman at the French court. But all of these personal objections might have been overlooked had the king believed that the match would benefit him politically. Instead, he seemed to believe that the exact opposite was true. Naples was a fief of the papacy. Once Cesare had gotten a foothold in the kingdom by marrying Carlotta, what was to prevent this arrogant young man from seeking to have his father invest him with the crown itself?

Though Frederic was at times remarkably outspoken in his opposition to the proposed marriage, he did not wish to antagonize the pope by an outright refusal. And so he placed the responsibility for the final decision upon his daughter. If Carlotta agreed to marry Cesare, all well and good. However, her father would not seek to influence her. The stratagem was fairly obvious. Nevertheless, Alexander went along with it, probably because he was confident that he would find a way to break down Carlotta's resistance. Since the princess was at the French court, he asked Charles VIII to persuade her to accept Cesare.

Relations between France and the papacy had improved considerably, and Charles had no objection to acting as matchmaker. In fact, it was he who had suggested Carlotta as a possible wife for Cesare in the first place. As it turned out, however, Charles had little chance to use his powers of persuasion. On April 7, while inspecting his new chateau at Amboise, the near-sighted young monarch struck his head against the lintel over one of the doorways. Nine hours later he was dead. A week before his death, he'd beheld a serpent and a dragon in a dream. His astrologers had assured him that the serpent meant that he would once again invade Italy and that this time he would be successful. After his death, they decided that the serpent had foretold the advent of his successor.

Thirty-six-year-old Louis XII was a distant cousin of the deceased and the grandson of Valentina Visconti of Milan. Although as Valentina's heirs Louis's family had a far more valid claim to Milan than that possessed by the Sforzas, Louis's father, the poet prince, Charles of Orléans, had not considered the duchy worth fighting for. Louis, however, had nothing better to do with himself. At his coronation at Rheims he made his intentions clear by assuming the title of duke of Milan as well as that of king of Jerusalem and the two Sicilies.

At the time he assumed these titles, Venice, Milan, and Florence were involved in a dispute over Pisa. In any case, rather than forget the question of Pisa and unite with the other states to discourage Louis's designs on Milan, Venice lost no time in seeking to conclude an alliance with the king. Florence also hailed his pretensions.

Although Alexander sent an envoy to France to warn Louis not to attack either Milan or Naples, the pope must have realized that with the states of Italy as divided as they had been in 1494, a French invasion was inevitable. Nor did Alexander have any chance of successfully opposing it. In fact, his position appeared so weak that when Christopher Columbus settled his estate on his son Diego, he commanded Diego to use his money "to assist the Pope if a schism in the Church should threaten to deprive him of his seat or his temporal possessions." Germany and Spain were both expected to withdraw their obedience from the Holy See momentarily; whole sections of the papal states were on the verge of anarchy, and the Orsini and the Colonna were once again at war. After paying no attention to the Pope's repeated efforts to arrange a truce, in July 1498 the leaders of the two families suddenly asked Frederic of Naples to mediate their dispute. So that there would be no mistaking the purpose of this new move, someone posted a notice on the door of the Vatican Library:

> A firm arrangement has united the enemy armies. Kill the bull who is laying waste the frontiers of Italy, tear out the monstrous beast's horns. Avenging Tiber, drown the calves in your fast-flowing waves! May the bull perish, a huge sacrifice on Jupiter's altars!

To make matters worse, Frederic, who that June had affianced his nephew to Lucrezia and should have been helping the pope, was secretly encouraging his rebellious barons. Meanwhile, Louis's envoys in Rome brought Alexander a most interesting proposal. The marriage of Anne of Brittany to Charles VIII had given the French control over the previously semi-independent appanage of Brittany. To retain that control, Louis wished to marry his predecessor's widow. Unfortunately, the king already had a wife: Anne's sister-in-law, Jeanne de Valois, whom Machiavelli describes as "deformed, hunchbacked on both sides and barren." In a display of cruelty that made the treatment of Giovanni Sforza seem benevolent by comparison, Louis swore that he had married Jeanne "against his will and for fear of her father Louis XI," that he had never consummated his marriage nor was his wife capable of consummating it, that she was a cripple afflicted with scrofula and repellent both in body and mind. Were the pope to give him a dispensation to divorce Jeanne and marry Anne, Louis promised to raise the county of Valence to a duchy, to bestow it upon Cesare along with the county of Diois, and to help the pope's son win the hand of Carlotta of Aragon, or, in the event that this was impossible, to give him the hand of a French princess. Under the circumstances, the temptation to make capital out of Louis's marital difficulties proved irresistible. Less than three weeks after Lucrezia's marriage to Alfonso, the pope concluded a secret agreement with the French king.

On August 17, Cesare appeared before the College of Cardinals. He had been admitted to the Sacred College on the express findings of a committee that he was the son of his mother's first husband, Domenico di Rignano, which was not true, he told the cardinals. Since, moreover, he had never had any calling for the priesthood and since his personal life ill-consorted with the high office he held, he believed that it would be in the best interest of the church for him to return to lay status. Because of the opposition of the king of Spain, the cardinals refused to vote on the matter. Instead, they left the decision up to the pope. That afternoon Alexander issued a *dispensa* allowing his son to surrender his cardinal's hat. A few hours later, Louis's royal patent investing Cesare with the duchy of Valentois arrived. Cardinal of Valencia when he arose that morning, he was duc de Valentois when he went to bed that evening.

"The ruin of Italy is confirmed—observe the machinations of this father and son!" Gian Lucido Cattanei declared in a letter to the marchesa Isabella written on October 1, the day the newly invested duc de Valentois set sail for France.

But despite all the evidence to the contrary, the pope was still not really committed to a French alliance. Rather he sought to play the various opposing factions one against the other and to benefit from their weaknesses, determined that a new invasion not find him in the same isolated position in which he'd placed himself in 1494. It cost him 200,000 ducats to outfit his son for the trip to France. Half of this was spent on Cesare's suite and the rest on the young man himself. But Alexander had always believed in putting on a good show to get what he wanted. And if we are to believe the rumors then circulating, not all the money came from his own pocket. Some of it was obtained by confiscating the estates of a bishop lately accused of heresy.

Cesare's spectacular entry into Chinon with the brief granting

Louis permission to marry Anne of Brittany could only have glad-
dened the heart of the new duke of Valentois who, for so long, had
seen himself relegated to the sidelines while his brother Juan occupied stage center. After a seemingly endless procession of mules,
all richly accoutred in red and yellow—Cesare's own colors—and all
bearing chests and coffers and tubs loaded with gifts for the bride
and other expensive paraphernalia, came great chargers covered
with red and yellow brocade; pages and lackeys most of them in red
velvet, but two, whom the watching crowd immediately dubbed *les
mignons,* in curled gold; still more mules; and then thirty gentlemen,
some in gold brocade, some in silver; followed by three musicians in
gold brocade carrying silver instruments with short gold chains. To
the accompaniment of their music, Cesare rode over the castle draw-
bridge to where the king's emissaries waited to greet him. An eyewitness reported:

> He was mounted on a great charger richly harnessed with a robe
> of parti-colored red satin and gold brocade and bordered with
> many large pearls. In his bonnet in two rows there were five or
> six rubies as large as beans which showed a great light. At the
> edge of his biretta he also had a large quantity of jewels down to
> his boots which were all fringed with gold strands and edged
> with pearls. And a collar which, to describe it truly, was worth
> a full thirty thousand ducats. . . . The horse he rode was
> weighed down with gold leaves and covered with fine jewelry,
> with many pearls and precious stones.

Louis, who watched the whole gorgeous display from one of the
windows of the castle, found it a trifle ridiculous. Although he
received Cesare with all due honor, he and his courtiers secretly
made merry over "the vainglory and stupid bombast of this duke of
Valentois."

In Rome, meanwhile, Ascanio Sforza accused the pope of bringing
ruin upon Italy by sending his son to France. "Are you aware, Monsignore, that it was your brother who invited the French into Italy?"
Alexander replied.

When the Spanish and Portuguese envoys demanded that the pope
recall Cesare from France and restore him to the College of Cardinals, Alexander threatened to have one of their party thrown into

the Tiber. Nevertheless, the pope was not as confident as his defiant words would indicate, for despite all Louis's assurances, the king had been unable to persuade Carlotta to marry Cesare. Although by then he bore the marks of the French disease on his face, Cesare, like his father, was enormously attractive to women. Nor was Carlotta immune to his charm. But it soon became obvious that despite all the talk of her being allowed to make up her own mind, she really had no say in the matter.

According to the journal of Machiavelli's assistant, Biagio Buonaccorsi, King Frederic had ordered his daughter not to consent to the marriage until the pope and the king of France conjointly granted him peaceful possession of the kingdom of Naples. Since Louis considered himself the lawful king of Naples by reason of his Angevin ancestors, he refused to make any such grant. Whether, as Buonaccorsi seemed to believe, his refusal was the sole cause for Carlotta's adamant refusal to marry Cesare, or whether the princess had some other reason for not wishing to have the pope's son as her husband, Alexander laid the blame for her rejection of Cesare upon the king of France. On February 4, the pope wrote that he feared that he would become the laughingstock of Italy if the question of Cesare's marriage was not soon settled, and Cesare himself talked of quitting the French court. On February 13, the pope begged Ascanio Sforza to persuade King Frederic to agree to the marriage. The pope appeared very much afraid of Spain and thoroughly distrustful of France, Ascanio reported.

That the two powers had decided to make Italy their battleground was obvious even to more or less apolitical persons such as Lucrezia's court poet L'Unico Aretino. Seeing Lucrezia with the Spanish and French ambassadors, L'Unico hastened to offer them a suggestion:

> Messer Bernardo Accolti to the ambassadors of France and Spain having between them the daughter of Pope Alexander VI to whom the poet makes love.

> Unconquered and able kings, it now seems clear to me that you desire to dominate the whole of Italy for she whom you have between you conquers more with her eyes than we do with our arms.

Let the expense and fatigue of the fatal machines you are bringing be spared.

For where she turns her gay glance
She will break down not only ramparts
And marbles, but even heaven itself.

All that spring Alexander appeared to vacillate between France
and Spain. If Cesare had not been in France, the pope would have
allied himself with Milan, the Venetian envoy wrote on March 12.
Whether Alexander's indecision was real or whether it was a way of
confusing Naples and Milan while putting pressure on Louis to find
another bride for Cesare, there is no way of knowing. Certainly the
pope appeared to have little faith in the success of Louis's negotiations to marry Cesare to Charlotte d'Albret, the sister of the king of
Navarre. Then, on May 23, a courier arrived in Rome with the news
that Cesare had married Charlotte at Blois on May 12. The marriage
had been consummated that Sunday, and the young husband had
given eight successive proofs of his virility *("octo vices successive"),*
Burchard wrote in his diary. However, the memoirs of Robert III of
La Marck, lord of Fleurange, appear to cast doubt upon this splendid
performance. According to La Marck, Cesare "requested pills from
the apothecary so that he might regale his lady." But through an
oversight he was given laxative pills instead, "and thus he went to
the privy without cease throughout the night as the ladies reported in
the morning."

Although an Italian who saw Charlotte d'Albret many years later
found her "more human than beautiful," at the time of her marriage
she was reputed to be one of the loveliest princesses in France. According to the *De Gestis Regnum Gallorum,* Cesare entered into
marriage with her very enthusiastically, not only because the
marriage was expedient, but because "the beauty of the lady was
equalled by her virtue and the sweetness of her nature." And
whatever happened on their first night together, his winsome
seventeen-year-old bride would look back on the four months she
spent with her handsome husband as the happiest months of her life.
But the exigencies of politics required that he return to Italy that
September. Whether out of fear of the unknown or for some other
reason, Charlotte kept finding excuses not to follow him. Although

he continued to write to her and to send her expensive gifts, the two never saw one another again. Nor did Cesare ever see the daughter his wife bore him the following spring.

While the negotiation for Cesare's marriage had been taking place, King Louis had concluded a treaty with Venice for the partition of Milan, leaving it up to the pope to sign if he wished. Upon learning that Cesare had married Charlotte, Alexander hastened to sign. To many it seemed that his sole reason for signing was his desire to aggrandize his son. At the Sorbonne, thousands of students made merry over a parody of Cesare's marriage. In another parody performed at the French court, a comic Saint Peter threw away his keys as a sign of love for his son, after which the twelve apostles danced a round.

But if Alexander had taken advantage of Louis's marital difficulties to advance his son, Cesare's advancement was not the only reason for concluding an alliance with France. From the beginning of his reign, the pope had been hampered by the disloyalty of his supposed vassals: not only the Orsini and the Colonna and the other Roman barons, but the semi-independent vicars of the Romagna as well. In exchange for Alexander's support of a French conquest of Milan, King Louis promised to give the pope a French army of 1,800 cavalry and over 4,000 Swiss and Gascon infantry to assist Cesare in overthrowing these unscrupulous vicars.

"Before Pope Alexander VI had crushed the petty tyrants that ruled the Romagna," says Machiavelli, "that country presented an example of all the worst crimes. The slightest causes gave rise to murder and every species of rapine; and this was due exclusively to the wickedness of the princes, and not to the evil nature of the people as alleged by the former. For these princes, being poor yet wishing to live in luxury like the rich, were obliged to resort to every variety of robbery."

By seeking to get rid of them, Alexander was doing what every pope before him had sought to do. That he intended to make Cesare the ruler of a unified Romagna goes without saying. He had always wanted to give his son a territory in Italy. There was, moreover, no one else he could trust to carry out his bidding. But although the pope used French aid to achieve his ends, he never ceased to have misgivings about his alliance with France. Over and over he pleaded with the Venetians to join him in a league of Italian powers which would contain or possibly evict the foreigners. "For the love of God let us have an end to our differences. Let us understand each other a little and busy ourselves with the welfare of Italy," he implored the Venetian ambassador, Antonio Giustiniani, in 1502. Nevertheless, he was far too practical to risk losing everything by opposing the French in 1499 when Spain had agreed to remain neutral and his only allies would have been Ludovico Sforza and Frederic of Naples, neither of whom he trusted and neither of whom trusted him.

There was, moreover, enough of the *arriviste* in Alexander for this second son of a minor Spanish nobleman to relish being able to marry a son of his to a French princess. Burchard tells us that soon after the news of Cesare's marriage reached Rome, Alexander ordered many fires kindled in the city, including one in front of Lucrezia's palace. "This took place as a sign of rejoicing," says the master of ceremonies. "In fact it was a great dishonor, a great shame for His Holiness and the Holy See."

That Alexander should have failed to appreciate the unseemliness of a pope's publicly celebrating the marriage of a son who also happened to be an ex-cardinal was typical of the man. That he should have been sufficiently indifferent to his daughter's feelings to order a fire lit in front of her palace is more surprising. Not that Lucrezia didn't love her brother enough to rejoice at his good fortune, but she was the wife of a Neapolitan prince. And Cesare's marriage obviously meant the end of friendly relations with Naples. What with Louis's constantly reiterated claim that he, not Frederic, was the lawful ruler of Naples, it was only natural that the pope's alliance with France should make Alfonso feel out of place in Rome. His uneasiness must have increased when he learned that Ascanio Sforza had fled the city. Alfonso was only eighteen and he had no one but the Neapolitan ambassador to advise him. When, a few days after Ascanio's flight, a number of other cardinals sympathetic to Naples also fled Rome, Alfonso decided that it would be folly for him to remain there any longer. On the morning of August 2, he saddled his horse and headed for the Colonna fortress at Genazzano. No sooner did he arrive there, than he wrote to his wife urging her to join him. But Alexander had sent out troopers to bring his son-in-law back, and although they failed to overtake him in time, they did succeed in intercepting his message to Lucrezia.

"The Duke of Bisceglie, Madonna Lucrezia's husband, has secretly fled and gone to the Colonna in Genazzano; he deserted his wife who has been with child for six months and she is constantly in tears," said Marino Sanuto. Others said that she put on a good face for what had happened. What is most likely is that she smiled in public and cried in private.

Tears are the refuge of the helpless. Lucrezia could not expect her father to terminate his alliance with France simply because it was repugnant to Alfonso. On the other hand, she could not expect Alfonso to remain with her now that her father had allied himself with an enemy of the Neapolitan royal house. During pregnancy the young mother-to-be is more emotionally fragile than usual, even under the best of circumstances. Each movement of the baby within her would remind Lucrezia that events completely beyond her control had caused its father to abandon her. Although at times she would tell herself that it was only natural for Alfonso not to have trusted her enough to let her know what he was planning, at other times his lack of trust would appear insupportable. She had, of course, no way of knowing that Alfonso had written to her from Genazzano. And so she cried.

But if, despite her tears, she made an effort to understand the reasons for her husband's behavior, Alexander could not. In truth, he could never understand why political differences should affect personal relationships. That Alfonso should leave his wife because of the French alliance infuriated the pope. Since he could not vent his anger upon his son-in-law, he decided to vent it upon the young man's sister. A few days after Alfonso's flight, the pope sent Sancha back to Naples. Ignoring his daughter-in-law's protests that she wished to remain where she was, he declared that if King Frederic didn't want to leave his property with the pope, the pope didn't want anything belonging to the king. Nor would he give Sancha the money she needed to return to Naples. The Milanese envoy protested that this was adding insult to injury, that rather than send away his daughter-in-law, the pope ought to remove the causes of his son-in-law's flight, but Alexander ignored him. Because Alexander must have hoped that a change of scenery would take Lucrezia's mind off her absent husband, he decided to send her away from Rome also. Nor was a change of scenery all that he contemplated.

Since the middle of the fourteenth century, Spoleto had been ruled by a series of papal governors. In an unprecedented move, the pope gave his daughter a letter addressed to the priors of Spoleto in which he informed them that he had entrusted "to . . . the noble lady Lucrezia de Borgia, Duchess of Bisceglie, the office of keeper of the castle as well as the government of our cities of Spoleto and Foligno and the county and district around them."

The new *governatrice* of Spoleto was then nineteen. Although she did not know it as yet, her father was already making plans to confiscate the lands of his rebellious barons and to bestow at least some of them upon her. Hence, he felt that it was imperative that he give her some experience in government. That any number of persons would object to his giving a woman such responsibility did not appear to trouble him. In fact, one of the reasons women must have found the pope so attractive was that although he was obviously only too aware of them as females, he also liked and respected them as people. His daughter was not merely sweet and eager to please and adorably feminine, she was also extremely intelligent; and Alexander knew it. Besides discussing affairs of state with her from the time she had been a child, he had also let her observe him listening to the complaints brought by ordinary citizens, and he must have realized what an asset her unfailing graciousness would be in dealing with just such matters.

Although Geoffredo was to accompany his sister to Spoleto, it never seems to have occurred to the pope to confer any similar responsibility upon him. A few months before, while crossing the Ponte Sant' Angelo with an entourage of twenty-five Spaniards, the seventeen-year-old Geoffredo had quarrelled with the *bargello* and received a wound in the thigh for his insolence. When Sancha demanded that the persons responsible for wounding her husband be punished, Alexander told her that Geoffredo had gotten what he deserved. Undoubtedly the incident with the *bargello* confirmed the pope's already low opinion of his youngest son. When Cesare had found himself passed over by his father in favor of the duke of Gandia, he had made no secret of his resentment. Geoffredo, however, was made of milder stuff, and there is no record of his ever having protested the appointment of his sister as *governatrice* of Spoleto.

Spoleto is an ancient Umbrian town in the central Appennines 126 kilometers northeast of Rome—a long journey for a young woman in her sixth month of pregnancy to make on horseback. However,

Alexander showed his usual concern for his daughter's welfare by providing her with a litter equipped with a mattress of crimson satin embroidered with flowers, white satin cushions, and a canopy to protect her from the sun. Should she prefer to rest in a sitting position, he also gave her a satin upholstered palanquin which could be fitted on to her horse's saddle and was furnished with its own footstool.

On August 8, just six days after Alfonso's flight to Genazzano, Lucrezia and Geoffredo set out upon their journey. With them went a large company of noblemen, ladies-in-waiting, and attendants, as well as forty-three carts laden with clothes and other supplies. After receiving the pope's blessing, the company crossed the Ponte Sant' Angelo and made their way to the Porta del Populo where they picked up the Via Flaminia, the old Roman highway connecting the Appennines with both the capital and the seaports of the Adriatic. Five years before, Lucrezia had taken the Flaminia up the valley of the Tiber past the ruins of the villa of Livia Augusta and the walled *castelli* of Umbria to Pesaro. As once more she set out upon that same highway, it was inevitable that she should be reminded of that earlier journey and of how, despite all the differences between Giovanni Sforza and her beloved Alfonso, both husbands had eventually abandoned her in the identical manner.

Because of her fear of bringing on another miscarriage by overexerting herself, it took the party six days to reach Spoleto. On the afternoon of the sixth day, they stopped for lunch at Porcaria, where four commissioners and four hundred infantrymen from Spoleto waited to escort the new *governatrice* to their city. The Italians are unabashedly inquisitive, and they love a good show. It was not every day that a small provincial city tucked away in the Appennines had the opportunity to play host to the pregnant daughter of a pope, a young woman who at nineteen had already divorced one husband and had been abandoned by another. From the moment the new *governatrice* rode through the Porta San Matteo mounted upon a white mule accoutred in red and gold, she was surrounded by crowds who made no secret of their interest in every detail of her appearance. As she and her escort wound their way through the impossibly steep and narrow streets under papier-mache arches built for the occasion, the bells of Spoleto's fourth-century basilica of San Salvatore and twelfth-century cathedral, joined the bells of the city's ten parish churches in a resounding greeting; fireworks went off on every side and local musicians insisted upon playing for her. When finally she reached the Rocca Albornaziana, the castle of Spoleto, the sun was beginning to set. Hence, it was not until the next morning that she had a chance to appreciate the spectacular beauty of her surroundings.

Spoleto is built upon a hill which rises out of the Umbrian plain. From the terrace of the Rocca Albornaziana at the hill's summit, the still taller hills which encircle the city on all four sides appear to shield it from the world beyond. There is only the city and the plain, with Perugia a barely discernible dot to the north and Trevi, Assisi, and Foligno to the south. Great stone walls, parts of which were hundreds of years old when Hannibal attacked Spoleto, clamber up the city's western slope. To the east, a deep gorge cut by the Tessino River separates the town from the ilex-covered heights of Monte Luco. Spanning this gorge at a point almost directly below the castle is a massive Roman aqueduct, a sudden slab of white in that sleepy blue-green countryside. In summer, wild flowers push their way up between the pockmarked stones, and flocks of birds build their nests in the slender Gothic arches of the fourteenth-century bridge that uses the aqueduct as its foundation.

Although Lucrezia must have wished that she could share all this beauty with her beloved, she had little time to brood over his absence. Her father granted public audiences to the Romans every Tuesday. Besides attending to administrative matters, she, too, let it be known that she would hear complaints and attempt to settle them. The historians of the Commune of Spoleto describe her as *"un auditor sec,"* by which they mean one whose judgments were both decisive and impartial. Among the cases she was called upon to settle was one involving the theft of goods from the castellan of Todi. The priors of that town were so impressed by the good sense with which she handled the matter that they next asked her aid in controlling a notorious local princeling who from his fortress at Aquapendente was in the habit of making raids upon Todi and the neighboring towns.

While she was dealing with these matters, her father was trying to persuade Alfonso to return to her. Soon after the young prince's flight, the pope sent Juan Cervillon, the Spanish captain who had held the sword over Lucrezia's head at the time of her marriage to Alfonso, to speak to King Frederic. By then French troops had crossed the Alps and were preparing to attack Milan. Frederic, who had promised his ally Ludovico Sforza that he would declare war upon the pope, decided to placate him instead by allowing Alfonso to return to his wife.

Shortly before sunset on the evening of September 19 Alfonso rode into the great court of the Rocca Albanorziana. He and Lucrezia were sufficiently in love with one another for any awkwardness they may have felt upon seeing one another again to soon pass, dispelled by Lucrezia's tears or by a sudden rush into one another's arms. After four days together in Spoleto, they bade good-bye to the priors and the people and set out for Nepi, where the pope was awaiting them.

Nepi is a walled Etruscan town off the Via Cassia some forty kilometers from Rome, a somber, lonely place overlooking a deep ravine. While still a cardinal, Alexander had rebuilt the eighth-century castle opposite the waterfall at the entrance to the town, reinforcing the thick tufa outerwalls and enlarging the two rectangular towers. After his election as pope, he had given the castle to Ascanio Sforza. When Ascanio fled from Rome, Alexander decided to bestow Nepi upon Lucrezia. On September 4, his treasurer, Francesco Borgia, took the town over in her name. The pope arrived on September 25, and Lucrezia and Alfonso joined him shortly thereafter. Alexander had always been extremely fond of his son-in-law. During the few days they spent together in Nepi, he must have assured Alfonso that he had no intention of allowing the alliance with France to affect their relationship. On October 1, the pope returned to Rome leaving his children behind in Nepi. Ten days later, he sent a brief to the residents of the city commanding them to obey Lucrezia as their lawful sovereign.

Not only was she now *governatrice* of two important papal cities, but also by reason of her marriage to Alfonso, she was duchess of Bisceglie and princess of Salerno. Neither she nor her husband desired any further territory. Had their marriage contract not compelled them to live in Rome, they would undoubtedly have divided their time between the four territories they already possessed with an occasional visit to the capital to see the pope and to savor the brilliant life of his court. Wherever they would have gone, they would undoubtedly have welcomed poets and writers to their court;

they would have entertained the local nobility and been entertained by them; and, as Lucrezia had done at Spoleto, they would have tried to attend to the needs of their subjects. Because they were young and ardent and fertile, they would also have raised a large family. But the pope's desire to have his daughter close by at all times made such an existence impossible.

Alexander was then almost sixty-eight. Although the great difference in age between Lucrezia and him caused Alexander to take unusual delight in her sheer physical presence—her bright smile, her gracious manner, her dancer's walk, her really quite moderate share of beauty—and to be constantly concerned when she was away, he also had other more practical reasons for wanting her in Rome. From the beginning of his reign and perhaps even before that, the pope had been given to partial and transient losses of consciousness, or *sincopi*. The first of these to come to public attention occurred on the day of his coronation. As the procession reached the Lateran, according to Pietro Delfino, the general of the Camaldolese Order:

> The pope, half dead with fatigue, lost consciousness and it was necessary to wait for a long time before he could enter the Basilica. Finally, supported by two cardinals, he advanced to the altar of the Sancta Sanctorum chapel; but barely had he seated himself upon the papal throne when he leaned his head on Cardinal Riario's shoulder and fell into a faint; water was sprinkled on his face and a good deal was needed to bring him around.

On November 7, 1496, Gian Carlo Scalona informed the marchese of Mantua: "This morning after consistory the Pope had one of his attacks so that his son and daughter ran up to him." Burchard reports similar attacks during the visit of Charles VIII and during the Corpus Christi Day processions of 1498 and 1499.

From Alexander's symptoms it seems fairly certain that he was suffering a *petit mal*, which is a mild attack of epilepsy, but doctors then could neither diagnose nor treat it. Although the pope tended to be unusually serene in the face of illness, it would be only natural for him to wish to have his daughter within reach when these attacks occurred. Nor would he feel that he was being either selfish or unreasonable in expecting this of her; what difference could a few years spent in Rome really make? That it might be dangerous for his daughter and her husband to remain in the city would strike the pope as absurd. The alliance with France had ended the feud between him and Orsini, at least for the time being. In addition, Lucrezia and Alfonso were not really important enough to have enemies who would wish to get rid of them. If any one of the pope's children had to guard against the fate of the duke of Gandia, it was Cesare. Or at least so the pope must have reasoned, if, indeed, he gave the matter any thought at all.

On October 14, Lucrezia and Alfonso returned to Rome. At two o'clock on the morning of November 1, 1499, Lucrezia gave birth to a son whom she and her husband decided to name Rodrigo, in honor of the pope. Alexander was beside himself with joy. On his orders, says Burchard, "the news was announced to all the cardinals, ambassadors and their friends at their homes before daybreak." To show his gratitude to Alfonso for having given him a grandson, and perhaps also to further reassure him, the pope gave him a command in the papal army.

The pope's shield bearers led the way when baby Rodrigo, "dressed in appropriate baptismal garments of gold brocade," was brought to Saint Peter's to be baptized on November 11. After the shield bearers came the chamberlains in red robes, musicians with their pipes and other musical instruments, and two special grooms—the one on the right bearing a gold bowl and jug, a gold salt cellar, a flask of muscatel wine, and a towel, the one on the left holding "a great taper of white wax some three pounds in weight gilded and very beautifully decorated." The governor of Rome was also there alongside the Spanish captain Don Juan Cervillon, who carried the baby. They were followed by ten priests walking in pairs and a large number of foreign envoys. Much to Burchard's annoyance, "a crowd of Roman women, old men, youths, and young ladies tagged along behind the priests," and these interlopers "were given places where there was room in the chapel at the feet of the noble dignitaries; and it was as a result of this overcrowding that the cardinals were compelled to sit on the third and highest bench with their feet on the stone floor." The master of ceremonies also noted that although the walls of Cardinal Zeno's chapel in Saint Peter's had been decorated with two great tapestries in honor of the occasion, the cloth on the altar was dirty and torn.

Other observers were more shocked by what they regarded as the excessive pomp and ceremony on the occasion than by such minor oversights. "There was much murmuring through all Christendom" said the Venetian diarist Girolamo Priuli, "and it was said that the pontiffs, the heads of the Christian religion, were making a public demonstration of their love and affection for their families and that the Pope officially was declaring himself the father of his children." But Alexander was too euphoric to care, and Lucrezia and Alfonso, although not at all arrogant, apparently saw nothing incongruous in the honors heaped upon their firstborn.

Renaissance women took a long time to recuperate after their confinements. Lucrezia did not leave her palace until November 28, when she went to Saint Peter's to thank God for having given her a son. By then the basilica was being refurbished for the approaching jubilee year. Ever since Boniface VIII had proclaimed the first Christian jubilee in 1300, the jubilees, or Holy Years, had been the occasions for hundreds of thousands of pilgrims from every part of Europe to flock to Rome to receive the special jubilee indulgence. They were of every age and condition, from princes and kings to peasants and tradesmen and beggars; from elderly matrons to nubile young maids. And it had not taken the popes long to realize how lucrative their devotion could be. To receive the "freewill offerings" of the pilgrims in 1500, Alexander ordered that "strong large casks" be placed next to the chapel of Sant' Andrea and Gregorio in Saint Peter's and that they be provided with three different locks and keys. Similar casks were placed in every church in Rome and in parish churches throughout Christendom. The Venetians kept all the money collected in their territory for the war against the Turks. But much of what was collected in the rest of Italy went to support Cesare's troops in the Romagna.

Ludovico Sforza, who only a short time before had boasted that the pope was his chaplain, the Venetians his treasurers, the Emperor Maximilian his condottiere general, and the king of France his messenger, had found no one willing to help him stave off a French invasion of his duchy. Even before Louis's troops entered Milan on October 6, Ludovico had fled to the Tyrol. Soon afterward the pope published a bull, in which he declared that after trial it had been found that the lords or vicars of Rimini, Pesaro, Imola, Forli, Camerino, and Faenza, with other feudatories of the Holy See (including the duchy of Urbino) had never paid the yearly tribute due the church and were therefore deprived of all their rights. By December, the 1,800 cavalrymen and over 4,000 Swiss and Gascon infantrymen that Louis had promised the pope in exchange for his support of a French takeover in Milan were helping Cesare in his campaign to unseat Ludovico's niece Caterina Sforza, countess of Imola and Forli. When, on January 15, the news that the countess had been taken prisoner reached Rome, the pope ordered bonfires lit throughout the city.

Although as a member of the house of Aragon Lucrezia's husband could not really share her family's joy at Cesare's victory, on February 26 Alfonso rode out to the Porta del Populo along with Geoffredo and a large number of cardinals and other dignitaries to greet his brother-in-law upon the latter's trumphal return to Rome. Cesare arrived at the Porta del Populo between three and four in the afternoon. Both sides of every street through which he would pass on his way to the Vatican, from the Via Lata (now the Via del Corso) to the Campo dei Fiori to the Piazza del Ponte to the newly laid Via Alessandrino (now the Via del Borgo Nuovo) were lined six or seven deep with pilgrims eager to catch a glimpse of the victorious young commander.

After a seemingly interminable procession of Swiss and Gascon infantrymen and cavalry officers, of German lansquenet and noblemen, he came into view riding behind his brother and brother-in-law. He was flanked on either side by a member of the College of Cardinals and surrounded by a hundred black-clad grooms, each carrying a new halberd. His knee-length coat of black velvet, with its severely simple collar, did more to accent his good looks and superb physique than all the pearls and rubies and gold strands he had worn on the day he rode into Chinon to meet King Louis. When he came within sight of the Castel Sant' Angelo, trumpeters stationed upon all the towers announced his approach to the crowd, and the guns of the castle thundered forth a salute. "Some two hundred or more explosions in turn shook the area," says Burchard, "coming first from the tower in the castle garden, then from the round tower facing the bridge with reverberations that brought down some windows and shutters, then from the tower facing Santo Spirito, next along the whole length of battlements and finally from the highest tower in the castle." Alexander was so happy to see his son that he laughed and cried at the same time.

The following day, which was the fifth Sunday of Lent, the triumph of Julius Caesar was presented in Piazza Navona in honor of Cesare. After circling the piazza, eleven triumphal chariots similar to the ones used in Roman times were driven to the Vatican. One contained a depiction of the crossing of the Rubicon; another a laurel-wreathed effigy of great Julius himself.

Although the pagan nature of these celebrations and the honors Alexander heaped upon his children disturbed some of the pilgrims—this same pope had at that time a daughter who lived in Rome in great pomp, and they could tell many things of her, one of their number wrote—others adapted readily to the mores of this worldly and wicked old Holy City. They made the required number of visits to the high altars of the basilicas of Saint Peter and Saint Paul, Saint John Lateran, and Santa Maria Maggiore, received the jubilee indulgence for their pains, and ended their stay with a visit to one of Rome's approximately seven thousand courtesans.

On March 29, those who managed to get into Saint Peter's saw the pope appoint Cesare captain-general and gonfalonier of the Holy Roman church and bestow the golden rose—the highest honor the church could give—upon him. "For all faithful Christians this flower, the most beautiful of all, symbolizes the joy and the crown of the saints. Receive it very dear son, you who add great virtue to nobility," Alexander told him.

So great was the admiration of Lucrezia and Geoffredo for the exploits of their older brother that Geoffredo put on the duke's spurs for him and Lucrezia welcomed him into her marriage bed, Paolo Capello said spitefully. Even those who did not believe the rumors of incest were convinced that the new captain-general of the church must resent his sister's husband if only because Alfonso's cousin Carlotta had spurned him. Nor was the resentment one-sided. On the sixth of April, Alexander granted the king of Hungary a divorce from his wife Beatrice, the daughter of the late Ferrante I of Naples. Naples, of course, opposed the divorce; Venice and France favored it mainly because Venice needed Hungary's assistance in fighting the Turks. A short time after it was granted, the Florentine orator reported overhearing Alfonso complain at great length to the Neapolitan ambassador. Sancha, too, showed her displeasure at the Borgia's close ties with France, ties for which she and her brother must have held Cesare responsible. When a Burgundian and a Frenchman had a duel, Sancha offered twelve scudi and a cross of Saint Andrew to the victorious Burgundian in what appeared to be a deliberate taunt to Cesare, who had vociferously championed the Frenchman.

"The Duke is a good-natured man, but he cannot tolerate an insult," Alexander would say of his son a few years later. And Pandolfo Collenuccio wrote that he was "terrible in revenge."

Cesare's reputation for vindictiveness caused men to fear him and to attribute every unsolved murder to him. When the Spanish Captain Juan Cervillon was stabbed to death on his way home from a supper party, when Cesare's cousin Giovanni Borgia the Younger died of a fever, when the Portuguese bishop Fernando d'Almaida succumbed to wounds received in battle, it was whispered that in reality Cesare had done away with them.

"I know that at the age of twenty-six I am in danger of ending my life in arms and by arms, and since this is so, I must live to enjoy the time," Gian Lucido Cattanei overheard Cesare tell some of his companions.

He seemed to have a constant need to prove himself by performing impossibly daring feats, and his bravado made men fear him all the more. On June 24, six wild bulls were let loose in a specially erected enclosure in one corner of the Piazza San Pietro. Armed with only a light lance, Cesare entered the enclosure on horseback and killed five of them. He then dismounted, exchanged his lance for a double-handled sword, and beheaded the sixth at a single stroke.

"In court he is unrivalled in splendor or magnificence," Machiavelli would say later. "In arms he is so enterprising that there is nothing so great it does not seem small to him; whenever he is concerned with the acquisition of glory or land, he can no longer know any rest, fatigue or peril; when he arrives no one knows from whence he came; he makes himself loved by his soldiers and has handpicked the best in Italy; all these are the things which make him formidable." His father was proud of his achievements, but he neither understood him nor did he seem really to like him. And Cesare, who was naturally closemouthed, complained that the pope talked too much.

A few days before the bullfight in the Piazza San Pietro, Alexander had experienced another one of his *sincopi*, one that turned out to be longer and more serious than usual. By June 29, however, he had resumed his normal activities. That afternoon he was seated upon his throne in the Hall of the Popes waiting to give an audience when a sudden strong gust of wind tore off part of the roof causing the section under which he was sitting also to give way. Fortunately, the balcony over his head held firm, and this protected him from the falling masonry, while the gold-embroidered hangings over his throne shielded him from the smothering dust. Although he sustained a head wound and became very feverish the night after the accident, it was obvious that he would recover. When the Venetian ambassador visited him on July 3, he found Lucrezia, Sancha, and Geoffredo at Alexander's bedside along with one of Lucrezia's ladies-in-waiting, whom the ambassador immediately labelled "the Pope's favorite." However great the pleasure Alexander may have taken in this reputed "favorite," during his convalescence it was his daughter whom he insisted upon having nurse him. Though this meant being separated from her husband and the seven-month-old Rodrigo, Lucrezia did not appear to mind. Her sister-in-law Sancha helped her care for her father, and Alfonso dined with them almost every evening. Their dinner on the evening of July 15 was much like all the other dinners they had had since the pope's accident. Shortly after it grew dark, Alfonso bade them goodbye. Accompanied by his gentleman-in-waiting, Tommaso Albanese, and his master of the horse, he left the palace through a door under the benediction loggia.

So common was it for pilgrims to use the steps of Saint Peter's as their sleeping place during that jubilee year that neither he nor his companions took any notice of the large numbers asleep there that evening. As the three young men began crossing the piazza, however, they heard what appeared to be a signal. Immediately thereafter, five of the supposedly sleeping figures jumped up, drew forth halberds from beneath their packs, and rushed at Alfonso. Before he had a chance to defend himself, they had given him a deep wound in the head and another in the shoulder, as well as lesser cuts in the thigh and arm. While his gentleman-in-waiting tried to ward off further attacks, Alfonso's master of the horse sought to carry the unconscious and bleeding prince across the piazza to Santa Maria in Portico. Finding the way blocked, he and Albanese decided to seek refuge in the Vatican. While waiting for the doors to open, they caught sight of a large number of men, some on foot and some on horseback, assembled at the corner of the piazza near the hospital of Santo Spirito. When, after what must have seemed an eternity, the doors of the Vatican finally opened and the palace guards appeared, these men rode off in the direction of the Porta Portense. Obviously, they had been part of the group sent to assassinate Alfonso. The prince, meanwhile, was brought up to the room where his wife and father-in-law were still chatting. At the sight of her husband, with his clothes in shreds and the blood pouring from his wounds, Lucrezia fainted. Her father had the wounded man put to bed in one of the rooms of the Borgia tower.

Because Alfonso was running a high fever and might not last the night, the pope sent one of his cardinals to administer the last rites of the church. Four days later the young prince's temperature was still so high that Alexander missed a consistory "out of concern for Don Alfonso." Although at that time Lucrezia, too, was running a fever, brought on no doubt by the shock of the assassination attempt made upon her husband and the critical condition in which it had left him, she seems literally to have willed herself better so that she could join his sister Sancha in caring for him.

The pope had stationed sixteen soldiers outside the sickroom, and Cesare had announced that anyone found carrying arms between the Castel Sant' Angelo and the Vatican would be executed. Nevertheless, both Lucrezia and Sancha were too stunned by what had happened to trust even these precautions. Alfonso had been placed in the Hall of the Sibyls, the first room one enters when visiting the Borgia apartments today. In that room of magificent blues and blue-greens with its sculptured stone fireplace, its trumpeting angels, its gilded bulls, and twenty-four lunettes depicting the stern-faced sibyls, and the somewhat more benevolent-looking old-testament prophets all announcing the coming of the Savior, the two princesses were like soldiers who have barricaded themselves in and are prepared for a long siege. Because they had determined never to leave Alfonso unattended even for an instant, they set up makeshift pallets beside his bed and took turns sleeping. Since they feared that someone might try to poison his food, they prepared his meals themselves.

Immediately after the attack, the pope sent one of his own physicians to care for his son-in-law. Later, King Frederic sent his surgeon, Messer Galliano de Anna, and his physician, Messer Clemente Gactula. The Colonna, too, sent one of their physicians. By July 28, these doctors had succeeded in bringing down Alfonso's fever. By August 6, the wound in his head had begun to heal, and the prince appeared to be feeling much better. As long as he remained in Rome, however, there was always the danger that whoever had attacked him would strike again. And this must have been the reason Lucrezia wrote to King Frederic asking him to get Alfonso out of the city as soon as he was strong enough to be moved.

It was probably with the intention to accompany the prince on his journey to Naples that his maternal uncle Giovanni Gazullo came to Rome around this time. According to a number of reports, Gazullo was with his nephew on the afternoon of August 18 when Alfonso died. That same evening the prince was buried next to Lucrezia's great uncle Calixtus III in the chapel of Santa Maria della Febbre. He was nineteen years old.

"The Duke of Bisceglie leaving the palace one night was assaulted on the steps of Saint Peter's and mortally wounded and he finally died of his injuries," Biagio Buonaccorsi wrote in his *Diary of the Most Important Events in Italy*. But Buonaccorsi is the only writer who attributes Alfonso's death to his wounds.

"He was gravely wounded in his head, right arm and leg . . . as he refused to die of his wounds, he was strangled in his bed about eleven o'clock on August 18," says Burchard. "The doctors of the defunct and a hunchback who had cared for him were taken to the Castel Sant' Angelo for questioning. The arrested men were freed because they were innocent. As was well noted, those who had sent them there knew who the guilty were."

A letter written by Alfonso's former tutor, Raphael Brandolinus Lippus, also gives strangling as the cause of death. Though like Burchard, Lippus refused to name the person responsible, his letter leaves no doubt as to the murderer's identity. On the advice of his doctors, Alfonso's wounds had been bandaged, says Lippus. He was in his room with his wife and sister and some close friends when Michelotto, "the most wicked minister of Cesare of Valentois and the prefect of his guard, broke into the room. He arrested Alfonso's uncle and the royal orator as well as those guarding the door . . . and handed them over to be thrown into prison." Astonished at the outrageousness of the deed, Lucrezia and Sancha "reviled Michelotto in womanly fashion." He excused himself by saying that he had to submit to the wish of another and suggested that they complain to the pope. While they were gone, Michelotto, "the wickedest of criminals, the most criminal of wicked men," strangled Alfonso. According to Lippus, Michelotto then made up a "most unlikely story" about his great crime, namely that Alfonso, seeing those close to him arrested and "dismayed at the greatness of his danger," had fallen to the ground "and from the wound which had been inflicted in his head blood flowed copiously and thus he breathed his last."

The Florentine envoy, Francesco Capello, also describes the arrest of Alfonso's "familiars" by Cesare's henchmen, but accepts the story of the fall as the cause of Alfonso's death: "Some say when these satellites entered the room, the duke [of Bisceglie] was on his feet and he fell; some say he was in bed and wanted to get up and fell and struck his head, and that he died of confusion and grief immediately thereafter." According to Capello, Lucrezia and Sancha were visiting their ladies-in-waiting when this occurred.

The Venetian ambassador, Paolo Capello, on the other hand, says that Alfonso was killed "because he had tried to murder the Duke of Valentois." Standing at the window of his sickroom overlooking the Belvedere gardens and seeing Cesare strolling along one of the paths, Alfonso shot at him with a crossbow. Whereupon Cesare immediately ordered his henchmen to go to Alfonso's room "and cut him to pieces." According to the pope, Alfonso's uncle later admitted that his nephew had tried to kill Cesare.

A few days after the supposed admission, the body of this same uncle, Giovanni Gazullo, was found in the fields near Castel Sant' Angelo. Whether he was murdered because he had talked or because he hadn't, or whether perhaps his murder was one of those unexplained acts of violence which everyone deplored but no one knew how to stop, it is impossible to say. In any event, no one save Paolo Capello mentions Gazullo's confession. And Capello's account of the murder changed considerably between the time he sent his original dispatches in August and the time he gave the signory of Venice a *Relazione*, or "summary," of the case in late September.

Whereas the original dispatches do not implicate Cesare in the first attack upon Alfonso, the *Relazione* says that the wounded man told the pope the identity of his attacker and that Alexander gave his son-in-law sixteen guards to protect him from Cesare. Despite these sixteen guards, however, "finally one day Cesare entered the chamber, drove out the terrified women and called in an assassin who strangled Alfonso in his bed." Later, the duke of Valentois told the ambassador that he had killed his brother-in-law because Alfonso had tried to kill him. Almost immediately after the murder, however, Francesco Capello, the Florentine ambassador, wrote that Cesare was making a great display of wearing black clothes, scarcely the behavior of a man who openly admitted having killed his brother-in-law.

Despite the numerous discrepancies between the various reports, all but two of them implicate Cesare in one way or another. But, and this is most important, with the exception of the *Relazione* of Paolo Capello, they implicate him only in the attack on August 18. And, as we have seen, the *Relazione* contradicts the report Paolo Capello made at the time the attack on Alfonso occurred. So that even if we assume that Cesare was responsible for Alfonso's death, we are still left with the question of who attacked the prince on July 15. "The duke [of Valentois] did not wound Alfonso, but if he had, Alfonso would have deserved it," Alexander supposedly told Paolo Capello soon after Alfonso was wounded. Did the pope mean that Cesare had good reason to attack Alfonso, or did he mean that Cesare would have attacked Alfonso only if he had had good reason to do so? Because in truth Cesare had so little to gain from a deliberate and cold-blooded attack upon Alfonso, some historians have concluded that the first attack must have been the work of the Orsini.

As a member of the house of Aragon, Alfonso had close ties with the Colonna, the hereditary enemies of the Orsini. As was noted at the time, the attack upon him was carried out in more or less the same manner as the attack upon the duke of Gandia. Not only had the Orsini gotten away with Gandia's murder, they had seen the accusation rebound and discredit the Borgias. Given Cesare's reputation, they could be certain that he would be blamed for this new attack. Since Alfonso's uncle, King Frederic, had taken Salerno away from the San Severino family and given it to his nephew, the attack could have also come from that quarter. The Gaetani family, too, were mentioned at the time because the pope had confiscated some of their land and given it to Lucrezia.

But even if we assume that one of these families did try to murder Alfonso on the evening of July 15, once he was placed in the Hall of the Sibyls with sixteen soldiers to guard him, it would have been impossible for them to get at him. Hence, either Alfonso died of his wounds or Cesare had him killed. If he died as a result of his wounds so long after receiving them, the only possible explanation is tetanus.

Since the victim of tetanus literally suffocates, this would account for the talk of suffocation or strangulation. To assume that tetanus was the cause of death when so many of the reports implicate Cesare is, however, presumptuous.

As we have seen, most of the reports mention Cesare's belief that Alfonso was conspiring against him. In the first report of Paolo Capello, Alfonso aims a crossbow at Cesare; in the others Cesare has heard of a conspiracy and seeks to find out more about it by arresting those close to his brother-in-law. Since it is highly unlikely that a young man recovering from a nearly fatal wound in the shoulder would have had the strength to wield a crossbow, we can dismiss the story of the crossbow as pure invention. That Alfonso believed that Cesare had sent the men who attacked him in the Piazza San Pietro and that he made no secret of his suspicions and even spoke of one day avenging himself is, however, entirely possible. And it is also possible that after hearing of these threats, Cesare sent some of his minions to arrest those close to Alfonso in order to find out what they knew. Out of a desire to protect his relatives and friends, Alfonso could very well have risen from his bed and then fallen, or he could have sought to restrain Cesare's henchmen and been strangled.

But if we accept this version of what happened, we are left with the question of why Lucrezia never expressed any resentment of Cesare, whereas she made no secret of her resentment of her father.

"The Pope is in bad humor, possibly because of what happened, possibly because of the King of Naples, or possibly because his daughter is in despair," Gian Lucido Cattanei wrote the day after Alfonso's death.

For two years Lucrezia had been as happy as is humanly possible, and now it was over. During the thirty-three days she and Sancha had cared for Alfonso there must have been times when she would tell herself that what had happened was a horrible nightmare from which she would awaken to find her husband whole and well beside her. But no matter how frightened and discouraged she had felt, there had been hope and the sound of his voice and the sight of his dear face. Now there was only a great emptiness and a sense of utter finality.

It is said that no one can escape a feeling of guilt at the death of a loved one. In Lucrezia's case the feeling of guilt would be particularly acute, for it would seem obvious to her that had Alfonso not married her, he would still be alive. The thought of the world in which she lived with its endless intrigues, its constant betrayals, and its gratuitous murders must have filled her with horror. And along with that horror would come a resentment of her father who, as head of that world, should have been able to prevent such enormities from occurring.

"Madonna Lucrezia who is wise and generous, was formerly in favor with the Pope, but now he no longer loves her and has sent her to Nepi," said Paolo Capello.

"The Pope has sent away his daughter and his daughter-in-law and everyone but Valentino because the sight of them grieves him," wrote Gian Lucido Cattanei.

If Alexander appeared no longer to love his daughter, if the sight of her grieved him, it was because her tear-stained face and unshakable sorrow made him feel guilty for not having been able to save her husband.

Lucrezia set out for Nepi on August 31, with only a small retinue. Less than a year before she had gone to that same castle with Alfonso, and every room, every piece of furniture, would remind her of the beautiful boy she had loved so dearly. Custom decreed that the walls of the castle be covered with sable draperies and that the widow cover her face with a black veil at all times. Lucrezia remained in mourning at Nepi for almost four months. Save for messengers from Rome, the only visitor she received during those months was Cesare.

Despite the hordes of women who worshipped at her brother's shrine and the great sacrifices a number of them were prepared to make for him, the only women Cesare seems to have really cared about were his mother and his sister. When at the end of September he set out from Rome with an army of ten thousand men to resume the campaign in the Romagna he'd begun the previous December, his first stop was at Nepi to see Lucrezia. The two of them had always been unusually close; nevertheless, it is difficult to see what they could have had to say to one another that fall. If Cesare had indeed been responsible for Alfonso's death, the very sight of him would be abhorrent. And even it he hadn't, in his sister's numb and frozen state she would find it a trial to laugh at his jokes and to entertain the entourage he had brought with him.

From the letters she wrote to Vincenzo Giordano, her servant in

Rome, it is obvious that her one real tie with the world of the living was the nine-month-old Rodrigo. In several letters, she asked Giordano to send clothes for the child. Other than that she was preoccupied with her grief. On October 28, she requested that prayers be said for her in all the monasteries "in recognition of this my new sorrow." On October 30, she told Giordano to pay what was necessary for a memorial service "for the soul of his Lordship, the duke my husband, may the glory of the saints be his." In another letter, she asked heaven to watch over her bed: "*La Infelicissima*," "the most unhappy one," she signed herself. And the girl who emerges from these letters is not only unhappy, but angry and afraid as well. She used pseudonyms and ciphers in her letters because using them made her feel safer and also because there was less chance of scandal that way, she told Giordano. Frequently, she asked that her letters be delivered secretly.

"I am so filled with misgivings on account of my returning to Rome that I can scarcely write, I can only weep," she confided in one letter. "And all this time when I found that Farina neither answered nor wrote to me, I was able to neither eat nor sleep, and wept continually. God forgive Farina, who could have made everything turn out better, and did not do so. . . . Again look well to the matter and do not let Rexa see this letter."

Gregorovius has suggested that Farina may signify Cardinal Farnese, and Rexa, the pope. Later, after Vincenzo told Lucrezia that he had spoken to her father, she wrote that everything was turning out better than she had expected, for which she thanked God and his glorious mother. Although she was back in Rome before Christmas, her return did not mean that she had ceased mourning for her husband, for to cease grieving would have been an admission that all was indeed over. And this she could not yet face.

To her father her grief seemed excessive and impractical. "The thing is over; it can't be remedied," he told the ambassadors who asked him about his son-in-law's death.

Alfonso had not been dead a month when Gian Lucido Cattanei reported that the pope was seeking a new husband for his daughter. One reason that Alexander was in such a hurry was that he was then almost sixty-nine, and he knew how important it was that Lucrezia find a husband while he was still alive. Otherwise, once he was dead, she would be a person of no importance, a helpless widow forced to rely upon Cesare for protection. The suitor whom the pope found and of whom Cesare also approved was Louis de Ligny, a cousin of the king of France. But misfortune had made Lucrezia more positive, less passive. She had no intention of ever going to live in France, she told her father.

Francesco Orsini, duke of Gravina, her next suitor, had already sought her hand once before. Undaunted by the fate of his successful rival, he came to Rome on December 6 to try his luck a second time. But when Alexander asked his daughter how she felt about becoming duchess of Gravina, she told him that she did not wish to marry.

"Why?" asked the pope.

"Because my husbands have been very unlucky," she replied. And, says Marino Sanuto, "she left in a rage."

Her father must have realized that her words were meant as a reproach. As he had done when she had shut herself up in the convent of San Sisto, he decided to bide his time. Lucrezia was a woman and a widow and as such had no rights to speak of. Had he really wanted to marry her to the duke of Gravina, he could have easily imposed his will upon her. But by that time he had another husband in mind. And this new husband was of so much more exalted a rank than the duke of Gravina or either of Lucrezia's previous husbands that when she heard his name, she would surely change her mind about remarrying. If perchance she didn't, Alexander would find ways to force the issue.

A Third Husband

Alfonso, in whom in rare proportion wisdom's joined with
goodness

Ariosto, Orlando Furioso, canto 3, stanza 51

Twenty-four-year-old Alfonso d'Este was the eldest son of Duke Ercole of Ferrara. After the birth of the famous Isabella d'Este, the first child of Ercole's union with Alfonso's mother, Eleanora of Aragon, there had been some rejoicing in Ferrara. After the birth of a second daughter, Beatrice, there had been none "because they wished it had been a boy." After Alfonso's birth, all the shops in the city remained closed for three days; the church bells rang continually; the city's artillery fired off salute after salute; and the people in their joy made bonfires of the benches in the *studium*, or university. Eleanora bore her husband three other sons, and Ercole also had a son by one of his wife's ladies-in-waiting. But it was upon Alfonso that the hopes of the house were centered. "*Il nostro dolcissimo primogenito; il nostro puttino*" ("Our sweetest firstborn son; our little cherub"), the duke called him at the time of his christening. In the *Orlando Innamorato*, Ferrara's great poet Matteo Maria Boiardo pictured Good Fortune "joyous in her semblance," kneeling at the young heir's feet.

> Sweet son, she seemed to say,
> Look at the mighty deeds of such great ancestors
> And at thy race renowned in the world.
> Wherefore among all make thyself glorious for
>   courtesy, for wisdom and for valor;
> So that thou mayst do honor to thy fair name.

In the *Orlando Furioso*, Lodovico Ariosto would trace the genealogy of the Estense back to King Priam of Troy and his son Hector. Others traced the line back to the Acci, a prominent family of Republican Rome, and still others to the Trojan Atenore. But in the *Antichità Estense*, the Italian annalist Lodovico Muratori later showed that if there was a legendary ancestor, he must have been Attila, not Atenore or Priam, for it was in Bavaria rather than in Troy that the family had originated.

In 961, the German Emperor Otho I gave the family the imperial fief of Este at the foot of the Euganean hills, forty miles north of Ferrara. In 1176, they were referred to as Marchesi d'Este for the first time. In 1196, Ferrara asked the Marchese Azzo VI to serve as its *podestà*. By the time Azzo's son Azzo VII died, the Marchesi d'Este—they did not become dukes until the reign of Ercole's half brother Borso—had made themselves the hereditary rulers of the city. Soon afterward they became lords of Modena and Reggio Emilia as well.

Like all Italian despots great and small, the Estense had no goal save to remain in power; and no means was too cruel to use against those who sought to displace them. When Obizzo, the nephew of Ercole's great grandfather the Marchese Alberto, conspired against him, Alberto had him and his mother beheaded. The marchese then ordered most of the other conspirators, including his half brother Giovanni, tortured to death in the streets of Ferrara and one noble lady burned alive.

Because Ercole's cousin Niccolò da Leonello disputed his claim to the dukedom, Ercole sought to have him poisoned. But at the last moment, Niccolò's seneschal, who had been persuaded to do the deed by the promise of two castles and a palace, lost heart and confessed to his master. A few years later, when Ercole was absent from Ferrara, Niccolò attempted a coup. Instead of acclaiming him as he had expected, the Ferrarese remained loyal to his cousin. After Ercole's return, eighteen of the conspirators were hanged from the balcony and windows of the palace of the *podestà* and five others from the battlements of the Castello Estense. The following night Niccolò and another accomplice were beheaded in the courtyard of the *castello*.

Wives who dared cuckold their husbands received equally summary treatment. The philandering of Ercole's father, Niccolò III, had earned him the title of Il Gallo di Ferrara ("the stud of Ferrara"). "*Di quà e di là dal Po son tutti figli di Niccolò"* ("On this side of the Po and on that, all are sons of Niccolò") said one popular ditty. The insatiable marchese was thirty-five when he took fifteen-year-old Parisina Malatesta as his second wife. At the Ferrarese court, Parisina came in daily contact with a number of her husband's bastards, including his favorite son Ugo, who was only a few months younger than she. The marchese, of course, was too busy with his affairs, amorous and otherwise, to pay much attention to his young wife. Shortly after the birth of her third child she and Ugo became lovers. When Niccolò learned what was going on, he had the then twenty-one-year-old Parisina and her twenty-year-old paramour imprisoned in the tower of the *castello.* After a trial during which the judges pleaded for mercy and Niccolò overruled them, Parisina and Ugo were both beheaded. Niccolò loudly bewailed the death of his son, but he wasted no tears on his wife. Because he did not want her to be the only one to suffer, says a contemporary chronicler, "he ordered the execution of a number of other Ferrarese ladies who were known to be serving their husbands as Parisina had served him."

Despite their frequent, egregious cruelty, the Estense sought to create a picture of themselves as benevolent despots concerned for the welfare of their subjects. Niccolò encouraged commerce and industry and tried to reduce taxes. His son Leonello built the Hospital of Santa Anna, a combined poorhouse, asylum, and medical facility. Leonello and his successor, the flamboyant and popular Borso, both commissioned hydraulic engineers to devise ways to manage the Po; and Borso initiated extensive drainage and reclamation works. Every morning before hearing mass, Ercole personally distributed alms to a dozen paupers. Once a year he and his courtiers went through the city collecting food and other offerings which they turned over to the poor. And all of the Estense, whether intellectual or not, were patrons of the new humanism.

In Burckhardt's *Civilization of the Renaissance,* the Swiss historian explains humanism as:

> An alliance between two epochs in the civilization of the same people. . . . As a competitor with the whole culture of the Middle Ages which was essentially clerical and was fostered by the state there appeared a new civilization founding itself on that which lay on the other side of the Middle Ages. Its active

representatives became influential because they knew what the ancients knew, because they tried to write as the ancients wrote, because they began to think and soon to feel as the ancients thought and felt.

As important as the revival of classical learning was the stress humanism placed upon the uniqueness of each individual and his freedom to shape his own destiny. To Burckhardt, this new individualism seemed the natural result of the growth of towns and the development of civic life in the Italy of the late Middle Ages: "At the close of the thirteenth century Italy began to swarm with individuality; the ban laid upon the human personality was dissolved; and a thousand figures meet us each in its own special shape and dress. Dante's great poem would have been impossible in any other country in Europe. . . . For Italy the august poet, through the wealth of individuality which he set forth, was the most national herald of his time."

Confirmed republican that he was, Dante had little use for the Estense. He relegated Obizzo II, fourth marchese of Ferrara, to the river of boiling blood where fierce centaurs hunt the damned souls of tyrants and murderers; consigned the *podestà* of Milan to the Evil Pits of the seducers of women for making his sister "do the Marchese's will"; and accused Obizzo's son Azzo VIII of parricide. But Petrarch accepted an invitation to live at the Ferrarese court in 1370. A few years later, Petrarch's friend Benvenuto da Imola dedicated his explication of the *Divine Comedy* to the marchese Niccolò II.

Niccolò's nephew, Niccolò III, reorganized the *studium*, or university, of Ferrara and engaged the renowned humanist Guarino da Verona to tutor his son Leonello. Leonello, whom one admirer likened to Plato's philosopher-king, invited the most distinguished scholars in Italy to teach at the *studium* and gave Ferrara its first public library. Leon Battista Alberti was his friend; Pisanello struck a number of medals for him; Jacopo Bellini painted his portrait; Roger van der Weyden's *Rugerius Brugeniensis* occupied the place of honor in his picture gallery. Although neither Leonello's brother Borso nor his half brother Ercole were as intellectual as he, both continued his support of the *studium* and invited artists and humanists to their court. It was for Ercole that the Belgian composer Josquin de Préz wrote his mass *Hercules Dux Ferrariae* and his *Miserere*. Ercole also encouraged other composers and recruited the best singers in Europe for his choir. But as much as the duke loved music, his great passion was the theater. For his production of the *Menaechmi* in 1486, he built a new stage with five houses painted as backdrops and a galley equipped with sails and oars. Subsequent productions included not only translations of the works of the ancients, but also the works of contemporary Ferrarese poets who wrote in the vernacular, such as Niccolò da Correggio, Boiardo, and Ariosto.

Ercole's love of the secular theater was not, however, an indication of any lack of religious fervor on his part. Although all of the Estense tended to be ostentatiously pious, none was more pious than he. During his reign, mystics flocked to the city; churches and monasteries proliferated; vanities were burnt; and the laws against blasphemy rigidly enforced. Whenever the duke was sick, he ordered a religious procession to pray for his recovery. No sooner did he recover than he ordered a procession to thank God for his goodness. During the jubilee year he organized solemn processions and novenas in all the cities of his duchy to implore divine mercy upon Italy and the liberation of Christianity from the Turks "for good reasons known to him and because it is always well to keep on good terms with God," said one Ferrarese.

His concern for keeping on the good side of God did not, however, prevent him from shamelessly seeking benefices for his third son, Ippolito. Ippolito was tonsured at six, received an archbishopric in Hungary when he was eight, and became a cardinal at fifteen. Although Ercole subsequently urged the pope to appoint the young cardinal to the archbishopric of Ferrara, his letters to his son reveal his dismay at Ippolito's worldly and licentious behavior.

Nor was Alfonso's behavior any more gratifying. Unlike his sister, the brilliant Isabella, the heir to the duchy of Ferrara took no interest in intellectual matters. Because he must have realized very early that he could never hope to compete with Isabella in that sphere, he had turned his back on book learning and was, says his biographer Paolo Giovio, "more interested in arms than in letters." His passion for casting guns and cannons and fashioning majolica plates made him feel more at home in foundries and bottegas where he could express himself in his work than at his father's court where he had to express himself in words. His dress was careless, his behavior rough, his taste in women rougher still. During his marriage to Anna Sforza of

Milan, who had died in childbirth, he spent considerably more time in brothels than in his wife's bed. Such reckless promiscuity brought its own reward. Like his brothers Ferrante and Sigismundo, Alfonso eventually came down with the French disease, and for a while it seemed as if gangrene would deprive him of the use of his hands. It could have been his anxiety over this possibility that made him so erratic. One hot afternoon in late July 1497 he and a few of his cronies walked nude through the streets of Ferrara. "He is accounted as having little sense," said the Venetian ambassador. When serving as regent of Ferrara in his father's absence, he appeared to derive pleasure from doing the exact opposite of what was expected of him. Although the duke had asked him to grant audiences and to eat in public so that the people might see him, he ate in secret and remote places and displayed little interest in governing.

A medal struck in 1492 when Alfonso was sixteen shows a scraggly-haired, coarse-featured youth with a prominent nose, a short, thick neck, and an insolent and stubborn bearing. Had he not been the hereditary prince of Ferrara, he would have soon received his comeuppance. As it was, Boiardo and Ariosto sang his praises in lines that were often so wide of the mark as to seem deliberate satire.

Although Alfonso's family held Modena and Reggio as fiefs of the emperor, Ferrara itself was part of the territory given to the popes by Pepin III in 756 and deeded to them again by the Countess Mathilda in 1107. Hence it was as papal vicars that the Estense ruled the city. Ferrara, located in the flat, marshy plain of the Po River midway between Venice and the Romagna, was included with the cities of the Romagna in the list of papal fiefs. When Alexander first began making plans to depose the lords of the Romagna, he also thought of taking Ferrara away from the Estense and giving it to Cesare. But the Venetians convinced him that this would be unwise because, said their ambassador, Ercole was old and beloved by his people and he had, moreover, sons who would not sit by idly if someone attempted to deprive their father of his state.

In truth, the Ferrarese did not love their duke quite as much as the Venetians supposed, for despite his good works and his religiosity, Ercole tended to be extravagant, aloof, and in the opinion of many people, excessively gullible. "He just takes all the pleasure that he likes and occupies his time with music, astrology and necromancy, only rarely giving audience to his people," said one contemporary critic. Nevertheless, there was a stability and a sense of governmental restraint that made Alexander and Cesare decide they would gain more from having him as an ally than from committing troops to what could turn out to be an unsuccessful attempt to depose him. They did not trust the Venetians. As an ally the duke of Ferrara would serve as a much needed buffer between Venice and Cesare's new states in the Romagna.

Although some historians claim that the pope and his son got rid of Lucrezia's second husband so that they would be free to use her to forward their plans, there is really no evidence that this was the case. Once Lucrezia did become a widow, however, they were far too practical not to seek to turn her misfortune to their advantage. The first mention of the hereditary prince of Ferrara as a possible husband for her occurs in a letter written just four weeks after the death of her second husband. The projected marriage was again mentioned in a letter which the Venetian ambassador sent to his government on November 26, 1500. Soon afterward Alexander began negotiations with Ferrara.

Ercole had hoped to strengthen his ties with France by marrying his son to Louise of Savoy, a princess of the French royal house. His own wife had been the legitimate daughter of a king. In the opinion of the duke of Ferrara, the house of Borgia was what Guicciardini would later call "a small private house," that is to say an insignificant dynasty in no way comparable to the ancient and glorious house of Este. The prospective bride was, moreover, the illegitimate daughter of a priest and her reputation was appalling. Not only had she already had two husbands (three if, as most people did, you counted Gasparo de Procida), but her father had disposed of one husband in the manner best calculated to humiliate him, and her brother was commonly believed to have murdered the other. Giovanni Sforza had accused her of incest; the correspondent of the Bentivoglio had spoken of her affair with Pedro Calderon; and Ercole's own correspondent in Venice had told him that she had borne an illegitimate child. Alfonso might spend his time in brothels, but like his grandfather Niccolo III, the hereditary prince of Ferrara expected his wife to be above reproach.

On February 14, Ercole sent a frantic letter to his ambassador in Paris. He would take it as a singular favor, said the duke, if the king of France made it clear that he had decided upon another match for

Alfonso. "Because to speak freely with his Majesty, we shall never consent to give Madonna Lucrezia to Don Alfonso; nor could Alfonso ever be induced to take her."

Although Ercole had no compunctions about speaking so openly to Louis, he had to be considerably more careful about what he said to the pope, for by then Cesare had added Pesaro, Fano, and Rimini to the list of his conquests in the Romagna, and there was no knowing whose territory he would decide to take next. "As far as we can foretell, we deem it certain that all of us, one after the other, will perish," said Ercole's son-in-law, Francesco Gonzaga, marchese of Mantua, speaking on behalf of his fellow despots. "We are like men led to the gallows who must helplessly watch others being hanged before our eyes."

When on February 18 the pope had one of his cardinals write to Ercole urging him to approve the marriage "on account of the great benefits that would accrue to his state from it," Ercole had no difficulty picturing the great disadvantages should he oppose the match. Soon after receiving the cardinal's letter, he learned that the apostolic commissary of Cesare's army was coming to Ferrara to discuss the matter with him. Obviously, Alfonso had to be provided with a fiancée before then, or he would have no legitimate excuse for refusing Lucrezia's hand. In another frantic letter to the Ferrarese ambassador in Paris, Ercole ordered him to beseech Louis "if he is urged by the Pope in this matter to tell him that he has already engaged Don Alfonso and cannot therefore set the Duke at liberty or whatever else will seem best to his Majesty, provided that he relieves us from this persecution of the Pope, and that he delivers us from his hatred."

Louis's ancestor Charles VII had given Niccolò III the right to include the lilies of France in the Estense coat of arms and the family has been pro-French ever since. Hence, the duke of Ferrara felt certain that he could count upon Louis's support in his struggle to avoid marrying his son to Lucrezia. "The Christian king need reck little if he does not gratify the Pope in this, since the Pope has more need of him than he of the Pope," Ercole told his ambassador.

As luck would have it, however, at that particular moment it was the Christian king who had need of the pope. On November 11, 1500, Louis had concluded a secret treaty with Ferdinand of Spain in which the two monarchs had agreed to partition Naples between them. Since Naples was a fief of the papacy, they had to have a papal bull approving the partition. Louis also required the pope's consent to move the French troops then stationed in Tuscany through the states of the church to Naples. Because the proposed partition would deprive the Colonna and the other Roman barons of the assistance they were getting from the Neapolitans, Alexander had every reason to give his consent. But like the consummate bargainer that he was, he insisted upon getting something in exchange, and that something was Louis's assurance that he would place nothing in the way of a Borgia-Este match.

Although the bull agreeing to the partition of Naples was not published until the end of June, the pope must have received Louis's assurance long before then, for in the papal consistory of May 8, Alexander spoke of the marriage as an accomplished fact. On June 23, Ercole's ambassador in Paris informed him that Baron de Trans, the most influential person at the French court, had advised him to agree to the marriage upon conditional payment of 200,000 ducats, remission of the 4,150-ducat annual tribute Ferrara was required to pay the Holy See, and receipt of certain benefices for the house of Este. The ambassador's letter was followed by a note from Louis himself informing the duke that he could not give Alfonso the hand of the French princess he had been courting and urging him to accept Lucrezia in her place. Deprived of the one excuse he had for refusing a Borgia-Este match, Ercole had no alternative but to give in. On July 8, he let the king of France know that he would do as Louis wished provided that a suitable agreement could be worked out with the pope.

Alexander, meanwhile, was gleefully supervising the downfall of his old enemies the Colonna and the Savelli. When these rebellious barons had learned that their protector, the king of Naples, was to be deposed and his kingdom divided between the rulers of France and Spain, they had decided to commit their lands and towns into the care of the College of Cardinals. But Alexander insisted that the lands and towns be given to him. On June 22, he ordered his cousin Francesco Borgia to take possession of Rocca di Papa and a number of other castles belonging to the Colonna. On July 27, the pope left Rome to inspect the castles himself. Before he left, says Burchard, "he turned over the palace and all the business affairs to his daughter Lucrezia authorizing her to open all letters addressed to him."

Lucrezia had been living in the palace of Santa Maria in Portico since the previous December. Because she was still in mourning, she had taken little part in the ceremonies of the papal court. Indeed, her return to the city, which had been the scene of so much past misfortune, had turned out to be every bit as painful as she had expected it to be. She considered Rome a prison, she would later tell the Ferrarese envoy. And it must have been her desire to turn her back on that prison forever that finally led her to agree to the match with Alfonso. If she did not expect to find the same bliss with him that she had found with her second husband, if the very thought of finding such bliss seemed a betrayal of that beloved spouse, she would at least be starting a new life far from the intrigues of the papal court. Her brief second marriage had given her a taste for poetry. What made Ferrara so attractive besides its distance from Rome was its reputation as a center of the arts. Like Urbino and Mantua, the city was also famous for the intellectual attainments of its women. Alfonso's sister Isabella d'Este Gonzaga, the marchesa of Mantua, was reputedly the most brilliant woman in Italy—*la prima donna del mondo* ("the first lady of the world"), the poet Niccolò da Correggio called her. Isabella's sister-in-law Elisabetta Gonzaga Montefeltro, the duchess of Urbino, had a reputation for culture and refinement second only to that of Isabella. Although Lucrezia was too modest to rank herself with these two famous ladies, she must have liked the idea of being included in their circle and emulating their patronage of the arts.

But if the opportunity to begin a new life at a court that she naively assumed to be more tranquil and more intellectual than the court of Rome counted for more with her than the prospect of becoming duchess of Ferrara, it was the title that her father coveted. Although the titles and the wealth Alexander had obtained for his children had twice brought disaster in their wake, the pope continued to equate happiness with rank and social standing. To see his beloved daughter enter the oldest ruling house in Italy as consort of its heir apparent, to know that a grandchild of his would one day sit upon the throne of Ferrara, filled him with uncontrollable joy.

Eleanora of Aragon, first duchess of Ferrara, had frequently served as regent in her husband's absence. It was to show that Lucrezia, too, was capable of handling affairs of state that Alexander left his daughter in charge of the Vatican when he set out for the Colonna castles that July. Although he entrusted her with the handling of temporal affairs only, many saw his action as yet another instance of that total disregard for the fitness of things which seemed to characterize his reign. Lucrezia, of course, was too close to the scene to realize how incongruous her appointment appeared, and she took it very seriously. She had been told that should she run into any difficulty, she must go to Cardinal Costa for advice. The eighty-five-year-old cardinal had known her since she was a child, and he was wont to treat her in that wry and teasing manner very old men frequently adopt with attractive young women. When one day she asked him to explain something that puzzled her, he found it difficult to conceal his amusement. "Perceiving that the matter was of no importance," says Burchard, "he told Lucrezia that when the Pope outlined proposals in consistory, the vice-chancellor or another cardinal was always present to write down suggestions and record the votes of each person. Consequently he thought there ought to be someone present to note what they were saying." Whereupon Lucrezia volunteered herself for the task. "But where is your pen?" asked the cardinal.

Realizing that he was joking, Lucrezia smiled "and in this suitable way the conversation ended." Although any young woman who was not an absolute ninny would have responded in the same fashion, the conversation has been passed down through the centuries as yet another instance of the incredible moral laxity of the pope's daughter.

Louis XII has advised Ercole to use the marriage to get as much as he possibly could out of the pope, and Ercole saw no reason not to follow Louis's advice. The duke of Ferrara lived on a grand scale. His production of the *Menaechmi* in 1486 had cost him 1,000 ducats; his numerous other theatricals, his religious processions, his charities, his music, his monasteries all required large sums of money. As he had been advised to do by Baron de Trans, he asked for a dowry of 200,000 ducats—almost six times the amount Lucrezia had brought to Giovanni Sforza and five times what she had brought to her second husband—reduction of Ferrara's annual tribute from 4,150 ducats to 100 ducats, transfer of the castles of Cento and Pieve from the archbishopric of Bologna to that of Ferrara, and a number of benefices for his son Ippolito.

The pope offered 100,000 ducats, and for the rest Ercole must trust him for he would grant them in time and would advance the interests of the house of Este so that everyone would see how high in his favor it stood, Ercole's ambassador in Paris wrote him on August 7. Alexander had urged the king of France to ask the duke to agree to these terms, said the ambassador, adding that it was really superfluous to tell Ercole all this, "for if this marriage is to take place, you will arrange it in such a way that much promising and little fulfillment will not cause you to regret it."

In truth, all that Ercole had promised was that if he got what he wanted, he would allow Lucrezia to marry his son, and in his opinion this was giving good value. On August 10, he protested that he was only asking what was reasonable "in such wise that it can be understood that we take more account of honor than of money." On August 21, he followed this up with a letter in which he told Alexander that the price the pope was being asked to pay for the privilege of making his daughter duchess of Ferrara was low enough, indeed merely nominal. Meanwhile, Lucrezia and Cesare pleaded with their father to accept the duke's terms; the Venetians expressed their disapproval of the match, and the Emperor Maximilian, who was Ercole's liege lord for Modena and Reggio, warned the duke not to allow the marriage to take place. The warning, of course, greatly improved Ercole's position, and he immediately mentioned it to the pope, at the same time assuring him of his determination to go ahead with the match. Alexander was too accomplished an extortioner himself not to know when he was beaten. Soon afterward he informed Ercole that he was prepared to settle all outstanding differences between them, and on August 26 the marriage agreement was signed in the Vatican.

Although Alexander persuaded Ercole to cut the size of the dowry to 100,000 ducats, the pope had to agree to give Lucrezia another 75,000 ducats in jewelry, clothes, silver, and other goods. He also had to agree to ask the next papal consistory to reduce Ferrara's annual tribute to 100 ducats, to settle the investiture of Ferrara on Lucrezia and Alfonso's progeny forever, and to transfer the castles of Cento and Pieve. In addition, the pope made Cardinal Ippolito archpriest of Saint Peter's and granted a number of benefices to other members of the Este clan.

Immediately after signing the contract, Alexander entrusted it to his datary to deliver to Ercole for his signature. The pope also sent his special envoy Don Ramiro Remolini to Ferrara. On September 1,

1501, in the lovely summer palace of the Estense known as Belfiore, with its shaded gardens, its artificial forest filled with wild boar and other game, and its world-renowned peacocks, Remolini served as Lucrezia's proxy when the contract was concluded *ad verba*. All that was needed now was an exchange of rings which the pope wished to have take place in Rome at the time the escort came to fetch the bride.

Ercole had driven a hard bargain, but he knew how to be gracious when the occasion demanded it. Although he had hitherto loved Lucrezia on account of her virtues and on account of the pope and her brother Cesare, he now loved her as a daughter, he told her in a letter written the day the contract was signed. A letter to her father said more or less the same thing and also thanked the pope for making Ippolito archpriest of Saint Peter's. But Ercole cast the mask of graciousness aside in the letter he wrote to his son-in-law the marchese of Mantua. "We have informed your Majesty that we have recently decided—owing to practical reasons—to condescend to an alliance between our house and that of His Holiness," said the duke. Then apparently feeling that "condescend" was a bit harsh, he crossed it out and wrote "consent" in its place.

Although Ercole consoled himself with the thought that an alliance with the Borgias would bolster his treasury and also protect his state from the incursions of both Cesare and the Venetians, the bridegroom and his sister Isabella could not hide their chagrin at seeing their father forced to admit a woman with so sullied a reputation into their house. In a letter to Isabella, one correspondent described Alfonso as being in *"una grandissima mosca"* ("the worst possible humor"). Only by warning him that if he refused to marry Lucrezia his father would be compelled to marry her himself had Ercole been able to get Alfonso to agree to the match. Although the prospect continued to put him in bad humor, he did hunt up a picture of himself to send the bride.

If upon receiving it she was prompted to make comparison—and under the circumstances comparisons were inevitable—they would all be in favor of that other Alfonso, who for over a year now had lain moldering in his grave in Santa Maria della Febbre. In August Lucrezia had discarded the widow's weeds she had worn since his death, replaced with silver ones the clay dishes out of which widows customarily ate, and commenced putting together her third trousseau. Those who had known and loved her second husband, including his former tutor Brandolinus Lippus, complained bitterly of what they regarded as her unseemly haste, and she, too, seems to have had her doubts about what she was doing. If for some reason this third marriage did not materialize, she would change her entire way of life and enter a convent, she told the Ferrarese ambassador a few months later.

But whatever her private misgivings, the image that Lucrezia presented to the public was one of a young woman delighted at her good fortune. The sun was just beginning to set and the churchbells were summoning the Romans to vespers on the evening of September 4 when a courier from Ferrara arrived at the Vatican with the news that the marriage contract had been signed at Belfiore. From that hour onward into the night, says Burchard, "there was a continual boom of cannon from the Castel Sant' Angelo." After dinner the next day, Lucrezia set out for the church of Santa Maria del Populo with an escort of three hundred horsemen and four bishops. Leaving her escort in the nave, she knelt before the high altar and prayed to the Blessed Virgin to protect her marriage. She was dressed in a robe of bright gold, and the veil she wore over her face was drawn back.

That evening the tower of the Campidoglio was illuminated and the great bell tolled continually from supper time until nine o'clock. The Castel Sant' Angelo, too, was illuminated, and bonfires glowed upon the parapets as well as in many other places throughout the city. "As a result," says Burchard, "the people became wildly excited, causing some anxiety."

Despite the anxiety, the celebration continued; in fact, it grew wilder and more frenzied. The following day, which was a Monday, two clowns, one on horseback, the other on foot, went through all the principal streets and piazzas. "Long live the duchess of Ferrara!" they shouted. "Long live Pope Alexander! *Viva! Viva!*" One of the clowns had been given the robe of gold brocade Lucrezia had worn the day before, a robe which Burchard valued at 3,000 ducats; the other had received an expensive dress from the future duchess.

Although the marriage was now a matter of public record and although Alexander let everyone know of his unbounded love for the Estense, Ercole's ambassador in Paris warned him not to trust the pope any further than was necessary. Consequently, the duke of

Ferrara made it clear that he would refuse to send an escort for the bride until he was sure that her dowry would be awaiting them along with the papal bulls lowering Ferrara's tribute and granting him the other concessions he had demanded. The two envoys he sent to Rome to discuss these matters with the pope arrived in the city on September 15. After presenting their credentials, they were taken to the palace of Santa Maria in Portico to meet their new duchess. Despite Ercole's sweet words at the time the marriage contract was signed, Lucrezia was, of course, fully aware of the commercial nature of the transaction by which she had become his daughter-in-law. But she was used to being bartered by then, and she was also desperately eager to get away from Rome. At her first meeting with Ercole's envoys she let them know that she would do everything she could to assist them. Perhaps because her father wished to show the Ferrarese the kind of duchess they were getting, he allowed her to be present at his daily sessions with them. She usually sat on a cushion one step below his throne, and he made a point of asking her opinion before committing himself. To the great delight of the envoys, Lucrezia favored their cause so consistently that, they told Ercole, she already seemed to them "a good Ferrarese."

The envoys had been in Rome only two days when Alexander summoned his cardinals to a secret consistory at which he asked them to grant Ercole's various requests concerning investiture and the lowering of Ferrara's tribute. Despite the pope's emphasis upon Ercole's devotion to the church and the benefits that would accrue to the Holy See from an alliance with Ferrara, a number of the cardinals, including the majority of those Alexander had appointed himself, appeared reluctant to oblige him. Those who did support him made it clear that they were doing so for reasons of friendship rather than for reasons of principle. Thus Lucrezia's old friend Cardinal Costa told his fellow princes of the church that he favored the bulls out of regard for her, and the cardinal of Naples said that he favored them out of regard for Ercole.

Although the eventual approval of the bulls reassured the greedy old duke, there was still the matter of the dowry to be settled as well as any number of other points, including the question of who was to accompany Lucrezia to Ferrara and who was to pay their expenses. But despite the inevitable haggling that characterized the daily sessions between the pope and Ferrarese, Alexander insisted that when evening came they forget their differences. There were parties and dancing every night, said the correspondent of the marchese of Mantua. In fact, Lucrezia danced so much one night that she had a fever the following morning, and the Ferrarese envoys appeared concerned for her health. "The illustrious lady continues somewhat ailing and is greatly fatigued," they told Ercole, and they attributed her condition to the frenetic pace set by her father. "Whenever she is at the Pope's palace the entire night until two or three o'clock is spent in dancing and at play which fatigues her greatly." But because Lucrezia knew how much pleasure Alexander derived from seeing her dance, she could not bring herself to object. Now that she would soon be taking leave of him forever, the resentment she had felt for so long seemed to vanish, and she appeared eager to do everything she could to please him during the brief time they still had together.

Alexander, for his part, was constantly singing her praises. They might see that the duchess was not lame, he told the Ferrarese after they had watched her and her ladies-in-waiting dance for the first time. She was always gracious, granted audiences regularly, and knew how to cajole, he assured them on another occasion. She had, moreover, ruled Spoleto to the satisfaction of everyone and always knew how to carry her point. There was nothing in the world he loved more than Lucrezia and Cesare, he declared. But whereas he was constantly finding new qualities to praise in his daughter, he found little to praise in his son at that time.

After Cesare had conquered Faenza and Castel Bolognese, Alexander had made him duke of Romagna. In the opinion of Machiavelli, the new duke "reconciled all the Romagna, unified it and restored it to loyalty." In fact, his government of the province, the famous *buon governo* of Cesare Borgia, was such an improvement over previous governments that it would be remembered for centuries. But Cesare was too restless to be satisfied with merely governing. He longed to add new cities to the list of his conquests, among them Florence and Bologna. Before he could launch a campaign against either one of these cities, however, Louis XII ordered him to assist the French in their campaign against Naples. To Cesare, the need to put the interests of the king of France ahead of his own interests underlined the tenuousness of his position. "He is displeased and uncertain because his affairs are held in the air. If the French win, they will not take him into account; if they lose and others defeat the

French, he will be in a bad way," said one correspondent who spoke to Cesare when he stopped in Rome on his way to Naples.

Cesare's inability to rid himself of the French disease also depressed him. When Ercole's envoy Pandolfo Collenuccio visited Cesare in Pesaro, he found him in bed suffering from pains in the groin. After the sacking of Capua in July 1501, Cesare became ill once more and had to summon two doctors from Rome to treat him. By then the mask which he wore to hide the pustules on his face had become habitual. Perhaps because he felt less conspicuous wearing it after dark, he conducted most of his business at night. According to Collenuccio, Cesare usually went to bed between three and five in the morning and rose at three the following afternoon. When, after the Neapolitan campaign had ended, he decided to live at the Vatican, his irregular hours exasperated his father. Cesare was in the habit of turning night into day, Alexander told the Ferrarese envoys, and "he severely criticized his son's mode of living."

Living in the palace with Cesare at that time was a little boy commonly believed to be his son. On September 1, the pope had, in fact, issued a bull in which this *infans Romanus*, or "Roman infant," as he was called, was described as a child of three and the "natural son" of Cesare Borgia, unmarried, and a single woman (*soluto genitus et soluta*). However, a second and secret bull issued that same day described little Giovanni's parents as Cesare, married, and a single woman (*coniugato genitus et soluta*), and then went on to declare that it was not because of Cesare that the little boy bore the stain of illegitimacy but because of the pope himself and the aforesaid single woman, "which for good reasons" His Holiness had not wished to state in the preceding instrument. Since Giovanni was said to be three years old at the time the bulls were issued, any number of people have concluded that he must have been Lucrezia's child by Pedro Calderon and that the pope issued a bull legitimating him that September to prevent embarrassing questions from the Ferrarese. But the correspondent who had informed Ercole of the birth of a child to Lucrezia had done so in March 1498, whereas Baron Pastor, the historian of the popes, gives Giovanni's date of birth as June 18, 1497, and a bull of Leo X makes him even older than that.

Those who accept the stories of Lucrezia's incestuous relations with her father assume, of course, that Giovanni was the fruit of that union. Although the bull describes the child's mother as an "unmarried woman," others have assumed that she must have been Giulia Farnese. But Giulia never showed the slightest interest in little Giovanni. Years later, when he came to Ferrara, Lucrezia referred to him as her brother, and Burchard, too, called him the pope's child *"cum quadum Romana"* ("with a certain Roman woman"), as did Sigismundo dei Conti and Girolamo Priuli. None of these writers, however, mentions the contradiction between the first sentence of the second bull in which Giovanni is referred to as Cesare's son and the second sentence in which he is referred to as the pope's son; nor do they say anything about the disparity between the first bull in which Cesare is described as "unmarried," which he was at the time of Giovanni's birth, and the second bull in which he is described as "married," which he was at the time that the bull was issued. Ever since the bulls were published by Gregorovius, however, historians of the Borgias have sought to resolve the discrepancies. Of the numerous exegeses, the most satisfactory remains that of the nineteenth-century Anglican bishop Mandell Creighton, who saw the two bulls as stemming from Alexander's wish to "provide as far as he could against all contingencies."

> We may either suppose [says Creighton], that in his desire to secure Cesare's bastard son against the possible claim of legitimate children, he [the pope] executed a second instrument in his favor; or we must hold that this child of three years old was the son of the Pope at the age of sixty-eight and that Cesare consented to recognize him as his own. In either case the Pope's conduct was scandalous and showed a shamelessness of inventive skill in moulding legal forms to suit his own purpose.

Seventeen days after the pope issued the two bulls legitimating Giovanni, he gave the child the dukedom of Nepi, including Palestrina, Frascati, and a number of other towns. At the same time the pope gave the dukedom of Sermoneta, which included both Albano and Nettuno, the Lucrezia's son Rodrigo.

Rodrigo was then two. In a letter to Ercole, the Ferrarese envoys described him as *"un bellissimo putto"* ("a most beautiful little cherub"). Although Rodrigo was then living in his mother's palace, it was taken for granted that he would not accompany her to Ferrara, for no woman took the children of a previous marriage with her when she remarried. "I asked her—in such a way that she could not mistake my meaning—what was to be done with him," one of the Ferrarese envoys told Ercole, "to which she replied, 'He will remain in Rome and will have an allowance of 15,000 ducats.'" But her letters to her son's guardians and the lengths to which she went to see the child again after she was in Ferrara show that she never reconciled herself to the separation. Indeed, there must have been times during those hectic months before Lucrezia took leave of Rodrigo when she wondered why she had ever consented to remarry and what good could possibly come of it.

Her future husband seldom wrote. When he did, his letters were so stiff and formal, so devoid of those endearing expressions men customarily included in letters to their betrothed, that they could have just as well been addressed to some anonymous government official. As if to compensate for Alfonso's indifference, Ercole wrote frequently and his letters were affectionate and confidential. They were also self-serving, for it had not taken the duke of Ferrara long to realize how eager his new daughter-in-law was to please him, and he saw no reason not to take advantage of her complaisant nature to get what he wanted.

What he wanted that fall, in addition to benefices and money from her father, were eight nuns—two from Narni and six from Viterbo. His wish for these particular nuns arose from his interest in religious reform in general and the cult of St. Catherine of Siena in particular. Like Savonarola, with whom Ercole had corresponded until it became dangerous to do so, St. Catherine had denounced clerical corruption and urged the pope to choose between the temporal power and the salvation of souls. Though she had lived and worked over one hundred years before the time of Alexander VI, her words seemed as appropriate during his reign as when she had first written them. Inspired by her teachings, women all over Italy sought to imitate her way of life. Like her, they went about robed in black and white; like her, they had visions; and again like her, many bore the stigmata on the second Thursday of Lent during matins and after-chronicler Matarazzo, Suor Colomba of Rieti, the most famous of the lot "neither ate nor drank save sometimes some jujube fruit and even then but rarely." Suor Osanna of Mantua had learned by revelation that the souls of all those who died fighting for the independence of Italy had been saved. Suor Lucia of Narni received the stigmata on the second Thursday of Lent during matins and afterward revealed such wondrous celestial mysteries that her fellow nuns could not find the words to explain them.

Alexander, who had been unimpressed by Suor Colomba when he had visited her during his stay in Perugia, was equally unimpressed by Suor Lucia. In his wonderfully down-to-earth and matter-of-fact way, he sent his doctor to examine her and later had the Father Inquisitor question her about her visions. Ercole, on the other hand, accepted both the stigmata and the visions at face value, and in a letter to his nephew, who was then governor of Viterbo, he emphasized how eager he was to hear of these "super-mundane and well-nigh celestial things." In fact, he was so eager to hear of them that he had Suor Lucia spirited out of Viterbo in a basket and brought to Ferrara, where he promptly built a convent for her. But a convent needs nuns. Because Suor Lucia tended to be autocratic and difficult, she could not find any in Ferrara willing to live under her rule. And so she asked Ercole to request the nuns with whom she had lived in Viterbo. However, the prior of her former convent told Ercole that he had no intention of parting with them. Nor did the sisters themselves, despite their protestations of love for Suor Lucia, appear at all eager to leave Viterbo to live under her rule. It was because Ercole thought Lucrezia would be able to overcome their opposition that he decided to seek her help. "Let not your ladyship wonder at this solicitation of ours, because, since we are in the state that we are, we attend more to affairs of the soul (like this is) than to other matters," he told her.

Lucrezia, of course, had no alternative but to oblige him. In fact, the special envoy whom Ercole sent to Rome to handle the matter found her so obliging that he told the duke he lived in hopes that she would bring the nuns to Ferrara "to make a desired present of them" to Ercole and "the venerable Suor Lucia." Although this is what eventually did occur, the nuns put up such a fierce resistance to leaving their convent that it took an order from the pope and over two months of constant negotiating to pry them loose. During this time, Lucrezia was also sitting in on Alexander's daily discussions with the Ferrarese and going to his nightly soirees in their honor. Besides these frequently lively gatherings, there was talk in Rome of other even livelier get-togethers to which the Ferrarese were not invited.

On Sunday evening October 30, for example, Burchard reported that Cesare had given a supper in his apartment in the Vatican. Among those invited were "fifty honest courtesans" ("*meretrici honeste*") by which was meant genteel courtesans more akin to the Greek hetaera than to the lowly streetwalker. These particular "honest courtesans," however, appear to have been misnamed, for after dancing with the servants a short while, they took off their clothes. Lampstands holding lighted candles were then placed on the dance floor "and chestnuts were strewn about which the prostitutes naked and on their hands and knees had to pick up as they crawled in and out among the lampstands." Watching the performance, according to Burchard, were "the Pope, Don Cesare and Donna Lucrezia. . . . Finally prizes were offered—silken doublets, pairs of shoes, hats and other garments—for those men who were most successful with the prostitutes. This performance was carried out in the Sala Reale and those who attended said that in fact the prizes were presented to those who won the contest."

Stories like this were, of course, nothing new. In a letter to Machiavelli written the previous July, Agostino Vespucci had told of twenty-five women observed riding pillion behind a number of horsemen to the papal palace every night between the Angelus and one in the morning "to say nothing of the Pope, who keeps his permanent little flock there so that the whole palace is being openly converted into a brothel for every kind of depravity." Although, like Vespucci, most foreign envoys accepted these stories and hastened to repeat them, at least one envoy, the Venetian Hieronimo Donado, did not. The pope led an orderly life and did not do the things he was said to do, Donado told his government. The expression he used was "*si dice,*" the insidious "it is said" that meant the informant was not speaking from firsthand knowledge but was repeating what he had been told by someone else who more than likely was repeating what he had been told.

Burchard begins his account of the famous supper by saying that it took place in Cesare's apartment and ends it by saying that it took place in the Sala Reale. Since Cesare's apartment was directly above the Hall of the Sibyls where Alfonso of Bisceglie had died, and the Sala Reale in which the pope usually gave his audiences was on the floor below, adjoining the Sistine Chapel, it is difficult to see how the party could have progressed from one to the other. In Burchard's account, he makes it clear that he did not attend the party, for at the end he speaks of "those who attended" telling him about the prizes. But even if his account was a *"si dice,"* for a stickler after detail like the master of ceremonies not to spot the obvious contradiction in the story was, to say the least, unusual, and gives rise to the suspicion that the story of the supper was inserted into the diary by someone else.

Shortly after the supper supposedly took place, a so-called "Letter to Silvio Savelli" began circulating in Rome. Silvio Savelli was one of the Roman barons whose lands had been confiscated by the pope. At the time of the letter he was living at the court of Emperor Maximilian, apparently in the hope of one day reaching an agreement with Alexander whereby the pope would return at least some of the confiscated lands. The letter to him, which was dated November 14 from the Spanish camp at Taranto, and which was translated into every important European language and circulated at every important European court, asked Savelli to abandon all hope of coming to terms with "this monster" (i.e. Alexander). Instead it urged the exiled baron to "lay the evil" that had proceeded from "this infamous beast" (once again the pope) before the emperor and the German princes. After calling Alexander a new Mahomet, "an enemy of God and an oppressor of the Christian faith," the letter went on to repeat every damaging story ever told about the pope and his family and to add a few new ones. It asked:

> Who is not shocked to hear tales of the monstrous lascivity openly exhibited at the Vatican in defiance of God and all human decency? Who is not repelled by the debauchery, the incest, the obscenity of the children of the Pope: son and daughter; the flocks of courtesans in the palace of Saint Peter? There is not a house of ill fame or a brothel that is not more respectable. On the first of November All Saints' Day fifty courtesans were invited to a banquet at the pontifical palace and gave the most repugnant performance there. . . . Rodrigo Borgia is an abyss of vice and a subverter of all justice human or divine.

"Abyss of vice" and "subverter of justice" though he may have been, the pope believed that Rome was a privileged place where everyone had a right to say what he pleased, and it is a tribute to the strength of his belief that even after the letter was read to him, he did nothing to keep it from circulating. His behavior would also seem to indicate that he thought the accusations it contained so preposterous that he could not see how anyone could take them seriously. Another reason for believing that the supper of the fifty courtesans never occurred is that there is no mention of it in the dispatches of the Ferrarese envoys, who were then seeing the pope almost daily and certainly had access to all the latest Vatican gossip. On the other hand, the Florentine envoy Francesco Pepi did tell his government that though the pope had a cold "this did not prevent him on Sunday night, the eve of All-Saint's Day, from staying up till twelve o'clock with the Duke [of Valentois], who had brought prostitutes and courtesans into the Vatican; and they passed the night with dancing and laughter." Pepi, however, makes no mention of Lucrezia's presence at the party nor does he say anything about chestnuts.

Both Burchard's diary and the "Letter to Silvio Savelli" place Lucrezia and her father at yet another explicitly sexual performance. This time, however, the performers were not courtesans and servants but mares and stallions. "On November 11th," says Burchard, "a countryman entered Rome leading two mares loaded with wood. When they reached the Piazza San Pietro some of the palace men-at-arms came up, cut through the straps, and threw off the saddles and the wood in order to lead the mares into the courtyard immediately inside the palace gate. Four stallions were then freed from their reins and harness and let out of the palace stables. They immediately ran to the mares over whom they proceeded to fight furiously and noisily amongst themselves, biting and kicking in their efforts to mount them and seriously wounding them with their hoofs. The Pope and Donna Lucrezia, laughing and with evident satisfaction, watched all that was happening from a window above the palace gate."

It scarcely seems the sort of performance a loving father would want his daughter to witness on the eve of her wedding. Nor is the "evident satisfaction" of the pope and his daughter consonant with Alexander's usually genial and dignified behavior or with the gentleness and goodness which Ercole's envoys invariably attributed to Lucrezia. Equally barbarous entertainments were, however, a commonplace at weddings throughout northern Italy. At the wedding of the gentle and cultured Elisabetta Gonzaga to the equally cultured duke of Urbino, a knight, nude to the waist, and a female cat were locked in a cage. After exciting and angering the cat, the knight was supposed to kill her without using either his hands or his teeth. The worse it went with him, the greater the enjoyment of the guests. On this particular occasion, the unfortunate knight selected to do battle with the cat was so badly mauled by his feline opponent that he had to be pensioned for two years.

The month of November, when Alexander supposedly arranged the rape of the mares by the stallions for the delectation of his daughter, was also the month when the pope finally grew so exasperated with Ercole's ever accelerating demands for money and benefices that he accused him of "behaving like a shopkeeper," to which Ercole protested. Although on November 24 Ercole had threatened to have the bridal escort return to Ferrara without the bride unless they received her dowry in cash as soon as they entered Rome, he protested against the use of the word *shopkeeper*. Nevertheless, he seems to have realized that he had perhaps overstepped himself and that he had best placate the pope. On December 1, he informed Alexander that the bridal escort would leave Ferrara on the ninth or tenth of December.

And what an escort it was! Although Ercole had not wanted this wedding, now that there was no getting out of it he was determined not to be outdone by the pope in pomp or brilliancy. Over five hundred persons set out from the cathedral square in Ferrara that chilly ninth of December to the joyous sound of thirteen trumpets and nine fifes. With them went innumerable carts, mules, and packhorses carrying the trunks in which were the velvet doublets and the shot velvet breeches, the sleeveless surcoats edged in fur, the colored hose, the great puffed caps, the linen handkerchiefs, the gloves, the lace ruffling, the belts, pendants, chains, and heavy jeweled crosses that the gentlemen going to Rome intended to wear at the ceremonies welcoming them to the city. Not to mention the ivory combs, the soap, and the perfume as well as the numerous presents for the bride, including diamonds that had once belonged to Alfonso's mother Eleanora of Aragon.

Although Alfonso would await his bride in Ferrara, his three brothers, Don Ferrante, Don Sigismundo, and Cardinal Ippolito, were all going to Rome. Because the twenty-two-year-old Ippolito was the first of his line ever to have been made a prince of the church, he had been given the honor of heading the procession. At his side rode two fellow churchmen of the house of Este: Niccolò Maria d'Este, bishop of Adria, who had kept Ercole up to date on the visions of Suor Lucia; and Meliaduse d'Este, bishop of Commacchio. There was also Count Ugo Ciccione dei Contrarii, first baron of the realm and husband of Ercole's niece, Diane d'Este; the duke's son-in-law, Annibale Bentivoglio of Bologna, who hoped that his presence in the escort would save his native city from Cesare's armies; as well as innumerable counts who lived in Ferrara and the surrounding provinces, including the Counts Rangone of Modena, the Counts Pio of Carpi, and the poet-statesman Niccolò da Correggio. So that all these noble lords would be well taken care of during the journey, there were also gentlemen-in-waiting and pages to help them in and out of their clothing; grooms to tend their horses; barbers to shave them and clip their locks; laundresses to do their linen; and secretaries to handle their correspondence.

Among these numerous lackeys was one attached to the train of Niccolò da Correggio who answered to the name of El Prete ("the Priest"). Shortly before El Prete set out for Rome with his master, he received a commission from the bridegroom's sister Isabella d'Este Gonzaga, marchesa of Mantua. All her life Isabella had been accustomed to being first. Despite some competition from her sister, Beatrice, it was Isabella who had been her mother's "dearest and sweetest daughter," her tutor's brightest pupil, her father's favorite child. And now that she was a grown woman she prided herself on being Italy's most elegant and cultured princess. But elegance and culture cannot be left to chance, especially when one wishes to be not merely elegant and cultured but the most elegant and the most cultured.

Besides a preceptor from whom she took lessons in science and Latin, the twenty-seven-year-old Isabella also had an agent who supplied her with the choice items she needed to maintain her reputation as a leader of fashion. Typical of what she expected from him was "blue cloth for a mantle such as shall be without rival in the world, even if it cost ten ducats a yard as long as it is of real excellence. . . . If it is only as good as those which I see other people wear, I had rather be without it."

Despite her concern for excellence, Isabella had to watch what she spent very carefully, whereas she knew that Pope Alexander had set no limit to what his daughter could spend on her clothes. It was to find out what kind of gowns Lucrezia wore and how she did her hair and which dance steps she favored and the nature of the trousseau she was bringing with her to Ferrara that Isabella engaged El Prete. For only by knowing everything there was to know about this unwelcome new sister-in-law could Isabella devise ways to outshine her.

Working for Isabella was no sinecure. She had threatened to imprison one unlucky artist for not meeting his deadline and had refused to pay any number of other employees because their work had not pleased her. Consequently, El Prete hastened to prove his worth. He would follow "the excellent Lady Lucrezia as a shadow follows a body," he assured his employer. He would even be able to tell the kind of imprint her feet left on the ground and where his eyes were unable to see his cunning would help him. "Your Excellency can judge what I have already achieved in Rome; although I have not left Ferrara, I can tell you that her ladyship goes out with shawls which cover her breast to the neck. She wears no curls, is modestly attired and for preference dances new steps and this with such lightness that one would think she was not moving." Delighted, Isabella called El Prete "her good hound."

Nor was she the only one eager to find out more about Lucrezia. Although Ercole's envoys had been unanimous in praising his new daughter-in-law, the duke of Ferrara could not forget the sinister rumors he had heard about her in the past. Before the bridal escort left Rome, he asked his councillor Gian Luca Castellini to observe Lucrezia carefully and then to let him know if in Castellini's opinion she could have been guilty of the acts attributed to her.

What with the size of their party and the bone-chilling winter rains that all but washed out the roads, it took the Ferrarese thirteen days to get to Rome. By the time they arrived at Monterosi, a castle fifteen miles north of the city, every last one of them was drenched and shivering and covered with mud. While they and their horses attempted to dry out as best they could, Cardinal Ippolito sent a herald to inform the pope that the Ferrarese were at his disposal. They were told to enter the city the following morning by the Porta del Populo. To everyone's delight the morning turned out to be clear and sparkling, an ideal morning for displaying the finery they'd brought with them across the Appennines.

Alexander's reign had accustomed the Romans to brilliant spectacles, but nothing they had witnessed during the nine and one-half years he had been pope, neither his coronation nor the entrance of Charles VIII nor Cesare's triumphal entry after the capture of Imola and Forlì, could compare to the welcome accorded the Ferrarese that twenty-third day of December 1501. The pope and his son tried to outdo one another in the magnificence with which they received the Ferrarese deputation, said the Florentine envoy, scarcely bothering to conceal his disapproval of the vast sums they were spending. As a minor instance of their extravagance, he cited the shoes of gold brocade which both had provided for their grooms. According to another observer, Cesare had spent at least 10,000 ducats outfitting himself and his horse for the occasion so "all one could see was gold, pearls and other jewels." Four thousand men accompanied him to the Porta del Populo to await the Ferrarese that morning, including one hundred mounted noblemen and two hundred Swiss halberdiers clothed in black and yellow velvet with black birettas on their heads and the papal arms prominently displayed on their persons. If one adds to this the two hundred men accompanying each of the nineteen cardinals who awaited the Ferrarese in the piazza on the other side of the Porta del Populo and the two thousand men who had accompanied the governor of Rome to the Ponte Milvio to greet them earlier that morning, the cavalcade whihc made its way down the Via del Corso in the direction of the Vatican after the welcoming speeches were finally over must have numbered at least ten thousand persons and taken several hours to pass. When the leaders of the procession reached the Tiber, the continual boom of cannons from the Castel Sant' Angelo on the opposite bank so terrified the horses, already unnerved by the din of trumpets and fifes and the crowds pressing in on them, that many refused to set foot on the bridge. Eventually, however, they were persuaded to do so, and the procession continued on its way.

Alexander's chamberlain met Cardinal Ippolito and his brothers at the steps of the Vatican and escorted them and the other important members of the bridal escort into the Sala del Pappagallo, where the pope awaited them with twelve of his cardinals. After the Ferrarese had kissed the papal foot, Alexander raised them and embraced them. Cesare then brought them to the palace of Santa Maria in Portico to meet his sister.

She had had weeks to prepare for this first meeting with her new in-laws, and she had obviously made up her mind to dazzle them. Leaning upon the arm of an elderly cavalier dressed in black velvet, she descended the steps of her palace as far as the entrance. Over her gold-embroidered white dress with its tight barred sleeves she wore a robe of dark brown velvet lined with sable. A ruby "of no great size nor of very fine color" hung from the string of pearls about her neck. The headdress of green gauze that completed her costume was held in place by a band of beaten gold which crossed with another band edged in pearls. After the introductions and the greetings were over, she ordered refreshments served and distributed small gifts of jewelry. The gesture delighted her in-laws. El Prete, who had managed to worm his way into Santa Maria in Portico along with his master, told Isabella that "the eyes of Cardinal Ippolito sparkled as much as to say 'She is an enchanting and exceedingly gracious lady.' "

Later that evening, Gian Luca Castellini paid her a second visit so that he might observe her more closely before reporting his impressions to Ercole. In a secret letter in which he told the duke that he considered it his duty to report the exact truth, he, too, described Lucrezia as "exceedingly gracious, most intelligent, modest, lovable, decorous," and what to Ercole must have been equally important, "devout and God-fearing." "In short," Castellini concluded, "her character is such that it is impossible to suspect anything sinister in her."

Both Castellini and El Prete continued to observe Lucrezia carefully all the time they were in Rome and to report her every move to their respective employers. Fortunately, Lucrezia did not know what was happening, for if she had, it would have added yet more strain to an already strained situation. "The illustrious Madonna appears in public but little because she is busy preparing for her departure," wrote El Prete. Always eager for additional news, on the evening of December 26 he insinuated himself into a group which accompanied Lucrezia's brother-in-law Don Ferrante on an unexpected visit to her palace. They found her in her chamber with twenty Roman women dressed à la romanesca, "wearing certain cloths on their heads," sitting in a corner, and ten of her ladies-in-waiting also present. A nobleman from Valencia and one of these ladies began dancing. They were followed by Don Ferrante and Lucrezia, who, said El Prete "danced with extreme grace and

animation. She wore a *camorra*, or smocked blouse, of black velvet
with gold borders and black sleeves; the cuffs were tight; the sleeves
were slashed at the shoulder; her breast was covered up to the neck
with a veil made of gold thread. About her neck she wore a string of
pearls and on her head a green net and a chain of rubies. She had an
overskirt of black velvet trimmed with fur, colored and very
beautiful." Two or three of her ladies-in-waiting were pretty, El
Prete continued. One danced well and another, Lucrezia's cousin
Angela Borgia, was charming. Without her knowing it El Prete had
picked her as his favorite.

Angela's charm would be the source of great tragedy in Ferrara,
and even then it must have been one of the reasons for the nightly
visits Alfonso's brothers made to Lucrezia's palace. Although
like their grandfather Niccolò III all three were indefatigable
womanizers, in most other respects they were utterly different one
from the other. Ferrante, the eldest, who was only a year younger
than Alfonso, was handsome but sluggish and showed neither a taste
nor an aptitude for the military life to which his father had consigned
him. Sigismundo, the youngest, was quiet, religious, and self-
effacing, and would have probably made a better cardinal than the
cruel and sybaritic Ippolito. Although at twenty-two Ippolito had
given proof of his virility an endless number of times on a seemingly
endless number of women, there was something almost effeminate in
the care he lavished upon his person. His long dark hair was always
carefully oiled and held in place by a set of ivory combs; his clothing
was immaculate; later the poetess Veronica Gambara would praise
his "beautiful little hands." Rumor put him in the bed of Cesare's
sister-in-law Sancha. But Cesare who, according to the gossips, was
also having an affair with Sancha, did not appear to mind. In fact he
insisted upon showing Cardinal Ippolito and Don Ferrante the sights
of the city.

So that the Ferrarese would not want for entertainment,
Alexander had allowed the carnival to begin early. As usual at
carnival time there were races scheduled: for old men, for children,
for prostitutes, for Jews, for wild boars, for donkeys, buffaloes, and
horses. There was also a tournament in a meadow where eight men
inside the barriers did battle with eight men on the outside using
edged swords and pointed lances. The battle lasted for two days
without either side being able to gain a victory, and said one ob-

server, "There were deaths on both sides, five very sturdy men, and this for nothing but pleasure and amusement."

Nor were the traditional rites commemorating the birth of the Savior neglected. On December 24, trumpeters went through the city to announce that the holy lance would be exhibited on Christmas Day and plenary indulgences granted. At the mass celebrated on Christmas Eve, the pope gave the Ferrarese precedence over the senators and the Roman nobles on the steps of the high altar. At the solemn Christmas mass the next day, Don Ferrante and Don Sigismundo were two of the four gentlemen selected to give the pope the water with which to wash his hands.

Although Lucrezia had been legally married to Alfonso ever since the marriage contract had been signed at Belfiore, Alexander announced that some learned doctors-at-law had advised him that the marriage should be celebrated again at Rome. In the absence of the bridegroom, his brother Don Ferrante would serve as his proxy at the ceremony in the Vatican on December 30.

The afternoon of the thirtieth a good part of Rome had turned out to watch the horse races in which first Barbary horses, then light Spanish mounts, and finally cavalry horses ran from the Campo dei Fiori to the Piazza San Pietro. The piazza was still filled with spectators when a sudden fanfare from the trumpets and fifes on a platform above the steps of St. Peter's basilica announced the approach of the bride. As the music continued, the doors of Santa Maria in Portico opened, and Don Ferrante and Don Sigismundo emerged leading Lucrezia by the hand. The sleeves of her gold brocade wedding dress touched the ground; her crimson velvet overgarment was trimmed in ermine, and her long train was borne by some of her fifty gorgeously attired maids of honor. About her neck she wore a string of pearls from which hung a pendant consisting of an emerald, a ruby, and one large pearl. A black band confined her long blond hair. Over it she had placed a light coif of gold and silk.

After crossing the piazza, she and the other members of the wedding party entered the Vatican and made their way to the Sala Paolina where they were greeted by Alexander and Cesare and thirteen of the cardinals. Alfonso's cousin Niccolò Maria d'Este, bishop of Adria, then began the wedding sermon. Though he had undoubtedly spent much time preparing it, Alexander found his delivery so dull that he "repeatedly urged him to hurry through more quickly." When the bishop had finally done speaking, a table was placed before the pope, and Lucrezia and Don Ferrante stepped forward.

Lucrezia was so used to being gracious by then, so used to smiling and playing a part, that it must have been impossible for any one of those present to tell how she really felt about this, her third wedding in nine years. Indeed, the absence of the bridegroom must have made the ceremony seem so unreal that she probably couldn't tell how she felt herself. Once again, as in the case of Giovanni Sforza and Alfonso of Bisceglie, she declared that she was marrying her husband "most willingly." Don Ferrante then slipped Alfonso's gold wedding ring upon her finger. The bridegroom had sent it of his own free will, Ferrante told her. "And I of my own free will accept it," she replied.

After her words had been attested to by a notary, Cardinal Ippolito brought in four rings—one diamond, one ruby, one emerald, and one turquoise—together with a small box containing the Estense family jewels. Generations of Ferrarese and Modenese peasants had worked their fields to pay the taxes that had permitted their rulers to buy the two pearl caps and the four diamond- and ruby-studded pearl collars, the jeweled pendant, the numerous exquisitely fashioned bracelets, and the four diamond crosses which the cardinal now presented to Lucrezia. When she admired their workmanship, Ippolito begged her not to despise them and assured her that after she had become duchess of Ferrara, her father-in-law would lavish still other presents upon her. Delighted, Alexander told Ippolito that his gallant words had enhanced the beauty of the gift. However, neither the pope nor his daughter had any idea of the care that had gone into formulating those gallant words. For Ercole, distrustful of the Borgias to the very last, wished to be sure that if anything happened to Lucrezia, if, for instance, she died in childbirth as had Alfonso's first wife, Anna Sforza, the jewels would not remain in her family or be given to her son by Alfonso of Bisceglie but would revert to the Estense. Hence, he had ordered Ippolito to be careful not to make an unconditional gift of the jewels and see to it that the notary's instrument did not mention them but spoke only of the receipt of a wedding ring from Alfonso.

After Lucrezia had received the jewels, the cardinals presented their gifts, and the entire company then withdrew to the adjoining room. El Prete, who, of course, had managed to wangle an invitation, told Isabella that the pope asked Cesare to lead the dance with Lucrezia "which he did most gracefully." And then there were comedies. "The first was not finished, as it was too long," said El Prete. "The second which was in Latin verse and in which a shepherd and several children appeared was very beautiful, but I have forgotten what it represented."

In the congested brilliance of the next few days, the other guests must have forgotten just as quickly, for what with the many plays and pageants, the parades and dances and eclogues and bullfights, one entertainment inevitably merged into another without leaving any but the most general impression. On New Year's Eve, Cesare and one of the cardinals both presented eclogues in honor of the bridal pair. On New Year's Day, Rome's thirteen districts, or *rioni* as they were called, each contributed a float to a parade which began at Piazza Navona and ended at the Vatican. Each of the floats represented an episode from the history of ancient Rome. "On one of them," said the Venetian ambassador, "was his lordship the Duke of Valentois richly attired, triumphant, happy and glorious." Later, Cesare appeared in a *moresca*, or Moorish dance, in which a jongleur dressed as a woman also danced to the accompaniment of tambourines. The pope was so happy during these performances that he laughed continually.

Although everything pleased him, it was obvious that nothing pleased him as much as seeing his daughter dance. On the same evening that Cesare appeared in the *moresca*, Lucrezia and her ladies-in-waiting also danced for the company. Lucrezia was wearing a dark velvet gown embroidered in gold that set off the strands of rubies and diamonds she wore about her neck. One of the two pearl caps given her by her father-in-law rested atop her golden hair. Her ladies-in-waiting, too, were sumptuously dressed in crimson velvet and gold brocade, and their colored cloaks were embroidered in gold silk.

It took hours to dress thus, but even in those last hectic days when she and her ladies were dressing for one entertainment after another, her father-in-law did not hesitate to ask new favors of her. One was for his illegitimate son Don Giulio. Before she left Rome would she be good enough to obtain from His Beatitude a promise that as soon as an occasion presented itself he would confer a good benefice on the said Don Giulio, such as a bishopric or a good abbey? There was also the matter of the nuns for Suor Lucia's convent. Because Ercole did not think it suitable for these sainted virgins to travel with the wedding party, he asked Lucrezia to have them leave two days earlier with one of the Ferrarese envoys and a company of crossbowmen to protect them. Not content with having his daughter-in-law attend to these arrangements, the duke also managed to have her bear most of the cost of the escort as well.

Ercole's envoys manifested the same determination to get as much as they could out of the Borgias. There were in those days two kinds of ducats in circulation: so-called chamber ducats and large ducats which, as their name implied, were larger and heavier. Quite naturally the envoys wished to have Lucrezia's dowry paid in large ducats. But Alexander was not such an easy mark as his daughter and he complained loudly of the excessive demands of the Ferrarese. Although there was talk of referring the matter to a lawyer, in the end the Ferrarese were forced to accept chamber ducats. Only when the last ducat had been put into Don Ferrante's hands would they write a receipt for the dowry, and Ercole commended them for their prudence.

Though the duke intended to give the bridal party a sumptuous welcome, he did not wish it to cost too much or last too long. Hence, he desired Lucrezia and her entourage to enter Ferrara on January 28. That way there would be only ten days of celebrating before Ash Wednesday put an end to the festivities. To make sure that the party did not arrive earlier, Ercole ordered it to leave Rome on January 6.

The Ferrarese had come by way of Florence and the Via Cassia. Because Cesare wanted his sister to see his newly conquered provinces in the Romagna, they would return by way of the Via Flaminia and the Adriatic Coast. At his own expense Cesare provided his sister with an escort of two hundred cavaliers and a number of buffoons and musicians whose duty it was to entertain her during the long journey. Not to be outdone, Alexander had a number of vehicles built just to carry her trousseau. He also gave her 150 mules and he permitted her to take whatever she wished with her. When his notary advised him to make an inventory, he refused. "I desire that the duchess shall do with her property as she wishes," he told the Ferrarese ambassador.

In Lucrezia's uncertain and apprehensive state, the accumulation of things seemed to provide a sort of security against the future. Besides the innumerable wedding presents she had received, she was taking at least 200,000 ducats' worth of household goods and clothing to Ferrara, one correspondent reported. There was silverware worth 3,000 ducats, jewels, fine linen, costly trappings for the horses, and in her wardrobe a trimmed dress worth 15,000 ducats, another worth 20,000 ducats, and a hat valued at 10,000 ducats. There were dresses of velvet and satin and brocade with hems of beaten gold. There were mantles lined with ermine and sable. The sleeves of several of her two hundred shifts were trimmed in gold fringe, and these sleeves alone had cost thirty ducats each.

Her uncle Francesco Borgia, archbishop of Cosenza—an elderly man and a worthy person, the Ferrarese called him—would accompany her through the papal states. She also had a retinue of 180 persons that included two sons of her married half sister Isabella, her first lady-in-waiting, Angela Borgia, and Adriana de Mila, the woman who for so long had been her surrogate mother.

Of Lucrezia's real mother there was no mention. By then Vannozza was once again a widow, a well-to-do lady of sixty who spent much of her time in prayer and donated much of the money she had accumulated from her real estate deals to churches and hospitals. Certainly, she was too proud of being the mother of the duchess of Ferrara not to have arranged a reunion with her daughter before Lucrezia left Rome. To Lucrezia the reunion could have meant little, for she scarcely knew the woman who had borne her. And realizing how unimportant Vannozza was to her, she would have a presentiment of how unimportant she would one day seem to the child she was leaving behind in Rome. There was no way to expain what was happening to the two-year-old Rodrigo. No more than the three-year-old Lucrezia had understood why Vannozza was leaving her, did he understand why his mother was leaving him. And if after embracing him for the last time, Lucrezia resented the unfairness of the choice she had been forced to make on this, her last day in Rome, she could not bring herself to resent the father whose complex diplomacy was in so large a measure reponsible for her predicament.

She found him seated on his throne in the Sala del Pappagallo waiting to say goodbye to her. At her entrance all his attendants left, and he motioned her to take her accustomed place on the cushion a step below his throne. Alexander had just celebrated his seventy-first birthday. Although he spoke of visiting Ferrara in the spring, he had to face the possibility that he might never see his daughter again. And so he would try to fix that beloved presence in his memory: the heavy golden hair, the sweet face, the ready smile, the incomparably graceful manner. As they talked, something in the tone of her voice or in what she said must have made him realize that despite all the differences they had had during the past few years, she was as uneasy about this separation as he was. When Cesare entered the room with the Estense brothers and she arose to leave. Alexander called after her telling her to be of good cheer and to write him whenever she wanted anything. Now that she was gone from him, he would do more for her than he had ever done for her in Rome, he assured her.

When her slender figure finally disappeared down the hallway, he went to the window to watch her take her place in the great cavalcade that awaited her. It was snowing, and she had put an ermine-lined cloak over her crimson and gold traveling dress. Her father saw her mount a white mule and fall into line between Cardinal Ippolito and Cesare. As the cavalcade began slowly moving in the direction of the Ponte Sant' Angelo, he went from window to window in the Vatican to watch his daughter and her retinue until the last horseman and the last gold- and brown-trimmed wagon disappeared from sight.

After leaving the Vatican, the cavalcade crossed the Ponte San Angelo and made its way down the Via del Corso to the Porta del Populo. Because of the storm the normally busy streets must have been hushed and empty. Nor were there any fishermen waiting to greet them along the banks of the Tiber when they left the city and headed for the Ponte Milvio. The pope had told Cesare and Cardinal Ippolito to accompany the party as long as they could. When finally the two young men took their leave, Lucrezia embraced her brother. After watching him ride back in the direction of the Porta del Populo until he had disappeared in the distance, she and her entourage continued on their way along the snow-covered Via Flaminia in the direction of Ferrara.

In the Castello of the Estense

All things change. Ferrara which of old, girt round by lowly
walls, on one side the green river bank, on the other the marshy
lagoon, in poverty held but slender resources, narrow houses and
narrow temples of the Gods . . . now stands out among the
neighboring cities as much as Father Appennine among the vine-
clad hills, or the Po among the rivers.

> Ariosto, epithalamium for the marriage
> of Alfonso d'Este and Lucrezia Borgia

Qui Parisina fu portata alla morte
Qui volse i chiari occhi ridenti
Lucrezia Borgia regina di eleganze

(Here Parisina was put to death
Here were turned the clear and laughing eyes
Of Lucrezia Borgia, queen of elegance)

> Inscription on the Castello Estense in Ferrara

The journey to Ferrara was hard on everyone. So great was the
pope's concern for his daughter, the Ferrarese envoys told Ercole,
that he demanded daily, even hourly, reports of her journey, and he
required her "to write him with her own hand from every city regarding her health." She must remember to dress warmly and to protect both her face and her person against the snow, Alexander told
Lucrezia in a letter written the day after she left Rome. Now that she
was gone from him forever, he began having second thoughts about
this marriage he had promoted so enthusiastically. He never ever
wanted to hear that Alfonso wasn't according his wife the love and
affection to which she was entitled, he told Cardinal Ippolito. In
fact, nothing would displease him more than the news that Alfonso
was neglecting to sleep with Lucrezia as he had neglected to sleep
with his first wife, Anna Sforza.

His Holiness need have no concern on that score, Ippolito replied.
If Alfonso had not slept with his first wife, it was because she had
claimed more than was her due and had not behaved as a wife
should toward her husband, whereas everyone knew that Lucrezia
was too prudent to make the same mistake. In short, though the cardinal did not say so in so many words, Alfonso had a right to as

many extramarital affairs as he pleased, and he expected his wife to overlook them as the unfortunate Anna apparently had not.

For perhaps the first time in Alexander's life he must have questioned the double standard by which he and every other man lived. But though he may have felt that his daughter deserved better of her husband, he knew that getting Alfonso to sleep with her on a regular basis was all that she could reasonably expect; and he did not protest. Lucrezia, of course, was unaware of his efforts on her behalf and would have felt humiliated had she learned of them.

Just as her father needed to be reassured constantly that all was well with her, so she needed constant reassurance that all was well with the son she had left behind in Rome. Even the cold and self-centered Ippolito was apparently sufficiently moved by her concern to send a messenger to look in on the boy one morning after mass. The messenger had found Rodrigo resting quietly and peacefully; thanks to God as beautiful and healthy as anyone could wish, Ippolito told her in a letter written on the sixteenth of January. If such letters served to assuage her anxiety about her son, nothing could assuage the the anxiety she felt about her first meeting with her new husband. As was only natural, she wished to look her best when they met. But she was not used to the saddle, and she found the journey along the icy roads exhausting. Because she dreaded looking worn-out and bedraggled by the time she reached Ferrara, she insisted upon a number of unscheduled stops: to wash her hair, to rest, to put her wardrobe in order. However, the size of her party and the eagerness of the various towns to ingratiate themselves with the pope by according her a sumptuous welcome made getting the desired rest far from simple.

At Foligno, which she had once governed along with Spoleto, the signors of the city, clad in red silk, were at the gate waiting to escort her to her inn on the piazza. Also at the gate was a float upon which stood a person, whether man or woman is not clear, who represented the Lucrezia of ancient Rome, clutching a dagger to her breast. In rough hexameters, this Roman Lucrece offered to yield her place in the Pantheon of virtue to the new duchess of Ferrara who, she declared, surpassed her in graciousness, modesty, intelligence, and understanding. As if this were not flattery enough for one day, further on was another float at whose summit stood a citizen of Foligno, representing Paris holding the golden apple. He had promised the apple to Venus, "the only one who excelled both Juno and Pallas in beauty," he told Lucrezia, but he now reversed his decision and would present the apple to her since she possessed greater beauty, wisdom, riches, and power than all three goddesses united. When, after accepting the apple, Lucrezia finally reached the piazza, she saw a Turkish galley coming toward her. Upon spotting her, one of the "Turks" standing on the bulwarks informed her that he had been sent by his sultan who, knowing how powerful Lucrezia was in Italy, had decided to surrender everything he had taken from the Christians.

Although Lucrezia was sensitive enough to appreciate the effort that had gone into extravaganzas such as this one even when, as the Ferrarese envoys put it, "the verses were not exactly Petrarchan" and the idea "not very happy," watching them required her to look her best and smile and make small talk with people she scarcely knew in near-zero weather for hours on end, thus adding to her fatigue and to her near panic about how she would look at the time of her crucial first meeting with Alfonso.

After spending an extra day in Foligno to recover from the effects of her reception, Lucrezia and her party continued on through the snow-streaked mountains of Umbria to Gubbio. Two miles outside this most medieval of all the Appennine hill towns, Elisabetta Gonzaga, duchess of Urbino, was awaiting them with a suite of fifty knights and ladies, including her constant companion, Emilia Pia, the sharp-tongued and witty Signora Emilia of Baldassare Castiglione's *The Courtier*. Elisabetta was then thirty, a large woman with a high-shaven forehead and heavy, lidded dark eyes, which gave her long, full face an expression that was at once aloof and melancholy. According to Castiglione, "the modesty and grandeur which ruled over all the acts, words and gestures of the Duchess, in jest and laughter, caused anyone seeing her for the first time to recognize her as a very great lady." And, it should be added, a most unhappy one. She had married Guidobaldo da Montefeltro, duke of Urbino, when both were seventeen. Although all Italy knew that her husband was impotent, Castiglione tells us that Elisabetta "uttered no word on the subject to a single soul," nor would she consider separating from him. Rather she appeared to pride herself on her faithfulness. Given the circumstances of her marriage, it was perhaps only natural that the conversations extolling platonic love that Castiglione reproduced in *The Courtier* should have taken place at her palace. Even if she had not belonged to a ruling class which regarded the Borgias as foreigners and interlopers, it would also be only natural for her to look askance at the thrice-married Lucrezia.

Urbino is not far from Pesaro. Hence it is possible that the two women had first met while Lucrezia was married to Giovanni Sforza. Because of Elisabetta's sympathy for the signor of Pesaro, she no doubt would have preferred not to greet Lucrezia. But Elisabetta's husband, Guidobaldo, was one of the papal vicars whose lands Alexander had threatened to confiscate. By entertaining his daughter and offering to accompany her to Ferrara, Elisabetta hoped to make the pope change his mind. Although Alexander was too shrewd not to realize this, he was also eager for Lucrezia to get to know this famous lady. Thus, he had provided his daughter with a comfortably upholstered sedan chair in which she and Elisabetta could travel side by side. Rather than make them better friends, there were times when this enforced proximity must have proved embarrassing to both; and one of those times was the evening they arrived in Pesaro.

Giovanni Sforza had never been popular with his subjects. Even before Cesare and his army appeared before the walls of Pesaro in October 1500, the Pesarese had turned against their ruler and forced him to flee. Although Lucrezia would have gladly avoided the city, Cesare had insisted that she stop there, and he had given orders that she be received royally. One hundred children clad in his colors were waiting at the gates with olive branches when she arrived. To their repeated shouts of *"Duca! Duca! Lucrezia! Lucrezia!"* the city officials accompanied her and Elisabetta to the palace where eight years before Lucrezia had lived with Giovanni. The memory of all that had happened during those eight years was more than she could cope with. Although she allowed her ladies-in-waiting to take part in the dances and other festivities arranged in her honor, she used the need to wash her hair as an excuse for remaining in her room during her entire stay, and she must have been relieved when on the twenty-second the wedding party left Pesaro. All the cities through which they passed between there and Bologna were under Cesare's rule, and all welcomed her enthusiastically: so enthusiastically, indeed, that at Faenza she announced that she would have to spend an extra day in Imola because she hadn't had a chance to wash her hair in eight days, and this had given her a bad headache. The headache, as she must have known herself, was occasioned not so much by the length of time she had gone without washing her hair as by the realization that they would soon reach Ferrara.

Before that, however, there were two days in Bologna. Like Guidobaldo da Montefeltro of Urbino, Giovanni Bentivoglio of Bologna lived in perpetual fear of being deposed by Cesare. And, like Guidobaldo, he had decided that honoring Lucrezia might be one way to save himself. Hence he personally escorted her around his city. Although Lucrezia was sufficiently impressed by his hospitality to write an enthusiastic letter to her father, whether she was inspecting Bologna's thousand-year-old university or admiring the two leaning towers in the Piazza di Porta Ravignano or dancing at the ball given in her honor, she must have been too concerned about her forthcoming meeting with Alfonso to really enjoy herself.

Ercole had decided that Lucrezia should meet her husband and Isabella at Malalbergo, a village on the canal which in those days ran through the flat and sparsely wooded countryside between Bologna and the Po di Primara outside Ferrara. Alfonso, however, had other ideas. He knew that Lucrezia and Elisabetta would spend the night before the scheduled meeting at Castel Bentivoglio, a villa near the Ferrarese border, and that Annibale Bentivoglio, the husband of Alfonso's illegitimate half sister Lucrezia, would serve as their host. Annibale had just shown the ladies to their quarters and ordered the torches lit when the hereditary prince of Ferrara galloped into the courtyard and asked to be announced to his wife.

She had intended to greet him in a flowing gown of crimson damask satin decorated with beaten gold and a sable-lined velvet cloak. Around her neck there was to have been a string of pearls with a ruby pendant; on her hair a golden headdress. As it was, she scarcely had time to brush the mud and dust of the day's journey off her riding dress and smooth her hair before she was being introduced to him. According to the Ferrarese envoys, she welcomed her husband "with many professions of esteem and most graciously," to all of which Alfonso responded "with great gallantry." Husband and wife remained together "speaking of various matters in a most pleasant manner" for almost two hours "in the presence of everyone." Lucrezia was so delighted with the way their meeting went that as soon as he left, she sat down to write a letter to her father, describing

Alfonso's visit. "The entire people rejoiced as did also the bride and her own following because His Majesty had shown a desire to see her and had received her so well—an indication that she would be accepted and treated still better," said one Ferrarese chronicler. But if Lucrezia had been reassured by her meeting with Alfonso, she still had his sister and his father to face. Early the next morning in her crimson damask gown and sable-lined velvet cloak with the golden headdress on her hair and the heavy pearl necklace around her throat, she entered the boat that would take her to Malalbergo, where Isabella awaited her.

Of the small number of likenesses of Isabella d'Este which are considered authentic, the most famous is the profile sketch by Leonardo, now in the Louvre. The serene and charming young woman in da Vinci's sketch wears a simple low-cut striped bodice that sets off her neck and shoulders to advantage. Her arms are crossed in front of her, and the hand that emerges from one billowing sleeve is fine and delicate, with long slender fingers. Although her nose seems a trifle too long and pointed and her chin too sharp, the directness of her gaze, the beauty of her hands, and her intelligent, alert expression make her unusually attractive. It is easy to recognize in this Isabella the young woman at the sound of whose name "all the muses rose and did reverence," the young woman who was interested in everything from affairs of state to Ariosto's *Orlando* and the latest discoveries in the New World; from fashions in dress to jewelry to the paintings of Mantegna, Bellini, and Leonardo. This is the Isabella who employed a learned Jew to translate the Psalms from the original so that she might satisfy herself that the text was correct; the Isabella who devoted a year to reading Herodotus; the dedicated collector who created for herself a *studiolo* filled with books and paintings and objets d'art where she could receive her friends and listen to poetry and music. It is also the Isabella who at seventeen took her ailing young sister-in-law Elisabetta of Urbino in hand and advised her "to resolve to think of nothing but her health in the first place and her honor and comfort in the second, because in this fickle world we can do nothing else, and those who do not know how to spend their time profitably allow their lives to slip away with much sorrow and little praise." Although she seems a shade too self-possessed, neither her expression nor her bearing gives any hint of the arrogant and frequently unpleasant Isabella who flattered her betters and badgered her inferiors, the imperious young princess who, like the queen in *Snow White*, was determined to be fairest in the land and would brook no competitors. The Italians call such excessive pride of self *superbia*, and Isabella's *superbia*, though not detectable in da Vinci's sketch, often prevailed over her better nature.

Partly because she feared Lucrezia as competition, partly because she was humiliated at seeing her brother forced to accept this bastard daughter of a foreign priest as his wife, Isabella had made up her mind to dislike her even before she met her. Although she rushed to Lucrezia's boat to embrace the bride, the letters she sent to her husband, the Marchese Gianfrancesco, who for political reasons had remained behind in Mantua, made it clear that she had no intention of ever being a friend to her brother's wife. As the boat continued through the flat, desolate countryside to Torre della Fossa where Ercole was awaiting them, the two young women had ample time to take stock of one another. Lucrezia wished only to be friends as she had been friends with Giulia Farnese and Sancha of Aragon. Isabella was determined to repel her every overture. Since Isabella's dear friends, Elisabetta of Urbino and Emilia Pia, were also in the boat, it was easy to turn the conversation to topics that would make Lucrezia feel excluded. It was not so easy to deny her grace and charm. Hence, it may have been to reassure Isabella that another friend, the marchesa of Controne, wrote a letter to Francesco. The bride was "sweet and attractive," she told him, and had many ladies with her including his own sister who was "very handsome," yet Isabella "was universally pronounced, both by our own people and those of the Duchess, to be by far the most beautiful, so much so that if the bride had foreseen this, she would have made her entry by torchlight."

At four o'clock in afternoon the party finally reached Torre della Fossa. Seventy-five crossbowmen in red and white livery were drawn up all in a row to salute the bride when she landed. Next to these crossbowmen stood a group of courtiers gathered around a tall, lame, gray-haired old man with a slit of a mouth and piercing blue eyes who, Lucrezia realized, must be her father-in-law. Ercole had walked "with limping gait" ever since he had been wounded in the foot at the battle of La Mulinella when he was thirty-six. This battle in which he and his troops covered the retreat of their Venetian allies was one of the few times in his life when he displayed real courage. In the portrait by Dosso Dossi now in the Galleria Estense in Modena he seems cold and inaccessible, which, in general, he was. He was also treacherous in politics, sentimental and even silly when it came to religion, and mean and petty in money matters. Nevertheless, he could, on rare occasions, be genuinely kind; and he knew how to be gallant, at least in public. When Lucrezia knelt on the damp grass to kiss his hand, he raised her up and embraced her.

To the merry sound of fifes, trumpets, and tambours, she and her entire retinue then entered the elaborately sculptured and luxurious Venetian galley known as the *Bucentaur* which the dukes of Ferrara customarily used on state occasions. After shaking hands with the foreign ambassadors seated therein, Lucrezia was given a place between the two most important: the ambassador of France and the ambassador of Venice. Isabella was forced to take second place between the ambassador of Venice and the ambassador of Florence. Elisabetta sat between the Florentine and Sienese ambassadors with the ambassador from Lucca nearby. As they talked, Isabella could hear her father and Alfonso laughing at the antics of Lucrezia's Spanish clowns who, Isabella told her husband, "paid the bride all manner of compliments." Finding it intolerable to listen to so much praise of her new sister-in-law, Isabella resolved to tip the clowns so that next time they would sing her praises as well.

At five o'clock "amid great cheering and the sound of trumpets and guns," the party reached the *casale*, or "country house," of Ercole's brother Alberto, where Lucrezia would spend the night. Waiting for her on the shore was Ercole's illegitimate daughter, Lucrezia Bentivoglio, "with a great company of ladies." After Lucrezia had greeted these ladies, Alfonso's seneschal introduced her to Madonna Teodorina who was to be her chief lady-in-waiting. Teodorina was accompanied by twelve other young Ferrarese noblewomen in crimson satin *camorras* and black velvet mantles lined with black lamb, who would also serve the new duchess. After greeting them, Lucrezia was next taken to see five carriages that were a gift from her father-in-law. One was hung with gold brocade and led by four horses, each, according to Isabella, "worth fifty ducats." A second carriage was hung with red velvet and led by roan horses; the other three were hung with purple satin and led by horses of different colors. So that Lucrezia and her party would be sure to get to Malalbergo on time, Ercole's envoy had awakened them before dawn.

Hence, she must have been very tired by then. Nevertheless, she managed to smile and to appear interested in everyone and everything until finally she was escorted to her apartment and left alone with her dear Adriana de Mila and the Spanish ladies-in-waiting she had brought from Rome. There wasn't much time for sorting out their impressions of the long, crowded day, for all needed to get some rest in preparation for the morrow when they would follow Lucrezia in the great procession that would mark her triumphal entrance into Ferrara.

No procession in which Lucrezia ever took part was as talked about or as brilliant as this one. As early as January 22, Isabella's correspondent in Ferrara had told her that seamstresses and tailors and poets and stage designers were working around the clock to get everything ready on time. From all over Italy, throngs of the curious poured into the city for the occasion, not to mention the hundreds of noblemen and noblewomen invited by Ercole, the bishops and other churchmen sent by the pope, and the ambassadors sent by the various powers. "All these gentlemen are busy preparing sumptuous dresses and gold chains, but the attire of the women will be splendid beyond words," Isabella wrote her husband. Although Lucrezia had none of Isabella's *superbia*, she knew that as the central figure she was expected to outshine them all. When Ercole and Alfonso came to fetch her at two o'clock that Wednesday afternoon, she was wearing a *camorra* of gold cloth with purple satin stripes and wide, flowing sleeves lined with ermine and an ermine-lined cloak of gold-embroidered cloth of gold open on one side. Around her neck gleamed the diamond and ruby necklace given her by her father-in-law. One of the two pearl caps he had given her rested atop her long golden hair.

The procession was to set out from Castel Tedaldo, a fortress which in those days stood on the banks of the Po across from Ferrara and was connected with the city by a pontoon bridge. First to cross the bridge were the seventy-five crossbowmen in red and white livery who had greeted her at Torre della Fossa the previous day. With them went three captains and eighty trumpeters, including six in cloth of gold and purple and white uniforms who had been sent by Cesare. Behind these trumpeters came the nobles and gentlemen of Ferrara. Isabella, who as her father's official hostess, watched the procession from a window of the ducal palace, later told her husband that seventy of these gentlemen wore chains worth at least 500 ducats each, and a few wore chains worth between 800 and 1,200 ducats. Following in the wake of these glittering and expensively dressed gentlemen was an equally well-dressed group belonging to the suite of Elisabetta of Urbino. After them came the bridegroom riding alongside his brother-in-law, Annibale Bentivoglio. Alfonso's great bay was caparisoned in purple velvet embossed with gold. He himself wore a suit of gray velvet covered with scales of beaten gold, which his price-conscious sister estimated was worth at least 6,000 ducats, and a black cap trimmed with white feathers and gold lace. His eight squires, in suits of gold brocade and purple velvet and red and purple hose, were almost as magnificently attired as he was. Lucrezia's gentlemen, who followed next, seemed drab by comparison. The twenty Spaniards among them were all dressed in black, and according to Isabella, only twelve of the entire company wore gold chains "and these not all large ones." After these dull fellows came five bishops and then the foreign ambassadors walking two by two—the Venetians in long mantles of crimson satin, the Romans in cloth of gold lined with crimson satin. When the last of their number had passed, six drummers and two jesters, wearing suits of variegated brocade, announced the approach of the bride.

Only those very close to her could see her face; to the others she must have seemed a mass of gold and jewels and ermine as she came into view mounted on a dappled gray horse splendidly caparisoned in crimson trappings embroidered with gold and a gilded saddle and bridle. Four professors from the University of Ferrara held a crimson satin canopy over her golden head. Eight of Alfonso's grooms in purple and yellow vests and hose attended her horse. At her side, but not under the canopy, rode the French ambassador summoned to his privileged place by the bride herself in recognition of all his king had done to promote her marriage. As she rode slowly past one of the churches just over the bridge, she was saluted by a number of blunderbusses fired from a decorated platform. The noise so terrified her horse that he reared and threw her. Obviously unhurt, she picked herself up and mounted a roan mule provided by her father-in-law. The little laugh with which she did this was so merry and unpretentious that it captivated her audience. "She is very beautiful, but her charm of manner is still more striking," one of Ercole's envoys had told him after meeting her in Rome, and all Ferrara seemed to agree.

"She pleased the people so greatly that they are perfectly satisfied with her, and they look to her Majesty for protection and good government," said one of those who saw her that afternoon.

After she had settled herself on her new mount, one of the grooms took the dappled gray by his gilded reins, and the procession continued on its way through the crowded, tumultuous streets to the cathedral. In addition to the customary triumphal arches and tableaux, including one with Europa mounted on the red bull of the house of Borgia, scaffolds of wood and paper and painted cloth had been erected at various points along the line of march. From these, garlanded actors recited "verses and panegyrics in honor of the bride and groom and the Pope." As Lucrezia had been doing during all the numerous celebrations that had marked her twenty-six-day journey from Rome, she smiled constantly, turning now this way, now that to acknowledge the praise of the actors and the cheers of the crowd. Her father-in-law rode behind her dressed in a purple velvet suit. Alongside him rode Elisabetta of Urbino in a black velvet robe adorned with triangles of beaten gold that were intended to represent various astrological symbols. They were followed by two of Lucrezia's ladies, also in black velvet, and by Adriana de Mila, whom Isabella described as "a widowed relative of the Pope."

After these three came twenty court carriages with covers of gold brocade and silk carrying various gentlewomen, some from Ferrara, some from Rome and Bologna; then twelve mares bearing the twelve young Ferrarese noblewomen who were to be Lucrezia's ladies-in-waiting; and finally seventy-two mules, two with elaborately worked silver and black trappings, the rest with velvet blankets, and all seventy-two of them carrying the bride's belongings.

Until Ercole's reign, Ferrara had been a town of cramped little houses and narrow winding streets, which began at the Po and ended at the great, looming, quadrangular red hulk of the fourteenth-century Castello Estense, built by the Marchese Niccolò II as a fortress to protect him and his family against popular uprisings. A covered passageway and a series of arcades in which fish was sometimes sold joined the castle with the ducal palace to the west. Facing the palace across the vast Piazza del Duomo stood the twelfth-century romanesque cathedral of San Giorgio. Running due north from the *castello* "wide and straight as a die" to the Wall of the Angels was the palace-lined Corso Ercole d'Este, the first really modern street in Europe. This famous avenue formed the heart of the Addizione Erculea or Terra Nuova, which the duke had added to the city to accommodate its growing population. Although Lucrezia had no doubt heard of the imposing dwellings, the fine new churches, and the leafy green parks that graced the new neighborhood, she had no opportunity to see them that Wednesday, for the wedding procession was confined to the medieval portion of the city south of the *castello*: the Via Grande along the banks of the Po, the arcaded Via di Santo Stefano, with its gloomy buildings where the sun seldom penetrated, and the Via del Paradiso, which would later house the university.

When, over two hours after leaving Castel Tedaldo, the procession finally reached the cathedral, two acrobats slid down from ropes attached to the high windows of opposing towers on the Piazza del Duomo "so quickly that the people thought it was a miracle." No sooner did they touch the ground than the doors of all the subterranean prisons in the neighboring *castello* were thrown open and the prisoners they held allowed to go free. Some had been imprisoned because they could not pay their taxes, some because they had blasphemed, others for more serious crimes. What all these forgotten men did after staggering out into the crowded torchlit city no one says. "So full was the piazza in every part," according to one observer, "that if a grain of millet had fallen to earth, it would not have reached the ground."

Directly across from the cathedral at the far end of the vast piazza there was then, and still is now, a rounded archway known as the Volta del Cavallo, flanked by a smaller arch supporting an equestrian statue of Niccolò III and a marble column supporting a seated statue of Niccolò's son Borso. It was of these statues that Ariosto wrote:

> *d'ogni cinque o sei mesi*
> *stato uno a passegiar fra il Duomo*
> *e le due statue dei Marchesi miei*

> (*Every five or six months*
> *I was wont to stroll between the Duomo*
> *and the statues of my two marchesi.*)

But when the enormous crowd moved back to allow Lucrezia and her retinue to pass through the Volta del Cavallo into the courtyard of the ducal palce that cold February evening, she must have been too filled with the strangeness and the excitement of the moment to even notice the two marchesi.

Immediately to the right of the arch was a covered marble staircase. As soon as Lucrezia's mule reached this staircase, the professors of the university lowered the canopy they had been holding over the bride's head for almost three hours, and the grooms helped her to dismount. Isabella was waiting for her at the head of the stairs. Like all the Estense, the marchesa of Mantua was an accomplished musician. To emphasize her interest in music, she had decided to appear in a gown of cloth of gold embroidered with musical notes, which she had designed herself. It proved an excellent choice, for it served to divert attention from the bride to her hostess when Isabella escorted Lucrezia into the great hall adorned with priceless hangings of silver and gold, where the members of Ercole's court were waiting to be introduced to her. Before the introductions could take place, however, protocol demanded that there be some sort of welcoming speech or poem.

Among those who had written pieces in honor of the new duchess was the twenty-seven-year-old Lodovico Ariosto. The poet's father had died only a short time before and Ariosto was desperately in need of a job that would give him time to write and also provide sufficient income for him to support his younger brothers and sisters. Apparently he hoped that Lucrezia would be sufficiently impressed by the epithalamium he had composed in her honor to engage him as her secretary. But as usual when he tried to flatter the great, Ariosto went too far. Not content with assuring her that there was nothing of which Ferrara boasted so much as receiving her as its mistress, the poet addressed the thrice-married bride as *pulcherrissima virga* ("most beauteous virgin").

Just when Ariosto read his poem to her is not clear. However, Pellegrino Prisciano, the elderly court astrologer and librarian who delivered the welcoming speech that night, was every bit as inept in his choice of supposedly flattering allusions and considerably more prolix. Prisciano began with the marriage of the elements, went on to a discussion of the Egyptians and Greeks, and then threw in a few quotations from Aristotle before getting around to the Borgias. After praising Lucrezia's great Uncle Calixtus III, he called attention to the accomplishments of her father, whom he likened to Saint Peter.

"Peter," he told his astonished audience, "had a very beautiful daughter Petronilla; Alexander has Lucrezia radiant with all grace and virtue. O unfathomable mystery of God, O men most blest. . . . " Alexander, whose tolerance of palaver was relatively limited, would probably have cut him short long before then, but Ercole appeared to derive real pleasure from the long and tedious glorification of the house of Este which followed.

When Prisciano had finished speaking, a by then thoroughly bemused Lucrezia was introduced to the ladies and gentlemen of her father-in-law's court. After the last nobleman had paid his respects, Isabella, Elisabetta, and all the ambassadors accompanied her to the bridal chamber. It was customary in Ferrara for the wedding guests to gather around the nuptial bed to tease the newly married pair in a ceremony known as the *serenata*. But Lucrezia or perhaps Adriana or some other member of her suite had let it be known that she wanted this ceremony omitted. When to the blare of trumpets she entered the bridal chamber, the doors closed behind her leaving everyone but her husband outside.

Nevertheless, those who wished to know what happened had their ways of finding out. "Last night our son the illustrious Don Alfonso and she [Lucrezia] 'kept company,' and we are convinced that both parties were thoroughly satisfied," said Ercole in a letter to the pope. Isabella was rather more explicit. "From what I have been given to understand," she told her husband, "Don Alfonso took her three times." Annoyed because not only the *serenata* had been omitted, but also the *mattinata* by which in Ferrara it was customary to salute the couple the following morning, Isabella described the nuptials as "very cold." When Lucrezia did not leave her bed until almost noon, Isabella's friend the marchesa of Controne decided that the "strenuous encounter" with a new spouse coming as it did after a long journey had caused the bride to sleep badly.

That she also felt humiliated by this first encounter with her husband is more than likely. Alfonso's long association with prostitutes had accustomed him to think only of his own pleasure. He had, moreover, not wished to marry his wife. Although he must have been pleasantly surprised by her graciousness, in the back of his mind there may still have lurked the suspicion that she was as much of a whore as his usual bed-mates. If he was an efficient lover, his subsequent behavior makes it clear that his approach to his wife was neither tender nor romantic. And what must have made his brusque and perfunctory lovemaking all the more unpalatable was the memory of how differently her second husband had treated her. Lucrezia would not have to say anything to Adriana de Mila or Angela Borgia or the others who knew her so well for them to sense her disappointment. Sensing it and realizing how difficult it was going to be for her to face all those curious strangers, Adriana would advise her to take her time about getting up and dressing.

When finally she made her appearance in a cloth of gold dress of French design and a pearl-embroidered cloak of dark satin bordered with little stripes of beaten gold, she was her usual good-humored and gracious self. "She is very gay and lighthearted and is always laughing," said one guest after seeing her alight from the dais in the great hall to dance Roman and Spanish dances "with rare grace." Although this guest did not find her "regularly beautiful," he thought "the whiteness of her skin together with her gentleness and winning manners" rendered her "most attractive."

As soon as the dancing was over, Ercole brought in 110 actors clad in togas and tunics of finest silk and of camlet—a rich-looking cloth made of goat's hair and silk. Where they could have stationed themselves remains a mystery, for according to Isabella the hall was so crowded there was scarcely room to dance. Nevertheless, the actors not only managed to get in, they also exhibited their costumes, for Ercole wished it understood that "the dresses had been made on purpose and that those which were worn in one comedy would not have to be used again."

After the leader of the actors, who appeared in the character of Plautus, explained the arguments of the five comedies which would be presented on successive evenings, the guests followed him through a covered passage to the great hall of the neighboring Palazzo Ragione, which had been transformed into an amphitheater capable of seating five thousand persons. Both the steps and the ceiling of this amphitheater were draped with green, red, and white cloth. Shields bearing the papal arms, the bull of the Borgias, the black and white eagles of the Estense, and the lilies of France respectively, hung from the wooden beams of the roof, and the places reserved for the duke and his party were covered with cloth of gold and protected by a golden canopy. Those who occupied them wore so much brocade and gold embroidery that, in the opinion of one spectator, they made the hall look "like a gold mine," and even the less important members of the audience wore silks and satins.

When the *Epidicus*, the play presented that evening, finally began, "so many chandeliers and candlesticks illuminated the stage that everything was seen in the fullest detail; the recitation took place in great silence and no one was sorry to go late to dinner." Or at least that was the verdict of the majority. Isabella, on the the other hand, thought "neither the verses nor the voices" very good, but she did think the *Moresche* dances between the acts were danced "with great spirit." The last was danced by Moors with lighted torches in their hands and was a fine sight. "It was not over till past ten, and then everyone went home to supper."

Eating was a serious business in Ferrara. For the wedding festivities, Ercole's chefs had prepared over fourteen bushels of preserves and set aside more than three hundred head of beef and as many large cheeses, as well as fifteen thousand chickens, ducks, and geese and so much game that they couldn't store it all and had to throw some of it in the river. The city's sumptuary laws limited the number of courses at an ordinary banquet to two soups, three roast meats, three boiled meats, one poultry dish, two tarts and meat pastries served between the courses, not to mention the wine and the salami for which Ferrara was famous. On special occasions, of which Lucrezia's wedding was assuredly one, confections and candied fruits were also permitted, and castles of spun sugar were placed upon the tables.

Although the supper did not begun until after ten and must have lasted until well past midnight, Isabella refused to believe that it was just fatigue that kept the bride in her room until late the following afternoon. "Madonna Lucrezia chooses to spend all these hours in dressing so that she may outshine the Duchess of Urbino and myself in the eyes of the world," Isabella told her husband.

While the guests were waiting for Lucrezia to appear, Ercole took a number of them, including the French ambassador, to visit Suor Lucia. After allowing those who wished to touch the bleeding stigmata on her body with their gloved fingers, Lucia graciously answered their questions. When they were about to leave, she gave one of the rags she used to staunch her wounds to the French ambassador. Since Lucia had no reason to favor him over his fellows, it seems obvious that Ercole had asked her to do this.

Because it was a Friday, there was no dancing when the guests returned to the palace. Instead, they were treated to a four-and-one-half-hour performance of the *Bacchides*, which, if we believe Isabella, was "long and tiresome," and brought "nothing but yawns and complaints from the spectators."

On Saturday afternoon, the French ambassador returned to the palace with the gifts sent by his king. There was a rosary of musk-filled gold beads for the bride, an expensive chain for her cousin Angela, and gold shields bearing enamelled portraits of Saint Francis for Ercole and Ferrante. Alfonso, too, received a gold shield, but instead of a portrait of Saint Francis, it bore a portrait of the Magdalen, because, said the ambassador, the king wished it known that the bridegroom had chosen a wife who was "a madonna of valor and gentle manners like the Magdalen." Such sly taunts were, of course, typical of Louis, who knew he was powerful enough to get away with them. So eager, in fact, was everyone to be in his good graces that his ambassador was the most sought-after man at the wedding.

When the ambassador had arrived in Ferrara at the end of January, Isabella had invited him to her apartment, and she and her ladies had spent three hours conversing with him. Since there was to be no play on the Saturday that he brought the wedding gifts to the palace, she invited him to dine with her that evening. "Because he could not refuse her invitation, he accepted it," said one of those with him. Although there can be no question that Isabella's principal reason for inviting the ambassador was to get him to put in a good word for Mantua with his king, she also relished the opportunity the supper party gave her to occupy stage center without competition from Lucrezia, and she wore a splendid gown of silver and white for the occasion. When the meal was over, she allowed her guests to "persuade" her to accompany herself on the lute. Later, she invited the ambassador into her private rooms where, in the presence of two of her ladies-in-waiting, she discussed the political situation with him. When it was time for him to leave, she slowly peeled off her long, scented gloves and offered them to him. Overwhelmed, or at least pretending to be overwhelmed, the ambassador told her that because the gloves had touched her hands, they were even more precious to him than the bloody rag given him by Suor Lucia and he would preserve them in a reliquary until the end of his days.

Having made such an important conquest, Isabella could not wait to flaunt him. That Sunday there was dancing in the Sala Grande for two hours, after which the guests filed into the amphitheater for a performance of the *Miles Gloriosus*. This tale of the braggart warrior who believes that he is irresistible to women is considered one of Plautus's best, but either because Ercole's guests were exhausted after two hours of dancing or because the play had been badly translated, they were so restless and talkative that the actors had to shout to be heard. Lucrezia, as befitted the guest of honor, seems to have tried her best to give the play her undivided attention. Isabella, on the other hand, showed her contempt for the production by turning away from the stage to laugh and chat with "a great foreign personality" who was obviously none other than the French ambassador. Finally, she ordered sweetmeats to be brought and shared them with her companion.

To the members of Lucrezia's party, her sister-in-law's behavior seemed a deliberate slap in the face of the bride in whose honor the play was being given, and they resolved to tell the pope about it as soon as they got back to Rome. That Isabella's behavior could also be interpreted as an insult to her father, who had lavished much care and money upon these productions, did not appear to disturb her. Although she found nothing to criticize in the production of the *Asinaria* that Monday, she made up for this lapse by her carping attitude toward the *Casina*. This play, which Ercole had reserved for the last day of the wedding festivities, derives a good part of its humor from the physiological peculiarities of the male organ. Although fairly predictable, the misunderstandings that arise when an elderly lecher finds in his bed a man disguised as the slave girl the old fellow has been lusting after, are frequently hilarious. Moreover, it is difficult to see how anyone with an ounce of sophistication could find them shocking, let alone the worldly marchesa of Mantua, who on at least one occasion would sit complacently by while one of her ladies-in-waiting rolled on the floor with an overeager lover. All the same, Isabella pronounced the comedy "lascivious and immoral beyond words" and would not allow any of her maidens to see it. Although as her father's hostess she felt obliged to put in an appearance, she made a point of looking pained by what was happening on stage. Lucrezia and her ladies-in-waiting, on the other hand, laughed heartily at the goings on, which, of course, gave Isabella an opportunity to look even more pained.

In fact, the only entertainment that Isabella allowed herself to enjoy that evening were the musical interludes between the acts. For the first of these, a globe fell upon the stage. From it the Virtues emerged to sing a quartet in honor of the bride. Alfonso and his illegitimate half brother, Don Giulio, then did a war dance for the spectators. Because of Alfonso's interest in cannons, a war dance seemed very much in character for him, but Lucrezia must have been genuinely surprised to see her gruff and sullen spouse return to the stage at the end of the play to join five other musicians in a performance of a concerto for six viols.

The next day, which was Ash Wednesday, the guests started preparing to leave. Before they left, however, Ercole had one last spectacle in store for them. While all Ferrara crowded into the Piazza del Duomo to watch, a blindfolded young acrobat with weights attached to his feet began walking along a rope strung across the great square from the tower of the bishop's palace to one of the high windows of the ducal palace. Moving from side to side as casually as if he were on terra firma, the acrobat pretended to fall and remained attached to the rope by one foot, then righted himself and continued to meander from side to side. Upon reaching the ducal palace, he returned to the bishop's palace via another rope, pausing to dance a *moresca* on the way.

Soon after his performance ended, the Venetian ambassadors went to Lucrezia's apartment to say their goodbyes. Finding Isabella and Elisabetta with her, the ambassadors made a speech in praise of Isabella's husband and the services he had rendered the state of Venice. Isabella's secretary who, like all those who served her, knew that she expected him constantly to sing her praises, told her husband that she replied to this speech "with as much elegance as if she had been a consummate orator" so that the "amazed" Venetians "confessed themselves her slaves." The ambassadors then turned to the duchess of Urbino who "also replied discreetly. Last of all, Donna Lucrezia spoke." Although, said the secretary, she had had more husbands than either of the others, "she could not attain by a long way to the wisdom of their answers." The link between the number of spouses a lady had had and her speech-making ability was admittedly tenuous, but if the marchese of Mantua showed the secretary's letter to his wife, Isabella would find the gibe at Lucrezia to her liking. And that, after all, was what counted.

Faced with Isabella's nastiness and Alfonso's indifference, it was only natural for Lucrezia to cling to Adriana de Mila and the other women she had brought with her from Rome. But in seeking to keep them in Ferrara after the wedding festivities had ended, she reckoned without her father-in-law. "These women by remaining cause a large number of other persons, men as well as women, to linger . . . and it is a great burden and causes heavy expense," the duke complained to his ambassador in Rome on February 14. Since the wedding had already cost 25,000 ducats, Alexander must be told in no uncertain terms that Ercole could stand no further expense, and "the Pope should therefore direct the ladies to return."

Soon after instructing his ambassador to deliver this message, Ercole decided that there was no point in waiting for the pope to act. On February 17, he sent Lucrezia a list of the 146 ladies-in-waiting, servants, and other attendants who would henceforth comprise her household. Prominent on the list were Teodora Angelini and the twelve young Ferrarese ladies-in-waiting who had been presented to Lucrezia when she first arrived in the city. Those not on the list, and this included most of the people who had made the trip from Rome with her, would be required to leave Ferrara by the end of the month. Lucrezia could have tried to fight the directive or at least have sought a compromise, but because she was still eager to please her father-in-law, she not only accepted the list he had given her but also went out of her way to be kind to her Ferrarese attendants. On February 18, Teodora Angelini, who only a few days before had complained to Isabella that she and her women felt like interlopers, wrote that Lucrezia was now seeing everyone willingly and had invited her (Teodora) to eat at her table during Lent, especially when fish was being served.

By then Lucrezia had been given an apartment in the Castello Estense. Although she must have liked the hanging garden outside her windows, the color scheme of her new apartment did not please her, nor was she happy with the indifferent housekeeping—the dust in the corners, the holes in the expensive satin draperies, the ragged sheets, and the lumpy straw mattresses that testified to her father-in-law's relentless penny-pinching; and she resolved to change all this as soon as possible. It was customary then for a princess who married into a reigning house to be allotted an annual stipend, or *appannaggio*. With this she fed and clothed herself and the members of her court, provided for the upkeep of her horses and carriages, gave alms, and entertained. The larger the dowry she had brought her spouse, the larger her *appannaggio*. Hence Lucrezia must have felt confident that she would have more than enough to redo her apartment. But once again she reckoned without her father-in-law.

Either because Ercole wished to make up for his son's indifference or because, as he had written the pope, he "was so pleased by the virtues and good qualities" he had found in his new daughter-in-law, the duke's carriage could be seen in the courtyard of the *castello* almost daily, waiting to pick her up for an outing. On February 26, there was a trip to the palace of Belfiore to watch a hunt. During the first week of March, there were tours of Ercole's favorite churches and monasteries. But much though Ercole might enjoy his daughter-in-law's company, he had no intention of allowing this to influence him when he drew up his budget. He was prepared to give her an *appannaggio* of 8,000 ducats a year, he told her. She could not manage on less than 12,000 and besides she was under the impression that the size of her dowry entitled her to that amount, Lucrezia replied. Whereupon Ercole asked Isabella how much she received. She managed very well on 8,000, Isabella replied. The praise of her own economy and that of her servants which she included in her letter to her father would have been more convincing if she had not just had to ask him for money because the cost of clothing herself and her maids of honor for Lucrezia's wedding had exceeded the allowance given her by her husband. Although Lucrezia may not have known this, she could be expected to know that the dowry Isabella had brought to Mantua was less than a third the size of the dowry she had brought to Ferrara. Hence Ercole, with a great show of magnanimity, offered to split the difference and give his daughter-in-law 10,000 ducats a year.

She had no head for bargaining, Lucrezia replied. She had been so accommodating about everything else her father-in-law had asked of her, including the matter of her retinue, that he must have been surprised by this reply. By then, however, it was obvious that Lucrezia realized that every time she made a concession in the hope of pleasing him, she paved the way for him to demand still further concessions. Since, moreover, even the household allowances given lower-class women were based on their dowries, she was genuinely outraged by Ercole's meanness. Her battle with the parsimonious old duke would have been less of a strain if she could have counted on her husband for support. But save for conscientiously visiting her bed, Alfonso showed no interest in her whatsoever. Nor did his attitude change when in the early part of March she announced that she was pregnant. By Easter week the loneliness of her situation and her resentment at the way she was being treated were more than she could handle. As she had done once before when faced with a life crisis, she sought refuge in the cloister.

The little red-brick church of Corpus Domini and the adjoining convent of the Clarisse, or Poor Claires, is on Via Pergolata, in one of the older sections of the city. When the daughters of noble houses wished to become nuns, it was to the Clarisse that they turned. And when their lay sisters needed to escape the pressures of the outside world, they, too, turned to Corpus Domini. Lucrezia had first visited the convent during one of her excursions with Ercole. When she came back to stay on Holy Wednesday it was because she needed a respite from her battle with her father-in-law. With her condition she may also have felt she needed a respite from her husband's impersonal lovemaking. But if her stay at Corpus Domini provided a temporary escape, it did not change anything. When she returned to her apartment in the Castello Estense the following week, Ercole was still insisting that she accept an allowance of 10,000 ducats, Alfonso was still indifferent, and Isabella was still unfriendly.

Feeling herself powerless to strike out against these cold, self-centered Estense, Lucrezia vented her anger on the Ferrarese in her service. Besides dismissing a number of the gentlemen that her father-in-law had recommended to her, she made it clear to Teodora Angelini and her other Ferrarese ladies-in-waiting that she would be perfectly happy not to see their faces "until Judgment Day." Although Adriana de Mila left for Rome in April and most of the ladies-in-waiting Lucrezia had brought with her from Rome were also gone, she had managed to keep Angela Borgia, a Sienese girl named Niccola, and a few others from her original retinue with her, and it was with these young women that she passed her days.

During the early months of pregnancy, a certain amount of lethargy is fairly common. Feeling no particular need to combat this lethargy, Lucrezia would have one of her maids prepare an aromatic bath for her and invite Niccola to share it. After spending the better part of the afternoon splashing about in the hot, scented water, the two would stretch out on cushions. Clad only in their shifts, with their damp hair confined by nets of gold mesh, they would while away the hours until supper, burning sweet incense in the braziers the maids set out for them. Since Niccola was being courted by Don Ferrante, it may have been of her relationship with the young prince that she and Lucrezia spoke during those langorous afternoons. According to El Prete, Niccola and Ferrante were "going strong but not sinning." To give them less opportunity to sin, Ercole had forbidden his son to visit Lucrezia's quarters more than twice a week. Besides Ferrante and his half brother Giulio, who was enamoured of Angela, the only other visitor Lucrezia received regularly that spring, with the exception of her husband and the duke, was the poet Ercole Strozzi.

Ercole Strozzi came from a well-to-do and noble Guelph family that had been expelled from Florence in the fourteenth century. His father, Tito Vespasiano Strozzi, belonged to the circle of intellectuals who had surrounded Leonello d'Este. Later, Tito became a judge of whom it was said that he and his sons were "universally detested . . . for their devouring of the people and their cruel oppression." Of these sons Ercole was the most talented and the most conniving. He might be unpopular with the common people, but he knew everybody worth knowing, from Isabella and Alfonso to Ariosto. At the age of thirty, he was already considered a better poet and Latinist than his father, and in spite of a congenital defect which made it necessary for him to walk with a crutch, he was extremely attractive to women.

At around the time that Lucrezia came to Ferrara, Ercole Strozzi set his heart on becoming a cardinal; and it may have been because he thought Lucrezia would be able to help him that he commenced making himself agreeable to her. It could not have taken him long to realize that the new duchess felt snubbed and isolated and in need of friends. Strozzi loved fine clothes and good perfumes, but like many noblemen, his tastes were too expensive for his pocketbook. By offering to help and befriend this wealthy young woman it must have seemed to him that he would also be helping himself. Whether he dropped the idea of becoming a cardinal in order to devote himself to Lucrezia or whether he devoted himself to Lucrezia because becoming a cardinal proved more difficult than he had supposed is not clear. In any case he soon found ways to be of use to her.

Because he was having an affair with a Venetian gentlewoman, he spent as much time in Venice as he did in Ferrara. The shops of Venice were noted for their beautiful and exotic goods. All that was newest and most elegant was to be found on the Rialto. As the duchess of Ferrara, Lucrezia was expected to be a leader of fashion, and Strozzi's taste was impeccable. When next he set out for Venice he offered to shop for her. That he would receive a commission for his efforts was taken for granted. Since Lucrezia had very little available cash until she settled the matter of her *appannaggio,* he suggested that she buy on credit. Wild shopping sprees are one way to alleviate boredom and depression. Prodded by Strozzi, Lucrezia ordered all sorts of expensive items that she could have just as easily done without. Later, she would say that she had spent 10,000 ducats on a hand-carved wooden cradle and a layette for her baby, not to mention the hundreds of ducats she spent on silks and satins and camlet from which to fashion new outfits for herself and her ladies-in-waiting.

Although her father did not feel he had the right to order Ercole to grant her the 12,000-ducat *appannaggio* that would enable her to pay for all this, he did put considerable presssure on the duke's ambassador in Rome. The pope had been so relieved to learn that Alfonso slept with his wife that he had willingly overlooked the young husband's persistent philandering. "During the day he goes where he likes, as he is young, and in doing this he does right," Alexander told the Ferrarese ambassador. But the pope was nowhere near as philosophical about the tales Lucrezia's attendants brought back from Ferrara. Was it true that Ercole had "chased these attendants away?" And what was this about Lucrezia having no money to spend and being forced to pawn her jewels in order to buy presents for her attendants before they left, he asked the Ferrarese ambassador. Nor did the ambassador's assurances that everyone in Lucrezia's new family loved her dearly carry much weight, for men such as L'Unico Aretino and his circle were all talking of Isabella's rudeness, and the pope had Lucrezia's letters describing her difficulties with Ercole. Finally, in answer to her repeated complaints, Alexander sent his daughter a brief in which he supported her demand for an allowance of 12,000 ducats. As he must have known she would, Lucrezia gave the brief to one of Ercole's gentlemen with instructions to show it to the duke. He would not change his mind about the *appannaggio* if God himself came to see him, was Ercole's only comment. In his exasperatingly detached manner he continued to send his carriage for his daughter-in-law and to visit her apartment regularly, until one day, unable to stand his chitchat any longer, Lucrezia told Ercole that rather than visit her, he would have done better to have stayed home "to settle his accounts."

While all this was going on, Louis XII decided to show his appreciation for the readiness with which Ercole had accepted Lucrezia into his family by giving the duke the castle of Cotignola, a castle, incidentally, which had originally belonged to Giovanni Sforza. To thank the king, Ercole announced that he would send Alfonso and his brother Sigismundo to France to accompany Louis on a projected trip to Milan.

With Alfonso gone, Lucrezia could see no reason to remain in her dingy apartment in the *castello*. As soon as she heard of her husband's proposed trip, she asked Ercole's permission to remove her court to Belfiore where, it seemed to her, she would be more comfortable. Because the duke was having work done on this palace and the rooms were filled with painters and other artisans, he refused. According to El Prete, who continued to keep Isabella informed of her new sister-in-law's every move, Lucrezia did not take the duke's refusal very well. In the end, however, she had to agree to go to the palace of Belriguardo instead.

Like the palace of Belfiore and the famous Palazzo Schifanoia, Belriguardo was one of the *luoghi di delizie*, or "pleasure palaces," of the Estense, a great sprawling place upon which it seemed to one visitor "a mountain of gold" had been spent. Though only nine miles from Ferrara, it gave the impression of being a world unto itself. Within its walls seven princes and their retinues could be accommodated comfortably at the same time. Its stables had room for five hundred horses; its courtyard was "as big as a meadow"; its fishing pond as big as a lake; one could spend whole days exploring its innumerable frescoed rooms and colonnaded secret gardens. Although one of the reasons Lucrezia had gone to Belriguardo was to escape her Estense relatives, the ever-resourceful El Prete found ways to keep an eye on her during her stay . She was attended by "that cripple of a Strozzi" and would receive no one else, he told Isabella. When her father-in-law's nephew the poet Niccolò da Correggio came to call, she had the servants tell him that she was sleeping and could not be disturbed.

It must have been while Lucrezia was at Belriguardo that she learned that Cesare had taken Urbino. Supposedly her brother and his army had set out from Rome intending to move against the neighboring town of Camerino. However, as Cesare explained in a letter to the pope, the realization that Guidobaldo of Urbino was conspiring with the lord of Camerino and sending him supplies made him decide to attack Urbino first. Although a letter the Ferrarese ambassador wrote Ercole appears to bear out Cesare's accusations against Guidobaldo, the duke of Urbino described the surprise attack upon his duchy as *"il gran tradimento,"* "the great betrayal." In order not to be taken prisoner, he fled to Mantua "with only his shirt and his doublet." Machiavelli was filled with admiration for the masterful way Cesare engineered the entire maneuver, but Lucrezia appeared to share the more prevalent opinion that her brother had betrayed a friend. She would gladly give 25,000 ducats not to have known Elisabetta of Urbino so as not to have to blush when she met her, she declared. And even so unfriendly an observer as Isabella's correspondent in Ferrara believed that she meant what she said.

Although Isabella also was sincerely upset by what had occurred, she was not so upset that she forgot her own interests. Some time before the attack on Urbino, Cesare had given Guidobaldo a marble torso of Venus and a sleeping Cupid. The Venus was of ancient origin; the Cupid an early work by Michelangelo, who was then just beginning to make a name for himself in Rome. In Isabella's opinion no other modern work could equal it. After Guidobaldo was driven from Urbino, she determined to get it and the Venus for her collection. And once she had succeeded in getting them, she would never consider restoring them to their rightful owner.

Lucrezia seems to have left Belriguardo soon after the capture of Urbino, but she was less than overjoyed at the prospect of being reunited with her father-in-law. Upon learning that he planned to meet her at a certain point along the road, she made it her business to keep him waiting. When soon afterward he asked her to take part in one of the religious processions he was constantly organizing, she did not show up until it was over.

May had been cold and wet. During Lucrezia's first week at Belriguardo, it had rained incessantly for four consecutive days and nights. The rain caused rivers to overflow, dams to burst, and crops to fail. It also filled every swamp in the vast, marshy plain that surrounds Ferrara. By the time Lucrezia returned to the city, swarms of mosquitoes hovered in the soggy air. Besides being a masterpiece of onomatopeia, *zanzara*, the Italian word for "mosquito,"rhymes with Ferrara, a coincidence that delighted the versifiers of the fifteenth century. What they failed to realize, however, was that besides being a nuisance, this wretched, bloodsucking *zanzara di Ferrara* was responsible for the epidemics of malaria that periodically decimated the city.

The disease struck without warning. Suddenly the victim would find himself alternately chill and burning with fever, his mouth dry, his body drenched with sweat, his teeth chattering. Because Lucrezia was in her sixth month of pregnancy that July, she was unusually susceptible. As soon as she began running a fever, her father-in-law sent his personal physician, Ludovico dei Carri, to care for her. Carri had cured Ercole's daughter Beatrice when she was stricken with a pernicious fever during one of her pregnancies. He had also treated Alfonso when syphilis threatened to deprive him of the use of his hands. At first Lucrezia's case seemed so simple to the learned doctor that he did not even trouble to issue any bulletins. Around the tenth of July, however, his patient suddenly took a turn for the worse. To Ercole, the news that she was vomiting bile and had lost the power of speech was unbelievably embarrassing, for he knew that if she died, her father would hold him responsible. Even before her condition grew so serious, he had decided to recall Alfonso to Ferrara. As he must have explained to his son, it would not do for him to be enjoying himself in the company of the king of France while his pregnant wife was lying ill in the *castello;* it might even give the pope the idea that he wanted her out of the way.

But if Alfonso went to Lucrezia's bedside for the sake of appearances, the sight of this semidelirious stranger to whom he had been making love for the past six months and the realization that not only her life but the life of his unborn child was at stake seem to have awakened a sense of responsibility and an unaccustomed tenderness. Carri,who was not much given to either flattery or exaggeration, reported that the young prince scarcely ever left his wife's bedside and that he caressed her "most lovingly."

Although Ercole had assured the pope that Carri could handle the case, Alexander insisted upon sending his private physician, the bishop of Venosa, to Ferrara, and Cesare sent the famous Gaspar

Torella, who arrived with four other doctors from the Romagna. "By God's grace," said Carri sarcastically, they all agreed with his diagnosis and treatment. Carri was noted for his attention to hygiene and his caution in administering drugs, especially to pregnant women who, in his opinion, were prone to hysterics. He also believed in having the patient drink large quantities of previously boiled cold water to bring down the fever. In Lucrezia's case this treatment seemed to work. By the end of July her fever had disappeared; she was sleeping peacefully and spent her days playing cards.

All that month Cesare had been in the Romagna awaiting the outcome of the battle for Camerino. When he learned that his troops had taken the city, he decided to go to Milan to discuss further conquests with King Louis. With the penchant for the dramatic that was so typical of him, he left Urbino secretly, disguised as a knight of Saint John of Jerusalem. Since he was still concerned about his sister, he decided to stop at Ferrara on his way to see the king. He arrived there on July 28, and in his impetuous fashion, burst in upon her unannounced. At the time she was dozing. When she opened her eyes and saw this knight of Saint John with her brother's face standing at her bedside, it was only natural for her to think that he must be another of those disturbing apparitions who visited her whenever the fever rose. "She became so agitated that she immediately began having pains in her stomach followed by a dysenteric flux and fever which gives us much to think about," Carri told Ercole.

Cesare had thought to cure her with the happy news of the great enterprise he was planning with Louis, and he was genuinely contrite. He remained in Ferrara until he was assured that his sister was out of danger; then set out for Modena taking Alfonso with him. Soon afterward Lucrezia had another relapse, and it was not until August 14 that her doctor considered her sufficiently recovered for him to cease sending bulletins to her father-in-law.

Two days later Carri himself became ill. Upon learning of his illness, Alfonso immediately rushed off to the house of Francesco Castelli, another of Ercole's court physicians, and insisted that he take the case. Castelli was not at all eager to do so. As he explained, he was suffering from dysentery, and besides Lucrezia, he would have to treat Carri and a number of other physicians who had also become ill. "I arrived more dead than alive," he told Ercole, "but it pleased the Omnipotent to deliver me of my diarrhea with a dose of rhubarb."

For the rest of that month Lucrezia continued to have sporadic attacks of fever. By the twenty-eighth of August, however, it seemed to Castelli that things had taken a decided turn for the better. In fact, he considered himself sicker than his patient, for despite the rhubarb, he still suffered from dysentery. Then at the beginning of September, Lucrezia's condition once again deteriorated. Her father's physician, the bishop of Venosa, attributed this relapse to depression, but Castelli had other ideas. "In my opinion there is a residue of bile which the patient cannot evacuate not only because she is pregnant, but because she is a woman. I believe your Excellency will understand what I mean," he told Ercole. The only thing he could possibly have meant was that because she was a member of the so-called weaker sex, she wouldn't even try to rid herself of the bile. Her condition was so bad by then, however, that it seems more likely that she simply couldn't. After two months of fever, she was literally wasting away: her feet, hands, and face were swollen, and she suffered from persistent nosebleeds. But there was worse to come.

On the morning of September 5, both Castelli and Alfonso were at Lucrezia's bedside when she began having mild labor pains. By afternoon they had doubled in frequency and were growing ever more violent. At six o'clock that evening she was delivered of a dead baby girl. Either because her husband thought she would fear that she had failed him or because he could not bear the thought of her having suffered so horribly for no purpose, he "solemnly" promised that "within four month's time" he would "console her with a boy." While she was in labor, said Castelli, Alfonso had served "as obstetrician, nurse, and maître d'hotel, prodding the cooks, besieging us with questions, and encouraging the midwife."

His exhausted spouse did not know that their baby was dead, nor did she hear his promise to give her a boy. Immediately after the delivery, Castelli began feeding her consommé enriched with egg yolks to restore her strength, and he continued to feed her this at intervals all that night. The next morning she felt well enough to have a light meal before falling asleep. As soon as she awoke, her concern was to find a satisfactory wet nurse for her daughter. She was also eager to know what the baby looked like.

—"Was she beautiful and well formed?"

—"She still had one eye open and the other closed," the doctor replied. "And every hour it was necessary to make up new stories about the child," he told Ercole. He had even had some country women brought in for Lucrezia to consider as possible nurses.

"Her Excellency has shown herself such a loving mother that she will experience the most terrible grief when she learns that the baby is dead," he wrote, obviously sufficiently moved to forget his misogyny.

Because the pope's doctor had also come down with the fever, Castelli had ended up with the entire responsibility for the patient. Despite his constant complaining and his snide remarks about her sex, he had spent every night at her bedside, and by then he was exhausted. He had also almost given up hope of saving her. On the morning of September 7, he noted that she had been agitated and feverish all the previous night and had narrowly escaped suffocating as the result of two violent attacks of catarrh. Everything possible had been done to help, her, but from now on her condition was in the hands of Providence.

Already rumors that she was dead or about to die were circulating throughout Italy. Her father was too old and too far away to do anything but worry, unable to face the possibility of a world that did not include his daughter; but her brother mounted his horse and galloped off at breakneck speed in the direction of Ferrara. Remembering what had happened the last time that he had visited his sister, he refused to enter her room until she was fully awake. Her condition was so bad by then that as a last resort the doctors had decided to bleed her on the right foot. "If her brother the duke had not held her leg, the operation would not have been possible," said Castelli. Although there is no scientific reason why the bleeding should have helped, her general state seemed "less bad" to him after it was done. To cheer her up, her brother remained with her for more than two hours "telling her stories that amused her and frequently made her burst out laughing." With childish pride he later boasted to his father that it was the enjoyment Lucrezia had derived from his visit that was responsible for her improvement.

Unfortunately, the improvement did not last. On the twelfth her pulse was so weak that she exclaimed, "Oh, good, I'm dead!" The following morning she announced that she was going to make her will. Although Castelli was not invited to be present when she did this, he resolved to find out as much as he could about the provisions she was making. "As I see it, the will was made at Rome before Her Excellency's departure," he told Ercole. "But I believe that what she is making now is a codicil designed to provide for the future of the three-year-old child born of the union with the unfortunate Alfonso of Bisceglie. A person who knows everything has promised to confide in me."

Whatever the doctor gave this all-knowing person in exchange for his confidence proved to be more than it was worth, for soon afterward it became apparent that Lucrezia would recover. By the twenty-eighth of that month Castelli was complaining that his patient ate everything in sight and talked of nothing but food from morn till night. "Thank God the fever has left her. As for me, I rejoice to be relieved of the care of a woman," he told Ercole.

If Castelli was weary of caring for her, her husband was no less weary. Until Lucrezia's illness, Alfonso's relations with women had been exclusively sexual. Now that Lucrezia was feeling better, the closeness that had developed between him and his wife while she was sick seemed to make him uncomfortable. When her fever had been at its height, he had vowed to go on pilgrimage to the shrine of the Madonna of Loreto as soon as she recovered. Partly because he wished to fulfill this vow and partly because he longed to get away, he asked his father's permission to leave. Lucrezia also was eager to leave the apartment where she had lain ill for almost three months. Since the rooms needed to be disinfected, Castelli urged the duke to allow her to spend some time in Corpus Domini.

The streets were lined with well-wishers when on the morning of October 9 Lucrezia set out for the convent on a litter borne by two white horses. Her husband and his brothers accompanied her to her cell. After taking leave of her, Alfonso set out for Loreto. Although he had vowed to make the journey on foot, Ercole succeeded in getting a special dispensation from the pope which allowed him to travel on horseback. Lucrezia was so grateful for the way in which Alfonso had behaved during her illness that she insisted upon going out to meet him along the road when he returned. But the distance he had always put between them before she took sick was back, and she must have realized that he preferred it this way. The distress that this caused her was, however, tempered by her illimitable joy at simply being alive. Like all who have recovered from an almost fatal illness, she felt herself a visitor in a new and delightful world that she had never fully appreciated, and she could not find it in her heart to be angry with anyone.

The leaves were almost all off the trees when, on October 23, Ercole drove up to the gates of Corpus Domini in his golden coach to take her home. During the ride back to the *castello*, the coach had to stop continually so that she might acknowledge the applause of the people. While she had been away, her apartment had been redone in the blues and deep browns that she loved, and this, too, added to her sense of well-being. One of Isabella's female cousins by marriage who visited Lucrezia at this time thought she looked "very pretty, though rather thinner." She had asked "with charming sweetness" after her sister-in-law, this cousin told Isabella, "begging to hear about your clothes, and especially about your headdresses. . . . And she expressed a wish that you would write to her sometimes and be more familiar in your intercourse with her. . . ."

In truth Lucrezia wished to be friendly with everyone that fall. Gone were the days when she would shut herself off with her Spanish ladies-in-waiting. After having been confined to her bed for so long, she wished to move about, to speak to people, to get to know the city that was now her home. She continued to see a great deal of Ercole Strozzi. While she was at Corpus Domini he had turned the Strozzi villa at Ostellato over to his fellow poet, Pietro Bembo. Bembo had gone to Ostellato to study, but Strozzi felt he needed some diversion. At the end of October or in the early part of November he suggested that Lucrezia and her ladies-in-waiting pay him a visit.

Pietro Bembo

It seems to me that to possess this beauty which he so much
praises without the body is a fantasy.

Castiglione, *The Courtier*, book 4

To many of those who knew Pietro Bembo, including his friend
Ercole Strozzi, he must have seemed fortune's darling. Besides being
rich, handsome, and well born, he was talented and likable, and, at
thirty-two, one of Italy's most promising men of letters. Nor had he
ever had to struggle to gain recognition. His first work, *De Aetna*, a
poem in dialogue form describing a trip from Messina to Taormina,
was an immediate success. The literati praised it for the quality of its
poetry, the scientists for its acute observations of the physical geog-
raphy of Mount Aetna. If they expected the tall, blond Venetian to
go on writing in this vein, however, they were mistaken. Of far
greater interest to the young poet than questions of physical geogra-
phy was the question of love: what it is and what it ought to be.

In *Gli Asolani*, his second work, which was still unfinished when
he arrived at Ostellato in October 1502, he used dialogue form to
dramatize the conflict between sensual or "depraved" love and spiritual or "virtuous" love. "Who can fail to see that if I love some gallant and gentle lady and love her for her wit, integrity, good breed-
ing, grace and other qualities more than for her bodily attractions
and love those attractions not for themselves but as adornments of
her mind—who can fail to see my love is good because the object of
my love is good?" he had his mouthpiece Lavinello say. "And on the

other hand, if I resolve to love some loose dishonest lady, or to love even one who is chaste, and causes loose dishonest thoughts, how can such a love be anything but wicked and depraved when the thing I seek is in itself depraved?"

There wasn't anything terribly new in all this. The same conflict between flesh and the spirit had produced Plato's *Phaedo*, Dante's mystical love for Beatrice as described in the *Vita Nuova*, and Petrarch's celebration of Laura. Like Petrarch, whom Bembo had chosen as his mentor, he wished to devote his life to courting some unattainable lady whom he could worship from afar even as he turned the incidents of their courtship into poetry. Like Petrarch, he was more interested in his lady's physical presence, her lips and breasts and skin and hair, than he cared to admit. And once again like Petrarch, he was "one of those who take joy in weeping" and was much given to self-pity and self-dramatization. But Petrarch, although he had two illegitimate children by other women, had only one Laura; whereas by the time Bembo arrived at Ostellato, he had already courted at least three women.

About the first of these, a mysterious M. G., almost nothing is known. Maria Savorgnan, the second, was a thirty-year-old widow with four children. Besides seventy-seven passionate letters and some equally passionate sonnets, Bembo sent her a little dog which he christened Bembino to remind her of his love. Although Maria was flattered, she found it hard to take him seriously. What she wanted more than all this crying and sighing was a husband who would care for her and her four children. Since in Bembo's opinion love and marriage were incompatible, the romance foundered, and he turned to Emilia Pia for consolation. Along with her in-laws Elisabetta and Guidobaldo, Emilia had sought refuge in Venice after Cesare's capture of Urbino. She was gay and witty and sympathetic, but she was also plain and dumpy, which was probably why her new lover found her an unsatisfactory substitute for the svelte and lovely Maria.

Astrology was then very much in vogue, and few people did anything without first consulting an astrologer. Bembo's astrologer advised him to leave Venice to seek his fortune elsewhere. During a stay in Ferrara he had become close friends with Ercole Strozzi and also gotten to know Ariosto and the other poets in his circle. Ercole d'Este, too, had been taken with him, so taken indeed that he had given him a suite at Belriguardo in which to do his writing. Hence it was only natural that he should decide to settle in Ferrara.

When he arrived at the Strozzi villa at Ostellato that October, it was with the intention of starting a new life, one in which women would play no part. "For many years I have searched for what I twice thought I had found, a faithful and certain heart. I will not search any further for I have come to believe that all women are cut from the same mold," he told Maria in one of those outbursts of self-pity so typical of him. Rather than involve himself in another unsatisfactory love affair, he would devote himself to his studies and put the finishing touches to his book. Or at least that is what he said. Secretly he longed for the pleasantly voluptuous feeling a love affair gave him.

When Charles VIII had invaded Italy, Bembo's fellow poet Matteo Maria Boiardo could see no point in continuing his *Orlando Innamorato*, that tale of unreal passion between knights and ladies in a medieval never-never land:

> Wherefore I leave you in this vain love of Fiordispina gradually
>   burning
> Another time if it be conceded to me I will tell you the whole in
>   full.

Like Bembo, most of the others preferred to go on writing about knights and ladies and unrequited love, content, as one critic has put it, "to live in sweet illusions of their own making." So absorbed was Ariosto in his *Orlando Furioso* that he walked halfway to Modena before he realized that he was still wearing his slippers. But even he was not so much the dreamer as to be content with fine words alone. Although in his Italian poetry he professed himself a disciple of Petrarch, in his Latin poetry he spoke of taking his lady in his arms, of "honeyed kisses so long desired," and "the good so long awaited." He also had two illegitimate children.

For a young healthy man such as Bembo to have been content with just the titillation of his platonic romances seems unlikely. Inevitably, there must have been times when, like Petrarch and Ariosto and all the other practitioners of "virtuous" love, he sought more substantial fare. But of these times he made no mention either in his letters or in his poetry. That he should have been curious about

Lucrezia even before he met her was to be expected. Her marriage to Alfonso d'Este was the talk of Italy. And what must have piqued his curiosity still further was the discrepancy between the stories then circulating in Venice and the enthusiastic reports of her charm he received from Ercole Strozzi and his other poet friends. When finally he met her, it seemed to him that she "exceeded all his expectations." Given his romantic temperament and his extreme susceptibility, it was inevitable that he should fall in love with her and wish to celebrate his love in verse. "Who would not extol a woman so beautiful, so elegant, and in no way narrow-minded?" he wrote to a friend that December. When he watched her "ivory hand" touch the harp or the zither, or saw her "nimble foot" skip to the music as she danced, he feared that some god would seize her from the depths of the castle and carry her through the air to make her the goddess of some new planet. Without knowing exactly what he expected from an affair with her, he could not wait to begin one.

. Like her father, Lucrezia loved music. When she played the harp or the zither it was under the direction of a violist so skilled in his art that Raphael would later use him as the model for the *Apollo on Mount Parnassus* in the Vatican. She also kept a company of singers and four flutists sent her by Cesare. Her father-in-law, too, supported a chorus of expert singers as well as a large number of musicians. Since Alfonso also played the viola, during the winter months concert followed concert at the ducal court. And Bembo was almost always one of those invited to attend. His friend Ercole Strozzi had no doubt told him of Lucrezia's difficulties with her new family. The concerts gave him a chance to observe the lack of sympathy between her and her husband for himself. Nor was it difficult to sense her irritation with her father-in-law. Realizing how alone and unloved she must feel could only increase the desire of this would-be Petrarch to make her his Laura.

Among the many pieces of jewelry she owned he had noticed an exquisite gold bracelet in the shape of a serpent. Ercole Strozzi had already written two epigrams in honor of this bracelet. In December, Bembo wrote five hexameters on the same subject. It was probably with these hexameters that he first captured Lucrezia's imagination. He had had many honors and kindnesses from the duchess and he had reason to believe that she thought highly of him, he told his

Portrait of Pope Alexander VI, fresco by Pinturicchio in the Borgia apartments, the Vatican.

The Disputation of Saint Catherine, fresco by Pinturicchio in the
Borgia apartments, the Vatican.

Portrait of a woman in the Congregazione della Carità, Rome, presumed to be Vannozza dei Cattanei. Artist unknown.

Portrait of Cesare Borgia in the Museum of Palazzo Venezia, Rome. Artist unknown.

Terra-cotta bust of Charles VIII by anonymous Florentine artist in the National Museum (Bargello), Florence.

Portrait of Ercole I d'Este
by Dosso Dossi in the
Galleria Estense, Modena.

Portrait of Alfonso d'Este
by Dosso Dossi in the
Galleria Estense, Modena.

View of the Castello Estense, Ferrara.

Portrait of Isabella d'Este
by Leonardo da Vinci.

The Virgin of Victory
(detail of Francesco
Gonzaga) by Andrea
Mantegna in the
Louvre, Paris.

The Mass of Bolsena (detail of Julius II) by Raphael in the Vatican.

Portrait of a cardinal by
Titian, presumed to be
Pietro Bembo.

brother Carlo that January. But it would be a long time before she admitted the true reason for her kindness either to herself or to him.

In January, the icy *tramontana* sweeping down from the Alps gave Bembo a good excuse for exchanging the villa at Ostellato for a house in Ferrara. Once the carnival season started, life in the city became a round of parties, balls, and masquerades, thus presenting him with innumerable opportunities to see his beloved. Much of the euphoria that Lucrezia had felt after her illness had worn off by then. To at least one courtier she appeared "eaten up" by resentment. Nor did her father-in-law's announcement that he would grant her the 12,000-ducat *appannaggio* she had been demanding for so long improve her humor; for 2,000 ducats would be in goods and services rather than in cash, thus giving the niggardly old duke innumerable opportunities to scrimp. El Prete, who continued to keep an eye on her for Isabella, reported that Lucrezia was perpetually out of sorts. At one of the numerous balls she attended that January, she insisted upon eating alone with her favorite Donna Angela and everyone noticed her frequent reproofs to the Italian members of her company. When the dancing began, she danced first with Don Ferrante, then with Don Giulio, and only at the very end with her husband. It was no doubt the only way she could think of to get back at him for his exasperating indifference, but one wonders if Alfonso cared enough to mind.

As yet there was no sign of the baby he had promised her, and this, too, must have contributed to her moodiness, for she knew that everyone was waiting for her to produce an heir. Her father was forever asking the Ferrarese ambassador if one was on the way. Ercole, too, wished to be informed at the first sign of a pregnancy. But even if no one had said a thing, her failure to conceive would have troubled her, for only another baby could compensate her for the child she had lost and give meaning to what must have seemed to her an empty and purposeless existence

Meanwhile, even when she was feeling most glum, she continued to dress up and appear at the duke's side on ceremonial occasions. As was his custom in February, Ercole presented a series of plays by Plautus in the Sala Grande. The chroniclers tell us that Lucrezia showed up at the first production "covered with jewels and most ornately [*ornatissimamente*] dressed." Certainly Bembo, who was a great admirer of the Ferrarese theater, must have made it his business also to be present. Even if Lucrezia did not get to talk to him, from her place of honor next to her father-in-law, she would spot this thin, sensitive face in the audience and be aware that he was watching her.

The cycle of plays had not yet run its course when Cardinal Ippolito returned to Ferrara. Although he said that the scarcity of goods in Rome had prompted his return, rumor had it that he had been forced to leave the city because Cesare could no longer tolerate his attentions to Sancha, whom Ippolito was supposed to have "known carnally." Despite these rumors the cardinal still appeared to be on good terms with Alexander and Cesare, and he made a point of being gallant to Lucrezia. Her nights belonged to Don Alfonso, but her days belonged to the cardinal, the Ferrarese ambassador told Alexander. In fact, she and the two brothers could be said to be "three bodies in one soul." Ippolito's actions would soon reveal the malevolence of his particular soul, but at that time he seemed merely another suave and lascivious young priest. Although Lucrezia must soon have realized that the principal reason for his attentiveness to her was his desire to be near her cousin Angela, she was nevertheless grateful for the interest he continued to show in her son. He had made his entire entourage wait while he stopped at little Rodrigo's palace to kiss the child goodbye before leaving for Ferrara, he told her.

Since Bembo remained in the city until the end of March, he also may have found excuses for visiting her that month. She could not have been very encouraging, however, for when he left for Ostellato, he announced that he would devote all his time to study. Then, at the end of April, Lucrezia suddenly and unexpectedly wrote to him. Bembo had confessed his love to Ercole Strozzi. After receiving her letters he could not resist gloating.

> Quite late yesterday evening when I was preparing to go out [he wrote], Lucrezia's letters were brought to me; alas! what a bad state they were in. May the gods punish their bearer! Not that they are as secret as you may suspect. They are addressed by Lucrezia's own hand. It distresses me that you make no mention of her in writing to me. Are you affected by jealousy? Would you use silence, O excellent man, to diminish our great joy?

Nevertheless, it was not until the beginning of June that the two began corresponding regularly. By then Alfonso had left on one of his
trips to inspect foreign cannon and artillery. Save for her desire to
become pregnant, Lucrezia had no reason to regret his absence, for
there was still no closeness between them. In those soft, languid days
of early June when the scent of roses and jasmine from the hanging
garden filled her rooms, she must have remembered that other Alfonso who had also been her husband and what it had been like to
love and be loved in return. She was only twenty-three and she still
had so much love to give. In one of her books of Spanish lyrics she
found a poem that seemed to give shape to her feelings.

> *Yo pienso si me muriese*
> *y con mis males finase desear*
>
> *Tan grande amor fenesciese*
> *que toldo el mundo quedase sin amar*
>
> *Mas esto considerando*
> *mi tarde morir es luego tanto bueno*
>
> *Que deuo razon usando*
> *gloria sentir en el fuego donde peno.*
>
> (I think that should I die
> And should desire end with my other ills
>
> Such great love would come to an end
> That the whole world would be bereft of love
>
> But when I consider this
> My tardy death becomes a thing so good
>
> That I should by reasoning
> Feel glory in the fire in which I suffer.)

Knowing of her interest in Bembo, did her ladies-in-waiting urge her
to send him a copy of this lyric, or did she send it off without telling
anyone, prompted by a barely acknowledged need to break the pat-

tern of her loveless existence? Whatever her reasons for sending the poem, Bembo saw her action as a clear invitation to court her, and he immediately dashed off two sonnets and a little Spanish song in her honor.

> *Tan buio es mi padescar*
> *I tan muerto mi spirar*
> *Que ni lo un puedo prender*
> *Ni lo ontro quiero dexar.*

> (So lively is my suffering
> And so dead my hope
> That the one cannot seize
> Nor the other seek to hold.)

He could tell her of nothing but the sloth and the half light of a solitary and secluded life which had held such sweetness for him in the past but was now less pleasing to him, he wrote in the letter which accompanied this. Perhaps Lucrezia ought to seek for the meaning of all this and what would result from it in her books. Meanwhile, he commended himself to her as many times as there were leaves in the garden which he saw from his window.

The summer, which until then had seemed to hold nothing, now gave promise of being unusually diverting. Lucrezia had had a goldsmith fashion a medal for her. Would Bembo provide a motto for it? "Your highness has asked me to compose a poem and I could give nothing better than my soul," he replied. "It is thus you may write 'Est Anima.' " Forgetting his decision to remain at Ostellato with his books, he made frequent visits to Ferrara. When courting Maria Savorgnan, he had suggested that they each keep one of those crystal globes in which it was popularly believed one could by concentrating see the image of the beloved. Now he made the same suggestion to Lucrezia. "If only my heart were like a lovely crystal," he wrote in a sonnet he sent her that July. Were she to look into her own crystal and tell him what she saw there, he would treat her confidence like a priceless treasure, the sweetest thing he had ever received.

Lucrezia seemed intrigued. "Messer Pietro Mio," she wrote, "As for your desire to know my feelings on meeting your or rather our crystal—for so we may call it—I know no better way of telling you than that this would be a unique event perhaps without equal in the past. Let this suffice and remain the truth for all eternity." Apparently she had decided that she needed to be more cautious, for she did not sign this letter. Henceforth, she told Bembo, her initials would be f. f. Since a medal of hers, the *amorino bendato*, bore the letters FPHFF on the tablet above the cupid, it has been suggested that f.f. symbolized something very close and intimate, something which represented the very essence of her being. As Lucrezia d'Este Borgia, future duchess of Ferrara, she had to be conscious of her position and the need to keep a certain distance between her and her would-be lover. As f. f. she could express her true feelings.

Because Bembo sent the letters he wrote to f. f. to one of Lucrezia's ladies-in-waiting who then showed them to her mistress, he, too, felt freer. "Now my crystal is more precious to me than all the pearls of the Indian Ocean," he told f. f. in his first letter to her. "Your magnificent gift to it was parity and fellowship. Let God know that nothing on earth could be dearer to me than that certainty. I know no other case, be it ever so great and wonderful, that I can compare to ours. The veneration in the depth of my crystal, which will appear anywhere and everywhere, is proof of this."

It must have been in July that Lucrezia sent him the famous lock of blond hair now in the Galleria Ambrosiana in Milan. "What joy for me!" Bembo exclaimed when he received it. "Every day you find some new way to fan my ardor. Today you did this with what had once adorned your lovely brow." When her doctor ordered her to leave Ferrara for a brief rest, the once happy lover grew distraught. "I cannot describe the gloom I feel at your departure," he told her. "I write to you, O light of my life, imploring you to take care of yourself and of your health, which I fear is affected, and to save me from dying of grief."

Soon after she returned to the city, he began running a fever, and it was her turn to be concerned about him. Since she was in the habit of visiting her courtiers when they were ill, there was nothing very daring about her decision to call on him. Her presence in the sickroom was, of course, conducive to some very unplatonic thoughts, but neither of them spoke of those.

"Fever had weakened me, but your coming restored me to health and strength. Your words so gentle, good, affectionate and gay brought comfort to me," Bembo wrote her afterward. "I kiss your hand, the gentlest hand ever kissed by man, and I shall not say the est, for a lovelier hand could never be." By then, however, the spread of malarial fever had made it dangerous to remain in Ferrara any longer. Bembo decided to go to Ostellato, and Lucrezia went to a villa owned by the Estense at Medellana. She had been there only a few days when she learned that her father was seriously ill.

During the year and a half that Lucrezia had been in Ferrara, she had seldom let a week go by without writing to the pope. As had been the case when she had gone to Pesaro at the age of fourteen, her letters were never long enough or frequent enough to satisfy him. "We think day and night in what way we can augment and benefit your condition," he told her in one letter. Even before she had left for Ferrara, he had talked of visiting her. At the beginning of April 1502, alarmed no doubt by the tales the wedding guests were bringing back, he had told her to expect him in June *cum tota curia* ("with all his cardinals"). But for a number of reasons he had been unable to make the trip as planned. Despite his panic during her illness and his concern over the painful stories of how shabbily she was being treated in Ferrara, it was not until that summer of 1503, when she was exchanging letters with Bembo, that her father once again talked of visiting her. Either because of his differences with the Estense or simply because he couldn't spare the time for a trip to Ferrara, he announced that their reunion would take place at the sanctuary of the Madonna of Loreto. Although he did not give her a date, he indicated it would probably be in September.

Alexander was then seventy-two. His exuberant good health and the success which attended his every venture were the despair of his enemies. "This Pope . . . grows younger every day; cares never weigh on him more than a night; he loves life; has a joyous nature and does what may turn out useful to himself," Paolo Capello had said a few years earlier.

With the help of Cesare's armies, Alexander had finally destroyed the last vestiges of Orsini power in Rome. Save for some opposition in Camerino, his son was undisputed master of the Romagna, and he was planning to seize control of much of Tuscany as well. "Some wish to make and crown him king of Italy, others wish to make him emperor; for he prospers so that no one dares forbid him anything," said one Venetian orator. In his famous essay on the Renaissance,

Jacob Burckhardt cites a remark that Alexander supposedly made to the Venetians—"I will see to it that one day the Papacy shall belong either to him or to you"—as proof that he wished to make Cesare pope. In *The Prince*, Machiavelli wrote that it was obvious that the pope's aim was to aggrandize "not the Church but the duke," although in the end "what he did resulted in the aggrandizement of the Church." But those close to Cesare said that he "merely wished to put down the factions and the despots and all for the good of the church only; that for himself he desired nothing more than the lordship of the Romagna, and that he had earned the gratitude of all the following popes by ridding them of the Orsini and the Colonna." In the opinion of the English historian Michael Mallett, Alexander's concern for Cesare and his other children and the pope's wish "to hand over to his successors a unified well-governed Papal state which could play a part in the future of Italy" were "so closely intertwined" that they became inseparable; inseparable to such an extent that it might well be argued that the ultimate Borgia aim was Borgia control of a strong papacy.

So that Cesare would be able to dictate the choice of his father's successor, Alexander had begun methodically packing the College of Cardinals with appointees favorable to his son. On May 31, he had named nine new cardinals, five of them Spaniards. But despite his hectic scheming on Cesare's behalf, the pope never forgot his dream of a league of Italian states which would expel France and Spain from the peninsula. "Although Spaniards by birth, and temporarily allied with France, we are Italians and it is in Italy that our fortune lies," he told the Venetian ambassador. When earlier that spring France and Spain had decided to go to war over how to divide up Naples between them, Alexander with his usual grasp of political realities had immediately sought an alliance with Venice.

> See how each of these two kings of France and Spain is striving to drive the other out of Naples [he told the Venetian ambassador]. . . . It would be an evil affair for us and for you if the Spaniards possessed this Kingdom, but it would be still worse if it fell totally into the hands of France, because they would have us bottled up here and would have us acting like their chaplains. Nor would it be any better for you.

The ambassador admitted that the pope appeared to mean what he said; nevertheless, he did not trust him, nor would his government consider an alliance with the papacy. Not long afterward the Spanish general Gonsalvo di Cordova entered Naples in triumph. Immediately, rumors began to circulate that Alexander intended to drop his alliance with France in favor of one with Spain. In fact, there were so many rumors and so much talk that it is impossible to determine exactly what the pope was planning. All that we do know is that on July 28, Alexander announced in consistory that Cesare would soon leave to join his troops in Perugia. Presumably, he intended to help the French retake Naples, but even this is not clear.

By then it had grown unbearably hot and humid in Rome. As usual the hot, humid weather brought malaria in its wake. "I myself am uneasy and almost out of my mind with fright; for so many are dying of fever," said one Florentine orator. In an effort to ward off the disease some misguided souls resorted to self-flagellation; butchers closed their shops; prostitutes refused to receive clients; and everyone who could possibly leave the city did so. Although Alexander also thought of leaving, the unsettled political situation made him decide to remain. But the decision troubled him, especially after his nephew, the corpulent and miserly Cardinal Giovanni Borgia of Monreale, died of fever.

"This month is a bad one for fat people," the pope was heard to say as he stood at one of the windows of the Vatican Palace watching the black-clad canons and priests bear his nephew's coffin across the piazza. Suddenly an owl flew into the room and fell at his feet. "A bad omen," he cried. Obviously discomposed, he rushed from the room. When the Venetian ambassador visited him on August 7, he was still depressed. The many deaths in Rome had alarmed him and he meant to take care of himself, he declared. The approach of French troops on their way to fight the Spaniards also disheartened him. "See how disastrous it has been that no understanding should have been arrived at between your Signoria and ourselves," he told the ambassador on August 11. It was the anniversary of the pope's election, and the ambassador was surprised to find him so glum on so joyous an occasion.

On Saturday evening, August 5, Alexander and Cesare had ridden out to Monte Mario to dine in the vineyard of one of the newly appointed cardinals, Adriano of Corneto. Below them the cupolas and towers of Rome seemed lost in an aqueous haze. But in the cardinal's vineyard there was a light breeze. If there were also a few mosquitoes, they were to be expected in this weather. Reluctant to return to the steamy low-lying Vatican, the pope and his son lingered over dinner until almost midnight. The following Friday at mass Cardinal Adriano suddenly began running a fever. On Saturday morning August 12 the pope, too, complained of feeling unwell. By afternoon both he and Cesare were feverish. Instead of presiding at the papal consistory as he usually did Alexander had to take to his bed. When by the following morning neither his fever nor the vomiting which accompanied it showed any sign of abating, his doctors decided to bleed him. Apparently the bleeding made him feel better, for he spent the rest of that day playing cards. The next morning, however, he felt worse again, and those attending him began to fear he might not survive.

Like the pope, the majority of his attendants were Spaniards. Even those who had not been in Rome in 1458 knew of the riots that had followed the death of Calixtus and the cries of "Down with the Catalans!" that had filled the city. Hence, it was only natural for them to want to keep the pope's condition secret as long as possible. "I have sought by all means to obtain information, but the more I seek the less I learn," the Ferrarese ambassador wrote Ercole on August 14. Since the pope's physicians, surgeons, and apothecaries were not allowed to leave his presence, the ambassador concluded that Alexander's malady must be "grave." That Cesare, too, was very sick with "fever, vomitings and disorder of the stomach" was only to be expected "for all the courtiers, especially those in the palace," were in the same state "by reason of the unwholesome conditions of the air."

In truth the doctors considered Cesare's condition even more serious than his father's, for his fever was so high that he had begun having convulsions. To bring down his temperature, they immersed him in a bath of ice-cold water. The shock took the skin off his body. Raw and smarting and still not entirely free of fever, he lay in the apartment above that of his father, now known as the Stanze Rafaello, waiting for news of the pope, for on Alexander's fate depended his own.

On the seventeenth one of the pope's physicians reported that the Holy Father had had a choking fit—no doubt similar to the catarrh that had afflicted his daughter—and was "going from bad to worse," so ill in fact that it was impossible to see how he could last "more than another day." Later, one of his bishops would picture the dying man "pierced by guilt over his deeds" weeping continually. Others said that he faced the end calmly. Certainly he had shown little fear a few years before when, caught in a storm at sea, it seemed that he and his crew must surely drown. "Alone in the turmoil," says Burchard, "His Holiness remained calm. Keeping his seat in the stern, he gazed firmly and fearlessly around on everything and only repeated the name of Jesus and made the sign of the cross when the sea in all its fury pounded against the galley."

Once the news got out that he was seriously ill, his enemies could not wait for him to die. But among those who were treating him there were some who had come to love the exuberant and genial old man. Early on the morning of the eighteenth, his chief physician, the bishop of Venosa, emerged from the sickroom with tears in his eyes and was heard to tell one of his people that the danger was "very grave." Later that morning the pope made his confession. Propped up in his bed in the small blue and gold bedroom where he could see the bull of the Borgias alternating with the papal tiara on the gilt beams overhead, he then received the viaticum. He felt very ill, he told the five cardinals attending him when the Mass was over. At the hour of vespers he was given extreme unction. Shortly afterward he died.

When Calixtus was dying, the then twenty-seven-year-old Rodrigo Borgia had held the dying man in his arms and sought to comfort him. Even had Cesare wished to perform a similar service for his father—and with a nature so closed in upon itself there is no way of knowing—he was much too ill to attempt it. Later, he would tell Machiavelli that he had taken account of every contingency that might befall him on the death of his father save that which actually happened, namely that he should at that moment be lying helpless, fighting for his own life. Ill though he was, however, he knew that there wasn't a moment to lose. Since he could not take matters into his own hands, he sent his most trusted lieutenant, Miguel Corolla, also known as Michelotto, and a party of equally trusted henchmen to close the doors that gave access to his dead father's rooms. A cardinal who had been with Alexander at the time of his death had not yet left when they arrived. Spotting him, one of Cesare's men threatened to cut the unhappy prelate's throat and toss him out the window unless he handed over the keys to the pope's treasury. After being given the keys, Michelotto and his henchmen unlocked the room where the treasure was kept and took all the silver they could find as well as two coffers containing about 100,000 ducats. While they were looting the treasury, the pope's valets were busy taking everything left behind in his wardrobe and apartments, so that by the time Michelotto opened the doors and announced that Alexander was dead "nothing of value remained except the papal chairs, some cushions and the tapestries on the wall."

Soon afterward Burchard arrived to take charge of the body. The master of ceremonies had prepared Sixtus IV and Innocent VIII for burial; hence, he knew exactly what needed to be done. Moreover, he enjoyed doing it. After substituting silken undergarments and vestments of red brocade for the workaday clothes in which the pope had died and replacing his shoes with red velvet slippers decorated with golden crosses, he put together a makeshift bier "assembled by covering a table with crimson cloth" and had the corpse brought into the Sala dei Pappagalli where "it spent the night completely alone with only two wax tapers burning." The next morning it was placed in the Sistine Chapel "whither came the monks of the city, the clergy of Saint Peter's and the canons bearing the cross. These carried the body from the chapel straight into the middle of the Basilica, going in procession out of the palace, through the courtyard into which the cardinals rode and by the main gate into the piazza, across to the fountain and shops opposite, and thence up the steps into the Basilica itself." No sooner had they set down the bier and begun the services than for some unknown reason the palace guards seized their tapers. In the ensuing free-for-all only Burchard remembered the body. With the help of three others he moved it into a position between the high altar and the papal seat.

But one of the bishops "wondered if the ordinary people might not climb up to the body there, which would cause a great scandal and perhaps allow somebody who had been wronged by the Pope to get his revenge." To prevent this, the body was transferred to the chapel entrance between the steps of the high altar. So that the feet could be touched, they were brought as close to the grating on the iron door as possible. And there the corpse remained through the day, with the door firmly closed.

If we believe Guicciardini, "all Rome thronged with incredible rejoicing to see the dead body of Alexander in St. Peter's, unable to satiate their eyes enough with seeing spent that serpent who in his boundless ambition and pestiferous perfidy and with all his examples of horrible cruelty and monstrous sensuality and unheard of avarice, selling without distinction sacred and profane things, had envenomed the world." But less than a century later, Sixtus V, when asked to name the most illustrious pontiffs replied, "Saint Peter, Alexander and Us." And in the seventeenth century, Urban VIII, with the same touching modesty listed Saint Peter, Saint Sylvester, Alexander, and himself.

To Alexander's contemporary the bishop of Viterbo, "he showed himself so great in so many things—in thought, word, action and decision—that he should have been a great prince if the virtues which graced him had blossomed freely and not been stifled by numerous vices." He was, as the cardinal readily acknowledged, "ever ready to deny himself rest, though thirsty for pleasures which yet were never an obstacle to bearing the burden of public interest, giving audience and dispatching by his word and presence all that required his attention."

But there were, of course, the vices, what Guicciardini, who hated him, called his "horrible cruelty, monstrous sensuality, and unheard of avarice." Looked at objectively, the "monstrous sensuality" doesn't seem all that monstrous. Although he had a few affairs when he was young, he remained reasonably faithful to one woman for almost eleven years, and he continued to be solicitous of her and her children all the rest of his life. His "criminal intercourse" with his daughter was pure fabrication. His affair with Giulia Farnese rests on only the flimsiest of evidence, as do the two orgies at which he is supposed to have been present. Although there are grounds for believing that he fathered the *infans Romanus*, there are also grounds for believing that he didn't. As for the many unsubstantiated stories about him that circulated during his reign, one can only conclude that the Italians, who always liked to think the worst of their popes especially when they were foreigners, derived a voluptuous pleasure from picturing him thus. Although it is true that he sinned, his sin, as one writer has very justly observed, "was not against nature, but against a rule of celibacy soon to be rejected by half of Christendom."

Those who had first sought to impose that rule upon the clergy had done so because they feared that a married priest would be tempted to appropriate church lands for his children. But they could not have imagined appropriation on so grand a scale as it was practiced by Alexander. "This Pope," said Sigismundo dei Conti, "if he had not had children and so much affection for them, would have left a better memory of himself." And that no one can deny.

That he was cruel and deceitful in his dealings with the Roman barons and the petty tyrants of the Romagna is also undeniable. But his aim, the restoration of papal hegemony over the territories of the Holy See, was a legitimate one. And, as one of his agents remarked, it could not be accomplished with holy water. It is moreover to Alexander's eternal glory that when Charles VIII invaded Italy, he, the Spaniard, was the only Italian prince to oppose the invasion. Had the other princes supported him, the need for much of his later duplicity would not have arisen, and Italy might have been spared two centuries of foreign rule. Assuredly he was not fit to be the successor of Peter, but then neither were most of the others in that motley crew who have worn the ring of the fisherman. And he was more tolerant and human than some whom his church has canonized.

August 19 was another sultry, humid day. In the stifling enclosure where the pope's body had been placed, the unbleached wax candles surrounding the bier soon burned down, and the complexion of the dead man grew "increasingly foul and black" so that "it horrified all who saw it." By the time Burchard returned to the chapel that evening, the color of the face had changed to mulberry and it was covered with blue-black spots. "The nose was swollen, the mouth distended where the tongue was doubled over . . . and the lips seemed to fill the face." When this hideous and putrefying corpse was brought to Santa Maria della Febbre to be buried, the carpenters discovered that the coffin they had prepared was too narrow and short to accommodate it. "And so they placed the Pope's miter at his side, rolled his body up in an old carpet and pummelled and pushed it into the coffin with their fists."

"Behold Alexander, a man of such fortunate good health in his whole body . . . lying these days on his humble bier, base, decaying and so horribly deformed." The words are from the address delivered at the pope's funeral service two weeks later. In so superstitious an age it was impossible for most men to believe that the rapid decomposition of the body could be due to natural causes. The marchese of Mantua, in a letter to Isabella, spoke of a pact with the devil by which the pope "purchased the papacy from him at the price of his soul. . . . There are some who affirm that at the moment he gave up his spirit seven devils were seen in his chamber, and his body began to putrefy and his mouth to foam like a kettle over the fire, which continued as long as it was on earth." Others spoke of a black dog running excitedly about Saint Peter's immediately after Alexander's death. But more persistent and more widespread than rumors of a pact with the devil were the rumors that the pope had been poisoned.

The ordinary people who had come to Saint Peter's to kiss the papal foot and had gone away shocked by the appearance of the face, had, of course, no idea when or how he had been poisoned. But they were prepared to accept what they were told. Soon after Alexander's death, a chronicler of Orvieto obligingly supplied the when. "The Pope and certain other prelates and bishops had been poisoned at a dinner give by Cardinal Adriano," this chronicler reported. The explanation of how they were poisoned was supplied that November by a writer named Pietro Martire who lived not in Rome but in Segovia at the Spanish court. According to this writer the pope had wished to poison Cardinal Adriano so that he might confiscate his goods. Consequently he had sent Cesare to the cardinal's villa with a flask of poisoned wine. This Cesare had left with the butler, along with a handsome bribe and instructions to pour a glass of wine for the cardinal. But like most servants, the butler was careless. Instead of putting the flask in some safe spot, he left it on the buffet where all could see it. It was still there when a hot and thirsty Alexander arrived for dinner and demanded that a servant—not the butler but someone else—pour him a glass. Not long afterward Cesare arrived. Since he, too, was thirsty, he, too, asked for a glass of wine. Why he didn't recognize the flask when he saw it was not explained.

Despite all the evidence that Alexander had died of malaria—the dispatches of the Ferrarese and Venetian ambassadors, the high incidence of the disease in the city, the reports of the doctors—it was this story of the poisoned wine with all its obvious discrepancies that was later taken up by Guicciardini and became the definitive account of how Alexander met his death. "It is clear [says Guicciardini] that both father and son had frequently and habitually made use of poisons, not only to take revenge against some of their enemies and secure themselves against suspicion, but because of their wicked greed to despoil the wealthy of their possessions, both among the cardinals and other members of the court." A few years after Guicciardini wrote his *History of Italy*, his contemporary, Paolo Giovio, drew up a list of the cardinals whom Alexander was supposed to have poisoned and identified the poison. According to Giovio this poison, which he called cantarella, was a sugared powder of a wonderful whiteness and a rather pleasant taste. "It did not overwhelm the vital forces in the manner of the active venoms by sudden and energetic action but by insensibly penetrating the veins it slowly worked with mortal effect."

In the opinion of the French writer Charles Flandin, if cantarella "were some form of arsenic acid, its action would be in its acute form either a violent inflammation of the stomach resembling cholera and causing death in from five to twenty-six hours or else a cerebrospinal infection ensuing in from one to twelve hours." But neither Alexander nor his son nor Cardinal Adriano became ill until almost a week after the supper party on Monte Mario, and their symptoms bore no resemblance to those described by Flandin. Nor did any of the other cardinals whom Alexander was supposed to have poisoned for their money exhibit symptoms consonant with the ingestion of arsenic. And in the case of Alexander himself, ironically enough, the rapid decomposition of the body was proof positive that he had not accidentally taken arsenic, for arsenic would have preserved the corpse. Even without all this scientific evidence, however, the numerous poisonings attributed to the Borgias would still be suspect simply because they make no sense. As Voltaire, for one, has pointed out:

> The Pope was on the verge of the grave. The Borgia faction was powerful enough to elect one of its own creatures: was it likely that the votes of the cardinals would be gained by envenoming a dozen of them? I make bold to say to Guicciardini, "Europe has been deceived by you, and you have been deceived by your feelings. You were the enemy of the Pope; you have followed the advice of your hatred. It is true that he used vengeance cruel and perfidious against foes perfidious and cruel as himself. Hence you conclude that a Pope at the age of seventy-two could

not die a natural death. You maintain on vague rumor that an aged sovereign whose coffers at that time contained more than a million of gold ducats desired to envenom several cardinals that he might seize their treasures. But were these treasures so important? The treasures of cardinals were nearly always removed by their gentlemen before the Popes could seize them. Why do you think that so prudent a pope cared to risk the doing of so very infamous a deed for so very small a gain; a deed that could not be done without accomplices; and that sooner or later must have been discovered?"

Although not even Guicciardini connects Lucrezia with the poisonings, her name has been linked with a so-called poisoned ring. In fact people who have no idea who she was or when she lived have heard about her famous poisoned ring. Unlike the story of Alexander's poisoning, which arose from the distortion of an actual event, the dinner at Cardinal Adriano's vineyard, the story of the poisoned ring suddenly appeared out of nowhere and there is no incident to which it can be traced. In one version the ring had a hidden point by means of which poison was injected into the body of the victim. Another version mentions a tiny capsule which broke when the unsuspecting victim brought the lady's bejeweled finger to his lips. But neither the point nor the capsule could possibly have held enough of any of the poisons then known to have killed or even maimed someone. Moreover, the only so-called poisoned rings which have come to light belong to a much later period. So much for the poison of the Borgias.

Cardinal Ippolito broke the news of Alexander's death to Lucrezia. Later, she would say that she had felt as though she, too, were dying. All she wanted at that moment was to be left alone to mourn the beloved figure who had filled her childhood. The conflicts she had had with him, the pain he had caused her were nothing compared to his immeasurable love. No one, it must have seemed to her, could ever love her as he had. And where his love had been there was now a fearsome void. Once again as she had done after the death of Alfonso of Bisceglie, she ordered her rooms draped in black. At first she refused to eat, nor would she allow so much as a single candle to relieve the gloom of her apartment. Her father-in-law made no pretense of sharing her grief. "Knowing that many will ask you how we are affected by the Pope's death, this is to tell you that it was in no way displeasing to us," he wrote his envoy in Milan. Alfonso decided to pay her a visit but saw no reason to hurry. It was otherwise with Pietro Bembo.

Though still not completely recovered from the fever which had stricken him, Bembo set out for Medeilana immediately to offer his condolences. But he was not prepared for the intensity of her grief. At the sight of her in her black gown, lying on the floor in that dark and airless room weeping, all the comforting words he had planned to use seemed inadequate. "Mumbling and speechless," he left. In a letter he sent her the next day, he sought to explain his feelings: "Perhaps this happened to me [he wrote] because you had need of neither my sympathy nor my condolences, for knowing my fidelity, you would be aware of the pain which I felt on account of your sorrow."

Poet though he was, he could find no better way to comfort her than by reminding her "that time soothes and lessens all our griefs." Although she had lost her father, who was so great that Fortune herself could not have given her a greater one, this was not the first blow she had received from an evil and hostile destiny. She had suffered so much before that her soul must now be inured to misfortune.

What would happen to her now that she could no longer look to her "great father" for protection? Bembo warned her that present circumstances required that she not give anyone cause to think she grieved less on account of the shock of Alexander's death than on account of anxiety as to her future position. Then, perhaps realizing that his warning could be misinterpreted, he apologized for his presumption, saying that it was foolish of him to write her thus. The thought that she might misconstrue what he had written continued to trouble him, however. In a letter he sent her later that day he sought to reassure her: "Though it would be my greatest joy to see you happy in everything always, I affirm and I swear that rather than diminish my ardor these misfortunes will quicken my desire to serve you."

By giving him an opportunity to prove his devotion, her misfortune transformed what had begun as a stylized flirtation into something more serious and more important to both of them. If

there was still a good deal of the usual romantic flimflam in the elegy
he sent her that September, the sheer goodness of the man and his
desire to raise her spirits were infinitely touching. All the more so
because so few besides him bothered to show her any sympathy in
her bereavement. At the beginning of October, Lucrezia must have
let slip some hint of what his devotion meant to her, for after that
Bembo alluded to what she had said repeatedly in his letters. "There
is no treasure I could value more than what I heard you say to me
yesterday, which you might properly have let me know sooner," he
wrote her on the fifth. In fact, her words had given him hope that she
would eventually prove the truth of a Spanish proverb he had found
among her papers. *"Que quien amatar perro spesso ravia la le-
vanta."* ("That in seeking to extinguish his ardor she had awakened
her own.")

When a week later Bembo had to leave for Venice, he was desolate. Although his father's problems kept him there longer than he
had expected, he assured Lucrezia that even while occupied with
them he continued to see the window which, along with the moon on
her balcony, bore witness to what she had told him. Referring to the
myth that every pair of lovers was at first a single being, in his next
letter he rejoiced that he would soon be seeing "his dear half without
whom he was not only incomplete but nothing, for in truth she was
not half of him, but all and would be forever." He had written almost the same thing to Maria Savorgnan, but Lucrezia, of course,
had no way of knowing that.

Because the danger of malaria had not yet abated, she was still at
Medellana. After Bembo's return there were more conversations on
her moonlit balcony and more letters. As he had done with Maria,
Bembo took it upon himself to serve as Lucrezia's cultural mentor.
She gave him Spanish coblas, and they discused how best to render
these in Tuscan. In July, he had sent her parts of *Gli Asolani*, and
they would also read and discuss these together. By then any number
of people knew of his infatuation. *"Bembo di Lucrezia"* ("Lucrezia's
Bembo"), was the way Ercole Strozzi's father referred to his son's
friend. But being at Medellana must have made them feel safe, for
Bembo continued to visit her, and as far as we know, Lucrezia did
nothing to discourage him. Had her need not been so great, she
would probably have realized that what she was doing was fool-
hardy, for she was then trying to persuade her father-in-law to help

Cesare, and she was too dependent upon the duke's assistance to risk displeasing him.

In the seventh chapter of *The Prince*, Machiavelli holds Cesare Borgia up as "an example to be imitated by all who by fortune and with the arms of others have risen to power. Cesare's designs, Machiavelli tells us, were frustrated only by the short life of Alexander and by his own illness. If at the death of Alexander Cesare had been well, everything would have been easy. As it was, "he was left with only the state of Romagna firmly established and all the other schemes in mid-air between two very powerful and hostile armies and suffering from a fatal illness." Because he was too ill to mobilize his troops, within two days of Alexander's death, the Orsini were back in Rome looting the shops in the Spanish quarter, burning the houses, and murdering the partisans of the dead pope. Within a week all those petty tyrants in the Romagna whom Cesare had deposed were also on the move seeking to win back their states, and the Venetians had given Guidobaldo da Montefeltro the troops he needed to return to Urbino. In an effort to help her brother, Lucrezia recruited a company of one thousand infantrymen and fifty crossbowmen, placed a Spanish captain at their head, and sent them off to reinforce Cesare's garrisons in Imola and Cesena. She also asked her father-in-law for assistance. Because Ercole didn't want the Venetians to gain control of the Romagna, he sent one of his most trusted advisers to urge the Romagnols to remain loyal to Cesare and offered to send him two hundred horses.

Meanwhile, by a series of hurried negotiations, the convalescent Cesare was trying to undo some of the damage his inability to act had wrought. There were negotiations with the Colonna, who agreed to join with him in opposing the Orsini; with the French, who agreed to help him hold on to the Romagna, and with the College of Cardinals who, in exchange for his oath of allegiance, agreed to allow him to continue as captain-general of the church. But they would not allow him and his army to remain in Rome during the conclave to elect a new pope. On September 2, Cesare set out for Nepi with a vanguard of thirteen carriages bearing his cannon and bombards, more than one hundred carts carrying his baggage, and all his cavalry. The drastic means used to combat his fever had transformed the handsome, blond giant, who had been wont to ride through

Rome so arrogantly, into an emaciated creature with a mottled purple complexion and swollen feet. But the love of display and the
theatricality that had always characterized him were still evident.
Twelve halberdiers bore his crimson velvet litter through the streets
of Rome on their shoulders. His riderless horse followed, magnificently caparisoned in gold-embroidered black velvet bearing his
arms and the ducal crown of the Romagna. Because Cesare could not
bear to have the Romans see him in his flayed and infirm state, he
kept the curtains of his litter drawn. But Vannozza and Geoffredo,
who accompanied him to Nepi, were on horseback and had to en-
dure the stares and gibes of the crowd.

The papal conclave was the usual free-for-all. "The electors were
running hither and thither like bees and intriguing in all directions,"
said the Mantuan ambassador soon after it opened. Louis XII wished
to have a French cardinal elected pope. Ferdinand of Spain quite
naturally supported a Spaniard. Ascanio Sforza, who had been
released from the prison at Bourges where he had been held since the
capture of Milan on condition that he vote for the French candidate,
had the support of a number of the Italians. Others supported
Giuliano della Rovere. Inevitably, with so many in the race no one
could gain a clear majority, and a compromise candidate had to be
found. Cardinal Francesco Todeschini da Piccolomini was the father
of twelve children, but that, of course, was neither here nor there.
The Spanish cardinals whom Alexander had appointed and who remained loyal to Cesare voted for Piccolomini because they thought
he would be friendly to Cesare. The others voted for him because he
was an old man with a bad leg, an ulcer, and no life expectancy to
speak of.

As the Spanish cardinals had expected, the new pope, who chose
to reign as Pius III, confirmed Cesare's appointment as captain-
general of the church and allowed him to keep his states in the
Romagna. Nevertheless, Lucrezia felt uneasy about leaving her son
in Rome. Before Alexander's death her father had made his cousin
Cardinal Francesco Borgia the child's guardian. Francesco was said
to be the illegitimate son of Calixtus III, although why with a son of
his own Calixtus should have lavished so much attention on his
nephews remains a mystery. Of Francesco's devotion to Alexander
and his children, there can be no question. In fact, his resentment of
the dead pope's enemies would eventually cost him his cardinal's
hat.

As soon as it had become clear that Alexander would not survive, Francesco had sent the four-year-old Rodrigo and the five-year-old *infans Romanus* to the Castel Sant' Angelo with their tutors and servants. The children were still there on September 9, when the Ferrarese ambassador, perhaps at Lucrezia's request, visited them. The cardinal intended to send little Rodrigo to Ferrara as soon as the election of a new pope made the roads safe, the child's tutor told the ambassador. By the beginning of October, however, Cardinal Francesco had changed his mind. In a letter to Lucrezia, he advised her to sell all her son's personal property and send him to Spain where it seemed to Francesco the child would be safer.

Because Lucrezia was not sure that this was what she ought to do, she sent her father-in-law a copy of the cardinal's letter and asked him for his opinion. Although she did not say so, she may have hoped that Ercole would suggest that she bring her son to Ferrara. Ercole, of course, did nothing of the sort. Instead he urged her to do what Francesco had suggested. "In fact," he wrote, "I think Your Majesty is bound to do as he advised because of the affection which he displays for you and the illustrious Don Rodrigo your son. . . . Although Don Rodrigo will be at a distance from you, it is better for him to be away and safe than for him to be near and in danger as the Cardinal thinks he would be." Anticipating her objections, he assured her that the mutual love between her and her son would in no way suffer by this separation. "When he grows up he can decide according to circumstances whether it is best for him to return to Italy or remain away."

There is, of course, no way of knowing if Ercole really thought it was in Rodrigo's best interest to send him to Spain or if he said this because he didn't want the child in Ferrara. But what is significant is the kindly tone of his letter and his appreciation of the anxiety that Lucrezia as a mother must feel. For until then, Ercole, like all the Estense, had been brutally indifferent to her feelings, and when her father had died, he had sent her only the most perfunctory of condolences.

Soon after Alexander's death, Louis XII, with the cruelty he so often displayed toward women, suggested that Alfonso find a way to divorce Lucrezia. "I know that you were never satisfied with this marriage; this Madonna Lucrezia is not Don Alfonso's real wife," the king told the Ferrarese representative at his court. Probably because a divorce would have meant returning Lucrezia's 100,000-ducat dowry, Ercole decided to ignore the king's suggestion. However, it is also possible that when he was called upon to make a decision, the old duke suddenly realized that he had come to like his daughter-in-law and did not want to lose her. This did not mean he would do anything to help her, unless by doing so he would also be helping himself. But from that time on he showed an unwonted consideration for her feelings, not only when, as in the case of her son, he could sympathize with her, but also when, as in the case of her brother, his own feelings were very different. If there was an element of hypocrisy in all this, it was a benevolent hypocrisy that Lucrezia found easier to handle than the callousness he had shown earlier and that both Alfonso and Isabella continued to show.

What with the excitement of the coronation and the strain of being pope, Pius III died even sooner than had been expected. Although Cesare could count on the support of the Spanish cardinals, this support did not enable him to handpick a new pope; on the other hand, "no pope could be created without his support." "In the creation of Julius II," says Machiavelli, "he made a bad choice. . . . For men commit injuries either through fear or through hate." And Giuliano della Rovere, who chose to reign as Julius II, hated the Borgias. In fact, he hated them so much that in 1507 he would move out of the Borgia apartments because, said his master of ceremonies, "he did not wish to see the face of his old enemy Alexander VI all the time; he called him a Marrano, a Jew and one of the circumcized." The laughter which greeted this statement so enraged the pope that he turned to the master of ceremonies "almost with rancor" and reproached him for not believing that Alexander was circumcized. When it was suggested that he remove the late pope's face from the wall if it was so displeasing to him, "he replied that he was opposed to this because it was not seemly, but that he refused to occupy papal apartments which brought back the memory of one so odious and scoundrelly."

In 1503, however, when Giuliano needed all the votes he could muster to be elected pope, he talked of the general good and pretended that the rancor he had always felt for the Borgias was a thing of the past. In exchange for the votes of the Spanish cardinals he assured Cesare that he would retain him as captain-general of the church and allow him to continue as duke of the Romagna. He also promised cash payments and other preferments to the Spanish cardinals as well as to anyone else who would give him his vote. "The agreements are being made publicly," said the Venetian ambassador, " . . . and they're not talking of tens of thousands, but of hundreds of thousands."

Machiavelli, who was one of the Florentine representatives in Rome at the time, reported that everyone was satisfied "because Giuliano promised them exactly the reward they asked for." As to meeting his promises, that was another matter. Why Cesare should imagine "that the word of others was more sincere than his own had been," Machiavelli could not understand. But illness and adversity had made the once proud and confident Cesare uncertain. *"Uscito di cervello"* ("out of his head"), Machiavelli called him on November 14, "a man who didn't know what he wanted, deceived and irresolute."

Cesare was at Ostia preparing to set sail on the first lap of a journey that would take him to the Romagna when the new pope's messenger arrived with a demand that he cede the fortresses he still held there to the church. His refusal to do so gave Julius the excuse he needed to arrest him. Despite the preelection promise to make Cesare captain-general of the church, Julius had given the post to Guidobaldo of Urbino, who was related to him by marriage. After Cesare's arrest, both Guidobaldo and the Orsini urged that the pope put an end to him. What probably saved his life was Julius's need for certain passwords that Cesare alone knew. For without these passwords the pope would never be able to persuade the commanders in the Romagna to give up their fortresses. By treating Cesare well and promising to free him as soon as the fortresses surrendered, Julius finally got him to reveal the passwords to Guidobaldo. "It seems to me that this duke of ours little by little is slipping down to his grave," said Machiavelli when he heard of what Cesare had done.

Despite the passwords, the castellans of the fortresses at Imola and Cesena refused to give them up as long as Cesare was being held prisoner. They also hanged the messenger who had asked them to do so. Julius was so furious he threatened to imprison Cesare in a dungeon in the Castel Sant' Angelo until the fortresses surrendered. In the end, however, the Spanish cardinals persuaded him to confine the prisoner in the room in the Borgia apartments where Alfonso of Bisceglie had died—a just fate in the opinion of those who believed that Cesare had murdered his brother-in-law. Machiavelli, who visited him there before returning to Florence, reported that he spent his days playing chess and ridiculed those who were afraid of "a sick man shivering with fever."

Soon after his imprisonment, two of the Borgia cardinals fled to Naples taking little Rodrigo of Bisceglie and the *infans Romanus* with them. Sancha of Aragon had returned to Naples immediately after Alexander's death, and Lucrezia must have been relieved to learn that her sister-in-law had agreed to care for the two children. But there was still the need to free Cesare. Besides pleading with Ercole to help her brother, Lucrezia also wrote to the king of France. But as Julius no doubt had realized, Louis was not one to help a fallen ally. And Ercole hesitated to do anything without the king's approval. When Julius suggested that he keep the prisoner at Ferrara until the fortresses in the Romagna surrendered, the duke agreed to do so but insisted "he must first know what he would have to do if the prisoner refused to give up the fortresses." In reality, Ercole was waiting for instruction from the French king. There was no longer any need to trouble himself about "that priest's bastard," Louis told him. Eventually, Cesare was sent to Ostia in the custody of one of the Spanish cardinals. When on April 19 the last fortress surrendered, this cardinal decided that the prisoner had met all his obligations. Without bothering to consult the pope, he allowed Cesare to leave Ostia. Nine miles down the coast three Spanish galleys were awaiting him. As soon as he got aboard, they set sail for Naples. When he landed, Geoffredo and the two Spanish cardinals, who had fled Rome in December, were there to greet him.

Cesare was then only twenty-eight. Although the pope had confiscated much of his fortune, he still had over 300,000 ducats deposited in Genoese and Florentine banks. Whatever his faults, Cesare had given the Romagna the only good government it had ever had. Were he to try to regain the states he had lost there, he felt certain that he could count on the support of the peasants and the townspeople. Gonsalvo di Cordova had given him a safe conduct which made him feel secure in Naples. Soon after his arrival, he began making plans to raise an army with which he could return to the Romagna.

In the middle of December when Cesare was still a prisoner in the Borgia tower and Lucrezia was frantically seeking to help him, her long stay at Medellana came to an end. The talks with Bembo, from which she had derived such consolation, would not be as easy to arrange once she was back in her apartment in the *castello*. Nevertheless, the poet assured her that he would continue to serve her "as often as I wish and I wish to do so as often as I am able."

But it was not to be. Less than two weeks after he and Lucrezia returned to Ferrara, a messenger arrived with the news that the poet's brother Carlo was seriously ill. Before leaving for Venice, Bembo went to the *castello* to say goodbye to Lucrezia. It was customary then to seek an augury of the future by opening the Bible and reading the first phrase that struck the eye. The phrase he read that day—"He fell asleep with his fathers and they buried him in the city of David"—turned out to be chillingly appropriate, for by the time he reached Venice, Carlo Bembo was already in his grave. The loss of this beloved only brother, "the support and solace of his life," and the need to comfort his "grief-stricken old father" would keep him in Venice indefinitely, he told Lucrezia. When she wrote that the news of Carlo's death had brought tears to her eyes, he assured her that those tears were the sweetest consolation he could have received. Just as she had once turned to him for support, so he now turned to her. In this, his terrible affliction, he would try to emulate the strength she had shown in the face of adversity. In the letters he wrote her that winter he spoke not only of his grief and pain but also of his love and his continuing wish to serve her.

Either because she did not write as often as he would have liked or because he found the letters she signed with her own name too impersonal, at the end of March he asked for a note from the pen of f.f. Like most of the letters Lucrezia wrote to him, her reply was addressed to *"Mio carissimo Mis. Pietro Bembo"* ("my dearest Mis. Pietro Bembo"). For a variety of reasons, wrote Lucrezia, f.f. could not oblige him at the time, so she (Lucrezia) was writing a few verses in her own hand and she hoped that these would set his mind at ease and provide some consolation. In closing she wished to assure him of f.f.'s continuing desire to serve him. Was she telling him that although the future duchess of Ferrara had to be more careful than ever about what she wrote, the woman within continued to love him? Or was it all a game, one of those private jokes lovers delight in sharing? Bembo sent her two replies: one addressed to the duchess of Ferrara and the other to f.f. The thought of her was a consolation to him every day, every night, every hour, in every place and in every condition, he told f.f.

While she and Bembo were engaged in this cautious long-distance love affair, Lucrezia was accessory to a far more passionate and open affair between Ercole Strozzi and a young noblewoman named Barbara Torelli. When only sixteen, Barbara had been married to Ercole Bentivoglio of Bologna. Although she found her husband cruel, brutal, and frightening, like most young wives she grimly accepted her lot until one day either out of greed or out of spite her enterprising spouse announced plans to sell her to a bishop for 1,000 ducats. When she refused to cooperate, he grew indignant and threatened to accuse her of trying to poison him. Soon afterward, Barbara fled to Mantua, where she sought refuge in a convent. Later, she transferred to the convent of San Rocco in Ferrara. Ercole's physician, the usually misogynistic and ill-tempered Francesco Castello, who visited her there, found her "very beautiful and clever." Apparently Ercole Strozzi agreed, for it was at about this time that he appointed himself her protector. Just when the two became lovers is not known.

In 1503, Barbara began legal proceedings for the restitution of her dowry. As was probably inevitable in that male-dominated society, the judges decided that since she had left her husband, he didn't have to give her so much as the money to feed herself. In the winter of 1504, she and the elder of the two daughters she had borne him were staying in the convent of Corpus Domini when her husband suddenly decided to marry his daughter to a Gonzaga. Rather than allow this daughter to submit to the kind of arranged marriage that had ruined her life, Barbara, presumably with the aid of Strozzi, hid the girl in Venice. When the marchese Francesco Gonzaga learned what she had done, he asked his father-in-law to banish Barbara Torelli from Ferrara until she had surrendered her daughter. Ercole was at first disposed to oblige him. After a talk with Lucrezia, however, he not only allowed Barbara to remain in the city, but he also gave her a small pension.

That spring was also enlivened by an ongoing battle between the duke and Cardinal Ippolito, who, in Ercole's opinion, was neglecting his interests at the court of the newly elected Julius II. The battle reached its climax on April 9 when a papal messenger arrived to ask Ippolito for the return of certain benefices, and the cardinal ordered him beaten. Upon learning what had happened, Ercole gave his son a choice between apologizing or being banished from the city. Rather than apologize, Ippolito fled to Mantua. During the following week the ducal messengers carried recriminating letters from Ercole to his son and from Ippolito to his father. "We fear that our Lord God, since you do not reverence His Majesty and are disobedient to your father, will give you some fitting chastisement for it," Ercole wrote on Sunday, April 14. But even as he wrote, Francesco Gonzaga was headed down the Po in a gondola to reconcile the duke and his son. As might have been expected, the reconciliation took place "with the greatest show of affection between father, son and son-in-law." Soon afterward, Isabella joined her husband, and the two remained in Ferrara for the horse races that marked the Feast of Saint George, the patron saint of the city.

The last time Lucrezia had seen Francesco Gonzaga had been eight years before, when he had come to Rome to receive the golden rose for his part in the battle of Fornova. Seeing him again under less glamorous circumstances, she may have been surprised to realize that the hero of Fornova was an ungainly man with great wet lips, bulbous eyes, and a swarthy face upon which the marks of the French disease were already evident. But there was a warmth and a geniality about him that soon made her forget his unprepossessing appearance. Cesare was still at Ostia then and in need of all the assistance he could get. Francesco Gonzaga was one of the chief condottieri of the king of France. Because he seemed so friendly and so accessible, she decided to ask him to help her brother. She had, of course, no way of knowing that Gonzaga believed that her father had made a pact with the devil or that the marchese had publicly denounced Cesare as "a priest's bastard." She knew only that there had once been talk of betrothing Cesare's daughter Louise to the Gonzagas' son Federico, and she took this as evidence of a bond between them. In truth, even if Gonzaga had wanted to help Cesare, there wasn't very much that he could have done. But he had always been a great womanizer, and he found this slim, golden-haired sister-in-law so appealing and was so flattered by her trust in him, that he could not resist giving her the impression that he would arrange to free her brother. One would not expect the daughter of Alexander VI to take such a carelessly given promise at face value, but Lucrezia seems to have done just that.

Nor did Cesare display any great acumen now that he no longer had his father to advise him. Rather than keep everyone guessing as Alexander would have done, he made no secret of his plans to launch an attack upon the states of the church. His behavior gave the pope a good excuse for complaining to Ferdinand and Isabella. Because Cesare had always been pro-French, the Spanish monarchs could see no reason to risk antagonizing Julius for his sake. Despite the safe conduct which their general Gonsalvo di Cordova had given Cesare, they ordered him arrested. The arrest took place on the night of May 26 just before he was to have set sail for the Romagna. For a while, one of Lucrezia's former ladies-in-waiting, who had accompanied him to Naples, was allowed to share his imprisonment. Later she was asked to leave. On August 20 her lover was placed aboard a Spanish galley which took him to Grao, the port in Valencia from which his great uncle Alonso de Borja, the future Calixtus III, had set sail for Italy seventy-five years before. Cesare's return to the land of his ancestors could not have been more humiliating. He had taken as his motto "Caesar or nothing," said one writer: "Fortune had replied by giving him nothing." He was imprisoned in the highest tower of the tallest castle in Seville: the Homage Tower of the Castle of Chinchilla, which rose to a height of 700 feet above the tiled roofs of the eponymous city below.

Lucrezia feared that he would never leave Chinchilla alive, and she pleaded with her father-in-law to do something. Besides assuring her that he wished to be a good father and a good brother to Cesare and bidding her place her hope in our Lord God "who does not abandon whoso trusts in Him," Ercole did nothing. Nor in truth was there anything he could do. But Lucrezia could no more accept the impossibility of helping her brother than she could accept her separation from her son or the futility of her affair with Pietro Bembo. If she tried hard enough and long enough, it must have seemed to her, she would surely succeed in freeing Cesare and being reunited with her son. As for Bembo, the best course was to think no further than the next letter or the next eagerly awaited visit.

Three weeks before Cesare was put aboard the galley which took him to Spain, Lucrezia's favorite lady-in-waiting, Niccola, was married to a young Ferrarese nobleman. At the time Bembo was putting the finishing touches to his *Gli Asolani*. Since the book had been inspired by the marriage of one of the ladies-in-waiting of the exiled queen of Cyprus, he decided to send Lucrezia a copy of the completed first draft to read with her maids of honor and courtiers during the wedding festivities for Niccola. In an accompanying letter which he would later use as the dedication "to Lucrezia d'Este Borgia, the most illustrious duchess of Ferrara, from Pietro Bembo," he described Lucrezia as one who "longing rather to dress out her soul with comely virtues than to cover her body with precious clothes devotes whatever time she can to reading or writing something, " and he expressed the hope that so much as her beauty surpassed that of other ladies, the attractions of her mind might eclipse those of her body and she might become "as it were, greater than herself, loving far rather to receive an inner pleasure than to please all others outwardly." Reading this, Lucrezia would be reminded of the earnest discussions about the purpose of life that she and Bembo had had and she would smile. The wish "to dress out her soul with comely virtues rather than to cover her body with precious clothes" was sincere and would grow stronger with time. But she knew that there had been a very special, almost voluptuous, pleasure in allowing this handsome blond poet to guide her.

Seeing her and talking such matters over with her were two of the firmest and sweetest mainstays of his life, Bembo had told her in April. Yet every time they arranged to see one another something always came up to make it impossible for them to do so. That October it seemed that Bembo would surely visit her at Ostellato or one of the other villas outside Ferrara where (although he did not say so) there would be less chance of Alfonso showing up unexpectedly. But at the last minute he heard that her father-in-law was ill. Since it did not seem to him that he could court her peacefully at such a time, he told her that on the advice of a friend he was postponing his visit until carnival began. But his letter was so apologetic that she must have wondered if he wasn't trying to convince himself that this was why he had put off visiting her.

Ercole died on January 25, 1505. When he realized that the end was near, he had summoned a harpsichordist to his bedside. While this harpsichordist played, the dying man had kept time to the music with his hand. Later, he spoke tearfully of his daughter Isabella and her husband. Of his sons he said nothing. In truth every one of them was a disappointment to him. Because they had always been so uncontrollable and there was so much bad blood between them, many in Ferrara feared that after the old duke's death the younger sons would contest Alfonso's right to succeed his father. Instead, to everyone's surprise, the transfer of power was remarkably peaceful.

After receiving the scepter and sword of office from Tito Vespasiano Strozzi, the head of the Council of the Wise, who nominally represented the people of Ferrara, Alfonso set out upon a tour of the city. He was mounted on a richly caparisoned charger and he wore a mantle of white damask lined with squirrel fur and a white damask cap. At his side rode Cardinal Ippolito and a representative of Venice. Behind them rode Don Giulio and Don Ferrante, followed by the most important nobles and judges of the realm with a company of crossbowmen and men-at-arms in attendance in case things got out of hand. It had been snowing since early morning, not the wet snow which is usual in Ferrara, but thick white flakes accompanied by icy gusts of wind. To Alfonso's secretary the storm seemed a bad omen, but the new duke's astrologer assured him that although his reign would be stormy, it would also be glorious. And despite the whirling snow and the biting wind, the streets were lined with people who cheered and applauded their frostbitten young ruler. Cardinal Ippolito administered the oath of office to his brother before the high altar of the cathedral, after which the crown of Ferrara was placed upon Alfonso's head.

From one of the balconies of the ducal palace, Lucrezia had watched the snow-covered procession enter the cathedral. As soon as she saw her husband leave after the coronation, she went to the door of the palace to greet him. At his entrance she knelt to kiss his hand in sign of submission, but he lifted her up and kissed her cheek. Taking her hand he led her up the covered marble staircase where Isabella had greeted her when she had first come to Ferrara three years before. Together the new duke and duchess entered the Great Hall to receive the congratulations of their nobles while outside the storm continued, and the wind piled the snow into great drifts against the sides of the buildings.

Soon after his coronation Alfonso told his wife that he planned to build an inner passage through which he could go from his apartment to hers without being observed. Although this may have been prompted by a wish for greater privacy, it could also have been prompted by a desire to keep an eye on her. Alfonso had never made any effort to conceal his dislike of her poet friends. Less than two weeks after he became duke, Ercole Strozzi was rumored to be "out of favor with him" and "in great danger." Strozzi was in the habit of confiding in Bembo, and he must have written to tell his friend of his problems with Alfonso and of the new duke's plan to build a passage between his apartment and Lucrezia's. How else explain the distraught letter which Bembo sent to f.f. on February 10?

Like many of the letters he wrote to f.f., this one was addressed to one of Lucrezia's ladies-in-waiting, who was to deliver it to her. It began with a reference to a letter Lucrezia had written him soon after he had left for Venice. No letter he had ever received was sweeter to him than that one, he told her, for in it she had let him know that he "lived in her heart." After reiterating his love for her and his unwavering desire to serve her, he begged her not to become discouraged now that so many things were working against their love. Nevertheless, he was forced to admit that "the day will come when fate will overcome us in spite of our efforts to prevent it. But then it will be sweet to remember that our love was strong and constant, and the memory will make us happy." Meanwhile she must be more careful so that

> the paths which lead to our love are not narrowed or cut off. Do not trust anyone until I, by some means, am near you if I am still alive. The bearer of these words, who is faithfully attached to me, will soon pass through Carpi and return to you to discover whether there is any command you wish to give me. In this way you will be able to send your reply quite secretly and it will be safe. I beg you to take this course; since we shall soon be able to speak together, be happy to converse with me now . . . and see that no one observes you writing for I know that you are watched.

In closing he kissed that sweetest hand to which his heart was linked and this gave him courage to kiss one of those two beautiful eyes that had first kindled his flame. His greatest happiness would be to know that he was loved by her who was "the harbor and sweet repose of his troubled ship," he told her. Nor did he stop there. He also sent her an Agnus Dei that he had worn at his breast. For love of him he wished her to wear it at night so that "the dear hospice of your precious heart (which I would bargain away my life to be able to kiss just once) will at least be touched by that which for a long time touched the hospice of mine."

"The senses reign and reason is dead," Petrarch had written in one of his *canzoni* to Laura. But Petrarch liked to exaggerate and so did Bembo. The truth was that even when he was swooning with desire, he still had enough reason left to know that he wasn't prepared to bargain away his life for any woman. He had, after all, just spent seven years writing a book which was coming out that March, and he couldn't wait to see how it would be received.

This letter, the longest and most passionate he ever wrote to f.f., was also the last. Perhaps the very act of writing it made him see more clearly the impasse that their love had reached. Certainly Lucrezia, no matter how much she loved him, must have realized that she couldn't allow him to go on writing to her like that. Only a short time before, she had learned that she was pregnant, and her pregnancy would sharpen the conflict between responsibility and desire that had been there from the start. It used to be thought that she and Bembo never saw one another again. However, Maria Bellonci has found evidence that Bembo visited Ferrara that April just as he had said he would and that he was there again in June. Obviously, he must have seen Lucrezia. What they said to one another we do not know, but it was the end of their affair. They continued to write to one another for many years, letters that were warm, friendly, and affectionate, but nothing more. f.f. had vanished. Only the duchess of Ferrara remained.

Lucrezia had not been the first woman in Bembo's life; nor was she the last. Although it is doubtful that he was ever as close to any of his other platonic flames as he had been to her, he went on crying and sighing and, incidentally, borrowing phrases from old love letters to put into new ones until he was almost fifty. It was then, according to one of his early biographers, that "so as to have more time for his studies, he decided to confine himself to one young woman whom he had seen in Rome." After that there was no more nonsense about platonic love. La Morosina, as she was called, bore him three children, and it was she, not Lucrezia, who was the great love of his life. The words he wrote after her death are considered by many the finest ever to come from his pen. Certainly they are among the least affected.

I have lost the dearest heart in the world, a heart which tenderly watched over my life, which loved it and sustained it neglectful of its own. A heart so much the master of itself, so disdainful of vain embellishments and adornments of silk and gold and jewels and treasures of price that it was content with the single (and so she assured me) supreme joy of the love I bore it. This heart, moreover, had for vesture the softest, most graceful and daintiest of limbs. It had at its service pleasant features and the sweetest, most graciously endowed form that I have ever met in this land.

For Lucrezia her affair with Bembo represented an attempt to recapture the love she had known with Alfonso of Bisceglie, the beautiful boy who had been taken from her before she had a chance to really know him. In Bembo she found the same gentleness, the same sensitive consideration of her feelings she had found in her second husband. Moreover, the poet had the advantage of being ten years her senior and immensely learned, so that he was able to introduce her to a world of ideas that she had scarcely known existed. She was only twenty-five when they parted. Ahead of her stretched a lifetime with a man whom she could not possibly love, a man who, in fact, did not even want her love. Although there must have been times when the thought of all those loveless years would terrify her, times when she would think of Barbara Torelli and wish that she, too, had the courage to flee and start a new life, in the end she accepted her fate and tried to make the best of it.

Francesco Gonzaga

Unhappy you! You who in the midst of so many evils have the
hope of being happy!

Petrarch, *De remediis utriusque fortunae*, book I, dialogue 108

When in April 1504 Francesco Gonzaga came to Ferrara to
patch up Ercole's quarrel with Cardinal Ippolito, Cesare was still a
prisoner at Ostia and Lucrezia had just assured Bembo of f.f.'s continuing desire to serve him. Although she was enough of a flirt to enjoy the marchese's obvious interest in her—all the more so because
he was Isabella's husband—neither his appearance nor his manner
was calculated to make her forget her poet. If Gonzaga had not
promised to help Cesare, she would probably have put him out of
her mind the moment he left for Mantua. As it was, she had her
ladies-in-waiting write to him almost immediately.

Now that they were deprived of his "divine virtues and exalted
and angelic manners," they were only half-alive, they told him.
Their mistress never ceased talking of him, said Madonna Angela
and a new lady-in-waiting who had come to Lucrezia's court from
Bologna, Madonna Polissena. In fact, said Polissena in a
letter describing one of Ercole's dinner parties, "every little pleasure
was but little pleasing to the most excellent lady [Lucrezia] and to me
who serves her because your illustrious Lordship was not present."

It was all nonsense, of course, the usual extravagant blandilo-
quence of the courts, and Gonzaga would have had to have been
dimwitted indeed to be unaware of what had prompted it. But

though he had no intention of helping Cesare, he was too much of a womanizer not to take advantage of the exchange of letters to further insinuate himself into his sister-in-law's good graces. Relations between Mantua and Ferrara had been deteriorating ever since the marchese and his father-in-law had found themselves on opposing sides in a quarrel between some local princelings—the Pio—over the strategic fief of La Mirandola. By cultivating Lucrezia, the marchese may also have thought he could find out what his opponents were up to. He had always had great faith in the power of poetry over the female heart. In the early days of his marriage to Isabella, he had deluged his wife with sonnets which, although they bore his signature, were usually the work of court poets. Soon after the exchange of letters with Lucrezia began, he promised to send her two sonnets; then had to apologize for not doing so because he'd been ill. He'd been ill, he told her, because he was deprived of the air of Ferrara which suited him so well and of Her Excellency's conversation, which he'd found so agreeable.

In October, Lucrezia's ladies-in-waiting invited him to meet their mistress at Comacchio, but for some reason he never got there. Lucrezia loved him like a brother, and most cordially, Madonna Polissena told him in November, and Lucrezia herself signed her letters to him "Your most dedicated sister, as much sister as servant." But the letters themselves contained none of the coquettish phrases her ladies-in-waiting tossed around so freely. Nor did she always seem to appreciate their efforts on her behalf. Soon after Polissena wrote the marchese that there were many other things she had to tell him (concerning Lucrezia's feelings for him) that couldn't be put on paper, Lucrezia sent her back to Bologna. And there matters stood on that snowy morning in January when Alfonso became duke of Ferrara.

The new duke had been a babe in arms when his cousin Niccolò da Leonello had taken advantage of Ercole's absence to ride into the Piazza del Duomo at the head of a company of seven hundred men and attempt to stage a coup. The story of how Alfonso's mother had taken him from his crib in the ducal palace and fled to the *castello* through a covered passageway, with Isabella and Beatrice behind her carried in the arms of her ladies-in-waiting, was one that he would never forget. He did not need Machiavelli to tell him that a prince must be "a fox so that he may know how to deal with traps and a lion that he may frighten wolves." Nor did he have any doubts about his ability to frighten wolves. His travels on the continent had convinced him that he knew more about artillery than most other European rulers, and even after becoming duke, he continued to spend time in his private workshop casting guns and cannon. Of his ability to withstand traps he was, however, far less certain. Because he sensed that he was temperamentally more fit to play the role of the lion than that of the fox, he relied on his brother Ippolito to play the fox for him. Where Alfonso was slow, Ippolito was quick. Where Alfonso was rough and often tactless, Ippolito was suave and remarkably adept at manipulating others. Although Alfonso raised the allowances of Don Giulio, Don Ferrante, and Don Sigismundo, all of whom had been kept in a state of near penury by Ercole, he did not give these brothers any similar responsibility in his government.

His mother had acted as chairman of the commission that examined the petitions of private citizens, and this is probably why he decided to give the same post to Lucrezia. Her affair with Bembo was coming to an end at this time, but the division between the public and the private person was so ingrained that no one who saw her presiding at the meetings of the commission or receiving the congratulations of the various foreign ambassadors could have had any inkling of her inner turmoil. "It was said that she had shown both intelligence and good grace at her first hearing," the Mantuan ambassador told Isabella.

Alfonso's willingness to give her this post indicated a certain respect for her ability. That spring he also showed occasional signs of what seemed like real affection. Because the court was in mourning for Ercole, there was no carnival. Instead the emphasis was on religious functions. The Monday after Easter, Lucrezia went to the church of Sant' Andrea for vespers with Angela Borgia and some other ladies of her court. No sooner were they settled in their places than two Capuchins stationed themselves behind them and tried to strike up a conversation. Sensing a joke, the ladies tried to learn the identity of the "monks" hidden within those voluminous brown cowls. After considerable repartée with the mysterious strangers, they were able to identify one of them as the Baron, a courtier famous for his pranks. Only much later did Alfonso reveal himself as the Baron's companion. Apparently delighted by Lucrezia's confusion, he began teasing her about what she'd said to the unknown monk, and the more she defended herself, the more amused he grew.

Not long afterward, however, he talked of dismissing all the Spaniards in her service, including Tromboncino, the famous singer she'd brought with her from Rome, and he continued to seek out prostitutes much as he had before becoming duke. His procurer in those days was a Gascon chaplain known variously as Giovanni Artigianove, Gianguascone, and Gian Cantore ("Gian, the singer"). This chaplain had been a ragged beggar boy who was singing sacred songs for alms when Ercole first came across him in France. Struck by the beauty of his voice, the old duke had brought him to Ferrara and given him a musical education. Although Gian Cantore proved an excellent student, Alfonso was less struck by the former beggar's musical ability than by his ability to ferret out complaisant women. Frequently, the young duke and his procurer visited brothels together. Alfonso could also depend on Gian Cantore to provide the kind of rowdy horseplay and buffoonery he required to take his mind off the terrible problems which faced him during that first year of his reign.

The year was going in reverse, said Maestro Tommaso Zerbinati, the supervisor of the mint, in an entry in his diary written the Christmas before Alfonso became duke. That December grapes were reported growing on the vines, violets bloomed, fresh beans were to be had, and the song of the cuckoo was heard in the land. The superstitious felt the unseasonably mild weather presaged disaster, and as it turned out, they were right. On New Year's Eve, an earthquake set the bells of the Rigobello tower to ringing for the length of an "Ave Maria." Around the same time a series of violent electrical storms accompanied by heavy rain caused the Po to overflow its banks, completely submerging one village and destroying large quantities of much-needed grain. Then in January came the snowstorm that ushered in Alfonso's reign. While the duke and his nobles were toasting the future, the poor in the vicinity of Modena were making do on oak bark, acorns, ground nuts, and grape seeds. To relieve their suffering, the new duke went to Venice to buy grain, which he then distributed to the needy. But the grain was of admittedly inferior quality and there wasn't enough to go around. That spring, says one chronicler, large numbers of poor people of both sexes and all ages combed the city for food from early morning until after the

Angelus had rung, crying aloud that they were starving and begging their fellow citizens to have pity on them. "And they ate the grass in the meadows and were so emaciated that they could barely stand on their feet, let alone work."

On the third of April a father was imprisoned for having killed two of his sons. They hadn't eaten for three days and he couldn't bear to see them suffer any longer, he told the authorities. Apparently he'd planned to kill himself but had been arrested before he could do so. It was said that the duke took pity on him and did not wish to see him die.

On the twelfth of May, foreign grain was being sold on the banks of the Po, but the quality was poor and the price the highest within anyone's memory. By the seventeenth no grain was to be had at any price. The experience of generations living with just such shortages had given rise to the old Tuscan proverb, "A full pot is the best remedy against malaria," for invariably famine opened the door to plague. On June 8, a ten-year-old boy dropped dead in the street. Since his mother had died two days before and his father the previous evening, no one would go near the corpse. Soon children were dying all over Ferrara, some on the streets, some in their mother's arms, and a few under the loggias of the ducal palace. Perhaps because the doctors feared that a panic would ensue, they continued to assure the people that the disease that was killing the children wasn't contagious. But when the mortality rate continued to rise and an ever greater number of adults also took sick, the learned gentlemen were forced to admit that this was indeed an epidemic.

A chronicler who went through the city at the end of June found most of the stores and workshops closed. The death rate was climbing so rapidly, he reported, that mass graves, some of them large enough to accommodate fifty or sixty corpses, were being dug in the sacristies of many of the churches. As usual, everyone who could do so sought to leave the plague-stricken city. The poor fled to the Lazzaretto del Boschetto, a refuge for beggars on an island in the Po three miles out of Ferrara; the rich fled to their villas in the surrounding countryside. Lucrezia, who was in her sixth month of pregnancy, went to Modena with her entire court, including her singers and clowns. When at the end of July the plague arrived there, the company moved on, through the vineyards of Rubiera to the Estense castle at Reggio.

Reggio is a small fortified town set in the midst of fertile green plains along the Via Emilia within sight of the Appennines. It had given Ferrara her two greatest poets, Matteo Maria Boiardo, whose castle at Scandiano could be seen in the distance, and Lodovico Ariosto. *"Reggio gioconda"* ("joyous Reggio") Ariosto called his birthplace. When Boiardo hit upon the glorious name of Rodomonte for the boldest of the Saracen chieftains in his *Orlando Innamorato*, the church bells had announced the momentous event to the people.

In this happy place Lucrezia appeared to feel freer to be herself than in any other town or village of her husband's realm. During a visit to Reggio the summer before, she had suggested that the town broaden its economic base by promoting silk-making and embroidery. Her own skill as an embroiderer was well known, and it had given her an appreciation of fine workmanship in others. On a visit to the atelier of a certain Messer Antonio, she had been so impressed that she had recommended him to the commune. When she returned to Reggio in 1505, she was suffering from an intermittent fever that worried her obstetricians. Nevertheless, she must have made it her business to visit Antonio's workshop once again in order to see the progress he had made.

Alfonso and his court were then at Belriguardo. Since the palace was certainly large enough to house Lucrezia's court, he must have had some special reason for allowing her to go to Reggio. The most logical reason would seem to be his anxiety over her approaching delivery. Alfonso had already had two stillborn children: one by his first wife and the other by Lucrezia. Although he would try to tell himself that his wives were to blame, the very fact that the same thing had happened with two different wives may have led him to wonder if he weren't in some way responsible. Hence it would be natural for him to wish to spare himself the anguish of being present at what could turn out to be yet another stillbirth. That his behavior placed an added burden on his wife did not appear to concern him.

Don Giulio followed Lucrezia's court to Reggio. This bastard son of Ercole's was by far the handsomest of the old duke's children, and he was ridiculously vain about his good looks, especially his dreamy brown eyes in which women seemed to find promise of a depth that simply wasn't there. "All the women were putting on airs so that I would dance with them," he told Ippolito after one ball. "The Lady Duchess [Lucrezia] did not dance at all except when I made her dance the torch dance."

Like Ippolito, Don Giulio had been destined for the church, but he had refused to consider taking Holy Orders. Nevertheless, his father had gone on seeking benefices for him, partly because a lucrative benefice would solve the problem of his son's support and partly because he wished to get Don Giulio out of Ferrara, where his idleness and lack of discipline could only cause trouble. After Ercole's death, Alfonso continued the search for a suitable benefice, but with no more success than his father had had. Meanwhile, Don Giulio kept himself busy chasing women in general and golden-haired Angela Borgia in particular. Although he accompanied Alfonso on a state visit to Venice and had been his father's representative in Rome during the papal conclave, he showed little interest in politics and even less in art and letters. What he loved besides women were expensive clothes and wild parties. When Ippolito was in Rome, Don Giulio had regaled him with hints of the *cose stomacose*, "the disgusting things," mostly sexual in nature, that went on during the carnival season. A vapid young man, and yet there must have been a certain sweetness about him, for both Isabella and Lucrezia enjoyed mothering him.

At the beginning of 1504, a chaplain by the name of Don Rainaldo was in Don Giulio's service. At the end of the year when Ercole was dying, Ippolito took this chaplain away from his brother, and for some complicated political reason known only to himself and Alfonso, imprisoned Don Rainaldo in a castle near Reggio. It wasn't until the following May that Don Giulio found out where the chaplain was. Either because Don Giulio was touched by the chaplain's predicament or because he wished to get even with Ippolito, or simply because he had nothing better to do with himself, he decided to free him. Since Don Ferrante was then fuming over Ippolito's preferred position in the new government and his own relatively minor role, he promptly agreed to help. Another person who agreed to help was Alberto Pio of Carpi.

Alberto Pio was the nephew of the famed Renaissance philosopher Giovanni Pico della Mirandola. He had studied Greek and Latin with the same tutor as Ariosto and was a good friend of Bembo and Ercole Strozzi. Lucrezia had met him during the carnival of 1504 when he gave a dinner in her honor. At the time of this dinner Lucrezia's son Rodrigo and his cousin Giovanni, the *infans Romanus*, were both in Naples being cared for by Rodrigo's aunt, Sancha of Aragon. Since there is no mention of Sancha in the accounts of the festivities celebrating Lucrezia's third marriage, it is likely that out of deference to the memory of her brother, she deliberately absented herself from Rome at that time. When she returned soon afterward, rumor once again linked her with Cardinal Ippolito. In October 1502, in what many interpreted as a protest against her loose morals, Alexander sent her and her court to the Castel Sant' Angelo. Just when he released her is not clear. In any case Sancha returned to the castle at the time of the pope's death along with Vannozza and the two children. Shortly thereafter, Prospero Colonna offered Sancha asylum in his fortress at Marino. When she sailed for Naples with him that December, everyone took it for granted that she had become his mistress. Although Geoffredo was in Naples at the time, according to some reports, Sancha refused to see her husband. But she did invite Cesare to dinner two days after his arrival, and she agreed to care for Rodrigo and the *infans Romanus* until other arrangements could be made for them. For some reason the earlier plan to send Rodrigo to Spain was dropped. Probably because Alfonso would not consider having the child in Ferrara, Lucrezia decided to entrust her son to the care of his father's half sister, Isabella of Milan, the widow of Gian Galeazzo Sforza, who was then living in Bari. But Lucrezia brought the *infans Romanus* to live with her.

Impressed by Alberto Pio's vast knowledge, she later sent the little boy to Carpi to be tutored by him. What she did not seem to know or what she pretended not to know was that besides being a scholar and humanist, Alberto Pio was also a petty, scheming politician who regarded Alfonso and Ippolito as his natural enemies and liked nothing better than harassing them.

Although Alberto would later say that he had had no idea why Don Giulio wanted the crossbowmen from him, he willingly provided them. With their help and the help of Don Ferrante, Don Giulio then stormed the castle where Don Rainaldo was being held, freed the chaplain, and as a taunt to his jailers, imprisoned the castellan in his place. After sending Don Rainaldo to Carpi for safekeeping, Don Giulio rejoined Lucrezia at Rubiera.

To Cardinal Ippolito the freeing of the chaplain seemed a deliberate insult to his authority, which, of course, it was; and he demanded that Alfonso do something about it. The cardinal's reaction was, in fact, so violent that it frightened Alberto Pio, who, though he liked to annoy Alfonso and Ippolito, had no in-

tention of giving them an excuse to invade his territory by continuing to shelter the chaplain in Carpi. At the end of July,
Alberto met with Lucrezia to see if the two of them could work
out a settlement of the chaplain's case that would be agreeable to everyone. Soon afterward, Alfonso, who didn't like his wife's
friendship with Alberto any better than he liked her friendship with
Bembo or Ercole Strozzi or Francesco Gonzaga, all of whom he regarded as in one way or another hostile to him, sent her a letter. The
letter ordered her to inform Don Giulio that as punishment for his
"presumption and guilt" in the matter of the chaplain, he must go to
the family estate at Brescello. He was to remain within a two-mile
radius of the estate at all times and report to Alfonso's resident com-
missioner every day. It was probably to make sure that Lucrezia carried out these orders that Alfonso visited her at the end of August.
By then Alberto Pio had persuaded Don Rainaldo to go back to prison by assuring him that his life would be spared, and it was. Certainly neither Alberto nor Lucrezia, the chaplain or anyone else involved in the affair could have had any premonition of the gruesome
tragedy to which it would eventually lead.

On September 19, Lucrezia gave birth to a baby boy whom she
named Alessandro in memory of her father. Soon afterward Alfonso
and his court came to Reggio to see the long-awaited heir. They were
joined by Don Ferrante and Isabella. Isabella had always been Don
Giulio's advocate within the family, and she persuaded Alfonso to
include their brother in the general amnesty he issued to celebrate the
baby's birth. Although baby Alessandro was a scrawny little thing
who would not take food and cried constantly, the doctors must
have assured his parents that he would survive, or they wouldn't
have celebrated as they did. Soon after Alfonso left for Comacchio,
however, the baby took a turn for the worse. A few days later he
was dead. The plague and famine in Ferrara were still as bad as ever,
and says one chronicler, "in the face of so many calamities, the University was closed and the courts ordered to take a holiday."

Perhaps Alfonso was too pained even to think of consoling his
wife. Perhaps he had convinced himself that she was to blame for
these moribund children. In any event, he left her alone at Reggio to
handle her grief as best she could. Bembo had written to congratu-
late her on the birth of this "*aspettatissimo* [most awaited]
bambino." Upon learning of the child's death, he wrote once more.

Although Lucrezia must have cherished his letter, it would awaken painful memories and make her loneliness all the harder to bear.

Reggio is a short distance from the Mantuan border. When Francesco Gonzaga heard that Lucrezia's baby had died, he was inspecting his citadel at Borgoforte on the Po. Partly because he was warmhearted enough to appreciate how desolate she must feel and partly because he was sufficiently attracted to her to relish playing the part of her consoler, he invited her and her court to visit him. A little over a month before, Lucrezia had written to ask him to speak to both the pope and the duke of Urbino about freeing Cesare. If he did this, she and her brother would be indebted to him for the rest of their lives, she had assured him. Under the circumstances, she could not possibly refuse his invitation without appearing both ungracious and ungrateful. On the other hand, as Gonzaga may or may not have realized, she knew that Alfonso would probably disapprove of the visit, and she used considerable ingenuity to circumvent his disapproval. At the time she received Gonzaga's invitation, she had already told her husband that she would return to Belriguardo at the beginning of November. Since the valley of the Po was then crisscrossed by innumerable canals which connected the river with its numerous tributaries, the simplest way to get from one place to another was by water. In planning her trip home, she arranged to have her boat pass Borgoforte, thus making her visit appear considerably more casual than it really was. And she did not tell Alfonso of her plans until it was too late for him to do anything about them.

Although Francesco Gonzaga was as sensual as his brother-in-law Alfonso, he preferred courting his women to procuring them. He was also romantic enough to enjoy the act of courtship even when, as in this case, he wasn't at all sure it would lead to the act of love. He felt "as if he had already gained a great treasure," he wrote Lucrezia after she accepted his invitation. Although Borgoforte was not equipped to receive "so radiant an apparition," he would do everything he could to make her stay comfortable.

It was the beginning of a romantic attachment that would last all the rest of their lives. If neither fell in love with the other, both enjoyed the illusion of love their meeting gave them, and both were sentimental enough to cherish the memory of their brief time together. One learned scholar has even suggested that they ended up in bed. But even if we assume that Lucrezia was willing—and this is debatable—they were only in Borgoforte for two days; she was still recovering from a difficult delivery; and there was also the problem of circumventing all those ladies-in-waiting and clowns.

Lucrezia had told Alfonso she would leave for Belriguardo on the thirtieth, but Gonzaga insisted that she first visit Isabella at Mantua. In fact, Lucrezia told her husband he insisted upon this with "such vehemence and determination" that though she used "considerable resistance," she was forced to obey. And so on the morning of the thirtieth, after leaving the rougher waters of the Po, their boat continued on the "smooth-sliding Mincius," past fields that had not changed much since Virgil's farmers cleaved the earth "with share and curving plough," to Mantua with its lagoons, its three lakes formed by the river, its arcades, now so battered and then so new, and its 450-room palace where Isabella was waiting to greet them.

When Isabella d'Este had come to Mantua at the age of sixteen, her romantic twenty-five-year-old husband had fallen in love with his slim golden-haired bride. And to judge by Isabella's letters to him she had returned his love. But she was so lacking in spontaneity, so studied and artificial in all her ways, that he soon began to wonder if she meant what she said or was merely playing the part of the perfect wife because she found it necessary to be the perfect everything. Nor did he like being reminded in numerous subtle and not so subtle ways of her superior political acumen and of her admiration for her brother-in-law Ludovico Sforza, a man far wealthier and more powerful than her husband. During the wars with the French, Gonzaga had served as captain-general of the army of Venice until in 1497 the Venetian senate dismissed him. Rightly or wrongly, he blamed Ludovico for his dismissal. When shortly afterward, Isabella left for Ferrara to discuss the matter with her father instead of remaining in Mantua with her husband, Gonzaga turned to another woman for consolation. Later, at a tournament in honor of the queen of Cyprus, it was this mistress who was at his side. Isabella pretended to "neither hear nor see." Although she and her husband continued to sleep together—she bore him six children—whatever love she had once felt inevitably turned to resentment as she saw him go from mistress to mistress. Once in a fit of rage she cut off the hair of one of her ladies-in-waiting "for playing the nymph with the Marchese."

And once, but only once, she let her husband know the pain he had caused her:

Knowing how much I deserve of you and how little I receive, I am tempted at times to alter my nature and to appear different from what I am. But even if you should treat me badly I would never cease to do what is right, and the less love you show me the more I shall always show you; because in truth, this love is part of myself, and because I became your wife so young that I can never remember being without it.

There were so many women available to a marchese of Mantua that eventually he would have been unfaithful to her in any case. But it was her tragedy never to understand how much her own shortcomings contributed to his unfaithfulness.

Although it would be only natural for Isabella to find her husband's attentions to Lucrezia infuriating, she did not allow her feelings to show. Instead, she insisted that her sister-in-law visit the famous *studiolo*, and she proudly pointed out the numerous treasures she had accumulated within its carved and gilded walls: the two allegorical paintings by Mantegna, the *Nativity* by Bellini, the many rare books and manuscripts, the "cupid" she had wangled from Cesare, the beautiful clavichord that had once belonged to her sister Beatrice. But despite the joy that she took in showing off her collection and Lucrezia's respectful admiration, she must have been glad to see her sister-in-law leave Mantua.

So that Lucrezia and her party would make up the time they had lost by visiting the city, Gonzanga insisted that they use his state barge. During the time he and Lucrezia had been together she had, of course, spoken to him of Cesare more than once. Although Francesco Gonzaga found his sister-in-law a charming young woman, and was, no doubt, touched by her devotion to her brother, it was also his policy to win over potentially dissident members of the house of Este by little acts of kindness. Before Lucrezia left for Belriguardo, he promised to send an envoy to speak to Ferdinand and Isabella about Cesare's case. In November, Lucrezia would thank him for having kept his promise.

Alfonso and Don Giulio were at Belriguardo to greet Lucrezia when she arrived there. By then both brothers had forgotten the incident of the chaplain. During those brisk autumn days, Don Giulio spent his time hunting in the surrounding fields, and he was, of course, delighted to resume his flirtation with Angela. Meanwhile, in the nearby villa of Vignano, Ippolito continued to brood over the presumption that this bastard brother of his had shown, and the piffling reproof he had received for it. Don Giulio's success with Angela also rankled the cardinal. Like most princes of the church, Ippolito had never allowed his cardinal's hat to interfere with his womanizing. "I am your pastor and you are my little sheep," he was fond of telling Lucrezia's ladies-in-waiting. And he could not understand why Angela should prefer to be his brother's little sheep rather than his. According to a legend which may or may not be true, when Ippolito asked her about this, Angela told him that it was Don Giulio's eyes that had made her fall in love with him. "Monsignore," she is supposed to have said, "your brother's eyes are worth more than the whole of your person."

The numerous chroniclers who repeat this conversation fail to say when it took place, whether in June before Angela accompanied Lucrezia to Modena, or at the beginning of November when she was at Belriguardo. In December, Lucrezia and her court would return to Ferrara, and in January the Mantuan ambassador would tell Isabella that he gathered "that the lady Angela gave birth to a child when coming here [to Ferrara] by ship." But he is the only one to speak of the birth, and there is no mention of who the father was or of what happened to the baby. If, however, the story is true, Ippolito would have confronted a very pregnant Angela that November at Belriguardo and would, of course, have assumed immediately that Don Giulio was the father. But even if Angela wasn't pregnant, there was still her remark about Don Giulio's eyes, a remark that a man like the cardinal must have found intolerable.

Ariosto, who was then in the cardinal's employ, would dedicate his *Orlando Furioso* to him, hailing him as the "good seed of Hercules," and "Ippolite the Good." But in the *Satires*, which he wrote when he was no longer dependent on Ippolito for a living, he pictures him as a monster of self-centeredness: "He does not consider his praises composed by me as worthy of any thanks. If I have praised him in my verses, he says, I have done so at my leisure; better if I had been at hand to wait on him."

When Ippolito was crossed, or when his pride was wounded, he did not hesitate to give physical expression to his rage. There was, for example, the time he had ordered his servants to beat up the pope's messenger. Don Giulio had already crossed his brother in the matter of the chaplain, and now this handsome bastard stood between him and the girl he wanted. On the afternoon of November 3— only two days after Angela's arrival at Belriguardo—Don Giulio was coming home from hunting in the fields when he met Ippolito and four of his attendants. "Kill that man! Tear out his eyes!" Ippolito shouted. Whereupon, the cardinal's attendants threw Don Giulio from his horse and dug their rapiers into his eyes. It was all over in a matter of minutes, and it is possible that Ippolito hadn't expected his attendants to obey him so unquestioningly—which does not, of course, excuse him. He could have left his brother to die. Instead he rushed to Belriguardo to tell Alfonso that he had found Don Giulio bleeding and wounded in the fields and did not know who had attacked him.

By November 8, however, he had changed his story. In a letter to the Ferrarese ambassador in Rome, he asked him to tell the pope "that when Don Giulio was at Belriguardo and riding for pleasure in the country round after midday, he was assailed by four men, formerly our familiars, who dragged him from his horse and with repeated blows strove to extinguish the light of his eyes—albeit we still hope that by the grace of God the affair will pass off well." And it was this explanation of the crime that Alfonso dispatched to all the courts of Italy.

In the dispatch he sent to Mantua, however, he included a postscript in which he told Isabella what had really happened. "I am much afflicted by this business," he wrote, "for to him [Don Giulio] this is more cruel than death and because this shameful act is an outrage against the name of our most illustrious house." And he urged her to speak of it to no one and to burn his postscript as soon as she read it. But Isabella considered this precaution pointless, since, as she told her brother, by then there wasn't a barber in the piazza who couldn't give a better account of what had happened than Alfonso had given in his postscript. Ippolito's henchmen fled to Venice, and the cardinal himself fled to Mantua, where he was given such a cold reception that he moved on to Mirandola. Both Isabella and her husband urged Alfonso to punish the guilty, as did Don Ferrante, to whom Isabella had shown the postscript.

Don Giulio was then in the *castello*. Alfonso had called in the best doctors in Ferrara to care for him, and Isabella had sent doctors from Mantua. After examining the patient, these doctors all appeared confident that they could restore partial vision to both eyes. But the once handsome Don Giulio had lost the lid on his right eye and his left eye was horribly swollen. Seeing him thus, Alfonso found it hard to keep back the tears. Nevertheless, he could not bring himself to punish Ippolito, because he did not trust himself to govern Ferrara without him. He may have also thought that, given his brother's fiendish nature, it was better to have him as a friend than as an enemy. Moreover, Alfonso knew that as a temporal ruler he lacked the authority to punish a prince of the church. He could, of course, turn Ippolito over to the pope, but Julius was no friend of the Estense and would use the case to discredit them. Nor did it seem right to turn a brother over to a third party for punishment.

By the middle of December, Ippolito was back in Ferrara. A few days before Christmas, Alfonso arranged for him to visit Don Giulio. To prepare Don Giulio for the visit, Alfonso sent the poet Niccolò da Correggio and two other courtiers to speak to him. They were still with him when Alfonso and Ippolito entered his darkened room accompanied by a boy holding a candle. It was the first time Ippolito had seen Don Giulio since the attack. He was grief stricken and penitent and wished to be a good brother, Ippolito told him. But the smoothness of his delivery belied his grief, and Don Giulio made no effort to conceal his bitterness. "Signore, Your Excellency sees how I am," he replied addressing the duke. "I have God and Our lady to thank for conceding me partial vision," he continued, now addressing Ippolito directly. "And although my case could not have been more cruel and inhuman, and although what was done to me was in no way my fault, I pardon Your Excellency and I will not fail to be the same goo d brother to him I always was." After that there was more talk of contrition and forgiveness and of how important it was for the brothers to forget their past differences for the good of the state. Niccolò da Correggio, who had known them since they were children, told them that he had spoken to them about this so many times and they knew his feelings in the matter so well that there was no point in his saying any more. But still Alfonso was not satisfied. Before he left, he asked for "some sign of love and peace" from them. At his urging, they kissed one another. After that Ippolito occasionally sent someone to his brother's room to ask him how he was getting on. "As well as could be expected" was Don Giulio's invariable reply. But those who visited him noticed his rancor.

The plague and famine had abated by then, and carnival time was approaching. Alfonso's sympathy for the misfortunes of others was at best limited. There had been no carnival the year before because of Ercole's death. To again have no carnival because of what had happened to Don Giulio would not help his brother, and it would deprive everyone else of a much-needed good time. Not only did Alfonso allow the carnival to go ahead as planned, he seemed determined to make it the liveliest ever. After rescinding his father's order prohibiting the use of masks, he had Lucrezia set an example by going through the streets masked, accompanied by two of her clowns and her new master of revels, Niccolò da Correggio. Thus encouraged, everyone in Ferrara was soon wearing masks. There were masked balls and masquerades as well as the usual dinner parties, plays, and pageants. In an eclogue coauthored by Niccolò da Correggio, Mercury announced that Ercole was rejoicing in heaven among the gods at seeing his son established as duke. . . . Let Alfonso, therefore, make merry with his glorious consort for in a very short time they would produce a new Ercole.

Mindful of the young duke's taste for horseplay, the resourceful Niccolò also arranged a mock battle in which two sets of courtiers, one armed with eggs and the other with sticks, fought one another in the Piazza del Duomo. Another day there was a pig fight modeled after one Alfonso had seen in Venice. The unfortunate pig chosen for the battle was placed under one of the galleries in the courtyard of the *castello* with one foot tied. To the blare of trumpets, a number of the duke's porters and hangers-on, clad in armor and with their eyes hidden by the visors of their helmets, were then led into the courtyard. They had been furnished with long clubs and told to seek out the pig and kill him, but because they could not see very well, they began hitting each other "in asinine fashion." Finally, one of their number spotted the pig. After jumping astride the poor, cowering beast, he clubbed him to death. Delighted, Alfonso arranged for another pig fight. This time a platform was built for the animal in the Piazza del Duomo, and the men sent to attack him wore blindfolds.

What with all these diversions, the government appeared to be at a standstill. According to the Mantuan ambassador, even the suppliants' court was dozing. Certainly Lucrezia could have had little time to listen to appeals. In addition to presiding at all the dances and theatricals and banquets given in the *castello* and watching the pig fights, she was also involved in arranging a marriage for her cousin

Angela. And because of the tragedy of which Angela had been the inadvertent cause, Alfonso wanted this marriage arranged as quickly as possible. There was, of course, no thought of marrying her to Don Giulio. In an effort to get Don Giulio out of Ferrara, Alfonso had asked Lucrezia to obtain a post and a benefice in the Order of Malta for her brother-in-law. The holder of a benefice could not marry.

Twenty-year-old Alessandro Pio of Sassuolo, the man the duke chose to be Angela's husband, belonged to that branch of the Pio family that had remained loyal to the Estense. In February, Lucrezia invited him to Ferrara to meet his bride-to-be. So that the young couple could get to know one another she left them alone in one of the rooms of her apartment for over two hours. To her husband's smirking courtiers it seemed obvious that they couldn't have spent all that time talking. "Surely conversation has led to copulation," said the baron. In any event they were betrothed.

To Don Giulio, the news of Angela's betrothal was one more reason to settle accounts with his brothers. By then Giulio was almost as resentful of Alfonso for not having punished Ippolito as he was of the cardinal for having attacked him. Although he was beginning to regain his vision, his eyes were still too weak to stand a strong light, and he continued to find it impossible to sleep because of the pain. Often during those sleepless nights he would hear the laughter of the masked merrymakers in the piazza below. Sometimes he would ask the servants to open the shutters so that he might catch a glimpse of what was going on. The thought of all the *cose stomacose* he was missing would torment him, especially when he pictured Ippolito, all elegance and perfume, his long hair held in place by the ivory combs Isabella had given him, going from party to party and from conquest to conquest. The most illustrious and reverend cardinal still had not visited him because he was too busy day and night with masquerades and other diversions, Don Giulio told Alberto Pio a few days before the end of carnival.

His brother Ferrante, on the other hand, visited him almost daily and had been doing so ever since the attack. Often Ferrante brought one of the captains of Alfonso's crossbowmen, a certain Gherardo de Roberti, with him. De Roberti's father-in-law, Count Albertino Boschetti, had served with Ferrante in the war against Pisa. The sexagenarian count had never gotten along with Ercole, and he hated

Alfonso for disputing his right to the fief of San Cesario, as well as for treating him like a person of no consequence. Were Ferrante to replace his brother as duke, there would be no more talk of taking San Cesario, and Boschetti would get the recognition he deserved, or at least so he must have reasoned.

In September, while Lucrezia was at Reggio, the count and his son-in-law had invited Ferrante and one of his lackeys, Roberto Boccaccio, to a meeting at nearby Le Lame. The upshot of this meeting was a decision to kill Alfonso and make Ferrante duke in his place. At first the conspirators proposed to kill Alfonso that fall at one of his villas near Ferrara. Later, they decided it would be easier to do away with him at carnival time. By the time carnival began, Ferrante and Gherardo had persuaded Don Giulio to join the conspiracy, and they had also recruited Alfonso's procurer, Gian Cantore. Why Gian decided to join them remains a mystery. Perhaps after having catered to Alfonso's lowest tastes for so long, he had come to despise him. Or perhaps, as Ariosto would later imply, this "fair fat Gascon" was filled with an all-encompassing hatred that made him love violence and discord for their own sake.

During the first weeks of carnival, the conspirators spent hours planning how they would kill Alfonso. But as they soon discovered, it was one thing to talk about killing him and another thing to do it. Once, when Alfonso was in a prostitute's room, Gian Cantore tied him to the bedpost with the intention to point him out to a hired assassin. But when Alfonso asked to be set free, Gian meekly obliged him. Another time the conspirators learned that Alfonso intended to return to the *castello* via a certain street and sent Gherardo de Roberti to lie in wait for him on the corner. Since Alfonso was masked and had only one servant with him, it should have been easy to take him by surprise. But when de Roberti saw him coming, he ducked into a barbershop in a neighboring street. There were still other ambushes and there was a hired assassin who arrived in Ferrara with two poisoned stilettos. The stilettos were never used; the hired assassin became disgusted with the pusillanimity of his employers and went home; the ambushes all failed. To Machiavelli, who discusses the ineptitude of the conspirators in the *Discorsi*, "Their neglect to profit by the opportunities afforded them for the execution of their design could have arisen only from two causes: Either the presence of the prince imposed upon them and filled them with fear, or they were disarmed by some act of kindness on his part."

At the end of March, Alfonso announced plans to go to Venice and then to visit the Spanish shrine of San Juan de Compostella. During his absence Lucrezia would serve as regent, assisted by Ippolito. When the conspirators learned of the proposed trip, they decided that Gian Cantore, who was to accompany the duke, should kill him while he was away from Ferrara. But on the day the galley was to set sail, Gian asked Alfonso if he could be excused from making the trip because he was prone to seasickness!

By then Don Giulio's doctors had long since pronounced him sufficiently recovered to return to his palace on the Via degli Angeli. Because Ippolito feared that his brother might be planning to avenge his injuries, he had arranged for one of Alfonso's former crossbowmen, a fellow with the reassuring name of Tuttobono, to enter Don Giulio's service. Besides acting as the cardinal's spy, Tuttobono probably also served as an agent provocateur. In any event, it did not take him long to find out about the conspiracy. All that remained was to gather enough evidence to convict the guilty. And it was to this task that Ippolito devoted himself while Alfonso was away. Whether Lucrezia had any idea of what he was up to there is no way of knowing. It was her first time as regent, and in May she had to deal with an outbreak of anti-Semitism.

The Jewish community in Ferrara was one of the oldest in northern Italy. Because the Estense were perpetually in need of money, they made it a policy to encourage Jewish banks and to discourage anti-Semitism. But despite the numerous laws they passed to protect the Jews, the latent prejudices of their Christian neighbors occasionally surfaced. The belief that the Jews used the blood of Christian children in their ceremonies was then prevalent throughout Europe and would be for centuries to come. During Ercole's reign, the rumor that a group of Jewish moneylenders had killed a Christian child in order to crucify her brought an angry mob to their bank near the Po. When Ercole's brother Sigismundo arrived on the scene, the mob had the bank surrounded and was battering down the oaken doors. Sigismundo attempted to calm them before Ercole appeared and ordered everyone to go home "on pain of the gallows." He intended to study the matter, he told them, but meanwhile he did not consider it right for people to molest Jews and destroy their houses. When someone shouted that it was a duty to kill those *"pessimi Zudein,"* Ercole drew his sword and the heckler quickly disappeared. Later, six hoodlums were arrested for having deliberately incited the people to riot in the hope of profiting from the disturbance.

Though not as serious, the outbreaks against the Jews in May 1506 also appear to have been the work of a few thugs. To discourage these malefactors and to prevent the outbreaks from spreading, Lucrezia instructed her officials to proceed *"virilmente"* by punishing all those who injured Jews in any place and in any way as severely as if these same malefactors had injured their fellow Christians. And she let it be known that she considered it "iniquitous" for these "delinquents" to harass and injure Jews in this fashion.

Shortly before Lucrezia issued this decree, Cardinal Ippolito arrested the spy Tuttobono. The reason for this arrest was not known, the Mantuan ambassador told Isabella, but he assumed that it was related to some plan the cardinal had for ruining Don Giulio. The arrest so terrified Don Ferrante that he wrote to Isabella begging her to persuade Don Giulio to come to Mantua "to avoid scandal." But Don Giulio seemed unperturbed. Tuttobono was still being held when, on June 13, Ippolito's crossbowmen arrested one of Don Ferrante's servants. On the nineteenth, both this servant and Tuttobono were released. That same day Ippolito's crossbowmen sought to arrest Gian Cantore, but he he fled the city without saying a word to anyone. Soon afterward, Ippolito decided to write to Alfonso. Their mother, Eleanora of Aragon, had been the aunt of Isabella of Milan, and Alfonso was then in Bari visiting his cousin. Since Isabella was caring for Lucrezia's little Rodrigo, Lucrezia seems to have hoped that her husband would bring the child back to Ferrara with him. After the arrival of Ippolito's letter, however, any plans Alfonso may have had for Rodrigo were quickly put aside. On July 3, he returned to Ferrara.

By then Don Ferrante had persuaded Don Giulio to go to Mantua. Save for complaining that Giulio had left the city without permission and asking that he return immediately, Alfonso gave no sign that he knew of the plot against his life until July 22, when he ordered an inquiry. On the twenty-fifth, Count Albertino Boschetti was brought in for questioning. On the twenty-sixth, it was Don Ferrante's turn. In his terror, Ferrante made no effort to shield anyone. Because he had been told that his life would be spared if Don Giulio were returned to Ferrara, he begged Francesco Gonzaga "that having more respect for my welfare than for that of Don Giulio you will do me this favor." But Gonzaga could see no reason to oblige him. Don Giulio remained in Mantua and Ferrante was imprisoned in the Torre Marchesana. Gherardo de Roberti was also arrested and imprisoned in the tower, as was Ferrante's lackey, Roberto Boccaccio. As a prince of the ruling house, Ferrante was spared the cord, but the others were tortured repeatedly to get them to reveal all the details of the plot.

Francesco Gonzaga's reasons for refusing to turn Don Giulio over to Alfonso were the same as the pope's reasons for refusing to turn over Gian Cantore, who was then in Rome in the service of one of the cardinals. He objected to Alfonso's pro-Venetian policy and could not see why he should oblige him in any way. Isabella, on the other hand, did not want her husband to surrender Don Giulio simply because he was her brother and she loved him. Although she could not condone the crime of *lese-majesty*, of which he was accused, she realized that it was Alfonso's failure to punish Ippolito that had led Don Giulio to conspire against them. And she must also have resented the ingenious way the cardinal had used the conspiracy to obscure his own iniquity and to reinforce his hold on Alfonso. Negotiations between Ferrara and Mantua continued for almost six weeks. Only after Alfonso promised to spare the lives of both brothers did Isabella and her husband finally agree to surrender Don Giulio. And even then Isabella could not at first bring herself to sign the extradition papers, probably because they contained a clause attesting to Don Giulio's guilt. In the end, however, her husband insisted that she sign, and Don Giulio was sent back to Ferrara in chains. Alfonso ordered him imprisoned in one of the dungeons of the *castello*, where he was left alone "with irons on his feet." That night, according to Alberto Pio, the duke sent one of his men to the cell "to spit in his brother's face, he [Alfonso] being present but hidden."

On the following Saturday, Count Albertino Boschetti, his son-in-law Gherardo de Roberti, and Ferrante's servant Roberto Boccaccio were beheaded in the Piazza del Duomo and their bodies quartered. As a warning to others, the heads of the executed men were stuck on lances and placed at the summit of one of the towers overlooking the piazza, where they would remain until they disintegrated. On October 18, the court sentenced Don Ferrante and Don Giulio to the same punishment, but in compliance with the promise Alfonso had made to Isabella, he commuted their sentence to life imprisonment. On October 30, the pope finally handed over Gian Cantore to the Ferrarese authorities. After being led around the city by the hangman and spat upon and tormented by the crowds who had come out to witness his humiliation, he was imprisoned in the *castello*. On the sixth of January 1507, the day of Epiphany, "the said Gian was placed in an iron cage and shown outside the Castel Vecchio. He was dressed in a doublet of light cloth and was fed with bread and wine; the weather was fine, and an icy north wind was blowing strongly." A week later he was found dead in the cage with a napkin tied around his throat. Although he was said to have committed suicide, most people assumed he had been strangled.

Don Giulio and Don Ferrante were assigned windowless rooms, one above the other, in a tower of the *castello*. Eighteen years later, they were moved to a three-room apartment in the same tower from which they could see as far as the hospital of Santa Anna. Don Ferrante died in this apartment at the age of sixty-three. Don Giulio was eighty-one when Alfonso's and Lucrezia's grandson, Alfonso II, set him free. According to one chronicler, the appearance of the still erect and handsome old man with his long beard and his elegant clothing cut in the style of half a century before "flabbergasted" the young people. It was then fifty-three years since Don Giulio had entered the tower. The two brothers who had condemned him, the sister who had sought to protect him, and the beautiful girl who had been the unwitting cause of his disfigurement were all long since dead, and he must have felt as alone in the world of strangers that confronted him on his release as he had felt in his solitary prison. He died two years later.

"He who does evil, so much the worse for him," Niccolò da Correggio had said at the time that the conspiracy was discovered. But the conspirators were so inept and so frightened that it is unlikely they would have ever gotten around to killing Alfonso. Had they not been discovered, they would probably have made a few more half-hearted attempts to do away with him and then given up. After they were arrested, however, the people were given to understand that their arrest had saved Ferrara from an imminent and bloody civil war. On August 3, the day the trial for conspiracy began, church bells all over the city announced the glad tidings to the people. That evening bonfires were kindled in the Piazza del Duomo and before the palaces of many of Alfonso's nobles. Inevitably, God was dragged into the festivities, and for the next four days shops all over the city remained closed so that everyone could join in a series of religious processions organized to thank him for allowing the malefactors to be discovered in time. Before setting out from the archbishop's palace each morning, Alfonso and Ippolito and the priests and nobles who accompanied them heard a solemn mass of the Holy Spirit. Although Lucrezia did not take part in the procession, the chroniclers tell us that "the duchess and all the noblewomen attended this Mass." We catch another glimpse of her a few days earlier when Gherardo de Roberti was led into the piazza of the *castello* "where the people were awaiting him, and at the windows over the covered way were the duke, the cardinal and the duchess."

As Alfonso's duchess, Lucrezia would also be present at the execution of Roberti and his father-in-law and at the sentencing of Don Giulio and Don Ferrante. But there are relatively few indications of how she felt about all this. In 1508, Don Giulio's former chaplain Don Rainaldo appears on the list of persons in her employ. In 1510 she and two of the courtiers paid a visit to Don Ferrante and Don Giulio "to comfort them both and to give them hope of a speedy liberation," a liberation that, as it turned out, she was powerless to arrange though she was then acting as regent. But even if at the time of their imprisonment she, like Isabella, was appalled at Alfonso's cruelty to his brothers, it would be only natural for her to be more concerned about the fate of her own brother. After an unsuccessful attempt to escape from the castle of Chinchilla, Cesare had been transferred to the even more inaccessible fortress of Medina del Campo in Castile. When in December Lucrezia heard that he had escaped, her joy was such that she could think of nothing else.

Cesare's escape had been worthy of the audacious commander whom Machiavelli had once labelled "magnificent." With the aid of a rope smuggled into his cell by a sympathetic local count, he had let himself down from his window seventy feet above the ground and, when the rope proved too short, had made a daring leap that landed him in the ditch surrounding the fortress. Because of his injuries he had to be carried to the count's stronghold at Villalon where he spent several weeks waiting for his broken bones to mend. After leaving Villalon, he made his way to the port city of Santander disguised as a wool merchant. On December 3, he arrived at the court of his brother-in-law Jean of Navarre. When the news of his escape reached Italy, banners bearing the bull of the Borgias appeared at windows all over the Romagna and cries of *"Duca! Duca!"* were heard in the streets. His former subjects had "good cause to love their duke," Guicciardini was forced to admit, "for he gave them the best government they had ever known." And the Spanish chronicler Zerita tells us that the news of Cesare's escape caused the pope "great anxiety," because the duke "was greatly beloved not only by men of war but also by many people in Ferrara and the States of the Church, something that seldom falls to the lot of a tyrant."

Although Francesco Gonzaga was then captain-general of the church and could be expected to share the pope's anxiety, both Cesare and Lucrezia seem to have been too elated to realize this. In fact, one of the first things Cesare did after arriving in Navarre was to send Gonzaga a letter informing him of all that had happened. With a childlike confidence in the marchese's continuing good will, he signed himself "your majesty's friend and younger brother," and Lucrezia wrote the marchese that she felt certain he would be as happy as she was at the news of her brother's escape. When Gonzaga came to Ferrara that January, everyone noticed "the great cheer and affection" with which the duchess greeted him. Although she had just learned that she was again pregnant, her pregnancy did not keep her from dancing with the marchese most of the evening. A few days later she miscarried. Alfonso immediately attributed the miscarriage to her "having been on her feet too much." According to the Mantuan ambassador, he was "more displeased [than] when the one who was born died because this time she is weakened in the spine." If Lucrezia was aggrieved, she did not show it. On February 6, one of the courtiers noted that "the duchess had been out at least three times since her misfortune."

When Cesare had set sail for Italy in September 1499, he had named his seventeen-year-old bride the administrator of his French lands. After his escape from prison he sent a messenger to the king of France to ask Louis's permission to return to the French court and to take possession of the duchy of Valentois and the other lands he had been granted. Besides writing to the king to second Cesare's request,

Lucrezia also wrote to the Ferrarese ambassador in Paris urging him to use his influence on her brother's behalf. But now that Alexander was dead, Louis could see nothing to be gained from helping Cesare. Under the pretext that he had failed the French during the second *impresa di Napoli*, the king had long since revoked his title to the duchy of Valentois. Nor would Louis consider giving Cesare the dowry he had been promised at the time of his marriage to Charlotte d'Albret. Deprived of land and titles, the two things that counted most in computing a man's worth, Cesare had no alternative but to offer his services as a condottiere to Charlotte's brother Jean of Navarre. After bringing Lucrezia the news of her brother's arrival in Navarre, Cesare's messenger went to Bologna, where Julius ordered him arrested. In a letter to Gonzaga, Lucrezia termed the arrest a "smaccamento" (an insult) and protested that her brother "would not think of doing anything to injure His Holiness." Despite her protest, however, she must have realized that Cesare would never be content to remain a simple condottiere and that he would constantly seek ways to get back what had once been his.

The Lenten sermon that year was preached by Fra Raffaele de Varese, a man whom the women of Ferrara found "truly useful to the soul." Like Savonarola and any number of lesser reformers, Fra Raffaele considered paint and powder the devil's handiwork. So impressed was Lucrezia by his words that she ordered her ladies-in-waiting to forgo the white compact foundation called *liscio* which they used as a base for rouge. To set an example, she had her alchemist prepare distilled water and the juice of aromatic herbs for washing and smoothing the face. On Good Friday, she and her ladies-in-waiting appeared in church without *liscio*, but, said one who saw them, "everyone wore rouge, beginning with the wise chief." Although the women of Ferrara were willing to follow "the wise chief's" example in the matter of makeup, they objected so vociferously to a suggestion that they cover their bosoms that the idea had to be dropped. Nor were the men any happier when, in response to the friar's urging, Alfonso raised the fines for blasphemy.

Soon afterward the duke left for Genoa to confer with Louis XII. It was while he was away from Ferrara and Lucrezia was acting as regent that she learned that her brother was dead. Death had come cruelly and unexpectedly while Cesare and his men were laying siege to the castle of Viana, a remote hilltop fortress near the Castillian border that belonged to Louis de Beaumont, one of the more obstreperous of Navarre's vassals. When Cesare learned that a company of soliders from Castile had smuggled provisions to de Beaumont, he and his horsemen rode out to confront them. Rather than do battle the soldiers fled. Calling to his men to follow, Cesare galloped after them. By the time he realized that he had outstripped all but one of his horsemen and sought to turn back, the enemy had him surrounded. Although he fought bravely, he was one against a multitude. The next day his soldiers retrieved his slashed and mud-spattered body, "bare as a hand," and laid it to rest before the high altar of Santa Maria de Viana. He was thirty-one years old. "Of his virtues and vices I shall say no more for they have been talked about enough," wrote a French soldier who had known him, "but I must say that in war he was a good comrade and a brave man."

> Cesare Borgia who was held by all
> To be a sun in courage and in arms
> Obliged to depart went whither Phoebus goes
> As evening falls towards the west.

The words are from the epitaph written by a poet of the Romagna. The inscription on Cesare's tomb was still more laudatory:

> Here lies in little earth
> The man the whole earth feared
> And who in his hand
> Held both peace and war
> O thou who seekest things worthy of praise
> If thou wouldst praise the worthiest
> Cease thy journey here.

"He controlled the Italian despots so well," said Abbé Brantôme, "that he stopped their capers . . . and there was hardly any more talk of those petty tyrants for which the Church is greatly in his debt." But the anonymous author of *The Pitiful Lament of the Duke of Valentois Son of Alexander VI* reproached him for his lack of moderation and for failing to realize that power without reason is worthless.

Fra Raffaele was given the task of breaking the news of Cesare's death to Lucrezia. By an ironic coincidence, she had just been telling one of Alfonso's cousins of the awful grief she had felt after the death of her father. Never again would she allow herself to give way to such uncontrollable grief, she declared. She heard Fra Raffaele in silence. "The more I try to do God's will the more he visits me with misfortune," she said when he had finished. It was a cry from the heart, a pathetic protest against unceasing calamity. Nevertheless, something in the friar's expression must have made her realize how close it came to blasphemy, for she made haste to add that she thanked God and was resigned to his will. Everyone paid tribute to her admirable behavior and staunch spirit," said the Mantuan ambassador. But at night in the privacy of her own room, or sometimes even during the day when she thought she was unobserved, her ladies-in-waiting would hear her endlessly repeating her brother's name.

"Give way to tears, a just cause, Borgia, has thou for grief. The chief pride of thy race has fallen, thy brother mighty in peace, mightier in war, whose arduous glory is equal both in name and deed to the great Caesars," said Ercole Strozzi in the funeral lament he addressed to her.

After her spontaneous outburst against God's indifference, she spent three days in Corpus Domini praying for her brother, and she ordered masses to be said for his soul. The page who had brought the news of Cesare's death and the priest who had helped him to escape from prison both found places in her service. The *infans Romanus,* who in those days passed for Cesare's son, had been removed from the tutelage of Alberto Pio the year before, probably at Alfonso's insistence, and was then in the *castello.* Later, Lucrezia would summon one of Cesare's illegitimate daughters—also named Lucrezia—to Ferrara. But none of these gestures by which she sought to honor her brother's memory could reconcile her to her loss. "I thank you as much as I am able for your condolences and I am trying to bear my grief with patience," she wrote Isabella at the beginning of May.

She had never been as close to her mother or to Geoffredo as she had been to Cesare. Her half sister Isabella Matuzzi was a stranger to her. Her son, the one person left in the world whom she really loved, was far away. In her terrifying loneliness it must have seemed to her that only Rodrigo's presence could ease her desolation. Alfonso, who had been so gruff and angry when she had miscarried in January, proved unexpectedly sympathetic. Although Rodrigo's very existence must have been disagreeable to him because it reminded him that another man had managed to give Lucrezia a living child, he allowed the little boy to come to Ferrara that summer. Rodrigo was then eight. During the five years he had been separated from his mother, she had watched over him most carefully. In 1506, for instance, there is mention in her account book of payment for some doublets of cloth of gold, berets *alla Francese,* and little swords of gilded wood and toy rapiers as well as little velvet-lined scabbards "for Don Rodrigo her son at Bari." And in other years there is mention of payment for embroidered shirts, silken belts, stockings, and still more doublets. Nor did Lucrezia forget those who cared for her son or helped him in any way. In the packages she sent to Bari, she always remembered to include skirts and linen for the nurse who had looked after him since infancy. Cardinal Lodovico Borgia, who had fled to Naples with Rodrigo after Cesare was imprisoned by Julius II, received four and one-half dozen masks and beards to be used during carnival and six harnesses for his greyhounds. But the most original and ingenious gift of all was a wooden doll "furnished with all her limbs" which Lucrezia sent to the seventeen-year-old daughter of Rodrigo's guardian, Isabella of Milan. With this doll came a wardrobe modeled after Lucrezia's own, including, among other finery, elaborate golden belts, a camorra with large sleeves, a tunic, and a pair of striped *zaraguelles*—the "wide-pleated harem-style stockings" she wore when she went riding.

Although Rodrigo would at first be shy with the beautifully dressed blond stranger whom he had been instructed to call mama, he would soon be won over by her gentleness and charm. The records show that he was in the *castello* all that August and September, and he may have been there even longer. As his playmate he had the eleven-year-old *infans Romanus.* While the two little boys played at war in the hanging garden that overlooked the moat, Lucrezia set the tailors and seamstresses to work preparing a whole new wardrobe of shirts and doublets for her son to take back to Bari. Although the thought that he must soon leave her again would be unutterably painful, the pain must have been eased somewhat by the knowledge that she was again pregnant. And this time she seemed so robust that her doctors were confident she would carry the baby to term. Nevertheless, they insisted that she limit her activities as much as possible. Partly to keep herself busy and partly to fill the void created by Rodrigo's departure for Bari, she spent the winter preparing for the new arrival.

After examining innumerable designs for the baby's crib, she finally settled on one of gilded wood with four delicate pillars supporting a classical architrave. Leafy and flowery branches of beaten gold crisscrossed over this architrave to form a glittering pergola. The curtains of the crib would be of white satin, the pillows of fine linen bordered with gold, and over all would be a red and white striped satin awning intended to keep out drafts.

To make Lucrezia's apartment worthy of this sumptuous crib, workmen reupholstered the walls in brown and gold cloth enlivened with a touch of crimson; a seamstress sewed a canopy of silver linen edged with colored silk for the bed of the mother-to-be; a goldsmith fashioned a cage of gold filigree for her parrot, and Benvenuto Tisi, better known as "il Garofalo,"prepared two works in gouache for the ceiling of a newly added room known as the "room at the turn of the Torre Marchesana." In response to Lucrezia's demand for something "new and gay," Garofalo pictured the ladies and gentlemen of her court in all their gorgeous and insouciant idleness, and he placed them within gilded frames that evoked memories of the gold and the glitter of the Borgia apartment in Rome.

Lucrezia's love of the glitter and gold that she remembered from her girlhood were also evident in a pair of gilded columns and a gilt-framed picture of the Madonna, which the Venetian painter Bartolommeo Veneto had painted for her the previous March. So that she would not catch cold during her pregnancy, she had the room where she took her bath lined with gilded wood and she installed a small stove. In the Middle Ages people had bathed at home in wooden tubs "ringed like barrels," and in addition there had been public baths. But syphilis and the resulting fear of contagion had made the public baths unpopular. With their decline, says one social historian, "the whole idea of bathing began gradually to disappear in the West." In a world where perfume did the work of soap and water, Lucrezia's insistence upon her daily bath seemed shocking and almost immoral and served to remind people of her Spanish upbringing, for the Spaniards had copied the practice from the Moors.

Ercole Strozzi was still in Lucrezia's service, and she relied upon his advice and support in making these changes in her apartment. To his friend Bembo and no doubt to Lucrezia as well, Strozzi, despite his bad leg and his crutch, suggested the image of a swan, a sensitive and artistic being enamored of all things beautiful. But to many in Ferrara this lame and perfumed poet seemed an unscrupulous conniver, constantly seeking ways to increase his income. Even his love for Barbara Torelli appeared suspect to them. In 1506, Barbara's first husband had died, and in September 1507 she married Strozzi. Since one of her daughters by Ercole Bentivoglio had married Strozzi's brother Lorenzo, she was in the awkward position of being her daughter's sister-in-law. Surely the Strozzi brothers had arranged these marriages in order to lay hands upon the not inconsiderable dowries of mother and daughter, said their detractors.

In justice to the two brothers, however, it should be pointed out that their reputation for greed had first arisen when their father, Tito, had served as judge of the Council of the Wise, and that these judges were invariably hated by the Ferrarese. Ariosto and his family suffered for years because of the obloquy heaped upon the poet's father during his term as judge. When the elder Ariosto was finally relieved of his post, the people lit bonfires in the piazza and hailed the duke for delivering them from "a rapacious wolf." Galeazzo Trotti, who succeeded him, was equally detested. Just as Ercole d'Este had increased his popularity by getting rid of these hated officals, so Alfonso increased his by removing Tito Strozzi and his sons from the Council of the Wise. He also took away the villa at Ostellato which his father had given them and their monopoly on fishing in Comacchio. Although he must have wanted Lucrezia to dismiss Ercole Strozzi and may have even asked her to do so, she continued to treat the poet like a dear and trusted friend. Which brings us to a mysterious exchange of letters between Strozzi and Francesco Gonzaga during that winter and spring of 1508.

Rather than being addressed to Gonzaga, as were numerous other letters which Strozzi wrote to the marchese, these letters were addressed to the poet's brother Guido, who lived in Mantua. After receiving them, Guido or his brother-in-law Uberto degli Uberti would deliver them to Gonzaga. Although the letters are all in Strozzi's handwriting, they are signed Zilio, which Alessandro Luzio, the man who discovered them in the Gonzaga archives in Mantua, interpreted as dialect for *gigolo*. And if we follow Luzio's reasoning, as many of Lucrezia's biographers do, the name is appropriate; for in

Luzio's opinion the letters are love letters which Lucrezia dictated to Strozzi (or asked him to write for her), and which he then sent to Gonzaga. So that no one would have any idea who he was talking about, he referred to Lucrezia as Madonna Barbara, Alfonso as Camillo, Ippolito appropriately enough as Tygrino, and Isabella as Madonna Lena. In the letters Zilio (Strozzi) repeatedly asssures Guido (Gonzaga) of the great love Madonna Barbara (Lucrezia) bears him, and he urges Gonzaga to prove his love by paying her a visit. But this talk of love is interspersed with talk of disagreements between Mantua and Ferrara which both Madonna Barbara and Zilio seem eager to patch up. In fact, the principal reason Madonna Barbara wishes Guido to come to Ferrara is that she feels that a meeting between him and Camillo (Alfonso) would be the best way to settle their dispute, which raises the possibility that Ercole Strozzi was using his privileged position as Lucrezia's confidant to effect a reconciliation between Mantua and Ferrara, and that the letters he sent to Mantua rather than being love letters, were reports in code on the progress of the negotiations.

Strozzi and his brother Lorenzo were then in the midst of a legal battle with the Bentivoglio family over the dowries claimed by Barbara Torelli and her daughter. Though Julius II had driven the Bentivoglio from Bologna, they were still powerful. When the matter of the dowries came up before the Roman Rota, the Strozzi must have decided it would be wise to have the support of some powerful lord. Ercole Strozzi had always been friendly with Francesco Gonzaga, and he knew that Gonzaga was looking for agents in Ferrara. Hence it would be natural for him to offer his services to bring about a reconciliation between Mantua and Ferrara in exchange for Gonzaga's support. Since Lucrezia looked upon the marchese as her brother's benefactor, Strozzi may very well have told her about what he was doing. Although Lucrezia would not want Alfonso to know, she would see nothing wrong with repaying Gonzaga's kindness to Cesare by helping Strozzi in any way she could. To flatter the marchese, Strozzi would imply that her desire to help was motivated by a stronger emotion than mere gratitude. "If you come [to Ferrara] it will be worth more to her than 25,000 ducats," he told Gonzaga in one letter. A strange way to measure love and one that seems alien to Lucrezia's nature. Since, moreover, she was then in her eighth month of pregnancy and Gonzaga was suffering from a flare-up of syphilis, the very idea of a tryst seems grotesque. But it was the nature of courtiers to use flattery indiscriminately and the nature of great lords to accept it as their due.

That besides seeking to effect a reconciliation with Alfonso, Strozzi performed other services for the marchese is evident from a letter Isabella sent to Alfonso in August 1507:

> Messer Hercule [Strozzi] is related by marriage to Uberto degli Uberti, the biggest ruffian in the land and my enemy. He has offended me and his only concern is to offend me as I will tell your lordship by word of mouth when I can speak to you. He often goes to Ferrara and was there recently after Messer Hercule was here. I have no doubt that he came to spy as that is obviously his office. I have said what I have to say. I pray you that my letter may be burnt as I burn yours for the sake of my honor and benefit.

Isabella frequently conspired with her brothers against her husband. A few years before, they had arranged the murder of one of Gonzaga's advisers. Though she had hoped that once her husband was deprived of Il Milanese, as this adviser was called, he would turn to her for advice, he had turned to his secretary instead. If she could not get at this secretary she could at least get at Uberti. Although her letter did not question Strozzi's good will, it may very well have made Alfonso and Ippolito decide to keep a closer watch on him. Some writers think they may have also found out about the Zilio letters. Whether they did or not, Zilio's efforts to bring about a reconciliation met with little success. At the beginning of April, when Alfonso left for Venice, he told Lucrezia that should the baby be born during his absence, she was to send an announcement of the birth to Isabella, but under no circumstances to send one to Gonzaga. Mortified, Lucrezia asked Zilio (Strozzi) to apologize to the marchese. "The duchess is expected to give birth any hour," Zilio wrote Guido (Gonzaga) the next day, "and Madonna Barbara [Lucrezia] hopes that you will pardon her for not letting you know, and will be assured of her good will."

On April 4, the future Ercole II was born, a wonderfully healthy baby with an obvious will to live. In the city-wide free-for-all that followed, the crowds made bonfires of "the gates of the notary's palace, the courtrooms, the door and the windows of the Palazzo Ragione, and the benches in the public schools, as well as all the benches reserved for women in the cathedral and the other principal churches of the city." Alfonso was so euphoric that his need to boast overcame his desire to snub his brother-in-law. Before setting out for Ferrara, he sent Gonzaga an announcement of the birth. Once back in the *castello,* the proud father replied to the congratulations of the various ambassadors by thrusting his naked babe at them so that they might see that "he was well provided for in all things." After a few days of this, however, Alfonso grew bored and announced that he was going to France. Though his joy at having an heir must have made him more tender than usual toward his wife, there was still so little intimacy between them that Lucrezia had no reason to regret his absence.

A little over a week after he set out for France, Zilio once again invited Guido to visit Madonna Barbara.

> I give you my word that she loves you, and if you continue as I have told you, you will certainly achieve what you desire. If not, blame me—I give you leave to do so. Show that you love her warmly, for she wishes for nothing else. When you answer me, do not refer to this, because I do not want her to think that you need to be pressed to love her; I know that this would seem to her lack of love on your part. Show every diligence in hastening to come where she is and then you will understand if I tell you even less than what is true. . . . She recommends herself to you exceedingly and says that Camillo [Alfonso] said before he left that he hoped to be reconciled so that you can come where she is. . . . Write to her in any case so that it should not appear that you are cold. I am writing you another letter of my own that you can show.

Although this has been interpreted as a love letter which Lucrezia asked Strozzi to write for her, his insistence that Guido (Gonzaga) make no mention of it to her and his offer to send the marchese another letter which he could show make it seem more likely that she knew nothing of this letter. Certainly Gonzaga, who had just been told to keep away from his wife because his syphilis was once again contagious, would find the reference to achieving what he desired ironic. But as Strozzi must have been shrewd enough to realize, the news that Gonzaga's lovely young sister-in-law was pining for him would be especially welcome to the marchese at such a time. Since Strozzi knew that Lucrezia did not love her husband, and since he also may have suspected that she was fonder of Gonzaga than she cared to admit, he would have had no compunctions about distorting the truth somewhat in order to please the marchese. On the other hand, he must have been relieved when Gonzaga decided not to visit Ferrara after all.

On the thirteenth of May, Alfonso was back in the *castello*. Either because of his presence or because Barbara Torelli was expecting a child and Strozzi could think of nothing else, there were no more letters to Mantua. On May 24, Barbara gave birth to a baby girl. When Lucrezia had given birth, Strozzi had composed a genethliacon, or birthday ode, in honor of her newborn son. At the time of his daughter's birth, he was working on an elegy which, according to those who had seen it, was concerned with the idea of death. He was destined never to complete it. On the evening of June 5, after several hours at his desk, he told his wife he was going out "for a breath of fresh air." The next morning his body was found wrapped in his cloak lying beside the wall of Casa Romei not far from the Strozzi Palace. He had been stabbed twenty-two times and his throat had been cut. Whoever had killed him had torn out great tufts of his hair, and these were arranged in a neat circle around his head. His crutch lay nearby.

"The great pity of it torments me, the sacrifice wracks me," said the Ferrarese humanist Celio Calcignani in the funeral oration he delivered in the cathedral, and he went on to speak of "the brilliant mind, the subtle acumen, the love of letters and the suave poetry" that had characterized the deceased. "Is it surprising therefore that he was so appreciated by Lucrezia Borgia, the wife of the prince, to whom he always showed a most religious devotion?"

But despite this "almost religious devotion" or perhaps, as some people thought, because of it, the prince himself did nothing to find the murderer. In despair, Strozzi's widow and his two brothers wrote to Francesco Gonzaga urging the marchese to "take vengeance upon him who had slain so very faithful a servant." Gonzaga offered a 500-ducat reward for information leading to the arrest of the killer and immunity to whomever revealed his identity. But as the Mantuan ambassador told Isabella, no one was talking so as "not to have his head against the wall."

"The magistrate never wanted to get to the bottom of the mystery," Alfonso's biographer, Paolo Giovio, would say later. Because the magistrate was responsible to the duke, many people took it for granted that Alfonso had ordered Strozzi's death. The duke was in love with Barbara Torelli and wanted her for himself, said some. He was jealous of Lucrezia's devotion to Strozzi, said others. And a few, remembering the rumors about Lucrezia's past, assumed that she had arranged the murder because she resented Strozzi's love for Barbara Torelli. A couplet written at the time—"Ercole Strozzi to whom death was dealt / for having written about Lucrezia Borgia"—has led one recent biographer, Maria Bellonci, to conclude that the Zilio letters were responsible for Strozzi's death. Bellonci sees an ominous connection between the murder of the poet and the murder the night before of the priest who had aided Cesare and who, it will be remembered, Lucrezia had taken into her service. Was it all part of a plot to isolate her? Perhaps.

But Barbara Torelli, who must have known of the Zilio letters, never blamed them for the murder. In an obvious reference to her former in-laws, the Bentivoglio, she told Francesco Gonzaga: "He who has taken my husband from me is causing his patrimony to be reft from his children and to do me harm in life and make me lose my dowry."

Given the concept of masculine honor at the time, the wonder is not that the Bentivoglio killed Strozzi, but that they waited so long to do it, for not only had the poet shielded Barbara, he had cuckolded her husband. For Strozzi then to marry her and claim her dowry must have been the last straw. Alfonso was related by marriage to the Bentivoglio and may not have wanted an investigation for fear of what it would reveal. He may have even thought that under the circumstances the Bentivoglio had every right to kill Strozzi. In the face of the duke's indifference, it would have taken a brave man to demand that the poet's murderer be brought to justice and there were no brave men in Ferrara. "One for fear, another for personal interest, not anyone has been found to defend his [Strozzi's] good memory nor his children save myself as is my duty," Barbara told Gonzaga. Feeling herself shunned and persecuted in Ferrara, she took her infant daughter and several of Strozzi's illegitimate children with her to Venice. *"Rara donna,"* Bembo called her.

Before his murder Strozzi had written a sonnet describing how wretched he felt when separated from his beloved:

> Ah! Why cannot the irksome body fly with thee to
> those two beautiful eyes, and with her, like thee,
> stay nights and days
> although nigher to her it feels more pain.

Now that death had separated them forever, Barbara answered him in one of the most famous of all Renaissance love poems:

> Why may I not go down to the grave with thee?
> Would that my fire might warm this frigid ice
> And turn with tears, this dust to living flesh
> And give to thee anew the joy of life
> And then would I boldly, ardently confront
> The man who snapped our dearest bond and cry
> O cruel monster see what love can do.

Later Lucrezia would offer to underwrite a complete edition of Strozzi's poetry by the Venetian printer Aldus Manuzio. At the time of the murder, however, she did nothing. Nor given Alfonso's wish to forget the matter and her own lack of power was there anything she could do. Her behavior during the Corpus Christi Day parade the week after Strozzi's death reveals her desperation. She had been invited to watch the parade from the Palazzo Pareschi on what is now Via Savonarola, across from the Casa Romei. The first-floor windows of the palace overlooked the spot where the poet's body had been found, and she was evidently unprepared for the effect the sight of that little square of pavement would have upon her. Besides reminding her of the murdered poet, it must have reminded her of the beautiful young husband who had been carried into her father's bedroom with the blood streaming from his head on that summer evening so long ago, the brother who had been slashed to death in Navarre the year before, and the other brother who had been fished from the Tiber: a whole company of ghosts who bore witness to man's cruelty and God's indifference. As the solemn procession of barefoot friars advanced through the street below, she began to cry and could not stop. Although the suspicion of God's indifference which she had first expressed after Cesare's death was undoubtedly one cause of her tears, it did not lead her to renounce him; instead it drove her to pray all the harder in the hope that he would finally hear her.

As is common when trying to deal with sorrow and depression, Lucrezia also felt a great need to get away. Leaving her infant son in the care of his nurses, she moved her court to Reggio for the summer. L'Unico Aretino, the flamboyant poet who had sung her praises when she was married to Alfonso of Bisceglie, was in Reggio then, and he immediately began paying court to her. Although Lucrezia found his poetry a consolation, it could not make her forget the shock of Strozzi's murder. Nor could she discuss what had happened with L'Unico, for he was familiar with neither the people nor the circumstances. Because Reggio is so near to the Mantuan border, it was natural for her to begin thinking of Francesco Gonzaga. Surely if she spoke to her brother-in-law, she could persuade him to launch an investigation into the murder. And even if she didn't, it would be comforting to talk things over with this warmhearted and genial man.

That Lucrezia still remembered Borgoforte and longed to be courted as she had been courted then was something she would not want to admit to herself. At the end of June she had written a letter of reference for Lorenzo Strozzi, who was replacing his brother as Gonzaga's Ferrarese agent. In August, she asked Lorenzo to invite the marchese to Reggio because she had something to talk over with him. When Strozzi told her that the marchese was in bed and could not possibly visit her, she replied that she was having so many prayers said for him both at Reggio and at Ferrara that he must surely recover. All very charming and perhaps a trifle too ingenuous, but either because Gonzaga really was ill or because he suspected that she wished to talk about the murder, he did not come to Reggio.

He had heard with great joy of the prayers she was having said for him, his secretary told Strozzi, and one of his principal reasons for wishing to be cured was so that he might see Her Excellency once again. Lucrezia thought of visiting him but did not. Soon afterward she returned to Ferrara. She found the five-month-old Ercole "beautiful and soft and white like a little pudding." But even the baby's toothless smiles and his comical efforts to investigate his small world could not dispel the listlessness his mother felt the moment she entered the *castello*. The courtiers noted that the duchess appeared "perturbed" and that she received no one and showed no desire to hold court. Alfonso, too, must have been troubled by her depression, for he dined with her more frequently that fall. But his presence would only remind her of how little they had to say to one another.

On December 1, she sent Lorenzo Strozzi to Mantua with a message for Gonzaga. Not finding Gonzaga at Mantua, Strozzi wrote him a note asking him to come to Ferrara because Lucrezia had something to discuss with him. From the letter which Strozzi sent him at the end of the month it seems likely that she wished to discuss the murder. But by then history had stolen a march on them all.

A little over two weeks before Gonzaga received her letter, a treaty between the Emperor Maximilian and the kings of France and Spain was confirmed in the Cathedral of Cambrai. Although the published clauses of this treaty spoke of perpetual peace and confederation, there were a number of secret clauses which, Guicciardini tells us, "were ambitious and to a great degree and in many ways contrary to the pacts which Maximilian and the King of France had with the Venetians." One of these clauses stated that "within three months the Duke of Ferrara, the Marchese of Mantua, and any who claimed that the Venetians were occupying any lands of theirs might be nominated to join the League [of Cambrai] and that once having been nominated they would enjoy all the benefits of the League as much as the principals and would have the right to seize by themselves those things which they had lost."

In the wholesale slaughter on Italian soil which this clause made inevitable, the murder of a single poet on the streets of Ferrara would seem unimportant indeed.

The League of Cambrai
and Other Abominations

Lords of Italy you compass your own destruction. . . .
Italy's divisions are laying waste the world's fairest land
And we are paying foreigners to shed our own blood.

Petrarch, *Italia Mia*

Over a century and a half elapsed between the writing of Petrarch's *Italia Mia* and the formation of the League of Cambrai. But despite the numerous disasters that occurred during that interim—the invasion of Charles VIII, the French conquest of Milan, the partition of Naples, the clear intention of the other European powers to make the Italian peninsula their battleground—the lords of Italy, including the pope, were as governed by "shortsighted interest" in 1508 as they had been in 1343. The only difference was that in Petrarch's time the Vatican was empty and the pope was living at Avignon under the protection of the king of France; whereas Julius II was determined to be "lord and master of the world's game."

In the famous portrait of Julius II by Raphael now in the Palazzo Pitti in Florence, the pope with his almost snow-white beard and his weary, introspective gaze seems a sweet, even saintly, old man, which he wasn't and had no wish to be. For the very unsaintlike Julius who emerges from the descriptions of his contemporaries, we must turn to the kneeling figure of the pope, which Raphael painted for the *Mass of Bolsena* in the Stanze Rafaello of the Vatican. There is no hint of weariness or introspection in this grim, tight-lipped old man with the sparse white hair, the florid complexion, the cold, hard gaze, and the outthrust chin. Rather, there is something perfunctory about the way he communes with his God, as if he is too restive to find prayer congenial and would like to be elsewhere.

The pope's explosive energy and turbulent spirit made the Italians call him Il Papa Terribile, by which they did not mean *terrible* in the English sense of the word, but unique and hard to handle. According to the Venetian ambassador, it was impossible to describe how strong and violent and difficult to manage he was.

> No one has any influence over him and he consults few or none. One cannot count upon him for he changes his mind from hour to hour. Anything that he has been thinking overnight has to be carried out immediately the next morning, and he insists on doing everything himself.

Like many difficult people, Julius had discovered very early in life that being difficult was one way to throw others off balance and get what he wanted. When he had one of his temper tantrums, and sometimes even when he didn't, his language was so vile that "the Pope used strange words" became the accepted euphemism for describing what he had said. Some of his choicer expressions may have been the result of drinking more than he could hold. The amount the Vatican spent on wine rose precipitously during his reign. Nor was wine his only vice. Although it was customary for the popes to expose their feet for adoration on Good Friday, Julius refused to expose his, because, says the papal master of ceremonies, "they were completely deformed *ex morbo gallico*" ("by the French disease"). If Julius was not as nepotistic as Alexander it was because his last son had died the year before his election. His surviving daughter was married in the vice-chancellor's palace; he made a nephew prefect of Rome and later appointed him captain-general of the church; and he bestowed cardinals' hats on a number of other relatives.

Although Alexander had used violent means to subdue the Roman barons and the vicars of the Romagna, he had done "as much as anyone to avoid the foreign invasions and the international wars which were beginning to destroy Italy." At the time of Julius's election, the only war being fought on Italian soil was the seemingly interminable but nevertheless purely local war between Florence and Pisa. The new pope soon changed all that. "Christianity being at peace," says Rabelais, "he took it upon himself to foment a cruel and treacherous war."

Because of his hatred of the Borgias, it had taken Julius awhile to realize that the principal threat to papal control of the Romagna came, not from Cesare, but from the Venetians. While he was trying to compel Cesare to surrender the fortresses he held, Venice seized control of a number of Romagnol cities, including the strategic cities of Faenza and Rimini. After Cesare's imprisonment, the pope demanded that the cities be returned to the Holy See. When the Venetians refused to give them up, Julius sent envoys to France and Spain urging them to unite with him to recover the "ill-gotten gains" of Venice. Their participation would cost them nothing, he assured them, because the spoils "would pay the expense and be a rich recompense for the undertaking." So that the Emperor Maximilian would not feel left out, he, too, was invited to enter Italy and to come to Rome to receive the Imperial crown. That what little independence was left in Italy might be crushed under the wheels of the remorseless juggernaut that the Pope was setting in motion did not appear to disturb him. "Let the world perish so long as I get my wish," he told the Venetian envoy, and he boasted that he would make of the ambassador and his countrymen "the simple fishermen ye once were."

Only after the three great European powers had ratified the League of Cambrai and the king of France and the Emperor Maximilian were preparing to send their troops into Italy did Julius seem to realize the nature of the monster he had wrought. Although he had been the principal instigator of the league, he waited three months before joining, because, say Guicciardini: "On the one hand there was his desire to recover the lands of the Romagna and his hatred of the Venetians, and on the other was his fear of the French king. Furthermore, he felt that it would be dangerous for himself and the Apostolic See if the emperor's power should spread too far in Italy."

When, on March 23, the pope finally did enter the league, Alfonso d'Este and Francesco Gonzaga entered with him. Since Alfonso ruled Ferrara as a papal vicar, for him to have refused to follow the pope into the league would have been to risk being lumped with Venice as an enemy of the Holy See. And even if this hadn't been the case, there was the lure of the spoils he had been promised.

Ever since the twelfth century, Venice had treated Ferrara more like a colony than an independent state. Although the lagoons that

Ferrara owned at Comacchio produced salt in abundance, the Ferrarese were compelled to get their salt from the Venetian works at Cervia. To make sure that no contraband salt was sold in Ferrara, Venice kept a representative known as a visdomino in the city, and there were other humiliations as well. While Alfonso was still a boy, Ercole had gone to war to break the Venetian hold on his duchy. Rather than win him any concessions, the war had cost him the Polesine of Rovigo, a strategic territory between the Adige and Po rivers. In return for joining the League of Cambrai, Alfonso was to get back the Polesine as well as the town of Este, the ancient seat of his house; and he would also be allowed to mine salt at Comacchio and to expel the visdomino.

Francesco Gonzaga, for his part, was to receive the town of Peschiera and a few small places on the Venetian border. Gonzaga had never forgiven the Venetians for dismissing him. More important than territories he hoped to acquire by joining the League was the opportunity to avenge the wrong that had been done him. To men like Gonzaga and his brother-in-law, who had been trained for war since childhood, the prospect of a good fight was also exhilarating. Although Gonzaga was still crippled by the French disease, he must have dreamed of once again winning the acclaim that had been his after the battle of Fornova. Alfonso, for his part, was eager to use the cannon he had been perfecting for so many years. Nor were the representatives of the church any less bellicose. Ippolito could not wait to show his mettle in battle, and the sixty-seven-year-old vicar of the Prince of Peace, whom Rabelais would remember "not at prayer, but wearing his metal warrior's cap," obviously thrived on the taste of blood. In Gonzaga's case there was another, softer, side which occasionally led him to have misgivings about the cruel necessities that war imposed. But he had long since learned to rationalize these misgivings with words such as *honor* and *duty,* and there is no evidence to indicate that the others even questioned the loss of lives and the bloodshed that getting back a few miserable cities entailed.

Although Lucrezia had grown up surrounded by warriors and politicians, like many sensitive people, she had no taste for war and little interest in politics. While Alfonso and his allies prepared for their grisly *divertissement,* she was still trying to arrange a meeting with Gonzaga to discuss the murder of Ercole Strozzi. Because she did not want Alfonso to know what she was up to, Ercole's brother Lorenzo referred to her as the "falconer" in the letters that he wrote to the marchese on her behalf. But nowhere is there any explanation of what made them pick this particular pseudonym. "I beg your Excellency to send a note to that 'falconer' who is always complaining to me that you don't write, and who angrily accuses me of not delivering the letters I get from him," Strozzi wrote that February. Whether Gonzaga ever got around to sending her the short note that Strozzi assured him would satisfy her, there is no way of knowing.

Despite the certainty of war, the carnival of 1509 was as lively as ever. For the carnival the previous year, Ariosto had written his *La Cassaria,* which the Mantuan ambassador called "a merry jape the which from beginning to end was as elegant and delightful as any I have ever seen." In 1509, the poet presented *I Suppositi,* the first play set in fifteenth-century Ferrara to be played at court. Instead of Greek slaves and their masters, Ariosto showed doctors at the university, corrupt ducal officials, and bullying customs officials in a *roman à clef* that delighted his audience. Although Lucrezia must have been present when *I Suppositi* had its debut, in general she seems to have kept to herself that winter. During the Lenten season, she went to hear the sermons in the cathedral only once or twice, and when she did go, she and her ladies-in-waiting sat in a tent which she had ordered set up for the occasion. Not since her first winter in Ferrara had she appeared so estranged from the world in which she lived. Certainly the preparations for war going on all around her must have contributed to her estrangement. She was then twenty-nine and again pregnant, so that there would also be a sense of the passing of youth and of opportunities missed, for at thirty a woman was considered middle-aged.

On April 16, just two days before her twenty-ninth birthday, the French dispatched a herald to proclaim war formally on Venice. On April 19, the pope named Alfonso standard-bearer of the church. Two days later, the great banner of the church was sent to Ferrara. The new standard-bearer received it in a solemn religious ceremony in the cathedral, a ceremony that gave the people the impression that God approved of what their duke was doing. More important than God's approval, however, was the approval of the king of France. Louis might be the pope's ally, but everyone knew he did not trust him. And because he did not trust him, he was not at all pleased to hear that Alfonso had become his standard-bearer. So great was his displeasure, in fact, that Alfonso thought it best to make a special trip to Milan where Louis and his army were then quartered. Only after Alfonso had given the king repeated assurances that Ferrara's first loyalty was to France would Louis agree to protect the duchy. His protection cost Ferrara 30,000 ducats, but Alfonso needed the French too much to object.

The duke had left for Milan on the first of May. By the tenth he was back in the *castello*. Because the attack on Venice had already begun, he hastened to move his army into the field. While he was gone, Lucrezia would govern at the head of a Council of Ten with Ippolito at her side. Since the cardinal left for Milan a few days later, both he and Alfonso obviously trusted her to govern on her own. This does not mean that she could do as she pleased. The conduct of foreign affairs was at all times the province of Alfonso and Ippolito. The collection of taxes and the supervision of the forced labor the *contadini* contributed to the war effort were left to the Council of the Wise. And there was a large administrative bureaucracy. Lucrezia's task was to see that this bureaucracy kept things running smoothly and to maintain public order. Although she never had enough power to make any great changes, she was always available to hear petitions and complaints, and she used what power she did have to help the *popolo minuto*, the "little people," who in Ferrara, as elsewhere, were generally mere makeweights in the struggle between the *grandi*, or "nobles," and the *grassi*, or "wealthy merchants."

As a prince "careful of the material wealth of his people," her father has been ranked "with the best of his age." Cesare also was unusual in that he sought, not only to conquer cities, but to govern them in the interest of the conquered peoples; so that in a sense Lucrezia's concern for the common man was a family tradition. But an even more powerful influence than the examples of her father and brother was a growing conviction that in good works lay the path to salvation.

On the reverse side of the *amorino bendato*, the famous medal which Filippino Lippi is supposed to have struck at the time of Lucrezia's marriage to Alfonso, the artist placed a Cupid with outstretched wings bound to a laurel tree. From one branch hung a violin and a role of music; from another the god's broken quiver. Cupid's bow with the cord snapped lay on the ground. The Latin expression accompanying this—*Virtuti Ac Formae Pudicitia Praeciosissimum*—is best translated as "Chastity, a thing most precious for virtue and beauty." "Perhaps," says Gregorovius, "the artist by this symbolism wished to convey the idea that the time for love's free play had passed and by the laurel tree he intended to suggest the famous house of Este."

Lucrezia had spent almost seven years trying to escape her destiny. As she approached her thirtieth birthday, however, she seems to have reconciled herself to the absence of romantic love in her life. While she was still too young to give up the search for romance entirely, more and more she would find the purpose of her existence in serving others. According to one of Alfonso's biographers, "She put aside the pomp and vanities of the world to which she had been accustomed from childhood and gave herself up to pious works and the founding of convents and hospitals." Although Lucrezia's newly acquired social consciousness has been criticized for being too closely linked to an unquestioning religiosity, during the Renaissance there were very few, even among those who did question, who were able to relinquish the consolation they derived from the sacraments and ceremonies of the church. "If heaven is eternal, I don't wish to go there," Ercole Strozzi had written in a moment of despair. But even so sharp a critic of the church and the Christian ethic as Machiavelli asked to receive the sacraments before he died. Although Lucrezia also faced the possibility that God was not there to hear her, she had neither the intellectual underpinning nor the will to explore so terrifying a prospect. In the doctrine that good works are the path to salvation, she found a way to resolve her doubts. Like many women who were dissatisfied with their lives and needed a sense of purpose, Lucrezia joined the Third Order of Saint Francis, a lay order which allowed its members to live in the world while sharing certain prayers and offices of the convent. As a faithful daughter of Saint Francis, she vowed to live peaceably, visit the sick, pray for the dead, and accompany them to their last resting place. Later, it would be said that she also wore a hair shirt under her clothing, but this seems unlikely, for she was never a fanatic but merely had a sincere desire to please God and serve her fellows.

Because the Venetians had not taken the League of Cambrai seriously, they were left "without a single ally" to oppose "a combination more powerful than any that Europe had known since the time of the Crusades." Nevertheless, they appeared confident of victory. That May they sent their 40,000-man army into battle with the motto *Defensio L'Italia* embroidered on their banners and the cry of *"Italia Libertà"* on their lips. On May 14, they faced the armies of the league at Agnadello near Cremona. The battle of Agnadello lasted less than three hours. When it was over "upward of 6,000 lay dead on the field of whom the greater part were Italians." Because Louis XII interpreted the league's victory as a sign of God's favor, he immediately ordered a chapel—Santa Maria della Vittoria—erected on the spot. Soon afterward the pope's nephew retook the cities which Venice had captured in the Romagna; Alfonso got back the Polesine, and Maximilian seized control of Padua, Verona, and Vicenza.

Although almost half the Venetian army had escaped unscathed from the field at Agnadello, the rulers of Venice were so demoralized that they immediately sought to make peace with the pope. "Your Holiness knows the state to which Venice has been reduced," wrote the doge at the beginning of June. "Let the bowels of your compassion be moved; remember that you are the earthly representative of Him who was gentle and who never casts away suppliants who flee to His Mercy." But mercy was not Julius's forte. Besides, he had no intention of breaking up the League of Cambrai until he was sure that there was nothing more to be gained from it. Although he agreed to negotiate with Venice, he put every obstacle he could think of in the way of a settlement. To the Venetians, his behavior appeared "devilish and unreasonable." Venice would send fifty envoys to the Turk before she would do what the pope asked, said the son of the doge.

That summer the Venetian army took back Padua from Maximilian and defeated the German guard that Alfonso had left at Este. Although these victories came as a surprise, they did not discourage the members of the league.

Francesco Gonzaga had been too ill to fight at Agnadello, but he had the satisfaction of taking Verona for Maximilian, and he had annexed Peschiera to the state of Mantua. Despite the evidence of the enemy's renewed will to fight, he decided also to annex the Venetian stronghold at Legnano. The battle for Legnano had not yet begun when Gonzaga and some of his men were surprised by enemy troops while they were asleep in a farmhouse outside the city. The seminude

Gonzaga fled through a window and hid in a cornfield. When a peasant discovered him there, Gonzaga offered the fellow a huge reward if he would help him escape. After agreeing to do so, the peasant led the Venetians to his hiding place. When the pope heard what had happened, he threw his cap on the floor and began cursing Saint Peter *"in orrende bestemmie"* ("with horrid oaths").

The capture of Gonzaga did wonders for Venetian morale. Everywhere along the road from Legnano to Padua he was met by groups of jeering peasants who had left their fields to celebrate. When he disembarked at Venice, a huge crowd was waiting for him in the Piazza San Marco. By then, however, Gonzaga had grown used to the cries of "Rat in a Cage," "Hang the traitor," and *"Turco! Turco!"* (his own war slogan) that greeted his appearance. Although crestfallen, he was by no means crushed. Hearing someone shout "Welcome, Marchese of Mantua!" he pretended not to know who the man could be talking about. "The person before you is Francesco Gonzaga and not the Marchese of Mantua who is in Mantua," he replied. What he meant, of course, was that if anything happened to him, his nine-year-old son Federico, who was safe in Mantua, would succeed him. And, in fact, one of the first things Isabella did after learning of his capture was to send Federico out riding through the countryside so that the people might see him. She was reassured by the "marvellous" reception they gave him, she told a friend.

While her husband was in prison, she would serve as regent. After asking the brothers of the Carmelite monastery in Mantua to pray for her, she turned to her astrologer for guidance. He discovered that there would be a "remarkable conjunction between the star of Jove and the Dragon's head on Saturday evening the 18th of August at three minutes before half-past seven." If Isabella knelt down at that precise moment and with hands clasped and eyes raised to heaven, repeated the Confiteor three times, and asked God to restore her dear husband safe and well to her side, the blessing she sought would be granted.

Isabella might have been gullible when it came to astrology, but in general she was not easily gulled. When Louis XII and Maximilian offered to send troops to Mantua to "protect" her from the Venetians, she realized that once the troops arrived, she would never be able to get rid of them, and she firmly but tactfully refused to have them. In truth her task as regent was not an easy one. Besides negotiating for her husband's release, she had to be careful not only of avowed enemies such as the Venetians, but also of supposed friends, such as the king of France and the emperor. And she had to insure that the Mantuans remained loyal to her son.

The Venetians had provided new bolts and locks for the apartment in the Torresella tower of the ducal palace which served as Gonzaga's prison. While in prison, he became ill once more. In the letters he wrote to Mantua, he asked his courtiers to pray for his liberation. To relieve the monotony of his days, Isabella sent his favorite tenor and a number of other musicians to Venice to entertain him. She also wrote letters to the pope, the king of France, and the emperor, urging them to do what they could to have him freed. But she forbade the commanders of the fortresses on the border between Mantua and Venice to open their gates "even if the Venetians led her husband to the foot of the glacis and murdered him before their eyes." Since in the long run it was obviously more important to save the state of Mantua than to save the marchese, Isabella's policy made a good deal of sense. But it was precisely because it was so sensible that it infuriated her husband. "We are ashamed to have as wife a woman who is always ruled by her head," he would tell her later. Rightly or wrongly, he never forgave her. During the eleven months that he spent in prison, it was Lucrezia, not Isabella, who was his consolation.

Lucrezia was almost at the end of her ninth month and, as usual, feeling somewhat ill when she heard of Gonzaga's imprisonment. Partly because it was her nature never to forget anyone who had done her a kindness, and partly because she was sentimentally attached to her brother-in-law, she ordered prayers said for him in all the monasteries, and she herself went to Corpus Domini to pray for his release. She also made up her mind to write to him. Who delivered her letters and what she sent him besides letters we do not know. Since both Alfonso and Ippolito treated his imprisonment as a joke, she had to be careful not to let them suspect what she was up to. But by then she had grown adept at keeping things from them. Besides, they were too occupied with the war to pay much attention to her activities. When on August 25 her second son was born, Alfonso was in the Polesine supervising the defense of his new province. Soon after the birth of the child, who was named Ippolito in honor of his uncle, the cardinal left Ferrara at the head of two hundred men-at-arms and two thousand Italian foot soldiers to join Maximilian before Padua. Ippolito went through the camp "upon a chariot like Darius, although in military dress," said one who saw him there.

But after a month's siege, the emperor, realizing that Padua could not be retaken, retreated to Verona. Although Julius had promised Este to Alfonso, because the town was a fief of the emperor, the investiture had to be obtained from him. Before beginning the retreat to Verona, Maximilian sold the investiture of the ancestral home of the Estense and of the town of Montagnona to Alfonso for 40,000 ducats. Since Alfonso had already paid 30,000 ducats for the protection of the king of France, he decided to raise another 100,000 ducats by levying a new tax. "The ducal stewards have given orders that each citizen shall bring his portion to the treasurer of communes, just as if we were all bankers who had money in chests," Ariosto grumbled. All the people high and low were murmuring bitterly, he told Ippolito, and there had been tumults of the *contadini* against the Council of the Wise, "complaining of the ever-increasing forced labor and threatening to fly from Ferrarese territory."

The Ferrarese had scarcely begun paying the tax which was to offset the cost of the investiture of Este and Montagnona when Montagnona was retaken by the Venetians. Soon afterward they also took the Polesine. In retaliation for what they termed "Ferrarese excesses," their fleet then entered the Po. As the eighteen galleys, two galleons, and three hundred smaller craft headed up the river toward Ferrara, the landing parties of Slavonian troops, whom they carried with them, ravaged the countryside, setting fire to the buildings and robbing and murdering the country people. Those who managed to survive sought refuge in the city.

The need to defend their city against the common enemy made the Ferrarese forget their resentment of the new taxes. In a show of solidarity almost never seen in peacetime, *grassi, grandi,* and *popolo minuto* all rallied behind their duke. With their help, Alfonso and his artillery drove the two Venetian galleys down the river opposite Polisella, where the rest of their fleet was anchored. In retaliation, the Venetian commander closed off the Po with a chain of tree trunks. He then put his men to work building two bastions, one on the Venetian side of the river, the other on the Ferrarese side. When Ippolito and his men tried to take the still unfinished bastion on their side of the river, they were driven back. Soon afterward, heavy rains raised the level of the Po and Ippolito captured the great dikes opposite the fleet. Because the Venetian commander assumed that the capture of the dikes was meant to check the looting of his Slavonian ground troops, he fired only a few shots. But Ippolito's plans were far more grandiose. Later, under cover of darkness, he brought up his artillery. After piercing the earthworks he planted his guns in a long line behind the dikes with their mouths at the level of the water. While he was doing this, Alfonso armed a huge flotilla of boats with his deadliest cannon and brought this flotilla within shooting range of the Venetian fleet. At dawn on December 22, Ippolito's artillery opened fire on the Venetian vessels while at the same time Alfonso's fleet swept down on them. Trapped in the crossfire between guns and cannon, one of the Venetian powder ships exploded. Any number of other ships either sank or caught fire. Many of the soldiers and sailors who tried to save themselves by jumping overboard were struck down by the arrows of Ippolito's crossbowmen. Those who did make it to shore were pursued by crowds of country people seeking revenge for what the Slavonians had done to them. "Before evening the Venetians will be utterly smashed with the help of the Lord," Ippolito exulted in a note he dashed off to Isabella. Alfonso was so delighted he jumped ashore and "tenderly embraced his valorous brother."

By close of day all but five of the Venetian galleys with sixty banners, and a bireme "of extraordinary grandeur," not to mention any number of smaller craft, a larger supply of artillery and ammunition, the shield and mast of the Venetian flagship, and a huge number of prisoners were in the hands of the Ferrarese. The evening of the twenty-seventh the laurel-clad victors brought the captured vessels up the Po to the gates of Ferrara. On the largest of the galleys stood Alfonso, surrounded by eighty guards of honor in gilded helmets. Overhead waved the insignia of the standard-bearer of the church, the eagles of the Estense, and the banners taken from the Venetians. Close behind followed a much smaller boat bearing Ippolito. In contrast to the other victorious warriors, all of whom were still fully armed, he wore his red cardinal's robes, and his vessel was devoid of either spoils or banners. But, as he must have known it would, this artful self-effacement made him more conspicuous than he would have been had he insisted upon sharing the triumph with his brother.

All Ferrara had crowded onto the ramparts to greet the returning heroes. As soon as the first galley came into view, the people began applauding while the ringing of the church bells, the blare of trumpets, and the salvo of cannon provided a thunderous salute. When Alfonso disembarked at the Porta Santa Barbara, Lucrezia was there to meet him dressed in cloth of gold. Twenty coach-loads of sumptuously dressed gentlewomen had accompanied her to the gate to join in welcoming the returning warriors. After the kissing and hugging and the applause, everyone set out for the cathedral to thank God for the glorious victory. The prows of the captured vessels were hung on the walls as votive offerings, and the hulls were left on the banks of the Po for all to see.

Soon after the battle of Polisella, the Venetians informed the pope that they were willing to accept all but two of his terms. By then Julius had come to realize what a mistake it had been to invite the French into Italy—"These Frenchmen are trying to reduce me to being their king's chaplain, but I mean to be Pope," he would say later—and "he was resolved [says Guicciardini] to expel the King of France from all those lands which he possessed in Italy." Apparently the pope counted on persuading Ferdinand of Spain to help him with the task. The question of who would then drive Ferdinand out of Italy would have to wait until the French were taken care of. And before the French could be taken care of, the pope had to make peace with Venice. When the war with Venice had first begun, Julius had published a bull of excommunication which deprived the Venetians of the sacraments and ceremonies of the church. By absolving Venice and withdrawing from the League of Cambrai, he boasted that he had stuck a dagger into the heart of the French king. Although the pope insisted that the Venetians no longer keep a visdomino in Ferrara, the treaty of peace he drew up for them to sign made no mention of the Polesine. Partly because Alfonso had been promised the Polesine at the time he had joined the League of Cambrai and partly because he did not wish to break with the king of France, he made up his mind to continue the war against Venice with Louis's help.

Among Alfonso's distinguished forebears were two saints: Beata Beatrice I and Beata Beatrice II. At the first sign of impending disaster, Beata Beatrice I was in the habit of warning her descendants. In 1479, when Ercole had joined France in a war against Julius's uncle, Sixtus IV, she had cried aloud in her tomb. No sooner did Alfonso make up his mind to defy the pope than "on the 12th of

March 1510, the day of Saint Gregory, she was heard knocking in Sant Antonio [the church where she was buried] and many other times was she heard that year by various nuns."

Unlike Ercole, who had set much store by the saint's admonitions, Alfonso paid no attention to them. That spring, with the help of troops sent him by the French and the emperor, he retook the Polesine and the towns of Este and Montagnona. Soon afterward, he and his French allies laid siege to Legnano. Among the artillery they took with them were two cannon Alfonso had cast himself: il Gran Diavolo ("the Big Devil") and il Terremoto ("the Earthquake"). The pleasure he derived from using these dangerous toys and his indifference to the havoc they wrought are both evident in a letter he wrote to Ippolito:

> I am stupefied by the cannon. [They] fire with *il Diavolo;* and if I were not tired to death, I should never have been so happy. I have become a real cannoneer and do my duty; our cannons fire splendidly, thirty-five to forty shots the day. Yesterday one of my cannoneers was killed. Your Lordship does not know him.

Shortly after Alfonso dispatched this letter, the pope ordered him "as a vassal and standard-bearer of the Church" to cease molesting Venice and to break with France. The duke was a tyrant in his own state; he had murdered Ercole Strozzi and a rich priest and he was to be deprived of his fief; let the French take arms to help him if they dared, Julius told the Ferrarese envoy in Rome. That August the pope began drawing up a bull of excommunication and deprivation against Alfonso. "It will be more terrible than the Bull against you for you were not our subjects, but he is a rebel," the pope told the Venetians. Besides calling Alfonso a "son of iniquity" and a "root of perdition," the bull declared his dignities and fiefs forfeited, anathematized all his adherents, and subjected the entire duchy of Ferrara to an interdict which deprived the people of most of the sacraments of the church, including the mass, and denied them a Christian burial.

Lucrezia, of course, had had no voice in her husband's decision to continue the war. Although the pope had betrayed her brother and reviled her father, as a good Catholic she felt compelled to make a distinction between the man and his office. Julius the man might be treacherous and warlike; Julius the pope was the anointed vicar of Christ on earth and as such entitled to respect and obedience. While Alfonso occupied himself with his troops and his cannons, she founded a convent dedicated to San Bernardino in the Casa Romei, which in those days was the property of Corpus Domini. This beautiful little palace with its arcaded balconies overlooking a secluded court of honor was well suited to its new role. Perhaps in converting it into a house of God when she did, Lucrezia was making up for her husband's defiance of the pope. Although as far as we know she never told Alfonso how she felt about his policies, she did confide some of her misgivings to Francesco Gonzaga.

Unlike Ferrara, Mantua had withdrawn from the League of Cambrai and was then supporting the pope. Despite this support, however, the Venetians had not released Gonzaga from prison until the middle of July. That August he was trying to decide whether to accept a Venetian offer to serve once again as captain-general of their army. When the post had first been offered to him the previous February, he had still been a prisoner in the Torresella tower. Because Isabella had feared that both the king of France and the emperor would seek to take over Mantua if he accepted the Venetian offer, she had begged him to put off doing so. If he would just tolerate his imprisonment a little while longer, she felt certain she would be able to work out an agreement that would allow him to go free without making any dangerous commitments.

At first Gonzaga seemed disposed to do as she asked. Although he continued to show an interest in becoming captain-general of the Venetian armies, he assured his wife that his interest was merely feigned and that he had no intention of accepting the post. As his imprisonment dragged on, however, he gradually lost faith in Isabella's ability to negotiate a settlement. In May, he let the Venetians know that he was ready to accept their offer. Although they were pleased to have him, they decided that they needed some guarantee that once he was back in Mantua he would not go over to the French. Hence they asked that Isabella send the ten-year-old Federico to Venice as a hostage. To Gonzaga the request seemed reasonable. But Isabella would not hear of it, because, she told her husband, she feared that once the Venetians had father and son in their hands, they would be tempted to do away with both of them. Not only did Gonzaga fail to see her point, he threatened to strangle her with his bare hands if she didn't do as he asked. "I have lost my state to that bitch!" he moaned.

Ironically, it was the normally explosive Julius who sought to calm him. The previous winter the Gonzaga's eldest daughter, Leonora, had married the new duke of Urbino, who was the pope's nephew and captain-general of the papal army. Since Isabella did not trust the Venetians to free her husband once they had his son in their hands and she was not reassured by the insistence of the Venetian signoria that Venice was incapable of such perfidy, Julius proposed to put her mind at ease by handing Federico over to his sister and brother-in-law, the duke and duchess of Urbino. Surely Isabella would have no objections to such an arrangement? But she did. Julius immediately let everyone know that he would make no further excuses for "that whore of a Marchesa." Her husband had every right to be furious with her, for he was "no longer a prisoner of the signoria, but of his wretched bum of a wife."

Although Isabella had told the pope that certain incidents made her wonder if it was in the best interests of the state to send Federico to Rome, from a letter she wrote to her representative in Ferrara it is clear that what was really bothering her was that her husband would have to accept the post of captain-general of the Venetian army in exchange for his freedom. And to many gentlemen in Mantua her opposition to his becoming captain-general was proof of her blind devotion to Alfonso and Ippolito and her willingness to sacrifice the interests of the house of Gonzaga to the political interests of the house of Este. But neither the attacks on her policy nor her husband's repeated threats to strangle her had any effect upon Isabella. Only after Julius had persuaded the Venetians to send their prisoner to Rome without first obtaining any commitment from him would she consent to send Federico to the Holy City as a hostage.

Before leaving Venice, Gonzaga assured the doge that he could count on help from Mantua in the forthcoming *impresa* against Ferrara. When Gonzaga arrived home, however, he discovered that Isabella was doing everything she could to assist her brothers. Although she had assured her husband that once he was safe in Mantua he would be free to accept the post of captain-general of the Venetian armies if he wished, she did her best to dissuade him from taking it. Rather than share her concern for Alfonso and Ippolito, Gonzaga resented them for not having done anything to help him while he was in prison. Nevertheless, he was reluctant to lead an army against them, if only because he wondered how long he would be able to hold on to Mantua once Ferrara fell to the pope. It was while he was trying to make up his mind what to do that Lucrezia wrote to him. She had more faith in him than in any other person in the world, she told him; and she begged him not to abandon her in "these times." Gonzaga must have promised to do what he could, for after the Venetians took back the Polesine, she told Lorenzo Strozzi that "were it not for the hope I have in the Lord Marchese that he will help me and protect me in my need, I would break my heart with sorrow."

Not long afterward, papal troops occupied Modena. Lucrezia had so little faith in her husband's ability to keep them from occupying Ferrara that she began packing her valuables with the intention of fleeing with the children. Alfonso did nothing to stop her until the Ferrarese let him know that if his wife and children left, every last one of his subjects would also feel free to do as he pleased. And so she was forced to remain, a most unwilling symbol of resistance and fortitude, in what she obviously considered a suicidal war.

After the capture of Modena, all the surrounding countryside went over to the pope, and Julius himself arrived in Bologna. Among the prisoners taken by the papal troops was a certain Masino del Forno, otherwise known as Il Modenese, whom the pope described as "an accomplice and perpetrator of the treacherous assassinations of the Cardinal of Ferrara." On September 26, Francesco Gonzaga received a letter asking him to come to Bologna immediately because the pope wished to speak to him "about certain abominable deeds revealed during Masino's trial." What these were the archdeacon who wrote the letter had been forbidden to say under pain of excommunication, but he hinted at "unspeakable" things directed against Gonzaga by his brothers-in-law. Certainly Gonzaga must have found them unspeakable, for no sooner did Julius tell him about them than he accepted the post of captain-general of the Venetian armies and agreed to replace Alfonso as standard-bearer of the church.

On his return to Mantua, however, he informed the pope that he had had a recurrence of the French disease and would be unable to lead the papal forces until he recovered. At first Julius was sympathetic. As one who had been incapacitated by the disease himself, he warned Gonzaga against using unguent of mercury which was "worthless" and might even do some harm. But when the invalid's condition failed to improve, the pope grew suspicious, so suspicious, indeed, that he sent one of his own doctors to Mantua to examine him. According to some writers, Isabella gave this doctor a handsome bribe to get him to say that her husband was really ill. Why Gonzaga should have agreed to the deception remains a mystery.

Before the pope and his allies could take Ferrara, they first had to take the fortress of Mirandola to the west of the city. By the end of December, Julius had grown so tired of waiting for Gonzaga to be well enough to assume command of the troops besieging Mirandola that he resolved to lead the assault upon the fortress himself. "Now we will see whose balls are bigger, mine or Louis's," he told his companions when he set out from Bologna in his litter on January 2. Despite a snowstorm that lasted for six days and frost so severe "that the ditches of Mirandola were frozen more than two full feet thick and a cannon which fell with its carriage from the brink above did not break the ice," the pope obviously relished his new role. Clad in armor, he rode around the batteries stirring up the ardor of his artillery men. "I don't care to repeat the words he uses," said the Venetian envoy.

Less than three weeks after the pope's arrival, Mirandola capitulated, and Julius began making preparations to besiege Ferrara. As soon as Francesco Gonzaga heard the news, he wrote to assure the pope that were Alfonso to seek refuge in Mantua, he would immediately turn him over to the papal troops. However, Gonzaga added, he would like to make a plea for the maximum of clemency "for the lady duchess." In fact, he would like the pope to turn her over to him, "and this because of the loving and loyal terms that she alone amongst all our many relatives used to us at the time we were prisoner in Venice and which oblige us in these days to show her gratitude, for had the providence of your Holiness not helped, there was no one else who showed that they held us in compassion as much as this poor girl."

Gonzaga was then forty-seven. His illness, his quarrels with his wife, his inability to make up his mind about leading an army against Ferrara were beginning to make him feel old and useless. Appointing himself the protector of "this poor girl" who had placed her trust in him appealed to his romantic spirit and gave him the feeling that he really mattered. Julius must have had no objection to letting him have Lucrezia, for Gonzaga immediately set about preparing an apartment for her in a palace near the meadows of the Te. In his enthusiasm, he could not resist describing the apartment to Lucrezia, without, of course, letting her know under what circumstances she would be living there. "Let us hope that we shall enjoy it together after so much tribulation," Lucrezia replied. It was the guarded response of one who suddenly realized that she had encouraged a man to expect far more than she was prepared to give.

By then all the shops in Ferrara were closed and everyone from great lords and ladies to public courtesans was working to reinforce the city's ramparts. "The duke himself passed to and fro among them, bearing his share like an ordinary laborer and at nightfall leading his workman off to the beating of drums to eat and drink together at his expense." Although the main body of French troops had been too busy defending Reggio to give him much help during the siege of Mirandola, King Louis had sent Alfonso a small contingent of soldiers under the command of the famous Chevalier Bayard. To his serving man, Bayard was *"le bon chevalier sans peur et sans reproche,"* and this loyal *serviteur,* as called himself, would later recount the exploits of his chivalrous master in a touching biography. Like the knights of old whom he sought to emulate, Bayard was too patriotic ever to question the *why* of the war he was waging on behalf of his king, but he insisted that the *how* conform to a complex ethical code which frequently bewildered the more prosaic Alfonso. Since the chevalier also proved to be a first-rate tactician, the duke soon learned to respect him in spite of his ethics.

After the fall of Mirandola, Alfonso had expected the papal troops to make a direct attack upon Ferrara. Instead Julius decided to starve the city into submission. While the Venetians cut off all supplies coming up the Po from points below Ferrara, papal troops planned to cut off all supplies coming down the Po from points above the city. However, there still remained a third source of foodstuffs which could be cut off only by capturing the fortress of Bastida twenty-five miles from Ferrara in the Polesine of Saint George. Since Bastida's commander had less than fifty men with him, Julius expected no problems. Nor would he have had any had Bayard not come up with an ingenious plan for dispatching troops to the beleaguered fortress. Between four and five thousand foot soldiers and more than sixty men-at-arms died during what the loyal serviteur calls "the glorious Battle of Bastida." "Nevertheless," says the serviteur, "it was necessary to venture it or the duke and the French had been lost."

If Lucrezia had had her way, her husband would never have gone to war against the pope in the first place. But this did not keep her from honoring the men who drove back the papal troops. "Above all persons," says the loyal serviteur, "the good Duchess, who was a pearl of this world, gave them a particular reception, and every day held banquets and feasts in their honor after the fashion of Italy with marvellous splendor." The graciousness, the warmth, and the gaiety which life in the *castello* of the Estense had all but stifled seem to have blossomed anew under the admiring gaze of these Frenchmen. "I make bold to say," continued the loyal serviteur, "that in her days and long before, there was not to be found a more glorious princess, for she was fair, good, sweet and courteous to all men. And nothing is so certain that although her husband was a wise and brave prince, the said lady by her sweet grace hath been the cause of many great and good services that were done to him."

But if, as the serviteur seems to imply, Lucrezia's grace compensated for her husband's lack of it, Alfonso's churlishness made it impossible for him to acknowledge her worth or to show her any real affection. And it was because she needed affection so desperately that Lucrezia continued her correspondence with Francesco Gonzaga, that strange correspondence in which she seemed so often to be fleeing the responses her own words evoked. She was delighted with the gift of citrons he had sent her, Lorenzo Strozzi told Gonzaga in February, and she constantly praised him to the French and to anyone else who mentioned his name. But when Gonzaga took this as an invitation to express his feelings for her more openly, she let him know that the "all too human terms" His Excellency had used in writing to her seemed unsuitable, for she looked upon him as her lord and brother. Gonzaga, of course, had had too much experience with women to take such a reprimand seriously, and he went on with his preparations for receiving her in the apartment by the Te.

That spring, however, the conquest of Ferrara, upon which all his plans for their future together depended, began to appear less and less certain. Not only did the French retake Mirandola, they drove the pope's troops out of Bologna. The same citizens who had cheered the victorious pontiff when he had entered the city three years before decided to celebrate his defeat by removing Michelangelo's bronze statue of the pope from its place over the door of the cathedral. After dragging the statue around the city and kicking it and spitting upon it, they finally broke it into pieces. Later, the French commander sent these pieces to Alfonso to use in fashioning a new cannon. As a final taunt to the pope, Alfonso called the cannon la Giulia (in Italian the feminine for *Giulio*, or "Julius"). But the new cannon was destined to remain idle for many months while her namesake negotiated with the king of France for a peace which neither really wanted.

During the lull in hostilities, the French returned to Ferrara. With them they brought one of the king's nephews, the twenty-two-year-old duke of Nemours, Gaston de Foix. This flamboyant and good-looking young man was used to being the center of attention. Men found his bravado infectious; women were both amused and touched by his exaggerated gallantry. Besides the inevitable banquets in his honor, Alfonso arranged a number of jousts and tourneys in the courtyard of the ducal palace. The first of these, "a mortal combat between two Spaniards," proved so bloody that Lucrezia, who was seated next to de Foix, "clasped her hands" and begged him "to cause the combatants to be parted." Despite his love for her, said the gallant young man, he could not, nor ought he "to make prayer to the victor against reason." Nevertheless, he must have been touched by her compassion, for soon afterward he decided "to wear a scarf of her colors as a mark of his admiration." Although Lucrezia was pleased, she found her role as hostess so exhausting that in September she went to Reggio to recuperate. As usual, when she was away from the *castello* she hated the thought of returning. At the beginning of October, she asked her husband for permission to remain where she was and to have the three-and-one-half-year-old Ercole and the two-year-old Ippolito brought to her. By then, however, Julius had persuaded Ferdinand of Spain and Henry VIII of England to join him in a Holy League directed against Ferrara and the French. Under the circumstances, Alfonso decided he wanted his wife and children with him.

Soon after Lucrezia returned to the *castello*, the troops of the newly expanded Holy League entered the Romagna. Although a number of towns across the Po from Ferrara went over to the enemy immediately, the mood of the city was carefree, even frivolous. Lucrezia's hairdressers devised "unheard of fashions" for her and her ladies. When Alfonso had to have his hair shaved off as a result of a scalp wound received in a skirmish with the enemy, any number of his gentlemen had their hair cut off too. And the appearance of this "shaven company" caused more talk than the war. The carnival in Ferrara that year was so colorful and so packed with entertainment that a group of Spaniards asked for a safe-conduct which would permit them to attend, but Alfonso would not hear of it. Young Gaston de Foix continued to wear Lucrezia's colors even after he was made supreme commander of the French forces in Italy. He was still wearing them when he and his men rode out to take Brescia from the Venetians that February. As soon as the news of their victory reached Ferrara, the people rushed into the streets shouting for joy, the church bells began ringing, fireworks went off all over the city, and the *contadini* working on the ramparts were given leave to go home to celebrate. That evening the ducal singers entertained the victors at an all-male dinner in Alfonso's rooms. Not to be outdone, Lucrezia gave a reception and a masked ball in their honor. Like everyone else, she seems to have preferred not to think of the war and of the Swiss soldiers whom Julius had called upon for help. In Paris, however, Louis XII could think of nothing else. At the beginning of Holy Week, the king ordered Gaston de Foix to put an end to the war in Italy "with a single battle" before the Swiss invaded Milan and the Spaniards attacked southern France.

On Easter Sunday, April 11, 1512, the combined armies of France, Ferrara, and the Emperor Maximilian met the armies of the Holy League on the marshy plain between Ravenna and the sea "in a flat countryside without any impediments of water or shelter, which might hinder the action, or any place to take cover." The battle of Ravenna lasted from eight in the morning until four that afternoon. "There have been many battles since God created heaven and earth," said the loyal serviteur, who was there with his master Bayard, "but never was one . . . so bloody, so furious, or better fought on both sides." Absorbed as the serviteur was in reporting his master's acts of heroism, he did not realize, or at least he failed to note, that this was the first battle in the history of warfare in which artillery decided the outcome. The commanders of the Holy League opened fire with cannon and two hundred *arquebuses à croc*, "mounted on wheels." But their weapons were no match for Alfonso's cannon. After moving these to a position on the enemy's extreme right, Alfonso caught the Spaniards by surprise with a sweeping gunfire which all but blasted their foot soldiers out of the trenches. "It was horrible to see how every shot made a lane through the serried ranks of the men-at-arms sending helmets and heads and scattered limbs through the air," wrote Jacopo Guicciardini in a letter to his brother Francesco. And one of Ariosto's elegies spoke of fields "red with barbarian and Italian blood," and of "one dead so near another that without treading on them, the soil for many miles hardly left a path."

Alfonso had made Ravenna regret his expertise, said the poet in the *Orlando Furioso*. It was because of his thrusts "so shrewd and bold," that the "lily [of France] was not broken or deflowered." But despite a few lines in praise of il Diavolo and il Terremoto, Ariosto was appalled by the effect of the cannon. Later, when he was no longer dependent upon the Estense for his livelihood, he made clear his true feeling about this "accursed and abominable tool."

> O hideous invention! By what means
> Did you gain access to the human heart?
> Because of you all glory's fled long since
> No honor now attaches to the art of soldiering;
> All valor now is pretense:
> Not Good but Evil seems the better part
> Gone is all courage, chivalry's gone,
> In combat once the only paragon.
>
> How many lords!
> How many more among the bravest of our cavaliers
> Have died and still must perish in this war
> By which you brought the world to bitter tears
> And Italy left stricken to the core?
> This is the worst device in all the years of
>   the inventiveness of humankind.
> Which e'er imagined was by evil mind.

Of the 45,000 men who went into battle at Ravenna that morning, 10,000 were corpses by close of day. And of those 10,000 corpses, two-thirds had been soldiers in the army of the Holy League. When the league's commander realized that he had lost the battle, he mounted his horse and "never drew reign until he reached Ancona."

But two of his generals were taken; one of them, Fabrizio Colonna, by Alfonso, who later brought him to Ferrara, where he was treated more like a friend than a prisoner. The French captured the army train of the league, as well as the league's artillery and banners. But whatever joy the victors took in their spoils was muted by the loss of Gaston de Foix, dead on the battlefield with "fourteen or fifteen wounds from his chin up to his forehead."

That morning the impetuous young commander had promised his troops rich booty, not only in the Romagna, but in the Holy City "where the boundless riches of that wicked court extracted for so many centuries from the bowels of Christians will be sacked by you: so many stately ornaments, so much silver, so much gold, so many precious stones, so many rich prisoners." And he had called for "divine justice to punish the pride and the enormous vices of that false pope Julius." When news of the French victory reached Rome, the cardinals begged the pope to make peace with the victors, and Julius himself thought of flight. But before the pope could flee, another messenger arrived with the news that there was nothing to fear from the French for the death of Gaston de Foix had left them too demoralized even to think of marching on Rome. Rather than abandon the city, the pope resumed his negotiations with the Swiss and by so doing transformed a humiliating defeat into a great victory.

At the end of May, 20,000 Swiss soldiers arrived in Verona, and Maximilian decided to recall the German foot soldiers who had aided the French at Ravenna. Ten weeks later, the king of France had lost everything he owned in Italy, including Milan and Asti. "The soldiers of Louis XII have vanished like mist before the sun without having fought a single battle and almost without having defended a single town," said one incredulous observer. The Swiss had shown themselves "the best doctors for the French disease," said Julius. He who, both as a cardinal and as pope, had done more than anyone to establish the French in Italy, found himself hailed as his country's liberator. "Now God has left us nothing more to ask from Him," he declared with unbecoming humility. But, of course, he didn't mean it, for he could not wait to get his hands on Ferrara.

When Alfonso realized what the pope was up to, he appealed to Louis XII for help. But Louis had "the whole world against him," and he could promise nothing. Even with il Diavolo, il Terremoto, and la

Giulia, Alfonso dared not face the combined power of the Holy League alone. Fabrizio Colonna, who was still his prisoner, advised him to throw himself at the pope's feet and ask for mercy. Isabella also advised an appeal to the pope, and she undertook to get him a safe-conduct which would enable him to go to Rome without fear of being attacked. On the day she delivered this safe-conduct to her brother, a nun in the convent of Sant' Antonio claimed to have a vision of Beata Beatrice I pointing to Alfonso, blindfolded and about to fall into a deadly trap. Because of the way Julius had betrayed Cesare, Lucrezia, too, feared the worst, and during Alfonso's absence she asked the nuns of San Bernardino to offer daily prayers for his safe return.

Alfonso arrived in Rome on July 4, the same day that Reggio, the third city of his realm, surrendered to the pope. As an excommunicated person he was not allowed to move freely about the city, nor was he allowed to speak to anyone outside the Gonzaga palace where he was then staying. On the ninth, he knelt before the papal throne and asked for absolution. After he had sworn upon the crucifix, Julius read the form of absolution to him. But the pope made it clear that the absolution would be valid only if Alfonso obeyed his will in all things. What his will would be Julius did not say, for he had first to consult a committee of six cardinals.

Alfonso's twelve-year-old nephew, Federico Gonzaga, was still a hostage in Rome then and something of a favorite with the pope. While Alfonso waited for the cardinals to decide his fate, Julius allowed Federico to entertain his uncle at a banquet in the Vatican. After being shown Pinturicchio's frescoes in the Borgia apartments, and perhaps marveling over the resemblance between the figure of Saint Catherine and his wife, Alfonso asked to see Michelangelo's frescoes in the Sistine Chapel. With the lordliness of a twelve-year-old who realizes how difficult adults find it to refuse him anything, Federico summoned Michelangelo and asked him to serve as Alfonso's guide.

Michelangelo had originally come to Rome to work on the pope's tomb, which Julius wished to be more magnificent than that of any previous pontiff. Later he decided that it would be unlucky to have his tomb built while he was still alive, and he asked Michelangelo to paint a series of frescoes for the flat vaulted ceiling of the Sistine Chapel instead. Because Michelangelo considered himself a sculptor rather than a painter, he approached his new task with considerable misgiving. "I've grown a goiter by dwelling in this den," he wrote in a poem describing what it was like to work lying flat on his back with the paint dripping in his face.

> My beard turns up to heaven: my nape falls in,
>   Fixed on my spine: my breast bone visibly
>   Grows like a harp: a rich embroidery
> Bedews my face from brush-drops thick and thin.
> My loins into my pannels like levers grind:
>   My buttock like a crupper bears my weight:
>   My feet unguided wander to and fro;
> In front my skin grows loose and long; behind,
>   By bending it becomes more taut and strait;
>   Crosswise I strain me like a Syrian bow,
>   Whence false and quaint I know
> Must be the fruit of squinting brain and eye;
> For ill can aim the gun that bends awry.
>   Come then, Giovanni, try
> To succor my dead pictures and my fame,
> Since foul I fare and painting is my shame.

At the time that Michelangelo brought Alfonso and his party in to see the work, the scaffolding was still up and the paintings for the lunettes were not finished. Nevertheless, Alfonso could not satiate himself with gazing at those figures, wrote one of Isabella's correspondents in a letter in which he tried to recapture the wonder that all of them had felt at seeing the great work spread out above them. Although Julius had not yet told Alfonso what he expected of him, the duke must have been confident that it would entail no great sacrifice on his part, for after seeing the frescoes in the Sistine Chapel, he commissioned Michelangelo to paint a picture for him.

A few days later, Julius cast aside the recommendations of the cardinals studying Alfonso's case and demanded that the Estense surrender Ferrara to the Holy See. The pope would give them Asti instead (which was worth 15,000 to 20,000 ducats a year), and he wanted the prisoners (Don Ferrante and Don Giulio), Alfonso told Ippolito.

Julius was then in the Castel Sant' Angelo, and Alfonso had agreed

to deliver his reply to the pope in person. Should he refuse to accept
the terms he had been given, Julius intended to imprison him. To
make sure that he wouldn't escape, the pope doubled the guard at the
gates of the city. But he made the mistake of confiding his plans to
one of the cardinals, who in turn confided them to Fabrizio Colonna.
Wishing to repay Alfonso for the kindness he had shown him when
he was a prisoner in Ferrara, Fabrizio sent a contingent of soldiers to
get him past the guards. The duke had left the city on a "pleasure
trip" because he had found the air in the city unhealthy, Fabrizio told
the pope. Later, Julius's spies captured Lorenzo Strozzi, who had accompanied Alfonso to Rome. But they could not find the duke, who
remained hidden in the Colonna fortress at Marino for almost three
months.

While Alfonso waited for the opportunity to get safely through
the papal states and return to Ferrara, Ippolito prepared to defend
the city from a possible attack by papal troops, and Lucrezia attended to civil affairs. On a Monday morning in early September
that must have begun much like other mornings, a morning when
Lucrezia, as was her custom, stopped in the nursery to see the
children before going to the Palazzo Ragione to read petitions and
grant audiences, a messenger arrived from Bari with the news that
Rodrigo of Bisceglie had died of malaria at the end of August. There
was no question of going on with her audiences or trying to put up a
brave front. Somehow or other she managed to summon a coach to
take her to San Bernardino, where she could be alone with her sorrow. She was so bowed with grief there was no way to console her,
the nuns told the Mantuan ambassador. Ippolito visited her as soon
as he heard what had happened. Although he remained with her for
a long time and sought to comfort her, she was too numb to re-
spond; and his suave manner and glib condolences could only end
by irritating her. "I am wholly lost in bitterness and tears on account
of the death of the Duke of Biselli, my dearest son," she told a friend
a few weeks later.

To a parent the loss of a child is the loss of a dream, the dream of
the man or woman that the child will one day become. In Lucrezia's
case, that dream must have been that in her son she would see rein-
carnated the beautiful boy who had been her first and dearest love. If
part of the bitterness she felt was directed at her God for having deprived her of that dream, part was surely directed at the society that

would not allow her to raise her own son, and part also at herself for having failed him as she had failed his father. But the news that Alfonso had left Marino and would be home by the middle of October made it necessary for her to veil her grief and bitterness and pretend to a joy she could not possibly feel.

Disguised now as a hunter, now as a domestic, and now as a friar, Alfonso had accompanied the troops of the Colonna as far as Tuscany. There he was met by Ariosto and a few of the gentlemen of the court with whom he continued on to Ferrara. "I cannot rid myself of fear, knowing as I do that I am constantly pursued by bloodhounds. May God deliver us from their fangs," Ariosto wrote to a friend. By the time they reached the gates of Ferrara, Alfonso was in rags and had to have a change of clothing sent out to him. The news of his arrival spread through the city so rapidly that by the time he reached the Piazza del Duomo, the great square was as full as it had been on the night of his wedding. No sooner did the crowds catch sight of him than they began cheering and shouting. The cheers and shouts grew louder, mingling now with the clanging of the church bells, as Alfonso mounted the stairway to the ducal apartment where Lucrezia and the children were awaiting him.

Ever since his departure for Rome, Lucrezia had asked the nuns of San Bernardino to pray for his safe return, and there must have been a sense of relief at seeing her prayers answered as well as a sympathy for the dangers he had faced. There may also have been the realization that although she did not love him, he and the children were all that remained to her. She had put aside her mourning for the occasion and was dressed in brown. Because she must have known how much her husband disliked being reminded of her past, she did not revert to black afterward. While she occupied herself with the painful task of breaking up her son's court and settling his estate, Alfonso prepared to continue his war against the pope. Although Lucrezia had originally opposed her husband's decision to go to war, she now seemed as determined as he was to preserve the duchy of Ferrara for their children. So that there would be money to continue the war, she willingly gave her jewels to Isabella to pawn. To raise further money, Alfonso sold his silver plate. That winter he and his family ate off terra-cotta dishes which he fashioned and painted in his own workshop.

Julius had already ordered his nephew the duke of Urbino to lead the armies of the church against Ferrara, but Isabella begged her son-in-law to spare the city. Apparently he was more concerned with pleasing her than with pleasing his uncle, for he agreed to put off the attack as long as possible. Meanwhile, Venice began negotiating with France, and the Swiss also appeared to be considering a French alliance. To complicate matters further, Ferdinand of Spain seemed eager to move into northern Italy. Undaunted by these setbacks, Julius made plans to step up his campaign against Ferrara in the spring.

While the pope was mulling over these plans, he suddenly complained of feeling unwell. "The Pope is not exactly ill," said the Venetian ambassador that January, "but he has no appetite. He eats but two eggs in the whole day; he has no fever but his age makes his condition serious." Feeling that the end was at hand, Julius insisted that the cardinals confirm a bull against simony. It was the finest act of his pontificate. Some time during the night of February 20, or the morning of the following day, he died. Supposedly his last words were: "Out of Italy French! Out Alfonso d'Este!"

In *Julius II Exclusus*, a dialogue attributed to Erasmus, the author pictured Julius trying to storm the gates of heaven much as he had stormed the gates of Mirandola. "I am not surprised that so few apply here for admission when the Church has such rulers," Saint Peter concludes after turning him away. "Yet there must be good in this world too, when such a sink of iniquity can be honored merely because he bears the name of Pope."

To the Ferrarese, Julius's death seemed a blessing. Although Alfonso advised restraint, Lucrezia journeyed from altar to altar to thank God for delivering the world from "this Holofernes" and sending him to wage his wars elsewhere. Three weeks later, the cardinals met to elect a new pope. As usual there was a seemingly insoluble split, this time between the older cardinals and the younger ones. What finally induced some of the older cardinals to support the mild-mannered and myopic thirty-eight-year-old Giovanni dei Medici was the knowledge that he had an incurable ulcer and was not expected to live long. He chose to reign as Leo X, but after Julius he seemed "more like a gentle lamb than a fierce lion." Although he would grow less lamblike as time went on, at the beginning of his reign he seemed eager to please everyone, and he readily agreed to lift the ban of excommunication that Julius had renewed against Al-

fonso and Ferrara. At the new pope's coronation, Alfonso helped
Leo mount the snow-white steed that bore him to the Lateran Palace.
Federico Gonzaga was allowed to return to Mantua; his father closed
up the apartment in the palace by the Te; and the pawnbrokers returned Lucrezia's jewels even before they had received their money.
The affairs of Ferrara were now in another state from what they had
been when the jewelry had been given to them, they told Isabella.

Peace

Your chief desire as you yourself so nobly asserted is to stand approved of God and to be useful not only to the present age but to future time; so that, when you quit this life, you may leave behind you a monument that you have not lived in vain.

Aldo Manuzio in an address to Lucrezia Borgia
prefixed to his edition of the works of Tito and Ercole Strozzi

That spring of 1513, when Leo was elected pope and peace returned to Ferrara, Alfonso was thirty-five and Lucrezia thirty-three. Although two silver votive shields dedicated to Saint Maurelio, the protector of the city, in thanksgiving for the victory at Ravenna and still in the church of San Giorgio in Ferrara show husband and wife in stylized poses, they do give some idea of what they must have looked like at the time. In one of them— *Alfonso d'Este Kneeling before Saint Maurelio*—two young and insouciant grooms hold the duke's horse while Alfonso, in full armor with his sword tucked under one arm, receives the saint's blessing. What is most striking is the contrast between the bland, rounded faces of the three secondary figures and the harsh, angular countenance of the duke with its hooked nose, strong jutting chin, and deeply circled eyes. As in the more realistic portrait of Alfonso by Dosso Dossi in the Galleria Estense in Modena, he seems a hard, stubborn man with very little that was gentle or sensitive in his makeup, a man whom it would be easier to fear than to love.

The second shield—*Lucrezia Borgia Presents Her Son Ercole to Saint Maurelio*—has all the charm that the first lacks. Holding her small son by the hand, Lucrezia stands before the saint, who is in the act of blessing the child. Lucrezia wears a dress worked in gold with wide flowing sleeves, a round pearl-studded neckline, and horizontal bands of embroidery on the long, full skirt. In her free hand, she carries a fine lace handkerchief. Her blond hair is confined in a net of precious stones similar to the one she wears in the medal known as *Della Reticella* ("Of the Hairnet") which, like the better known *amorino bendato*, was struck at the time of her marriage to Alfonso. Although her profile shows the same receding chin and slightly aquiline nose, she looks, if not eleven years older, certainly less girlish and more dignified than in those earlier representations. Behind her the silversmith has grouped five of her ladies-in-waiting. All are very young and pretty, prettier in fact than their mistress. Nevertheless, it is Lucrezia with her erect carriage, her gentle, resigned gaze, and what one enthusiastic modern writer has called her "radiant voluptuousness" who dominates the scene: "the incarnation of sovereign beauty."

It was a beauty that depended less upon her features, which were irregular and not well proportioned, than upon her delicate coloring, her elegant wardrobe, and a careful attention to detail. An inventory of the jewels and goods she owned in 1516 listed 399 separate items. Among other adornments, it included 2,000 "large and beautiful pearls"; innumerable rosaries fashioned of silver and rubies and mother-of-pearl; flat diamonds to be pasted on the forehead; and a hundred buckles of gold and enamel. Perfume was considered an indispensable adjunct to any wardrobe then. Like Caterina Sforza and Isabella and any number of other great ladies of fashion, Lucrezia concocted her own, and one of her scents was sufficiently seductive to win the praise of the king of France.

As important as the perfume and the jewels and the exquisite clothes in creating the illusion of beauty were Lucrezia's physical grace and her unfailing graciousness. Her husband had seen the effect that her graciousness had upon the French, and he must have been aware that others thought her beautiful. But the gallantry of a Bayard or a Gaston de Foix was something he simply could not understand. Because he found it such a nuisance to pretend that he was seeking anything save sensual satisfaction from a woman, he had always preferred the company of prostitutes to the company of princesses. With the approach of middle age, however, he seems to have concluded that such indiscriminate whoring did not become a duke of Ferrara. Since he also wanted more children, he decided to try to confine himself to his wife. Large families were then the rule. Alfonso's mother had had five children; his sister Isabella had six and would have had more had her husband's illness not forced him to keep away from her. As a result of Alfonso's increased devotion to Lucrezia, she bore him three more children in a little over two and one-half years.

Alessandro, born in 1514 when she was thirty-four, was "a big baby with a huge head" who was sickly almost from the moment he entered the world and may have been rachitic. Fifteen months later, Lucrezia gave birth to a daughter whom she named Eleanora in memory of her husband's mother. In Dante's *Paradiso:*

> Nor yet did daughter's birth dismay the father
> For dowry and nuptial age did not exceed
> The increase upon one side or the other.

In the more mundane climate of Italy, however, the birth of a daughter was seldom greeted with anything but dismay. When Isabella gave birth to her second daughter, Lorenzo the Magnificent sent Francesco Gonzaga a letter of condolence; and Isabella replaced the gilded cradle she had prepared for the use of a son with a simple wooden one. But Lucrezia had already borne three sons, and whatever her husband's worries about the dowry he would one day have to provide, she had so longed for a daughter that she looked upon the birth of this little girl "almost as one of those proofs God occasionally gives of His Kindness to those who love him."

Such proofs, as she well knew, were few and far between. A year after Eleanora's birth, Alessandro had "a most cruel dysentery" which, because he was already ailing, ended by killing him. "The poor little one surrendered his soul to our Lord God at around the fourth hour," Lucrezia wrote Isabella, "and has left me much affected and full of immense sorrow as your most illustrious ladyship can easily believe, being a woman and a tender mother. In the same letter she also mentioned Alfonso's grief. Alfonso was far closer to Isabella than he would ever be to his wife. In fact, the reason that Lucrezia and Francesco Gonzaga were so drawn to one another was that the solidarity of the Estense made them both feel like interlopers. But in this particular instance, grief softened Lucrezia's resentment, and she must have hoped that Isabella could give Alfonso the sympathy he would never accept from her. She was five months pregnant at the time. That November she gave birth to another son, Francesco, a healthy, happy baby who by his very existence did more to help his father forget the loss of Alessandro than anything Isabella could possibly have said to him.

Despite the strain of these successive pregnancies and the responsibility of caring for an ever expanding brood, Lucrezia continued to hear complaints and to give audiences much as she had in the past. She also continued to write to Francesco Gonzaga. At one point just after the election of Pope Leo, Gonzaga had thought that he was cured of syphilis and had announced that he was "ready to consummate marriage." But it had not taken him long to realize that he was fooling himself and that he would never be completely well again. More and more as time went on he was confined to his apartment. The Venetian ambassador who visited him there in 1515 found him resting on a couch before the fireplace. His pet dwarf in gold brocade and three of his greyhounds lay at his feet. "Lest even a hair should fall on him," three pages stood nearby waving large fans. He had always loved hunting, and the walls were covered with pictures of his favorite horses and dogs; a number of hawks and falcons on leash were also in the room. But all these reminders of the life he had once led only served to depress him. Like Lucrezia, and perhaps at her urging, Gonzaga sought consolation in the teachings of Saint Francis. Instead of the romantic allusions with which his letters to her had been filled in the past, the letters he wrote her during these later years were filled with talk of God's grace and the miracles he had wrought.

Although, after one such description, Lucrezia congratulated him on witnessing "so great a proof of the power of God," she herself appeared to have no need of miracles to reinforce her faith. Nor was she blind to the drawbacks of the religious life. Upon learning that three of her ladies-in-waiting wished to become nuns, Lucrezia did her best to dissuade them. She didn't think they should enter a convent *"così presto,"* she wrote Isabella, because it was possible that they would later change their minds. Since one of the girls came from Mantua, she also thought that Isabella should know what the girl was planning to do and should inform her father. She herself would make another attempt to get all three girls to change their minds. On the other hand, seeing their fervor, she felt that perhaps it was not right to oppose their desire and the salvation of their souls. Isabella replied with an instance of similar religious fervor among her own ladies-in-waiting.

Isabella's behavior during her husband's imprisonment had convinced Gonzaga (and any number of other people) that she cared more for governing than she did for him. "It is I who am the Marchese of Mantua not you," he told her after his return. From being all powerful regent, Isabella suddenly found herself demoted to cast-aside wife with no say in the government whatsoever. Unable to bear the humiliation, she constantly found excuses to get away from Mantua. After the ouster of the French from Milan, her nephew Maximilian Sforza had been reinstated as duke. Since, unlike her husband, Maximilian was eager for advice on how to govern, she spent considerable time with him. She also made frequent trips to Ferrara to advise her brothers. Although she continued to encourage disparaging stories about Lucrezia, she no longer seemed to feel the same need to snub her that she had felt in the past. The letter about her ladies-in-waiting, for example, was straightforward and almost chummy. Nor did Lucrezia's friendship with Gonzaga appear to disturb her as much as it once had. In fact, Isabella occasionally asked her sister-in-law to request favors that Gonzaga could be expected to refuse were Isabella to request them herself. And if her ego suffered thereby, she did not let it show. At forty-two she was still so elegant that when she made a pilgrimage to the shrine of Saint Mary Magdalene in southern France, "wherever she was seen passing in the streets, all the men and women in every walk of life rushed to the doors and windows or stood still in the road gazing in wonder at her beautiful clothes and those of her ladies."

Like Isabella and Alfonso and most other people, Lucrezia had expected the new pope to bring peace to Italy, all the more so because Leo had chosen Bembo as one of his secretaries. And she must have rejoiced to learn that Messer Pietro's first task was to address eloquent eulogies of peace to all the rulers of Europe. But Maximilian and Ferdinand and Louis and Henry, though certainly literate enough to appreciate the new secretary's eloquence, were much too involved with plans for their own aggrandizement to pay much attention to what Bembo had to say. And Leo, smiling, chubby, mild-mannered Leo, who seemed so good-natured and eager to please, had plans for the aggrandizement of the Medici that made him as slippery as everyone else.

Despite all the pope's talk of peace, the Italian wars during his reign were even crueller and bloodier than those during Julius's reign. This time, however, Ferrara was not directly involved. On the other hand, the possibility that the duchy would be dragged into the wars was always there, for Leo was determined to give his family a kingdom in northern Italy that would include not only Parma, Piacenza, Modena, and Reggio, but Ferrara and Urbino as well.

During the wars with Julius, Alfonso had given Modena to the Emperor Maximilian for safekeeping. While he was negotiating for the return of the city, Leo suddenly offered the emperor 40,000 ducats if he would give Modena to him. Maximilian, who in the opinion of one writer, "would almost sell his own teeth for money," was only too happy to oblige. When Ippolito remonstrated with the pope for undercutting Alfonso, Leo swore "upon his breast as a true priest" that as soon as he had Modena he would restore it and Reggio as well to the Estense. Instead, he gave both cities to his brother Giuliano.

Because Alfonso feared that Ferrara would be next, he began strengthening the city's ramparts and refurbishing his cannon. Nor did his vigilance slacken after his French allies took Milan and made Leo promise to restore Modena and Reggio to Alfonso. However, the threat of war was not immediate, and it affected the life of the ducal court very little.

In winter there were the usual concerts and dinner parties and the excitement of the carnival with its masked balls and new plays performed in the Sala Grande. With the approach of summer there were the excursions to Belfiore and Belriguardo. More because Alfonso wished to have a place for which he would be remembered than because his family needed another pleasure palace, he built the *Delizia Estense* known as the Belvedere on an oval-shaped island in the Po above Castel Tedaldo. Although he continued to turn to Ippolito for advice, especially after his problems with Leo began, a page who was then in Lucrezia's service later wrote: "In their life and their habits the conduct of these princes was as different one from another as is day and night." To the page, the cardinal's court seemed "all rioting noise and feasting," whereas Alfonso did not even have a court in the usual sense of the word and preferred to spend his leisure fashioning majolica plates in his workshop, casting cannon, and embellishing the rooms of the *castello*. Because he had grown increasingly self-conscious about his lack of culture, Alfonso insisted that his children be given the classical education he had spurned. Ercole was only eight and one-half when he began studying Greek and Latin with a tutor selected by one of Lucrezia's poet friends. This tutor was so hard on his pupil that he satisfied even Alfonso, who believed in bringing up his children as strictly as possible. Although Ippolito II would not take kindly to this method of instruction, the more sedate Ercole appeared to thrive on it. He was just ten when, in the presence of his mother, he "recited many lines of Virgil, interpreted them and translated them into Italian." He then translated a page of Caesar's commentaries "and he answered brilliantly to his tutor's question in Greek."

By that time both Ercole and Ippolito II had their own rooms and were under the rule of their preceptors. But the two younger children were still with Lucrezia, petted and indulged by her ladies-in-waiting, her singers and dancers, her dwarfs and clowns. Sometimes in the evening after supper, one of the ladies-in-waiting would place a little bench on the table. This was the signal for Santino, the cleverest of the dwarfs, to seat himself thereon and begin one of Aesop's fables. To the delight of the children, he would act out all the parts, looking, as one courtier put it, "like a wolf preaching to sheep." Alfonso was then living in a small apartment overlooking the piazza. Although he did not take his meals with his family, Lucrezia and the two older boys would frequently join him after supper. In addition to chess and cards, there would also be reading aloud, usually excerpts from Boiardo's *Orlando Innamorato* or Ariosto's *Orlando Furioso*.

Ariosto's employer, Cardinal Ippolito, had been a child of eight when he was made bishop of Zagreb. Soon afterward, he had gone to Hungary, where he had spent his adolescence. In September 1517, Ippolito suddenly decided to return there for good. In addition to the 250 dogs, 4 stallions, 2 leopards, and 20 hawks and falcons he sent on ahead, he also took with him a number of courtiers, a mathematician, and a German theologian. He had planned on taking Ariosto, but the poet was in love with a young Florentine widow and did not wish to leave her. "Let those who would gad about, gad about, let him see England, Hungary, France and Spain, it pleases me to dwell in my own district," he wrote later. Ippolito accused him of being "faithless and loveless" and showed by words and signs that he "held his name in hate and scorn." He also took away two benefices that had provided most of Ariosto's income. The poet was still searching for a way to compensate for these lost benefices when, in the spring of 1518, Alfonso took him into his service. After that it was Ariosto himself who usually read aloud from the *Orlando*. According to his biographer, Giovanni Battista Pigna, "He read splendidly, bringing out all the fine qualities of the books and not like a man who takes pleasure in reading for the sake of hearing his own voice."

Ariosto's tribute to Lucrezia in the thirteenth canto of the *Orlando Furioso* has often been quoted in her defense:

> Alfonso's second wife Lucrezia she
> Whose virtue, fame and beauty every hour
> Increase, whom fortune and prosperity
> Combine to favor like a plant no less
> Which fertile soil and rain and sun all bless
>
> As tin to silver or as brass to gold,
> The poppy of the cornfield to the rose,
> The willow pale and withered in the cold,
> To the green bay which ever greener grows,
> As painted jewels to glass thus I hold
> Compared with her, as yet unborn all those
> Who hitherto for beauty have been famed
> Or models of all excellence are named.
>
> Both while she lives and after she is dead
> She'll be esteemed above all that she'll raise
> Those sons so royally that she'll have bred.

But Ariosto was so eager to please his patrons that he would have praised Lucifer himself had he been an Estense. Unless one is also prepared to believe his description of Alfonso as "just" and Ippolito as "magnanimous," there is no reason to set much store by what he says about Lucrezia.

More to the point and undoubtedly more gratifying to her was the tribute of the Venetian printer Aldo Manuzio, who praised the gravity and prudence with which she conducted public hearings—the *"acerrimum judicium"* ("very sharp judgment") and the *"acumen summum ingeneii"* ("great acumen").

Lucrezia had never been very robust, nor had she ever found childbirth easy. Rather than growing "ever greener," it was inevitable that she should begin to wilt under the strain of three births in so short a period of time. Although she would never admit it to herself, the frequent trips to the cloister that she made during those years provided her, not only with an opportunity to commune with her God, but also with the only reasonable way in which she could put off the next unwanted pregnancy. Without a knowledge of the days when conception was possible, however, the trips were a limited means of birth control. What probably saved her from becoming pregnant in 1517 was not the time she spent in San Bernardino, but an unexplained malady of her husband's.

According to one Ferrarese historian, at the beginning of 1518, Alfonso made a trip to Bagni d'Aboni "to cure himself of certain illnesses he had contracted in youth and in the performance of his military tasks," which could be a roundabout way of saying that he had had another flare-up of syphilis. Whatever his illness, unfortunately for his wife, the doctors soon pronounced him cured, and he returned to Ferrara ready to resume relations with her. That October Lucrezia was again pregnant. She would be thirty-nine in April and this was her eleventh pregnancy. Although she was obviously worn out, she made no effort to pamper herself, nor did her husband seem to think that she needed pampering.

Louis XII had died on New Year's Day, 1515. "Greedily making use of the most excellent beauty and youth of his new wife, a girl of eighteen, and not considering his own years and weak constitution, [he] was taken by a fever . . . and so departed this present life almost regretfully," says Guicciardini. In the autumn of 1518, Louis's successor, Francis I, concluded a treaty of peace with Henry VIII. Soon afterward, Alfonso received an invitation to be present at the French court when the treaty was proclaimed that Christmas. Although the pope had promised Francis that he would restore Modena and Reggio to Alfonso, he had not yet done so. Going to Paris would give Alfonso an opportunity to discuss the matter with the king and strengthen Ferrara's ties with France. As usual, Lucrezia would serve as regent while he was away.

Among those who went to Paris with him was Giovanni Borgia, the *infans Romanus*. Giovanni was then nineteen or twenty. In 1508, he had gone to Bari with Rodrigo of Bisceglie, and it had not been until 1517 that he had decided to visit Ferrara once again. Besides Cesare's illegitimate daughter, Lucrezia, who was a nun at San Bernardino, Lucrezia was also caring for one of her brother's illegitimate sons, Hieronymous, a little boy so lively and agreeable that he had managed to win over even Alfonso.

It was in the hope that some place could be found for Giovanni at the French court that Lucrezia sent him to Paris. As her husband had promised her he would, he presented Giovanni to the king. But Giovanni was too shy and tongue-tied to make an impression on that glib and glittering monarch, and nothing came of the visit.

Lucrezia's brother Geoffredo was then living in Squillace. Somewhat earlier he had sent one of his illegitimate sons to live with Vannozza. Since Vannozza was living alone, she was delighted to have the little boy with her. But she was also worried about what would happen to him after her death. And so she wrote to both Lucrezia and Ippolito asking that a place be found for him at Ferrara. Although Vannozza must have become even more anxious when, in 1517, Geoffredo suddenly died at the age of thirty-six, there is no record of what became of the child. Vannozza had made a good deal of money on her real estate transactions, and she also had an expensive collection of jewels, many of them given to her by Alexander. Increasingly, as she grew older, she used the money to endow hospitals and churches and gave the jewels to decorate altarpieces. To commemorate Cesare, her first and best-loved child, she had a silversmith fashion a massive silver bust of her son, which she placed in the Ospedale della Consolazione.

Vannozza died on November 26, 1518, at the age of seventy-six. She was buried in Santa Maria del Populo "with the highest honors, almost like a cardinal." A Venetian chronicler reported that the pope's chamberlain conducted the funeral service, which was "quite unwonted." Because she had left the Brotherhood of the Gonfalonieri so much money that they would "now be able to enjoy an income of four hundred ducats and put it to the advantage of the sick and needy," they decided to honor her "with a proud and splendid monument," and to celebrate a yearly mass on the anniversary of her death, as well as other ceremonies "for the purpose of commending her soul's salvation to God." For some unknown reason, the monument was never erected, but the masses were sung for over two hundred years, after which the soul of Vannozza was left to fend for itself.

Lucrezia received the news of her mother's death while she was acting as regent. After giving orders that no one was to speak of it to her, she sought refuge in San Bernardino. "She will not speak of it in case she disturbs the state. She will wear her mourning alone," said one of the courtiers. The loss of her mother was painful, not because she had been close to her, but because she hadn't. "Your happy and unhappy mother," Vannozza had signed herself. Happy to have a daughter who was duchess of Ferrara, unhappy to have had to give her up when she was little more than a baby, and unhappier still to have outlived three sons. All this Lucrezia would understand as she reflected upon her mother's life. But she could not mourn her as she had mourned Alexander, for she had never really known her and she had so few memories on which to base her grief. What she must have mourned instead was the passing of the last member of her original family and the feeling of unutterable aloneness this gave her.

Francesco Gonzaga was so ill by this time that he was unable to leave his apartment at all. He died on March 29, 1519. As he had wished, he was buried in the habit of a Franciscan monk. "I grieve for Your Excellency in this great sorrow and can never express how much grief it has caused me," Lucrezia wrote in the letter of condolence that she sent to Isabella. But Isabella's sorrow, if there was any, soon gave way to a feeling of relief. In a letter to Baldassare Castiglione, the author of *The Courtier*, she complained of how little authority her husband had given her during the last years of his life. "We were held so low in Mantua . . . that, ashamed of our abject treatment, we spent nine months away from home." Now that Gonzaga was dead, she would act as regent until the nineteen-year-old Federico came of age. That he would then reject her advice much as his father had was something she could not forsee. For the time being she was content.

For Lucrezia, Gonzaga's death meant another void that could not be filled. Perhaps because she wished to see the grave of her old friend, she talked of visiting Mantua. But she was really too weak to attempt it. By the end of May she felt so ill that she asked Alfonso's cousin, the bishop of Adria, to appeal to the pope for a special blessing on her pregnancy. Because she must have felt that there was no time to lose, she asked that a messenger set out for Rome with the bishop's letter immediately. It was a letter "full of all possible feeling that proved her humility and her devotion to the Pope, as well as the holy obligation she felt every day," the Ferrarese ambassador told Leo before reading it to him. Leo listened attentively. Then, with the smile that almost never left his face and an "air of great concern," he asked God to preserve her and traced a gesture of benediction in the air.

If the pope's blessing made Lucrezia confident that all would turn out well in the end, it did not improve her condition. Because she had always found the *castello* oppressive, she decided to go to Belriguardo. The poplars beside the huge fish pond had lost their blossoms a short time before and their long, stalked leaves were a pale, new green. Bees circled around the clover in the nearby meadow of Bologna, while in the fields magpies and swallows skimmed over the carefully tended furrows. Within the great courtyard, the air was fragrant with the scent of roses and the fountain plashed merrily. But Lucrezia was almost too weary to notice. Once settled in her room, she scarcely ever left it. Her doctors were thinking of inducing labor when, on June 14, she gave birth to a daughter. The infant was so puny and so reluctant to take nourishment that they decided they had best baptize her immediately. She was christened Isabella Maria.

The birth had been difficult, and Lucrezia developed a fever almost immediately after delivering. The doctors tried giving her purgatives, but these failed to bring down the fever. Lucrezia's head ached continually, and she complained of how heavy it felt. To relieve the heaviness, the doctors decided to cut off her hair. While it was being cut, her nose began to bleed. But neither the nosebleed nor the loss of her hair did much good. There was little hope of saving the duchess, the Mantuan envoy told Isabella on June 21. Alfonso remained at her bedside night and day, unable to conceal his anxiety. She had confessed her sins, received communion, and made her will. On June 22, she lost her sight and hearing, and the end seemed at hand. But in the evening she regained the use of her faculties and took a little broth. She was so tranquil that some of the courtiers thought she might pull through. But she knew otherwise. It was then, while she was still in possession of her faculties, that she dictated a letter to the pope asking for the blessing *in extremis*.

Most Holy Father and Honored Master:

With all respect I kiss your Holiness' feet and commend myself in all humility to your holy mercy. Having suffered for more than two months, early on the morning of the 14th of the present, as it pleased God, I gave birth to a daughter and hoped then to find relief from my sufferings, but I did not, and shall be condemned to pay my debt to nature. So great is the favor which our merciful Creator has shown me, that I approach the end of my life with pleasure, knowing that in a few hours, after receiving for the last time all the holy sacraments of the Church, I shall be released. Having arrived at this moment, I desire as a Christian, although I am a sinner, to ask your Holiness in your mercy to give me all possible spiritual consolation and your Holiness' blessing for my soul. Therefore I offer myself to you in all humility and commend my husband and my children, all of whom are your servants, to your Holiness' mercy. In Ferrara, June 22, 1519, at the fourteenth hour.

Your Holiness' humble servant,
Lucrezia d'Este

Religious serenity has been called the upper side of skepticism. The courtiers noted that Lucrezia did not ask to see her children. Was it because they were so very young that she wished to spare them so painful a leave-taking? Or was it because she feared that if she saw them, instead of approaching the end of her life "with pleasure," she would be moved to reproach "her most merciful Creator" for his indifference as she had done once before?

The death agony began the next morning. Because Alfonso did not know what else to do, or perhaps because he felt responsible, he ordered a religious procession. To those who saw him, his haggard face seemed proof of the great love he bore his wife. By the morning of the twenty-fourth, Lucrezia had once again lost her sight and hearing. But still she lingered. "The poor woman is having great difficulty letting go," said the courtiers. They were gathered at the foot of one of the great staircases along with her dwarfs and clowns and ladies awaiting news of their mistress. At eleven that evening, they heard someone come out of the sickroom and ask for a jug of rose water with which to wash the body of the duchess.

"It has just pleased our Lord to summon unto himself the soul of the illustrious lady the duchess, my dearest wife," Alfonso wrote in a letter he sent to his nephew Federico. "I cannot write this without tears, knowing myself to be deprived of such a dear and sweet companion. For such her exemplary conduct and the tender love which existed between us made her to me."

She was buried in Corpus Domini in the same vault as his mother. Alfonso fainted at the funeral and had to be carried into the sacristy, where he was revived with aqua vitae. "Her death has caused the greatest grief throughout the city and his ducal majesty displays the most profound sorrow," said Federico's uncle, Giovanni Gonzaga, who represented him at the funeral. And the doge of Venice said that he grieved for her as if she had been his own daughter, although his sorrow was somewhat mitigated by the remembrance of the award that awaited her religious and praiseworthy life. But these were the people who had known her and their words were soon forgotten. Twenty years before, the Neapolitan poet Giovanni Pontano, wishing to get back at her father for his treatment of the house of Aragon, had composed what he considered a fitting epitaph for her:

> Hic jacet in tumolo, Lucretia nomine sed re
> Thais. Alexandri filia, sponsa, nurus.

> (Here lies in her tomb a Lucretia in name,
> but a Thaïs in fact. Daughter, wife and
> daughter-in-law of Alexander VI.)

and thus her name has been passed down through the centuries.

Notes and Sources
Bibliography
Index

Notes and Sources

PROLOGUE

Lucrezia's father and two of her brothers: Latour, p. 130.
"The Messalina of modern Rome": Roscoe, p. 395.

ROME

3 "In the more than 1,100 years": Lea, "History of Sacerdotal Celibacy" gives a detailed account of what happened.
3 "So widespread": Gnoli, p. 5. See also Burchard (ed. Thuasne), vol. 2, p. 443, note 2.
4 "Although Burchard described the affair": *Ibid.* vol. 1, p. 322.
4 "Perhaps it was because": Infessura, p. 305.
4 "But the case": *Ibid.*, p. 243; also Burchard (ed. Glaser), pp.36–38.
5 "As one of them wrote": Pastor, vol. 5, p. 353.
7 "Because Burchard": Burchard (ed. Glaser), p. 7; also Burchard, *Diarium Innocentu.*
7 "After the conclave": Piccolomini, p. 81.
8 Papal states: Acton, chapter II; Mallett, chapters 1 and 2.
9 "Because there were no facilities": Burchard (ed. Celani), pp. 22–25; 45–46. (ed. Glaser), pp. 13–16.
9 "He and Cardinal Carafa": In describing the conclave of 1492, I have relied upon LaTorre unless otherwise indicated.

RODRIGO BORGIA

11 The pontiff-elect: Creighton, vol. IV, p. 184.
11 "Obviously, the election": LaTorre, p. 32.

12 "In fact, Infessura delcared": Infessura, pp. 281–82.
12 "The cardinal from Milan": Burchard (ed. Thuasne), vol. II, p. 610.
12 "For if Rodrigo Borgia": Guicciardini, p. 9.
13 "And once he had that many votes": LaTorre, pp. 52–55. In my opinion La-Torre successfully refutes the accusations of simony made by Picotti in his *Nuovi Studi a Papa Alessandro VI intorno*. See also Soranzo, *Studi intorno a Papa Alessandro VI*, pp. 24–28.
13 "Also, he was just": Pastor, vol. V, p. 387.
13 "Far more important": Garnett, "Cambridge History," pp. 19–21.
14 "Guicciardini tells us": Guicciardini, p. 10.
15 "Burchard noted": Burchard (ed. Glaser), p. 53.
15 "In front of one of the houses": Burchard (ed. Thuasne), vol. II, pp. 615–21.
16 "Then, when he was about twenty": Garnett, "English Historical Review," p. 312.
16 "Alfonso would later complain": Woodward, p. 6, note 1.
16 "A Roman friend": Latour, p. 19.
17 "If I do not vote": Piccolomini, p. 83.
18 "When he was in his twenties": Pastor, vol. II, p. 451.
18 Letter of Pius II: Gregorovius, p. 25.
19 "But he must have believed": DeRoo, vol. II, p. 123; copy of letter, pp. 431–32. The best discussion of the famous "orgy at Siena" appears in LaTorre, pp. 6–18. It is summarized by Mallett, pp. 86–87.
20 The same mother: Gnoli, *Un figlia sconosciuta*, pp. 7–12.
21 "In a document": Bellonci (1974 ed.), 610–12.
21 "In the secret archives": Archivium Secretum Apostol Vaticum. AA Arm I–XVIII 5027; also in Pastor, *Supplemento al* vol. III *Storia dei Papi*.
22 "Ferdinand Gregorovius": Gregorovius, p. 349.
22 "Therefore, I beg your Holiness": *Diverse Dame*, pp. 22–23; Pastor, *Supplemento*, pp. 505–06, letters 42–44.
22 "Because it was felt": "Not in God's Image," p. 63; Boulting, p. 181.
23 "Many of his letters": Queirazza, "*Gli Scritti Autografi.*"
24 "He would do his utmost": Pastor, vol. 5, p. 397.
25 "Because the two factions": Machiavelli, *The Prince*, p. 42.
26 "You would be astonished": DeRoo, vol. IV, p. 6.
26 "In an audience": Burchard (ed. Thuasne, vol. II), p. 626.
27 "I took Clarice": Rodocanachi, *La Femme Italienne*, p. 56.

LUCREZIA

28 "Her earliest memories": Gregorovius, pp. 15–16.
29 "They included among others": Gregorovius (French edition), pp. 423–25.
29 "Men and women": Kelso, p. 39.
30 "But a letter written": Bellonci (1960 ed.), p. 532.
30 "A year later": Soranzo, *Studii intorno*, pp. 97–98.
31 "Adriana ignored": Bouard (de), pp. 314–15.
32 "Lucrezia's hair": Gregorovius, p. 67.
32 "A recipe used": Putnam, p. 167.
33 "There isn't any real proof": Giovanni Soranzo, *Studii intorno a Papa Alessandro VI (Borgia)*, and *Orsino Orsini* takes this point of view. Though Picotti *Nuovi studi documenti a Papa Alessandro VI* points out some of the weak-

nesses in Soranzo's arguments, he does not really refute his basic premise. In fact, he concedes that Alexander may have been having a flirtation with Giulia rather than an affair.

34 "Legend also has it": Vasari, p. 170. See also Bérence, *Les Borgia*, p. 41, for the comments of Leo XIII when the Borgia apartments were reopened in the nineteenth century. One of the reasons Vasari's story gained acceptance was that the Borgia apartments were closed in 1507 by order of Julius II and not opened to the public until the reign of Leo XIII.

36 "Moreover": Bellonci (1974 ed.), p. 33.

36 "They danced in the great hall": Gregorovius, p. 52.

37 "We will make him a cardinal": Bellonci (1974 ed.), p. 36.

38 "On February 27,": Burchard (Parker edition), pp. 54–55.

38 "There would be pearls": Gregorovius, *Lucrezia*, p. 60.

39 "The chroniclers of": Burchard (ed. Celani), p. 445 note 2.

39 "On February 16,": Bouard (de), pp. 329–30.

39 "The Ferrarese ambassador": Gregorovius, *Lucrezia*, p. 57.

39 "When he was bypassed": Woodward, p. 116.

40 "According to Boccaccio": Bellonci (1974 ed.), p. 50.

41 "After these came gigantic": Rodocanachi, *La Femme Italienne*, pp. 76–78; Boulting pp. 81–86.

42 "Here, too, a throne had been": Burchard (Parker edition), pp. 64–67 gives the best account of Lucrezia's wedding.

44 "According to Stefan Infessura": Infessura, p. 286; see Bellonci (1974 ed.), p. 43 for a discussion of how to translate this.

45 "In a letter to the Duke": Bérence, *Lucrèce Borgia*, p. 108.

47 "Moreover, 'his King had' ": Infessura, p. 288.

47 "But says Sigismundo dei Conti": Delaborde, p. 260.

48 "Salt ruins the skin": Bellonci (1974 ed.), p. 39.

49 "Afterward, he would receive": Bellonci (1974 ed.), p. 59 and footnote to p. 59 on p. 565.

50 "When he finally married": Gardner, *Duke and Poets*, pp. 222–23 note 2.

51 "When the French envoy": Delaborde, pp. 281–83.

51 "In a characteristically": Pastor, vol. 5, p. 420.

51 "And in such confusion": Guicciardini, p. 32.

THE INVASION OF CHARLES VIII

52 "Everywhere rumors spread": Guicciardini, p. 44; also Delaborde, p. 317.

52 "He will pass over the": Delaborde, p. 316.

53 "He stutters": Pastor, vol. 5, p. 432.

53 "And, said the Comines": Comines (English ed.), p. 447.

53 "And, if later,": Nulli, p. 83.

53 "A prince, says Machiavelli": Machiavelli, *The Prince*, p. 84.

53 "As the King saw it": Delaborde, p. 314.

54 "*Sine luce, sine cruce*": Burchard (ed. Thuasne), vol. II, p. 89.

55 "You speak to me": Nulli, p. 78.

56 "How could Giovanni": Bellonci (1974 ed.), p. 61.

56 "I ask that your": Gregorovius, *Lucrezia*, p. 72.

58 "Long live King Alfonso": Burchard (ed. Parker), pp. 77–78.

58 "The King and the": Burchard (ed. Parker), p. 85.

59 "There were as many": Pastor, *Supplemento*, letter 5, p. 471.
60 "Giulia, dearest daughter": *Diverse Dame*, p. 30; Pastor, *Supplemento*, letter 10, p. 476.
60 "The streets were as": Cinelli, pp. 85–87.
61 "For we looked as if": *Diverse Dame*, p. 18; Pastor, *Supplemento*, letter 6, p. 473.
61 "We understand that at": *Diverse Dame*, p. 1; Pastor, *Supplemento*, letter 7, p. 474.
61 "In short in every": *Diverse Dame*, p. 6; Pastor, *Supplemento*, letter 9, p. 475.
62 "Through Giulia's estimate": *Diverse Dame*, p. 32.
62 "We thank God and": *Diverse Dame*, p. 29; Bellonci (English ed.), p. 53.
63 "The pope also wished": Bellonci (English ed.), p. 53.
63 "The pope then went": *Diverse Dame*, p. 30.
64 "However, it is done": Gregorovius, *Lucrezia*, p. 74.
64 "In the future be": Pastor, vol. II, pp. 477–78.
65 "If his holiness would": Pastor, *Supplemento*, letter 15, pp. 481–82.
65 "Should any word of": Bellonci (1974 ed.), note to p. 69 on p. 566.
66 "You may be certain": Gregorovius, *Lucrezia*, p. 74.
66 "The weapons they carried": Guicciardini, pp. 49–52.
66 "To Giacomo Trotti": DeRoo, vol. 4, p. 132.
67 " 'The Pope,' said": Pastor, vol. 5, p. 427.
67 "One of his kinsmen warned": Quierazza, p. 31.
68 "He was convinced that not": Pastor, *Supplemento*, letter 22, p. 490.
68 "Were Giulia to go to": *Ibid*., letter 24, pp. 492–93. See also letter 30, pp. 494–95; letter 31, p. 495.
70 "It is said that Giulia": Gregorovius, *Lucrezia*, footnote p. 88.
70 "He wore Spanish boots": Gregorovius, *Lucrezia*, p. 89.
71 "To one eyewitness": Woodward, p. 77.
71 "All along the Via Lata": Burchard (ed. Parker), p. 103.
71 "Everyone in Rome": Latour, p. 64. Burchard (ed. Parker), p. 106 also mentions the attacks on Jews.
71 "In answer to the king's": Gregorovius, *History*, vol. 7, pt. 1, p. 386.
71 "When Alexander": Burchard (ed. Parker), pp. 108–109.
72 "When Charles protested": Guicciardini, p. 72.
72 "Their march south": Comines (English ed.), p. 478.
72 "The pains were so intense": Latour, pp. 58–59.
72 "The disease is thought": Rosebury gives the evidence for and against the theory that syphilis was brought to Europe from the New World.
73 In China: Braudel, pp. 45–46.
73 "But the favorable": Comines (English ed.), p. 462.
73 "During the French": Bellonci (1974 ed.), p. 91.
73 "And whatever": DeRoo, vol. 5, pp. 216–36 gives the subsequent history of the two women and of Giulia's daughter Laura.
74 "Ludovico's nephew": Delaborde, pp. 426–27.
74 "Should Giovanni": Bellonci (1974 ed.), p. 97.
75 "I exhort you": *Ibid.*
77 "Because he was still": Luzio, Series V Book 1, p. 493.

DIVORCE AND OTHER STRANGE MATTERS

79 "The majordomo": Bellonci (1974 ed.), pp. 101–102.
79 "The countess of Pesaro": *Ibid.*, p. 103.

80 "Apparently the pope": Luzio, Series V Book 1, p. 489.
81 "Burchard tells us": Burchard (ed. Thuasne), vol. II, p. 280.
81 "To his horror": Burchard (ed. Glaser), pp. 87–88.
82 "On the first day": Burchard (ed. Parker), p. 120.
83 "His red velvet cap": Bellonci (1974 ed.), pp. 107–108.
83 "One anointed priest": Pastor, vol. VI, p. 17.
83 "More irksome than plague": Silenzi, p. 199.
84 "Wherever you may find": Bellonci (1974 ed.), p. 100.
85 "On January 15": *Ibid.*, p. 110.
85 "According to": Luzio, Series V Book 1, p. 493.
86 "That is to say": Rodocanachi, *La Femme Italienne*, p. 59.
86 "Tied to the": Creighton, vol. IV, p. 290.
87 "Although Burchard": Mallett, p. 135.
88 "In Spain": Mallett, p. 133.
88 "During the time": Woodward, p. 102.
88 "Rather than go": Sanuto, t. I, ed. 569, also Burchard (ed. Thuasne), vol. II, footnote to p. 386.
88 "The following day": Bellonci (1974 ed.), pp. 112–13.
89 "But Gian Lucido Cattanei": Luzio, Series V Book 1, p. 496.
89 "This is the chamberlain": Gregorovius, *Lucrezia*, p. 104.
90 "Your own good judgment": Bellonci (1974 ed.), p. 113.
92 "Mariano is moderation": Pastor, vol. V, p. 183.
92 "That he was so": Gregorovius, *Lucrezia*, p. 331.
93 "Some say she": *Ibid.*, p. 107.
93 "The sheriff": Luzio, Series V Book 2, p. 497.
93 "Because a bride": Rodocanachi, *La Femme Italienne*, pp. 231–48.
95 "According to a letter": Sanuto, vol. I col. 879.
95 "The two brothers": Burchard (ed. Parker), p. 144.
96 "At last however": Burchard (ed. Parker), p. 147.
98 "Although he could name": Sanuto, vol. I col. 1827; DeRoo, vol. I, pp. 227–40. Further discussion of the murder of the duke of Gandia in Pastor, vol. V, p. 521, and appendix letter 37, pp. 552–54.
98 "Or, if he did not": Bellonci (1974 ed.), p. 130.
99 "The most famous": Boulting, p. 263.
99 "I do not want to": Bellonci (1974 ed.), p. 131.
100 "Giovanni Sforza had": Malipiero, p. 490.
100 "The royal house of Salerno": Bellonci (1974 ed.), p. 139.
100 "Cesare had murdered": Guicciardini, p. 124.
101 "Obviously he intended": Creighton, vol. IV, p. 300.
101 "When the commission": Mallett, p. 144.
102 "Hence he must have": Bellonci (1974 ed.), p. 132.
102 "If, however": *Ibid.*, p. 133.
103 "Let him do": *Ibid.*, p. 134.
103 ". . . While it seems": Gregorovius, *Lucrezia*, p. 109.
103 "Because she had never": Bellonci (1974 ed.), p. 136.

ALFONSO OF BISCEGLIE

105 "Six days later": Burchard (ed. Thuasne), vol. II, p. 433.
105 "An entry in the diary of Marino Sanuto": Sanuto, vol. I, col. 883.
106 "Perotto was in prison": Pastor, vol. 5, p. 400. Pastor's interpretation of this is refuted by DeRoo, vol. I, p. 321.

106 "It has been vouchsafed from Rome": DeRoo, *Ibid*.
106 "With his own hand": Burchard (ed. Thuasne), vol. II, p. 433 note 1.
107 "When Giorgio Schiavi": Burchard (ed. Parker), p. 146.
107 "Soon after Alexander agreed to look elsewhere": DeRoo, vol. I, p. 323.
108 "Gian Lucido Cattanei had just written": DeRoo, vol. I, p. 325. Gregorovius, *Lucrezia* (French edition), pp. 311–18 reprints the entire contract.
108 "Capodiferro's epigram": Woodward, p. 130 note 1.
108 "The son on the other hand": Gregorovius, *Lucrezia*, p. 113.
109 "The daughter of the pope": Pastor. vol. VI, p. 612.
109 "According to Burchard": Burchard (ed. Parker), p. 163.
110 "While the guests were being seated": Bellonci (1974 ed.), p. 164.
110 "Later, a play was presented": Pastor, vol. VI, p. 12, letter 3.
110 "In fact, his private physician Gaspar Torella": Alvisi, p. 41 and Document #7m pp. 463–64.
111 "Burchard notes that Lucrezia's marriage": Burchard (ed. Thuasne), vol. II, p. 494.
111 Fausto Maddalena di Capodiferro: Bellonci (1974 ed.), pp. 171–75: and note to p. 171 on p. 579.
113 "Whether the foetus was male or female": Luzio, Series V Book 2, p. 425.
113 "Venus was jealous,": Bellonci (1974 ed.), p. 172.
113 "They had been married": Pastor, vol. VI, p. 612 letter 3.
115 "In fact, his position appeared so weak,": Pastor, vol. VI, p. 67.
115 Notice of the agreement between the Orsini and the Colonna: Pastor, vol. VI, p. 59: Ducas-Dubreton, p. 150.
116 Louis XII and the promises he made to Alexander: Woodward, pp. 132–33.
116 Cesare appears before the Sacred College to surrender his cardinal's hat: *Ibid.*, pp. 133–34; also Alvisi, p. 49.
116 "The ruin of Italy is confirmed": Luzio, Series V Book 2, p. 423.
116 "Cesare's spectacular entry into Chinon": Brântòme, vol. II, pp. 214–18.
117 "Louis, who watched the whole gorgeous display,": Burchard (ed Thuasne), vol. II, footnote beginning on p. 496.
117 "In Rome meanwhile,": Sanuto, vol. II, col. 279.
118 "According to the journal of Machiavelli's assistant": Buonaccorsi, pp. 9–10.
118 "The pope appeared very much afraid of Spain,": Pastor, vol. VI, p. 66.
118 Accolti's poem: Bellonci (English ed.), pp. 129–30.
119 "The marriage had been consummated that Sunday": Burchard: (Ed. Thuasne), vol. II, p. 532.
119 "However, the memoirs of Robert III": Burchard (ed. Thuasne), vol. II, p. 532 note 1.
119 "Although an Italian who saw Charlotte d'Albret": Sabatini, p. 188.
120 "At the Sorbonne": Latour, p. 92.
120 "Before Pope Alexander VI": Machiavelli, *Discourses*, p. 495.
121 "For the love of God,": Giustiniani, vol. I, pp. 242–43, December 12, 1502.
121 "This took place as a sign of rejoicing": Burchard (ed. Thuasne), vol. II, p. 532.
122 "The Duke of Bisceglie,": Sanuto, vol. 2. col. 1049.
124 "On the afternoon of the sixth day": *Storia del Comune di Spoleto*.
125 "The historians of the Commune": *Ibid.*
125 "Among the cases she was called upon to settle": Mancini, pp. 182–87.
127 "The first of these to come to public attention": Pastor, vol. V, p. 391; Burchard (ed. Thuasne), Vol. II, pp. 3–4.
127 "On November 7, 1496": Luzio, Series V Book 1, p. 491.

128 "At two o'clock on the morning of November 1, 1499": Burchard (ed. Parker), p. 163.
128 "To show his gratitude": De Roo, vol. I, p. 331.
128 Baptism of Rodrigo of Bisceglie: Burchard (ed. Parker), pp. 163–67.
129 "There was much murmuring": Latour, pp. 83–84.
129 "Soon afterward the pope published a bull": Pastor vol. VI, p. 147.
130 Cesare's entrance into Rome after the capture of Imola and Forli: Burchard (ed. Parker), pp. 179–82.
130 "This same pope had at that time": Pastor vol. VI, footnote p. 152.
131 "So great was the admiration": Alvisi, p. 110.
131 "A short time after it was granted": Burchard (ed. Thuasne), vol. III, p. 32 note 1.
132 "On June 24, six wild bulls": *Ibid.*, p. 64; Sanuto, vol. III col. 842.
132 "In court he is unrivalled": Woodward, pp. 238–39.
133 Attempt to assassinate Alfonso: Luzio, *Mantova e Urbino*, pp. 103–104; Burchard (ed. Parker), p. 183.
134 "In that room of magnificent blues": Sanuto, vol. III col. 845; Burchard (ed. Thuasne), vol. III, p. 68 note 1.
135 "And this must have been the reason": Bellonci (1974 ed.), p. 185.
135 "The duke of Bisceglie": Buonaccorsi, p. 51.
135 "He was gravely wounded": Burchard (ed. Thuasne) vol. III, p. 73.
135 Letter of Brandolinus Lippus: Brom, pp. 190–95.
136 "The Florentine envoy Francesco Capello": Burchard (ed. Thuasne), vol. III, pp. 436–37.
136 "The Venetian ambassador Paolo Capello": *Ibid.*, pp. 438–39.
136 "A few days after the supposed admission": Bellonci (1974 ed.), p. 189.
136 "Whereas the original dispatches": Sanuto, vol. III col. 671; Burchard (ed. Thuasne), vol. III, p. 73 note 2.
137 "Because in truth Cesare had so little": Pastor vol. VI, p. 77; Creighton. vol. V, pp. 295–301.
137 "If he died as a result of his wounds": Rolfe, p. 169.
137 The murder of Alfonso: The best summary of all the evidence is given in Creighton, vol. V, pp. 295–301.
138 "The pope is in bad humor": Luzio, Series V Book 1, p. 520.
139 "Madonna Lucrezia who is wise": Sanuto, vol. III col. 846.
140 Lucrezia's letters to Vincenzo Giordano: Gregorovius, *Lucrezia*, pp. 155–57 and Gregorovius, *Lucrezia* (French edition), pp. 334–38.
141 "Because my husbands have been very unlucky": Sanuto vol. III col. 1228.

A THIRD HUSBAND

142 "In the *Orlando Innamorato*": Gardner, *Dukes*, p. 293.
143 "But in the *Antichità Estense*": Muratori, *Antichità*, pp. 1–5.
143 The conspiracy against Ercole: Gardner, *Dukes*, pp. 143–47.
144 The story of Parisina: *Ibid.*, pp. 35–39.
144 The government of the Estense: Gundersheimer, chapters 2–5.
145 Burckhardt's definition of humanism: Burckhardt, pp. 148–53.
145 Dante's opinion of the Estense: Dante, *Inferno*, Canto 12, p. 66; Canto 18, p. 96.
147 Alfonso's character: Bacchelli, pp. 202–203; Chiappini, pp. 209–210; Gardner, pp. 251–52.

148 "Although some historians claim": Creighton, vol. 5, p. 301.

148 "On February 14, Ercole": Gardner, pp. 390–91.

149 Partition of Naples: Pastor, vol. VI, p. 83.

150 "On July 27, the pope left Rome": Pastor, vol. VI, p. 104.

150 Lucrezia in charge of the Vatican: Burchard (ed. Thuasne), vol. III, p. 154.

153 The dickering over the marriage contract: Gardner, pp. 392–95.

154 Letter to Francesco Gonzaga: *Ibid.*, p. 307; Gregorovius, *Lucrezia*, p. 186.

154 "In a letter to Isabella": Luzio, Series V Book 1, p. 532.

155 Celebrations in Rome after the signing of the marriage contract: Burchard (ed. Parker), p. 193.

156 "To the great delight of the envoys": Gregorovius, *Lucrezia*, p. 189.

156 "Despite the Pope's emphasis": Burchard (ed. Thuasne), vol. III, p. 163.

157 Letter to Ercole concerning Alexander's parties: Gregorovius, *Lucrezia*, p. 190.

158 "Cesare's inability to rid himself of the French disease": Gregorovius, *Lucrezia*, pp. 161–64.

158 Alexander's criticism of Cesare: *Ibid.*, p. 201.

158 The *infans Romanus*: Pastor, vol. 6, pp. 104–105; Creighton, vol. V, p. 22; Dal Re, footnote 1, pp. 90–91; Sanuto, vol. I col. 369 and Gregorovius, *Lucrezia*, p. 95 and pp. 194–95.

160 "I asked her": Gregorovius, *Lucrezia*, p. 195.

160 The story of the nuns: Gandini, pp. 285–340; Gardner, *Dukes*, pp. 401–405.

162 The supper of the fifty courtesans: Burchard (ed. Parker), p. 194; (ed. Thuasne) vol. III pp. 167–68; note 2 includes the letter of the Florentine envoy Francesco Pepi (see p. 164 of this text).

162 "In a letter to Machiavelli": Creighton, vol. V, footnote p. 57.

162 "Although like Vespucci": *Ibid.*, p. 299.

163 The letter of Silvio Savelli: Burchard (ed. Thuasne) vol. III pp. 182–87. A French translation of the famous letter appears in Funck-Brentano, pp. 189–98.

164 The incident of the mares and the stallions: Burchard (ed. Parker), p. 194.

164 "Equally barbarous entertainments": Rodocanachi, *La Femme Italienne*, p. 78.

166 "Typical of what she expected": Cartwright, vol. 1, p. 72.

167 Letter of El Prete: Luzio, Series V Book 1, p. 535 (English translation Latour p. 535).

167 Entrance of the Ferrarese into Rome: Letter of Zuane Battista Scabalino reprinted in Burchard (ed. Thuasne), vol. III pp. 176–77 note 1.

168 Lucrezia greets the Ferrarese: Letter of El Prete, Gregorovius, *Lucrezia*, pp. 211–12.

169 Castellini's letter to Ercole: *Ibid.*, p. 213.

169 El Prete's letter of December 26: *Ibid.*, pp. 214–15.

170 Ippolito's character: Hauvette, pp. 94–96.

170 "There was also a tournament": Latour, pp. 167–68.

171 Christmas rites: Burchard (ed. Thuasne), vol. III, p. 178.

171 Lucrezia's marriage ceremony: Burchard (ed. Parker), pp. 196–97; Pastor, vol. VI, p. 109.

172 The presentation of the Estense jewels: Burchard (ed. Parker), p. 197; Gardner, *Dukes*, p. 408; Gregorovius, *Lucrezia*, pp. 216–17.

173 "The first was not finished": *Ibid.*, p. 218.

174 "Ercole's envoys manifested": Bellonci (1974 ed.), p. 239 and p. 243; Gardner, *Dukes*, p. 408.

174 Lucrezia's trousseau: Beltrami; Gregorovius, *Lucrezia*, pp. 207–08.

175 Lucrezia leaves for Ferrara: Burchard (ed. Thuasne), vol. III, pp. 188–89.

IN THE CASTELLO OF THE ESTENSE

177 "She must remember to dress warmly": Bellonci (1964 ed.), note to page 245 on page 584.
177 "His Holiness need have no concern": Bellonci (1974 ed.), pp. 281–84.
178 Lucrezia's welcome at Foligno: Gregorovius, *Lucrezia*, pp. 230–31.
179 "According to Castiglione": Castiglione, p. 16.
182 According to the Ferrarese envoys: Zambotti, p. 312.
182 "It is also the Isabella": Cartwright, vol. I, chapters 5 and 6.
183 "Hence it may have been": *Ibid.*, p. 202.
184 "One was hung with gold brocade": *Ibid.*, p. 201.
185 Lucrezia's entry into Ferrara: *Ibid.*, pp. 202–205; Zambotti, pp. 313–14, pp. 322–24.
189 "Among those who had written": Gardner, *King of Court Poets*, p. 43.
189 Pellegrino Prisciano: Bellonci (English ed.), pp. 183–84.
190 "Last night our son": *Ibid.*, p. 185.
190 "From what I have been given to understand": Catalano, note to page 16 on pp. 54–55.
190 "When Lucrezia did not leave": *Ibid.*, pp. 543–44.
191 Celebration the day following Lucrezia's arrival: Cartwright, vol. 1 pp. 205–207.
192 "Eating was a serious business in Ferrara": Gilbert, vol. II pp. 3–9; Frizzi, pp. 206–207.
192 "Madonna Lucrezia chooses": Cartwright, vol. 1, p. 208.
192 "While the guests were waiting": Zambotti, p. 326.
193 The presentation of gifts from Louis: *Ibid.*, p. 327.
193 Isabella invites the French ambassador: Cartwright, vol. 1, p. 209; Zambotti, pp. 327–28.
194 Isabella's behavior at the performances of the *Miles Gloriosus* and the *Casina*: Bellonci (1974 ed.), pp. 304–307; Cartwright, vol. 1 pp. 210–12.
195 The visit of the Venetian ambassadors: *Ibid.*, pp. 212–14.
197 Lucrezia's problems with Ercole: Bellonci (1974 ed.), pp. 311–20; see also letter dated March 7, 1502, reprinted in Bellonci (1960 ed.), pp. 544–45; and Luzio, Series V Book 1, pp. 550–52.
197 "Whereupon Ercole asked Isabella": Cartwright, vol. 1, pp. 226–27.
197 Ercole Strozzi: Gardner, *Dukes*, pp. 469–70; see also Beltrami, which contains numerous references to items Strozzi bought for Lucrezia and Catalano, note to p. 24, pp. 60–61.
200 "Later, she would say": Bellonci (1974 ed.), p. 326.
201 "Though only nine miles from Ferrara": Gundersheimer, pp. 254–62.
202 Cesare's capture of Urbino: Woodward, pp. 232–38.
203 Lucrezia's illness: This is described in great detail in Gagniere and in Cabanes.
204 Cesare's first visit to Lucrezia: Woodward, p. 249.
206 "With childish pride": Giustiniani, vol. 1, p. 114.
208 "One of Isabella's female cousins": Cartwright, pp. 214–15.

PIETRO BEMBO

209 "Who can fail to see": Bembo, *Gli Asolani*, p. 156.
210 "Maria Savorgnan, the second": Meneghetti, pp. 20–36; gives a detailed account of Bembo's affair with her; see also *Carteggio d'Amore* and Bembo,

Lettere, pp. 145–278. Letter XV p. 163 and Letter LXXIII p. 262 both mention Bembino.

211 "For many years": Meneghetti, p. 40.

211 "Like Bembo, most of the others": DeSanctis, vol. 1, pp. 425–26.

212 "When finally he met her": Morsolin, p. 398.

212 "He had had many honors": *Ibid.*, p. 400.

213 "El Prete, who continued": Luzio, Series V Book 1, p. 697.

213 "The chroniclers tell us": Zambotti, p. 346.

214 "Her nights belonged to Don Alfonso": Bellonci (1974 ed.), p. 351.

214 "Quite late yesterday": Morsolin, p. 401; English translation Latour, p. 145.

215 "Yo pienso si me muriese": Bellonci (English ed.), p. 212.

216 "Tan buio es mi padescar": *Ibid.*, p. 213.

216 "As for your desire to know my feelings": Biblioteca Ambrosiana, *Lettere di Lucrezia Borgia*, Letter V p. 11 (English translation) Latour, p. 145.

217 "Since a medal of hers": Bellonci (1974 ed.), p. 356.

217 "Now my crystal is more precious": Morsolin, p. 404; English translation Latour, p. 145.

217 Famous lock of blond hair: Morsolin, p. 406. The lock, by now quite faded and brittle-looking, is on display in a reliquary in one of the glass display cases on the second floor of the Ambrosiana in Milan. It must have been more accessible in Byron's time, for he boasted of having filched a few hairs when no one was looking.

217 "I cannot describe the gloom": Bembo, *Lettere*, p. 279; English translation Latour, p. 147.

217 "Fever had weakened me": Morsolin, p. 408; English translation Latour, p. 146.

218 "We think day and night": Gilbert, vol. II, p. 250.

218 "This pope . . . grows younger": Pastor, vol. VI, p. 80.

218 "In his famous essay on the Renaissance": Burckhardt, pp. 88–89.

219 "In the opinion of the English historian": Mallett, p. 226.

219 "See how each of these two kings": Giustiniani, vol. I, p. 150; English translation Mallett, p. 180.

220 "In fact, there were so many rumors": This is my conclusion after reading the accounts of what happened in Mallett, Woodward, and Pastor.

220 "This month is a bad one": Pastor, vol. VI, p. 131.

220 "See how disastrous it has been": *Ibid.*

221 "I have sought by all means": Rolfe, p. 207.

222 "Later, one of his bishops": Garnett, *A Contemporary Oration*, pp. 311–14.

222 "Alone in the turmoil": Burchard (ed. Parker), p. 204.

222 "Later that morning": *Ibid.*, pp. 220–21.

222 "Later, he would tell Machiavelli": Machiavelli, *The Prince*, p. 29.

222 "Since he could not take matters into his own hands": Burchard (ed. Parker), p. 221.

223 "Soon afterward Burchard arrived": The account of all that happened to Alexander's body until it was buried is taken from Burchard (ed. Parker), pp. 221–26.

223 "If we believe Guicciardini": Guicciardini, p. 166.

224 "But less than a century later": Lucas-Dubreton, pp. 282–83.

224 "To Alexander's contemporary": *Ibid.*, pp. 237–38.

224 "Although it is true that he sinned": Durant, p. 436.

225 "And he was more tolerant ": I am thinking of Pius V, who was so rigid in his treatment of heretics that even the future Sixtus V trembled before him.
225 "Behold Alexander": Garnett, *A Contemporary Oration*, p. 311.
226 "The marchese of Mantua": Gregorovius, pp. 288–89.
226 Accounts of the poisoning: Rolfe, pp. 214–40.
226 "It is clear, [says Guicciardini]": Guicciardini, p. 165.
227 "In the opinion of the French writer Charles Flandin": Pastor, vol. VI, p. 136, note 3.
227 "The pope was on the verge": Rolfe, pp. 212–13.
228 "So much for the poison of the Borgias": For further discussion see Creighton, vol. 5 pp. 301–304; Rolfe, pp. 214–40; Pastor, vol. VI, pp. 135–36, including footnotes.
229 "Knowing that many will ask": Gardner, *Dukes*, p. 433.
229 "In a letter he sent her": Gregorovius, *Lucrezia*, pp. 291–92.
229 "Though it would be my greatest joy": Morsolin, p. 409.
230 "At the beginning of October": Bembo, *Lettere*, pp. 290–94.
230 "When a week later": Morsolin, p. 411.
231 "In the seventh chapter of *The Prince*": Machiavelli, pp. 23–30.
231 "Because Ercole didn't want": Gardner, *Dukes*, p. 253.
232 "The electors were running": Pastor, vol. VI, p. 191.
233 Ercole's letter concerning Rodrigo: Gregorovius, *Lucrezia*, pp. 297–98.
233 "Soon after Alexander's death": *Ibid.*, p. 287.
234 "In the creation of Julius II": Machiavelli, *The Prince*, p. 30.
234 "In fact he hated them so much": Latour, p. 170; Creighton, vol. 5, p. 85.
235 "The agreements are being made": Giustiniani, vol. II, p. 255.
235 "Machiavelli, who was one": Woodward, p. 343, note 2.
235 Guidobaldo of Urbino: There is a legend that Cesare grovelled before Guidobaldo and asked his forgiveness. See Woodward, pp. 435–36. On page 355 he calls the story "not wholly imaginary."
235 "It seems to me": Woodward, p. 355.
236 "When Julius suggested": Gardner, *Dukes*, p. 441.
237 "Nevertheless, the poet assured her": Morsolin, p. 413.
237 "Like most of the letters Lucrezia wrote to him": Biblioteca Ambrosiana, *Lettere di Lucrezia Borgia*, Letter III p. 10. The ending "Desiderosa gratificarvi" ("I desire to serve you") has been given a sexual connotation by certain writers, but as Gilbert, for one, points out, this was the usual ending employed in the letters of the period.
238 "The thought of her was a consolation": Bembo, *Lettere*, pp. 286–87.
238 Barbara Torelli: Catalano, pp. 62–65; Luzio, Series V Book 2, pp. 153–54.
238 Ercole's quarrel with Ippolito: Gardner, *Dukes*, pp. 446–50.
240 Cesare's arrest and subsequent imprisonment: Woodward, pp. 353–70.
240 "Besides assuring her": Gardner, *Dukes*, pp. 443–44.
241 The dedication of *Gli Asolani*: Bembo, *Gli Asolani*, pp. 1–3.
241 "Seeing her and talking": Morsolin, p. 411.
241 The death of Ercole: Bacchelli, pp. 343–44; Chiappini, p. 209.
242 Alfonso becomes duke: Frizzi, p. 219; Chiappini, pp. 213–15.
242 "Soon after his coronation": Bellonci (1974 ed.), p. 399.
243 "Like many of the letters": The text of this letter is in Bembo, *Lettere*, pp. 290–94; parts of the translation are from Latour, pp. 141–47; the rest is my own.

244 "However, Maria Bellonci": Bellonci (1974 ed.), pp. 393–94 and note to p. 393 on p. 592.
244 "They continued to write to one another": Biblioteca Ambrosiana, *Lettere di Lucrezia Borgia*, letters VII and VIII p. 13; Bembo, *Lettere*, pp. 27–37.
244 "It was then": Cian, p. 15.
245 "I have lost the dearest heart": Durant, p. 320.

FRANCESCO GONZAGA

246 "Now that they were deprived": Luzio, Series V Book 1, p. 705. Luzio makes much of this, apparently forgetting that Polissena had used the same kind of flattery in writing to Isabella (p. 547 of Luzio's work).
247 "He'd been ill": Bellonci (1974 ed.), p. 411.
248 "It was said": Luzio, Series 5, Book 1, p. 709.
248 "The Monday after Easter": Bellonci (1974 ed.), pp. 401–402.
249 "His procurer in those days": Bacchelli, p. 421.
249 "The year was going in reverse": *Ibid.*, pp. 346–47; 377–79. Frizzi: pp. 219–20.
250 Reggio: Gardner, *King of Court Poets*, p. 7.
251 Don Giulio: Bacchelli, p. 230; Bellonci (1974 ed.) pp. 387–88; 402–404.
252 The story of the chaplain: Bacchelli, pp. 359–92.
252 Sancha of Aragon: Bellonci (1974 ed.) pp. 339–40, 367, 379–82.
253 "But she did invite": Woodward, p. 361.
253 Alberto Pio and the matter of the chaplain: Bacchelli, pp. 386–87; 379–80; Bellonci (1974 ed.), p. 405.
254 "The plague and famine": Frizzi, p. 220.
255 "On the other hand": Bellonci (1974 ed.), p. 413.
255 "He felt as if he had already gained . . .": Luzio, Series V, Book 1, p. 711.
255 "One learned scholar": *Ibid.*, p. 718.
256 "Isabella pretended": Cartwright, p. 144.
256 "Once in a fit of rage": Bellonci (1974 ed.), p. 525.
256 "And once, but only once": Cartwright, vol. II, pp. 85–86.
258 "In December, Lucrezia and her court": Bacchelli, p. 393.
258 "He does not consider his praises composed by me": Ariosto, *Satires*, p. 5.
258 The attack on Don Giulio: Bacchelli, pp. 398–99; Gardner, *Dukes*, p. 499.
259 "In a letter to the Ferrarese ambassador": Gardner, *Dukes*, p. 499.
259 "In the dispatch he sent to Mantua": Latour, p. 149.
259 "But Isabella considered": Bacchelli, pp. 400–401.
260 Ippolito's visit to Don Giulio: Gardner, *Ibid.*, pp. 415–16.
261 "Not only did Alfonso allow the carnival": Gardner, *Dukes*, p. 502.
261 "Mindful of the young duke's taste": Catalano, notes to pages 30–31, pp. 73–74.
261 Angela's betrothal: Bellonci (1974 ed.), p. 423.
261 The condition of Don Giulio: Catalano, notes to pages 27 and 28, pp. 65–66; Bacchelli, pp. 417–18.
261 The conspiracy: Bacchelli, pp. 419–49; Gardner, *Dukes*, pp. 501–502; Machiavelli, *Discourses*, pp. 425–26.
264 "The Jewish community in Ferrara": Gundersheimer, pp. 124–26, 206–207; Balletti, pp. 11–13; Zambotti, pp. 92 and 124.
265 "To discourage these malefactors": Gregorovius, *Lucrezia* (French edition), #55 pp. 407–408.

265 "Save for complaining that Giulio": Bacchelli, p. 464.

265 "In his terror, Ferrante": *Ibid.*, pp. 464–56.

266 "Isabella, on the other hand": *Ibid.*, pp. 462; 504–508.

266 "That night, according to Alberto Pio": *Ibid.*, p. 509.

267 "On the sixth of January, 1507": Frizzi, p. 225; Bacchelli, pp. 511–12.

267 "According to one chronicler": Chiappini, pp. 221–22.

267 "After they were arrested": Bacchelli, pp. 476–77.

268 "In 1510 she and two of the courtiers": Luzio, Series V Book 1, p. 747.

268 Cesare's escape from Medina del Campo: Sabatini, pp. 442–44.

269 Italian reactions to Cesare's escape: Woodward, p. 474; Alvisi, p. 324. Gregorovius, *Lucrezia*, p. 320.

269 Letters of Cesare and Lucrezia to Gonzaga: Gregorovius, *Lucrezia*, pp. 320–21; Gardner, *Dukes*, pp. 511–12.

269 "When Gonzaga came to Ferrara": Bellonci (1974 ed.), pp. 434–35.

270 "The Lenten sermon that year": *Ibid.*, pp. 436–37; Luzio, Series V Book 2, p. 161.

270 The death of Cesare: Luzio, Series V Book 2, p. 152.

270 "It was while he was away from Ferrara": *Ibid.*

271 "Of his virtues and vices": Lucas-Dubreton, p. 280.

271 "Cesare Borgia, who was held by all": Bellonci (English ed.), p. 260.

271 "Here lies in little earth": Lucas-Dubreton, p. 279.

271 "But the anonymous author": Burchard (ed. Thuasne), Vol. III, pp. 450–55.

271 "Fra Raffaele was given the task": Luzio, Series V Book 2, p. 152.

272 "Give way to tears": Gardner, *Dukes*, p. 513.

273 The visit of Rodrigo of Bisceglie: Bellonci (1974 ed.), pp. 511–12; 607–608.

273 "During the five years he had been separated": Bertoni, pp. 92–93.

273 "Nevertheless, they insisted": Luzio, Series V Book 1, p. 749 note 2. With his usual eagerness to derogate Lucrezia, Luzio misinterprets this completely.

274 Lucrezia redoes her apartment: Bellonci (1974 ed.), pp. 451–53.

274 Bartolommeo Veneto: Bellonci (1974 ed.), pp. 452 and 610. Says that Veneto painted Lucrezia's portrait at about this time. However, neither the article by De Hevesy nor the work by Giacomo Bargellese, which Bellonci cites on page 610, offer any real proof that this was the case.

274 "In the Middle Ages": Braudel, p. 240.

275 "Even his love for Barbara Torelli": Luzio, Series V Book 1, p. 726.

275 "Rather than being addressed to Gonzaga": *Ibid.* Although most writers accept Luzio's interpretation of these letters, I find it impossible to do so. To me the relationship between Lucrezia and Gonzaga seems no more compromising than, for instance, the relationship between Isabella and Ludovico Sforza. But Luzio, with his usual insistence upon seeing everything Lucrezia did in the worst possible light, used words such as "inverecondia" ("shamelessness") to describe her behavior.

277 "Messer Ercole [Strozzi] is related by marriage": Bellonci (English ed.), pp. 269–70.

277 "In the city-wide free-for-all": Frizzi, p. 231.

278 "I give you my word that she loves you": Luzio, Series V Book 1, pp. 719–20; Bellonci (English ed.), pp. 267–68.

279 "The great pity of it torments me": Bellonci (English ed.), p. 272.

279 "In despair, Strozzi's widow": Luzio, Series V Book 1, p. 727.

280 "The magistrate never wanted": Gardner, *Dukes*, p. 519.

280 "A couplet written at the time": Bellonci (English ed.), p. 274.

280 "One for fear": Gardner, *Dukes*, pp. 521-22.
281 "Ah! Why cannot the irksome body fly": *Ibid.*, p. 518.
281 "Why may I not go down to the grave": Durant, p. 270.
281 "Her behavior during the Corpus Christi day parade": Bellonci (English ed.), p. 275.
282 "In August she asked Lorenzo": Luzio, Series V Book 1, p. 731.
282 "He had heard with great joy": *Ibid.*, pp. 731-32.
283 "On December 1": *Ibid.*, pp. 732-33.
283 "Although the published clauses of this treaty": Guicciardini, pp. 196-97.

THE LEAGUE OF CAMBRAI AND OTHER ABOMINATIONS

285 "According to the Venetian ambassador": Pastor, vol. VI, p. 213.
285 "Although it was customary": Roscoe, p. 300.
285 "His surviving daughter": Pastor, vol. VI, pp. 217-19, 260; Creighton, vol. V pp. 81-82. For some reason both these writers are considerably more tolerant of Julius's nepotism than they are of Alexander's. Thus Creighton, normally one of the fairest of historians, gives us the following piece of ingenious double-talk: "Though Julius II abandoned nepotism as a political weapon, he did not forget the claims of his relations." (vol. V, p. 81).
285 "Although Alexander had used violent means": Mallett, pp. 225-26.
286 "Let the world perish": Creighton, vol. 5, p. 110.
286 "Although he had been the principal investigator": Guicciardini, p. 198.
288 "I beg your Excellency": Luzio, Series V Book 1, p. 740.
288 Ariosto's plays: Gardner, *Dukes*, pp. 515; 522-23.
288 "During the Lenten season": Bellonci (1974 ed.), p. 475.
289 "His protection cost Ferrara": Gardner, *King of Court Poets*, p. 57.
289 "As a prince": Garnett, *Cambridge History*, p. 241.
289 "On the reverse side of the *amorino bendato*": Gregorovius, *Lucrezia*, pp. 359-60.
290 "If heaven is eternal": Bacchelli, p. 351.
290 "Like many women who were dissatisfied": Davidsohn, pp. 313-14.
290 "Because the Venetians had not": Roscoe, pp. 232-36.
291 "Your Holiness knows the state": Creighton, p. 119.
292 The capture of Francesco Gonzaga: Luzio, Series V Book 2, pp. 12-29; Cartwright, vol. 2, p. 32; Gardner, *King of Court Poets*, p. 59.
292 "After asking the brothers": Cartwright, vol. 2, pp. 33-34.
293 "But she forbade the commanders": Plumb, p. 366.
293 "She also made up her mind to write to him": Luzio, Series IV Book 15, p. 287.
294 "The ducal stewards": Gardner, *King of Court Poets*, p. 61.
294 The battle of Polisella: Frizzi, pp. 240-43; Bellonci (1974 ed.), pp. 480-81; Gardner, *King of Court Poets*, pp. 64-67.
296 "By then Julius had come to realize": Creighton, pp. 133-35; Guicciardini, p. 208.
296 "Among Alfonso's distinguished forebears": Gardner, *King of Court Poets*, p. 68.
297 "I am stupefied by the cannon": *Ibid.*, p. 71.
298 "When the post had first been offered to him,": Luzio, Series V Book 2, pp. 51-55.
299 "Julius immediately let everyone know": *Ibid.*, p. 66.
299 "And to many gentlemen in Mantua": *Ibid.*, p. 64.

300 "She had more faith in him": Luzio, Series V Book 1 (1914–15) pp. 741–42.
300 "Among the prisoners taken": Bellonci (1974 ed.), pp. 486–87.
301 "Now we will see": Creighton, vol. V, p. 143 note 1.
301 "In fact, he would": Luzio, *Archivio Storico Lombardo*, Series IV, 1911, p. 287.
302 "Let us hope": Bellonci (1974 ed.), p. 494.
302 "By then all the shops": Gardner, *King of Court Poets*, p. 81.
302 "Between four and five thousand foot soldiers": *History of Bayard*, p. 250.
303 "Above all persons": *Ibid.*, pp. 251–52.
303 "But when Gonzaga took this": Luzio, Series V Book 1, p. 745.
304 "As a final taunt to the Pope": Pastor, vol. VI, pp. 512–13.
304 "The first of these": *History of Bayard*, p. 266. In a footnote, the editor notes: "This prayer, like many other passages in this history, falsifies the reputation for cruelty which romantic literature has created for Lucrezia Borgia."
304 "Although a number of towns across the Po": Bellonci (1974 ed.), pp. 502–503.
305 "On Easter Sunday, April 11, 1512,": Guicciardini, p. 248.
305 "There have been many battles": *History of Bayard*, p. 332.
306 "It was horrible to see": Gardner, *King of Court Poets*, p. 87.
306 "And one of Ariosto's elegies": Ariosto, *Orlando Furioso*, Introduction, p. 23.
306 "O hideous invention!": *Ibid.*, pp. 22–23.
307 "That morning the impetuous young commander": Guicciardini, p. 244.
307 "Ths soldiers of Louis XII": Pastor, vol. VI, p. 416.
308 "On the day she delivered this": Gardner, *King of Court Poets*, p. 91 note 2.
308 Michelangelo: Pastor, vol. VI, pp. 513–20; sonnet, p. 518.
310 "She was so bowed with grief": Luzio, Series V Book 1 (1914–15), p. 743.
310 "I am wholly lost in bitterness": Gregorovius, p. 333.
311 "That winter he and his family": Frizzi, p. 268.
312 "In *Julius II Exclusus*": Julius Exclusus, pp. 149–51.
312 "Although Alfonso advised": Luzio, *Archivio Storico Lombardo*, Series IV, vol. 17, 1911, p. 417.
313 "The affairs of Ferrara": *Ibid.*

PEACE

315 "Nevertheless, it is Lucrezia": Catalano, p. 43.
315 "With the approach of middle age, however": Chiappini, p. 244. Though this was said of him at a later date, it seems to apply just as well at this time and to explain his new devotion to Lucrezia.
315 Lucrezia's jewelry: Bellonci (1960 ed.), pp. 555–78.
316 "But Lucrezia already had three sons": Gilbert, vol. 2, p. 332.
316 "The poor little one": Gardner, *King of Court Poets*, pp. 143–44.
317 "The Venetian ambassador": Cartwright, vol. 2, p. 137.
317 "Upon learning that three of her ladies-in-waiting": Luzio, Series V Book 1, p. 745.
318 "It is I who am the Marchese of Mantua": Bellonci (1974 ed.), p. 525.
318 "In fact, Isabella occasionally": Bellonci (1974 ed.), p. 526.
319 "While he was negotiating for the return of the city": Gardner, *King of Court Poets*, p. 132.
319 "Although he continued to turn to Ippolito": *Ibid.*, p. 126.
319 "To the page": Mosti, pp. 168–70.

320 "Ercole was only eight": Roscoe, p. 431. Letter to Trissino. (For an opinion of this tutor's discipline see Mosti.)

320 "He was just ten ten when": Luzio, Series V Book 1, pp. 748–49; Latour, p. 152.

320 "Soon afterward he had gone to Hungary": Frizzi, p. 280.

321 "According to his biographer": Gardner, *King of Court Poets*, p. 127.

321 "Alfonso's second wife, Lucrezia": Ariosto, *Orlando Furioso*, p. 407.

321 "More to the point": Luzio, Series V Book 1, p. 747.

322 "According to one Ferrarese historian": Frizzi, p. 281.

322 "Louis XII had died": Guicciardini, pp. 283–84.

323 Giovanni Borgia: Gardner, *King of Court Poets*, pp. 138–39; Bellonci (1974 ed.), pp. 542–46, but Bellonci's assumption that Giovanni had been in the Castello since 1506 seems to be refuted by Gregorovius, *Lucrezia*, p. 335. ("Both children, Giovanni and Rodrigo of Bisceglie, were again in Bari in April 1508 . . .").

323 The death of Vannozza: Gregorovius, *Lucrezia*, pp. 352–54.

324 "I grieve for your Excellency": Cartwright, vol. 2, pp. 157–58.

324 "In a letter to Baldassare Castiglione": Luzio, *Archivio Storico Lombardo*, Series V Book 1, p. 753.

325 "It was a letter": Bellonci (1974 ed.), p. 551.

325 "Because she had always found": This information is given in the little folder distributed by the nuns of Corpus Domini in Ferrara.

325 "There was little hope of saving the duchess": Luzio, *Archivio Storico Lombardo*, Series V Book 1, p. 751.

326 "Most Holy father and honored master": Gregorovius, *Lucrezia*, pp. 356–57.

326 "Because Alfonso did not know": Luzio, *Archivio Storico Lombardo*, Series V Book 1, p. 752.

327 "It has just pleased": Gregorovius, *Lucrezia*, p. 357.

327 "Alfonso fainted": Cartwright, vol. 2, p. 158.

327 "And the Doge of Venice": Brown, vol. III, p. 344.

327 "Hic jacet in tumulo": Roscoe, p. 496.

Bibliography

I. Written and Printed Material in Archives and Special Libraries

Archivio Segreto Estense, Modena, Sezione Casa e Stato Fasa 99/205 *Documenti spettanti alla famiglia Borgia.*
Archivium Secretum Apostol Vaticum
———. A A Arm I–XVIII 5027, *Lettere di diverse Dame scritte à Papa Alessandro VI.*
———. Vol II 5021 (other letters).
———. Arm XXXIX, vol. 9, Pius II *Brevia* (Letter of Pius II to Rodrigo Borgia concerning the party at Siena.)
Most but not all of the letters to the women and to the others have been reprinted in Pastor's supplement to volume III of the Italian edition of his *Story of the Popes* (see below). An English translation of the letter of Pius II to Rodrigo Borgia appears in Gregorovius's *Lucretia Borgia* and is part of chapter 2 of this text.

Biblioteca Ambrosiana, Milan.
Bembo, Pietro. *Versi à Lucrezia* (Borgia) *Estense.* H. 26 inf ors S.P. II 100.
———. *Versi spagnuoli e rimi à Lucrezia Borgia* (Autografo unito alle Lettere di Lucrezia Borgia).
———. *Lettere di Lucrezia Borgia à Messer Pietro Bembo.* Dagli Autografi conservati in un Codice della Biblioteca Ambrosiana Milan: coi tipi Dell' Ambrosiana, 1859.
Biblioteca Olivieri, Pesaro. *Memorie di Pesaro.* Tome 10. Manoscritto Oliveriano 944, IV, c. 263r.
Betti, Teofilo. "Delle Cose Pesaresi" dall'anno 1449 all'anno 1519.

II. General Works Covering the Entire Period

Creighton, Mandell. *A History of the Papacy From the Great Schism to the Sack of Rome*. Vols. IV & V. New York: Longmans, Green, 1911.

De Sanctis, Francesco. *History of Italian Literature*. 2 vols. Translated by Joan Redfern. New York: Basic Books, 1959.

Durant, Will. *The Renaissance (The Story of Civilization: Part V)*. New York: Simon and Schuster, 1953.

Guicciardini, Francesco. *The History of Italy*. Translated by Sidney Alexander. New York: Collier Books, 1969.

Hay, Denys. *The Italian Renaissance in Its Historical Background*. Cambridge: The University Press, 1961.

Luzio, Alessandro, and Renier, Rodolfo. *Mantova e Urbino*. Turin: L. Roux, 1893.

Machiavelli, Niccolò. *The Prince and the Discourses*. New York: The Modern Library, 1940.

Pastor, Ludwig. *The History of the Popes*. Vols. 2–6. Edited by Frederick Ignatius Antrobus. London: Routledge and Kegan Paul, 1950.

———. *La Storia dei Papi* (Supplemento al III). Rome: Desclee, 1912.

Plumb, J. H. *The Horizon Book of the Renaissance*. New York: American Heritage Publishing Company, 1961.

Sanuto, Marino. *I Diarii*. Vol. 1–7. Venice: F. Stefani, 1879.

III. General Works Dealing Primarily With the Social History of the Period

Boulting, William. *Women in Italy*. London: Methuen and Company, 1910.

Braudel, Ferdinand. *Capitalism and Material Life 1400–1800*. Translated by Miriam Kochan. New York: Harper & Row, 1973.

Burckhardt, Jacob. *The Civilization of the Renaissance in Italy*. New York: The Modern Library, 1954.

Castiglione, Baldassare. *The Book of the Courtier*. Translated by Charles S. Singleton. New York: Anchor Books, 1959.

Delumeau, Jean. *La Civilisation de la Renaissance*. Paris: Arthaud, 1967.

Fracastoro, Girolamo. *The Sinister Shepherd*. Translated by William van Wyck. Los Angeles: The Primavera Press, 1934.

Guicciardini, Francesco. *Ricordi (Maxims and Reflections of a Renaissance Statesman)*. New York: Harper & Row, 1965.

Himes, Norman E. *Medical History of Contraception*. New York: Schocken Books, 1970.

Kelso, Ruth. *Doctrine for the Lady of the Renaissance*. Urban: University of Illinois Press, 1956.

Putnam, Emily Jane. *The Lady*. Chicago: University of Chicago, 1970.

Rodocanachi, E. *La Femme Italienne a l'epoque de la Renaissance*. Paris: Librairie Hachette, 1907.

Rosebury, Theodore. *Microbes and Morals*. New York: The Viking Press, 1971.

Thompson, James Westfall, et al. *The Civilization of the Renaissance*. New York: Frederick Ungar, 1929.

Not in God's Image. Edited by Julia O'Faolain and Lauro Martinez. New York: Harper Torchbook, 1973.

Religion and Sexism. Images of Woman in the Jewish and Christian Traditions. Edited by Rosemary Radford Ruelher. New York: Simon and Schuster, 1974.

The Secular Spirit: Life and Art at the End of the Middle Ages. New York: E. P. Dutton, in association with Metropolitan Museum of Art, 1975.

Violence and Civil Disorder in Italian Cities 1200-1500. Edited by Lauro Martinez. Berkeley: University of California Press, 1972.

IV. General Works Covering the Roman Period

Acton, Lord. *Essays on Church and State*. Chapter II, States of the Church; Chapter III, The Political System of the Popes. New York: Thomas Y. Crowell, 1968.

Bouard, A. (de) *Lettres de Rome de Bartolomeo Bracciano à Virginio Orsini*. Melange d'Archeologie et d'histoire. Vol. xxxiii: (1913) 268-361.

Brântóme, Pierre de Bourdeille. *Vie des hommes illustres*. Vol. 3. Oeuvres Nouveaux. London, 1779.

Brom, Gisbert. *Einige Briefe von R. Brandolinus Lippus*. Romische Quartalschrift ii (1880): 190-95.

Buonaccorsi, Biagio. *Diario de successi più importanti seguiti in Italia & particolarmente in Fiorenza dall' Anno 1498 in fino all' Anno 1512.*

Burchard, Johann. *Diarium*. There is no complete translation of Burchard's diary in English.

———. *At the Court of the Borgia*. Edited and translated by Geoffrey Parker. London: The Folio Society, 1963. By far the better of the two partial translations.

———. *Pope Alexander and His Court*. Extracts edited by F. L. Glaser. New York: N. L. Brown, 1921. More summary than translation, but it does contain material describing the pontificate of Innocent VIII which is not included in the Parker translation.

———. *Diarium Innocentu*. Volume Unico. Florence: Biblioteca Dante, 1896. Describes the death of Pope Sixtus IV.

———. *Liber Notarum*. A cura de Enrico Celani in Muratori Rerum italicarum scriptores. Nuova, ed. t 32 pt. 1 fasc. 1 Città di Castello: S Lapi, 1907, Considered the most accurate edition of the *Diarium*. It is in the original Latin and much additional material is to be found in the footnotes.

———. *Diarium*. Introduction, notes, appendices et index par L. Thuasne. Paris: E. Leroux, 1883-1885. Also in the original Latin. Has some innaccuracies, but it is valuable for a French summary of the events it covers and for the letters and other primary material in the appendix and footnotes.

Cecini, Nando. *Pesaro*. Pesaro: Azienda autonoma di soggiorno Pesaro.

Cessi, R. *Dispacci degli ambasciatori veneziani alla corte di Roma presso Giulio II.* Venice: Reale & Deputazione di Storia patria per le Venezie, 1932.

Cinelli, Carlo. *Collennuccio e Pesaro à suoi tempi*. Pesaro, 1880.

Comines, Philippe de. *The History of Comines*. English edition by Thomas Danett. Vol. 2. New York: AMS Press, 1967.

————. *Memoires*. Edites par Joseph Calmette. Tome III (1484–1498) Paris: Sociétè D'Edition "Les Belles Lettres," 1965.

Corio, Bernardino. *Storia di Milano*. Milan: Alexander Minutianus, July 15, 1503.

Dal Re, D. *Discorso critico sui Borgia con l'Aggiunta di documenti inediti relative al pontificato di Alessandro VI*. Archivio della Società Romana per la Storia della Patria IV (1881): 78–97.

Delaborde, Henri François. *L'expédition de Charles VIII en Italie*. Paris: Firmen, Didot et Cie, 1888.

Ehrle, Francesco, and Stevenson, Enrico. *Gli affreschi del Pinturicchio nell'appartamento Borgia*. Rome, 1897.

Gandini, L. A. *Lucrezia Borgia nell'imminenza delle sue nozze con Alfonso d'Este*. Atti e memorie della R. deputazione di Storia Patria per la Romagna. Per 3 v. 20 (1902): 285–340.

Garnett, Richard. *Rome and the Temporal Power*. Cambridge: Modern History. Vol. 1, chapter VII. Cambridge: Cambridge University Press, 1907.

Giustiniani, Antonio. *Dispacci*. Vol. I & II. Florence: Successori Le Monnier, 1876.

Gnoli, U. *Cortigiane Romane*. Arezzo: Edizione Della Rivista I1 Vasare, XIX. 1941.

————. *Una figlia sconsciuta*. L'Urbe ii (1937): 7–12

Gregorovius, Ferdinand. *History of the City of Rome in the Middle Ages*. Translated by Mrs. Gustavus W. Hamilton. Vols. 7 & 8. London: G. Bell, 1903–12.

Infessura, Stefano. *Diario della città di Roma di Stefano Infessura*. Nuova edizione a cura di Oreste Tommasini. Roma: Forzani, 1890.

La Torre, Ferdinando. *Del conclave di Alessandro VI, papa Borgia*. Rome: Olschki, 1933.

Lea, Henry Charles. *History of Sacerdotal Celibacy in the Christian Church*. London: Watts, 1932.

Marc-Bonnet, Henry. *Les Papes de La Renaissance*. Paris: Presses Universitaires de France, 1969.

Matarazzo, Francesco. *Chronicles of the City of Perugia*. Translated by E. S. Morgan. New York: Harper & Row, 1969.

Negri, P. *Le missioni di Pandolfo Collennuccio à Papa Alessandro VI*. Archivio della Società romana di storia patria. xxxiii (1910): 333–439.

Paschino, Pio. *Roma nel rinascimento*. Bologna: L. Cappelli, 1940.

Piccolomini, Aeneas Sylvius. *Memoirs of a Renaissance Pope: the Commentaries of Pius II*. An abridgement. Translated by Florence A. Gragg. New York: Putnam, 1959.

Picotti, G. B. *Ancora Sul Borgia in Rivista di Storia della Chiesa in Italia*. Anno VIII no. 3 (Sept.–Dec. 1954): 313–55. A review of the Borgia Pope by Orestes Ferrara.

————. *Nuovi studi documenti intorno à Papa Alessandro VI*. Rivista di storia della Chiesa in Italia. Vol. 5 (1951): 199–243.

Priuli, Girolamo. *I diari in Muratori; Raccotli degli storici italiani*. Vol. 24 part 3 fasc. 1–14. Città di Castello: S. Lapi, 1912.

Rodocanachi, Emmanuel. *Histoire de Rome. Une cour princière au Vatican pendant la renaissance*. Paris: Hachette, 1925.

Silenzi, Fernando. *Pasquino Quattro secoli di satira romana*. Florence: Vallecchi, 1968.

Soranzo, Giovanni. *Orsino Orsini, Adriana de Mila sua madre e Giulia Farnese sua moglie nei loro rapporti con Papa Alessandro VI.* Archivi D'Italia e Rassegna Internazionale degli Archivi. Ser. II xxvi (1959): 119–50.

———. *La più grave accusa fatta à Papa Borgia.* Archivi d'Italia e rivista internazionale degli Archivi. Ind serie xxviii, 1961.

———. *Studi Intorno à Papa Alessandro VI (Borgia).* Milan: Pubblicazione Delle Universita Cattolica del Sacro Cuore. Vol. 34, 1950.

Tommasini, Oreste. *Evangelista Maddaleni di Capodiferro Academico e Storico* in Atti della R. Accademia dei Lincei Ser. IV, 1892. Memoire 10: 3–20.

Vasari, Giorgio. *Lives of the Artists.* Abridged and edited by Betty Burroughs. New York: Simon and Schuster, 1946.

The Borgia Apartment and contemporary Art in the Vatican monumenti, musei e gallerie pontificie, 1974.

Storia del Comune di Spoleto dal secolo 12 al 17. Achille Sanse, Parte II. Foligno, 1884.

V. General Works Covering the Ferrarese Period

Alighieri, Dante. *The Divine Comedy.* Translated by Laurence Binyon in *The Portable Dante.* New York: The Viking Press, 1947.

Bacchelli, Riccardo. *La Congiura di Don Giulio d'Este.* Rome: Arnoldo Mondadori, 1966.

Battelli, A. *Gli Ebrei e gli Estense* in Atti e memorie *Deputazione Modenese Storia Patria.* Ser. V vol. VII (1913): 161–397.

Bertoni, G. *Un "putino de legno" di Lucrezia Borgia.* Archivium Romanicum II: 91–93.

Brown, Rawdon (ed.). *Ragguagli sulla vita e sulle opere di Marino Sanuto.* Parti II e III. Venice: Dalla Tipografica di Alvesopoli, 1838.

Cabanes, A. *Le Journal des couches de Lucrèce Borgia.* Dans les coulisses de l'histoire prime serie (1929): 30–44.

Cappelli, A. *Notizie di Ugo Caleffino notaio di secolo XV con la sua cronaca in rima di Casa d'Este ed altri documenti.* Atti e memorie Regia Deputazione Modenese di Storia Patria vol. II (1864).

Chiappini, Luciano. *An Illustrated Guide to Ferrara.* Terni: Stabilimento Poligrafico Allerocca S.p.A.

Cionini, C. *Angela Borgia una pagina di storia patria per le provincie modenesi vi* (1910): 48–97.

Erasmus, Desiderius. *Julius II. Exclusus. A Dialogue. Voices of the Past Readings in Medieval and Early Modern History.* New York: the Macmillan Company, (1967): 149–151. Though Erasmus was suspected of being the author, this is still uncertain.

Fedele, P. *I gioelli di Vannozza.* Archivio della Società Romana di Storia Patria XXVIII (1905): 452–63.

Frizzi, Antonio. *Memorie per la storia di Ferrara.* Con giunte e note del conte Avv. Camillo Laderchi. Seconda Edizione Vol. IV. Ferrara: Presso Abram Servadio Editore, 1848.

Gagniere, A. *Le journal des médecins de Lucrèce Borgia.* La Nouvelle Revue LIV (1888): 295–313.

Gardner, Edmund G. *Dukes and Poets at Ferrara*. New York: E. P. Dutton, n.d.

Gundersheimer, Werner L. *Ferrara the Style of a Renaissance Despotism*. Princeton: Princeton University Press, 1973.

Hauvette, Henri. *L'Arioste et la poesie chevaleresque à Ferrara au debut du XVIe siecle*. Paris: Librarie Honore Champion, 1927.

Morsolin, B. *Pietro Bembo e Lucrezia Borgia*. Nuova Antologia. Volume LII (1885): 388–422.

Mosti, Agostino. *La vita Ferrarese nella prima metà del secolo decimosesto*. Edited by A. Solerti. Atti e memorie della R. Deputazione di Storia Patria per la Provincie di Romagna. Series III, vol. x (1892): 168–73.

Noyes, Ella. *Story of Ferrara*. London: J. M. Dent, 1904.

Zambotti, Bernardino. *Diario Ferrarese dall'anno 1476 sino al 1504*. Muratori, Rerum Italicarum Scriptores Vol 24–Part VII. Bologna: Nicola Zanichelli.

———. *Diario Ferrarese dall'anno 1409 fino al 1502*. di autori incerti. Muratori, Rerum Italicarum Scriptores. Vol. 24. Bologna: Nicola Zanichelli.

History of Bayard. The Good Chevalier Sans Peur et Sans Reproche. Compiled by the *Loyal Serviteur*. Translated by Loredan Larchey. London: Chapman and Hall, 1883.

VI. Biographies and Other Material Relating to a Specific Person or Family

Alexander VI (Rodrigo Borgia)

De l'Epinois. *Le Pape Alexandre VI*. Revue des Questions Historiques. Vol. xxx (1881): 256–548.

De Roo, P. *Materials for a History of Alexander VI*. 5 vol. Bruges: Desclee, De Brower and Co., 1924.

Ferrara, Orestes. *The Borgia Pope*. Translated by F. J. Sheed. New York: Sheed and Ward, 1940.

Garnett, R. *A Contemporary Oration on Alexander VI* (Oration of the Bishop of Gallipoli at opening of the conclave that selected Alexander's successor). English Historical Review (1892): 311–14.

Mathew, A. H. *The Life and Times of Rodrigo Borgia*. London: St. Paul, 1912.

Quierazza, G. Gasa. *Gli scritti autografi di Alessandro VI nell'Archivum Arcis*. Turin: Rosenberg & Sellier, 1959.

Ariosto

Ariosto, Lodovico. *Orlando Furioso* (The Frenzy of Orlando). 2 vols. Translated with an introduction by Barbara Reynolds. Great Britain: Penguin Books, 1975.

———. *Satires*. Translated by Peter De Sa Wiggins. Athens, Ohio: Ohio University Press, 1976.

Gardner, Edmund G. *The King of Court Poets: A Study of the Work, Life and Times of Ludovico Ariosto*. New York: Haskell House, 1968.

Pietro Bembo

Bembo, Pietro. *Gil Asolani*. Translated by Rudolph B. Gottfried. Bloomington: Indiana University Press, 1954.

————. *Lettere di M. Pietro Bembo Cardinale à Principesse e Signori ed altre Gen-tili Donne scritte.* Volume Quarto. Milano: Società Tipografica De Classici Italiani, 1810.

Cian, V. *Un decennio della vita di Pietro Bembo.* Turin: Loescher, 1885.

Meneghetti, G. *La vita avventurosa di Pietro Bembo.* Venice: Tipografica Commerciale, 1961.

Carteggio d'Amore 1500–1501 [da] Maria Savorgnan [e] Pietro Bembo a cura di Carlo Dionisetti. Florence: Felice le Monnier, 1950.

Cesare Borgia

Alvisi, Eduardo. *Cesare Borgia.* Imola: Tip d'Ignazio Galeati e Figlio, 1878.

Bradford, Sarah. *Cesare Borgia.* New York: Macmillan, 1976.

Garnett, Richard. *Contemporary Poems on Caesar Borgia.* English Historical Review 1886: 138–41.

Sabatini, Rafael. *The Life of Cesare Borgia.* New York: Brentano's, n.d.

Woodward, William Harrison. *Cesare Borgia.* London: Chapman and Hall, Ltd., 1913.

Yriarte, Charles. *Cesare Borgia.* Translated by Wm. Sterling. London: F. Aldor, 1947.

Lucrezia Borgia

Bellonci, Maria. Three editions of Signora Bellonci's biography of Lucrezia have been consulted.

————. *The Life and Times of Lucrezia Borgia.* Translated by Bernard and Barbara Wall. New York: Harcourt Brace, 1953. Does not include much of the material to be found in the later Italian editions and contains no footnotes.

————. *Lucrezia Borgia la sua vita e i suoi tempi.* Rome: Arnoldo Mondadori Editore, 1967. Besides being an expanded version of the earlier edition, this edition reproduces a number of letters and papal briefs referred to in the text as well as an inventory of Lucrezia's jewels.

————. *Lucrezia Borgia.* Rome: Arnoldo Mondadori Editore, 1974. Omits the letters and the inventory but includes new material relating to Lucrezia's son Rodrigo and to Vannozza.

Bérence, Fred. *Lucrèce Borgia.* Paris: Payot, 1937.

Campori, G. *Lucrezia Borgia: una vittima della storia.* Nuova Antologia (1866): 628–35.

Catalano, Michele. *Lucrezia Borgia, duchessa di Ferrara.* Ferrara: A. Taddie, 1920.

Davidsohn, R. *Lucrezia Borgia suor di penitenza.* Archivio Storico Italiano. (1900): 313–14.

De Hevesy, Andre. *Bartolomeo Veneto, Les Portraits De Lucrezia Borgia.* Arts Quarterly of the Detroit Institute of Arts. ii (1939): 233–49.

Donizetti, Gaetano. *Lucrezia Borgia.* Libretto translated by G. Calcaterra. New Orleans: The Picayune.

Funck-Brentano, Frantz. *Lucrèce Borgia.* Paris: La Nouvelle Revue Critique, 1930.

Gilbert, William. *Lucrezia Borgia.* London: Hurst & Blackett, 1864. One of the first biographies favorable to Lucrezia.

Gregorovius, Ferdinand. *Lucrèce Borgia.* Traduction de l'Allemand par Paul Regnaud. Tome second. Paris: Sandoz et Fischbacher, Editeurs, 1876. Contains letters and documents not included in the English edition.

———. *Lucretia Borgia.* Translated by John Leslie Garner. New York: D. Appleton, 1903.

Mancini, Franco. *Lucrezia Borgia governatrice di Spoleto.* Archivio Storico Italiano. Anno 115 (1957): 182–87.

Polifilo (il). *La guardaroba di Lucrezia Borgia.* Rome: dall'Archivio, 1903.

Roscoe, William. *The Life and Pontificate of Leo the Tenth.* 6th edition. Revised by his son, Thomas Roscoe. 2 vols. London: Henry G. Bohn, 1853. Pages 393–404 of volume I are devoted to a Dissertation on the Character of Lucretia Borgia. Pages 431–34 of the appendix to the same volume contain letters from Lucretia to Gian Giorgio Tressino and a letter from Bembo to Tressino.

Rubinstein, Nicolai. *Lucrezia Borgia.* Rome: Istituto della Enciclopedia Italiana, 1971.

Swinburne. *Lucretia Borgia.* The Chronicle of Tebaldo Tebaldei. Commentary and notes by Randolph Hughes. Great Britain: the Golden Cockerel Press, 1942.

Le prime nozze di Lucrezia Borgia in una Lettera Inedito di Jacopo Gherardi. Rassegna Volterrana, 3–5.

Alfonso d'Este

Giovio, P. *La vita di Alfonso d' Este Duca di Ferrara.* Translated by G. B. Filli. Venezia, 1597.

Pistofilo, Bonaventura. *Vita di Alfonso I d'Este Duca di Ferrara, etc.* Edited by Antonio Capelli. Atti e memorie delle R. R. Deputazione di Storia Patria per le provincie Modenese e Parmensi. Serie I vol. 3, 1865.

Isabella d'Este

Cartwright, Julia. *Isabella d'Este.* 2 vols. London: John Murray, 1903.

D'Arco. C. *Notizie di Isabella Estense Gonzaga.* Archive Storico Italiano. Series I Appendix. Vol. 2. Florence, 1845.

Luzio, Alessandro. *Isabella d'Este e i Borgia.* Archivio Storico Lombardo. Serie Quinta. Vol. I (July 1914–March 1915): 467–553, 673–753. Vol II (June 1915–February 1916): 115–67, 412–64. Also published as a single volume. Milan, 1916.

———. *Isabella d'Este di Fronte a Giulio II negli ultimi tre anni del suo pontificato.* Archivio Storico Lombardo 4ª serie SVI (1911): 260–417.

———. *La Reggenza d'Isabella d'Este durante la pregonia del marito (1509–1510).* Archivio Storico Lombardo. Ser 14 Book 37 (1910): 5–104.

I ritratti di Isabella d'Este. Emporium M-G vol. II, 66, June 1900.

Petrarch

Bishop, Morris. *Petrarch and His World.* Bloomington: Indiana University Press, 1963.

Ludovico Sforza

Nulli, Siro Attilio, *Lodovico il Moro.* Milan: Casa editrice ambrosiana, 1949.

The Borgia family

Bérence, Fred. *Les Borgias*. Paris: Pierre Waliffe, 1966.

Gordon, Alexander. *The Lives of Pope Alexander VI and his son Caesar Borgia*. 2 vols. London: C. Davis & T. Green, 1929. New edition of a virulently anti-Borgia tirade first published in the seventeenth century.

Latour, Anny. *The Borgias*. Translated by Neil Mann. New York: Abelard-Schuman, 1963. Documents relating to the family connected by snippets of text which are not always accurate.

Lucas-Dubreton, J. *The Borgias*. Translated by Philip John Stead. New York: E. P. Dutton, 1956.

Mallett, Michael. *The Borgias: The Rise and Fall of a Renaissance Dynasty*. London: Paladin, 1971. The book jacket has a quotation from the economist calling this "the best general treatment of the family in any language." Though I do not always agree with Dr. Mallett's conclusions, I do agree with this description of his book.

Portigliotti, Giuseppe. *The Borgias*. Translated by Bernard Miall. London: George Allen and Unwin, 1928. Another virulently anti-Borgia tract.

Rolfe, F. W. *Chronicles of the House of Borgia*. New York: Dover Publications, 1962.

Yriarte, Charles. *Autour des Borgia*. Paris: J. Rothschild, 1891.

The Estense

Chiappini, Luciano. *Gli Estensi*. Dall'Oglio, Editore, 1967.

Muratori, L. A. *Della Antichità Estensi ed Italiane*. 2 vols. Modena, 1717–40. Modena: Stamperia ducale, 1717–40.

The Sforza

Collison-Morley, Lacy. *The Story of the Sforzas*. New York: E. P. Dutton, 1934.

Index